Also by Hazel E. Barnes

HUMANISTIC EXISTENTIALISM (*originally published as*
THE LITERATURE OF POSSIBILITY)
HIPPOLYTUS IN DRAMA AND MYTH (*in collaboration with*
Donald Sutherland)

Translated with Introductions
BEING AND NOTHINGNESS *by Jean-Paul Sartre*
EXISTENTIAL PSYCHOANALYSIS *by Jean-Paul Sartre*
SEARCH FOR A METHOD *by Jean-Paul Sartre*

AN
EXISTENTIALIST
ETHICS

AN
EXISTENTIALIST
ETHICS

BY

HAZEL E. BARNES

NEW YORK: *Alfred·A·Knopf*

1 9 6 7

THIS IS A BORZOI BOOK
PUBLISHED BY ALFRED A. KNOPF, INC.

First Edition

© Copyright 1967 by Hazel E. Barnes

Library of Congress Catalog Card Number: 66–19368

Manufactured in the United States of America

Acknowledgment is hereby made for permission to quote from the following: *Berkeley: The New Student Revolt* by Hal Draper, Copyright © 1965 by Hal Draper, by permission of Grove Press, Inc.; *Advertisements for Myself* by Norman Mailer, © 1959 by Norman Mailer, and *The Presidential Papers* by Norman Mailer, © 1960, 1961, 1962, 1963 by Norman Mailer, both by permission of G. P. Putnam's Sons; *The Way of Zen* by Alan Watts, © Copyright 1957 by Pantheon Books, by permission of Pantheon Books, a division of Random House, Inc.; *The Quarry* by Friedrich Dürrenmatt, Copyright © 1961 by New York Graphic Society, by permission of New York Graphic Society, Greenwich, Conn.; *Zen Buddhism: Selected Writings of D. T. Suzuki* edited by William Barrett, © 1956 by William Barrett, by permission of Mr. Barrett; *Naked Lunch* by William Burroughs, Copyright © 1959 by William Burroughs, by permission of Grove Press, Inc.

Preface

PREFACE

I have titled this book *An Existentialist Ethics*, stressing the indefinite article, for two reasons. First, what I have called "existentialist ethics" is certainly not *the* existentialist ethics. While it is not quite true that there are as many kinds of existentialist ethics as there are existentialist philosophers, we should undoubtedly have to distinguish an ethics originating in Kierkegaard's existentialist Christianity from one based on Heidegger's philosophy of Being and, even more, from an ethics that adopts Sartre's nontheistic premises. The existentialist ethics I present is humanistic, and it accepts as a starting-point the view of man and the world that Jean-Paul Sartre set forth in *Being and Nothingness*. Second, I do not presume to try to write the "Ethics" which Sartre promised as a sequel to that volume. Nor do I feel bound to agree with Sartre in every detail, certainly not with everything he has said on ethical, social, and political problems on various occasions throughout the three decades since he first published his major philosophical work. My own interests are quite different from his.

My purpose is not to show exactly how existentialism fits into the philosophical tradition. I have discussed writers whose names will never appear in any future history of philosophy. There are others whom I have ignored although any one of them might well be made the subject of a seminar in ethical theory. This is because I have determined to discuss the existentialist choice as a living option for real people in today's world, not as a proposition labeled X to be logically analyzed in relation to other abstract alternatives. In Part One I have attempted to demonstrate the possibility of an existentialist ethics and to indicate the nature of its initial choice and its basic commitments. The rest of the book discusses, from the viewpoint of one who has made this choice and these commitments, some of the ideas, trends, and problems that confront a person existing at our particular point in time and space. As I have taught my university classes and as I have lectured on existentialism to audiences of various types, one question I have been asked again and again is this: "I accept Sartre's existentialist description of man and his relation to the Universe. What sort of ethics naturally follows? If I am an existentialist, then what?" I have attempted to provide an answer to this question.

Finally, I wish to express my appreciation to the University of Colorado Council on Research and Creative Work. The Council granted me a Faculty Fellowship for the fall semester of 1964 so that I might have time free to do the preliminary work in writing this book and generously supplied funds to aid in the preparation of the manuscript.

H A Z E L   E .   B A R N E S

Boulder, Colorado

Contents

PART ONE

THE CHOICE

The Choice
To Be Ethical

Among the heroes and anti-heroes of existentialist literature, one who should never be forgotten is Dostoevski's Underground Man. His violently individualistic protest remains at the heart of the existentialist revolt in the twentieth century. His defiant rejection of any appeal to rational self-interest may serve for a touchstone as we examine the possibilities of an existentialist ethics.

In writing the novella *Notes from Underground*, Dostoevski was attacking the easy optimism of certain nineteenth-century liberals, their idea of inevitable progress, their insistence on viewing man as rational and inherently good. The Underground Man objects to these ideals, not out of cynicism so much as because they seem to him a travesty of that human dignity which they pretend to affirm. The Underground Man takes offense at this picture of man as a predictable creature who can be counted on to act rationally and to pursue his own self-interest—the assumption being, of course, that there is no contradiction between these two activities. Such a man is left with no freedom, with no will of his

3

own. In a flight of fancy, the Underground Man envisions a future society without conflict, one where all possible conduct is so rationally tabulated that everybody will quickly perceive what he ought to do for his own advantage—and do it. "Everything will be so clearly calculated and designated that there will be no more incidents or adventures in the world." The Underground Man rebels.

You see, gentlemen, reason, gentlemen, is an excellent thing, there is no disputing that, but reason is only reason and can only satisfy man's rational faculty, while will is a manifestation of all life, that is, of all human life including reason as well as all impulses. And although our life, in this manifestation of it, is often worthless, yet it is life nevertheless and not simply extracting square roots.[1]

The Underground Man imagines that amidst all the future general rationality, someone might rise up someday and declare, "What do you think, gentlemen, hadn't we better kick over all that rationalism at one blow, scatter it to the winds, just to send these logarithms to the devil, and to let us live once more according to our own foolish will!" He would be right. "One's own free unfettered choice, one's own fancy, however wild it may be, one's own fancy worked up at times to frenzy—why that is that very 'most advantageous advantage' which we have overlooked." No matter how stupid the caprice, even if it is certain to harm the man who acts by it, the Underground Man argues that it may still be more advantageous than all other advantages. "Because in any case it perserves for us what is most precious and most important— that is, our personality, our individuality."

The Underground Man does not represent a positive ethical ideal for Dostoevski or for me. His life is wretched in his own eyes and harmful to others. He remains an anti-hero. But he can be valuable to us. In the peculiarly negative quality of his self-assertion, he anticipates the form of rebellion which in recent decades has baffled guardians of the *status quo* and

[1] Fyodor Dostoevski: *Notes from Underground*, tr. Ralph E. Matlaw (New York: E. P. Dutton and Co.; 1960), p. 25.

disturbed all of us. Youthful revolt against authority, artistic bohemianism, delinquency, radicalism—these we have always known. They are in any case defined relative to their background; often the world is better because of them. What is new, at least in terms of the numbers involved, is the aggressive rejection of all that society has to offer—not only its materialistic comforts and its professed ideals of rationality, happiness, and altruism, but the very concept of community and ethical responsibility. As with the Underground Man, this stubborn defiance does not point toward any goal, nor is it motivated by anything except the bitter pleasure of asserting one's right to be against oneself. The inmost self is preserved but by a process of allowing only destructive relations to exist between it and the world. The purely arbitrary alone has value, and it is recognized chiefly in acts which sever not only self from others but the immediate choice of self from the moments of one's own past and future.

It is exactly this identification of the arbitrary with the authentic free choice of self which has been thought of as the insurmountable obstacle in the way of any humanistic existentialist ethics. If every man is free both to choose and to establish the value of what he chooses, then it is not easy to find any argument to convince the Underground Man that he ought to make a different kind of choice. But if he is right, even from his own point of view, in choosing to be miserable himself and to injure others, there appears to be no hope for either ethics or humanism.

There is a tendency today, more popular than strictly philosophical, to identify as "ethics" any personally chosen value system and code of behavior. This extreme of relativism is exactly parallel with what has happened to "religion." An age which is willing to apply the term "religion" to communism, aesthetic awe, devotion to one's fellow man, and allegiance to the impartial demands of pure science has no difficulty in labeling any guiding motif of choice a personal ethics. From this point of view, nobody is nonreligious or nonethical. Calvin O. Schragg, for instance, speaks of Sartre's "atheistic theology"![2] He is not the only critic to feel that Sartre's attitude must be religious because it is sincere and total. From this point of view, the only question we can ask is which religion and what kind of ethics. At most we might say that a person who scoffed at all ultimate concern is irreligious and amoral, but this very levity, because it is a total regulating principle of a life, is taken as constituting the person's individual value system and bona fide ethical code. Existentialism has often been interpreted as providing philosophical support for this position, attaching only one condition: that the decision to act and the choice of values must be authentic, embraced spontaneously rather than in a somnambulistic state of mingled fear and lazy habit.

For both ethics and religion, my objections to this all-inclusive use of the terms are the same. First, if no man can be non-religious or unethical, I cannot see that any positive meaning is left to the words "religion" and "ethics." It may be true that nobody is without some sort of driving force and total attitude toward the world and that everyone has within him at least a roughly formulated, haphazard hierarchy of values. This is to say nothing significant, and it is to blur irreparably any recognition of particular orientations which may be distinguished from all others as religious or ethical. Moreover, it is not true that every person is committed to his particular ultimate concern (his religion) or to a specific mode of conduct designed to further his personally selected values (his ethics). What characterizes many, if not most, people is precisely a lack of commitment and consistency. They do not have a coherent life plan either as ideal or reality. One cannot truthfully say even that they have chosen to respond spontaneously to each new situation as it occurs, for their responses are frequently not genuine but only what they feel is expected. To apply the term "religious" or "ethical" to this sort of aimless, desultory, semi-mechanical living is to do

[2] Calvin O. Schragg: *Existence and Freedom: Towards an Ontology of Human Finitude* (Chicago: Northwestern University Press; 1961), p. 94.

6

such violence to language as to destroy the possibility of communication. Although the nature and context of the religion we may choose are immeasurably varied, there remains always the distinct alternative of choosing not to be religious. Prior to embracing any particular ethics, there is the necessary choice of whether or not to be ethical. And here if anywhere we must recognize the truth of Sartre's claim that not to choose is already to have chosen. The refusal to choose the ethical is inevitably a choice for the nonethical.

Within a given ethical system, it is comparatively easy to establish certain obligations, prohibitions, responsibilities which follow as consequences from the premises of the system itself. In choosing between two ethical systems, both rational and irrational processes are involved. One finds that Ethics A involves a scientifically sound view of the world and human psychology whereas Ethics B seemingly rests on error. Or Ethics A alone is internally consistent. Or Ethics A, if followed, seems likely to realize the ends it sets up whereas Ethics B fails to show a clear pathway to its goals. On the other hand, I may simply feel that the way of life which A promises is intrinsically desirable whereas B offers as values things which have no incentive force for me. Admittedly in this choice as to *which* ethics, we have not hit upon any universal compelling factor that might serve as an absolute criterion. Nevertheless, even at this stage, we can see why a person might feel that from his point of view he ought to choose one rather than the other. In actual practice it is hardly conceivable that two ethical systems, significantly distinct from one another, could appear to the same person to be equally well-grounded in reality, both of them internally consistent, equivalent in their chances of fulfilling what they promised, yet each one postulating different but equally self-evident values as goods to be attained.

The most difficult problem lies in the question which seeks to remain outside all ethics. Why should I be ethical? Is there an *ought* which underlies the ethical choice itself? When we look at a specific ethics, we see easily that any seemingly

7

categorical imperative is contingent on our accepting the system as a whole. Take fundamentalist Christianity as an example. Before I am obliged to accept obedience to God's will as an absolute command, I must do more than accept the reality of an omnipotent Father, Creator of the Universe, and Prime Mover in History, the Revealer of Sacred Writ, and Judge of each man's eternal future. Even granting my literal belief in all of this, I will regard obedience to the divine will as an imperative only if my personal value judgments agree with those of traditional Christianity. Satan unrepentant is not the evident negative proof of the validity of the categorical imperative. He is the eternal challenge. If I do not find God's goodness to be the highest good, if I question His judgments, if I do not want His eternal bliss, then others may call me wicked, stupid, and misguided. They will neither coerce nor persuade me. God's commands are absolutes only when I accept the hypothesis that for His will to be done and for me to be in accord with it and to be happy in this accord are my ultimate value criteria. It is simple to demonstrate a parallel situation with regard to Platonic Ethics or Kantian or whatever other ethics one wishes to mention. All are ultimately hypothetical. Furthermore, all rest finally on the choice of the ethical itself as a value. If the original choice is for the nonethical life, then no system is compelling, no matter how logically consistent its structure or how apparently evident its values.

Is the choice to be ethical itself a categorical imperative? Or is this, too, conditional? And if so, on what is it contingent?

If we are to attempt an answer, we must first formulate some sort of working definition of the ethical. Usually the idea of ethics is associated with the notion of obligations, the necessity of recognizing that acts have consequences, and the idea that consideration of more remote aims may act as a check on immediate impulses. Ethics is thus an inner control which the individual exercises over himself. Or again, a system of ethics serves as a set of reference points, by which to adjudicate conflicts of interests—whether this conflict is within a single person or in personal relations with others.[3] While acknowledging the validity of both these claims, I believe that in the choice to be ethical there is something still more basic. This is the recognition of the need to justify one's life. To put it another way, the decision to be ethical is a choice of a particular value: the sense of satisfaction derived from knowing that one may judge his own life as he would judge another's and find it good. To justify one's life involves the belief that one's conduct is harmonious with the image which he has selected as the ideal pattern of a life he can admire or deem to be in itself a positive value. The ethical calls for continuity between the moment of decision, the act itself, and the later judgment passed upon it. In the justified life there is harmony and perfect continuity between the subjective process which one *is* and the objectified self which he has become in his relation with the world and others— outside himself. At this point we do not introduce the question of conformity with God's judgment or the opinions of other men. Such references are appropriate only within the sphere of a particular ethics. The choice to be ethical as such involves the bare idea of the inner demand for justification as a self-imposed necessary relation between actions and judgments by and within the same individual.

At this point I want to return to the Underground Man. Rebelling against the notion that man's salvation lies in realizing himself as what he essentially is—a creature dominated by rational self-interest, the Underground Man cries out that he is something in addition to reason, and he proclaims that he treasures this rest of himself. So far I think anyone would agree with him; what is nonrational is not necessarily bad. But the Underground Man goes further. He asserts that there is value in keeping his life independent of any rationally coherent plan. He refuses to link present and future in a

[3] The idea that an ethical system serves to adjudicate conflicts of interest is implied by most philosophers writing on ethics. The phraseology in which I have stated it is derived from a lecture, "Ethical Relativism," presented by Richard Brandt at the University of Colorado in November 1965.

pattern designed to perfect a self in which he may enjoy a creator's proud happiness. In other words he explicitly rejects the opportunity to justify his life; he deliberately chooses the nonethical as the higher value. The Underground Man clearly demonstrates the fact that the choice to be ethical is conditional, not categorical. He suggests that the nonethical may be preferable. Is he right? Can there possibly be any justification for the nonethical choice?

At first thought it may appear easy to answer No. If we define the choice to be ethical as a decision to justify one's life, the resolve not to do so appears to be outside all possibility of justification. Yet I feel that there is a problem.

Let us take the Underground Man seriously and try to determine exactly what are the opposing values between which he is choosing. He himself puts it as a choice of life over square roots. Some might call it emotion versus reason. I, for my part, see it as a choice between two kinds of self-realization. In saying this, I realize that I am departing from the philosophical neutrality which I have been trying to maintain up until now. Many schools of philosophy and of psychology would hold that the Underground Man's defiance is a total rejection of self-realization. For Freudian and Behaviorist psychologists, the choice is not free in any case, and the Underground Man, despite his protests, has no true understanding either of himself or his situation. He decides blindly, pushed by forces of whose very existence he is unaware. For both Eastern mysticism and Western Christianity, it is partly ignorance and partly willfulness which lead him to cling to his separate, partial, or illusory self in preference to recognizing his true Being in God. For the humanistic psychologies of self-realization (for example, that of Erich Fromm), the Self to be realized is a reservoir of positive potentialities, like the oak in the acorn. In this view, too, the Underground Man's decision is a refusal of Self, as though the acorn could will to rot rather than to grow.

Even in keeping with these positions, I think it is possible to argue that the Underground Man has chosen one kind of Self rather than another; the debate would be unprofitable inasmuch as all positive value would remain with the Self rejected. Furthermore, we would still have to admit that the choice was made in partial ignorance. Sartre's theory of consciousness seems to me to be the only one which allows us to postulate two genuine forms of self-realization so that we may find the Underground Man's choice to be knowing and intelligible—even though we continue to judge it nonethical and unwise.

Sartre's psychology is incomprehensible without reference to his fundamental distinction between Being-in-itself—which is all of nonconscious reality, and Being-for-itself—which is human Being, with consciousness. At times in his discussion of these two types of Being, Sartre almost but never quite seems to equate them with that other famous pair—with Being and Nothingness. The consciousness which sets man apart from the rest of Being is defined as the process of causing Nothingness to emerge like a hole at the heart of Being. Man is described as the being through whom Nothingness comes into the world. But neither consciousness nor man *is* Nothingness. He is that part of Being which is able to stand back and, by a sort of psychic withdrawal, assume a point of view on the rest of Being, to question it, to judge it and to establish a definite relation between it and himself. Sartre is certainly not the first to emphasize the idea that man is the only creature capable of detaching himself—at least mentally—from the rest of nature and able to achieve a clear sense of self-identity. What is distinctive in his philosophy is the peculiar emphasis which he places on the negativity of consciousness, and his corollary views of freedom and the Self.

Starting one step earlier than Descartes, Sartre claims that in its primary structure, consciousness is neither reflective nor personal. Descartes's *cogito ergo sum*, "I think, therefore I am," is both. It points to a well-grounded subject reflecting upon its own activity. It presupposes too much. Its role is played much later in the dialectical drama. According to Sartre, the first moment of consciousness, so to speak, cannot be expressed verbally as "I am aware of a bright light" or some such equivalent. One should say rather, "there is a bright light." The "there is" implies an awareness on the part of consciousness that the awareness and the object of awareness are not the same. Thus any act of consciousness involves two aspects: an implicit self-consciousness and the psychic distance which consciousness establishes between itself and its object. This subjective recoil Sartre called "nihilation." He speaks of consciousness as enfolding its objects in a shell or muff of nothingness.

Even on this nonreflective level, we see that consciousness introduces a separation which is the basis for all that complexity of differentiation, distinction, significance, and meaning which characterize the world as each conscious being knows and lives it. At this first stage, however, consciousness is not directly its own object. Nor is there any sense of "I" or "me." The first beginnings of a personalized consciousness come when consciousness reflects back upon its earlier awareness that "there is a bright light." At this point two things happen: First, consciousness recognizes that it establishes the same sort of relationship between its present and past awareness that it had set up between itself and its objects; second, it introduces a distinction which is expressed in the transformation of the *is* of "there is a bright light" into *was*. In short, consciousness has realized itself as both reflective and temporal. The future appears as soon as there is any movement of reaching toward or avoiding.

One thing more is required before consciousness may be properly called personal, and here Sartre differs from most Western psychologists. All, and Sartre too, would agree that the highly personalized Ego is slow and gradual in its development. For all but existentialist psychologists, consciousness or the psyche (which for Freudians would include the Unconscious as well) is some sort of entity and is identical with what we think of as the full person. This complex evaluation is determined partly by forces within—like the potentialities of the acorn—and partly by environmental pressures and the objective consequences of actions. The person *is* the complex of his personality traits, the product of his past, and cannot shed his weight any more than a snowball might strip itself of accumulated snow. Sartre does not make the mistake of postulating a consciousness which remains a tight entity untouched by its experience—like the vein of gold in the ore. Quite the opposite. Sartre says of man that because he has consciousness, he is the being who is not what he is and is what he is not. Consciousness is not entity but a process of attention, as William James put it, or of intention, to use the phenomenological term as Sartre does. Apart from its objects, consciousness is nothing at all. Consciousness is always consciousness of something. What prevents it from being one with its object is precisely nothing, and this nothing is that nothingness or psychic withdrawal which *is* the act of consciousness. Since consciousness is thus only a constant relating, the assuming of a point of view, there is nothing *in* consciousness, certainly no unconscious and no reservoir of determining traits or tendencies. The unconscious Sartre denies completely. Most startling of all, the accumulation of memories, habits and personal characteristics, even the strong sense of being and having been a definite "I" or "me" —all of this psychic material Sartre puts over on the side of Being-in-itself, making it the object and product of consciousness rather than an intrinsic primary structure of Being-for-itself.

If we leave the level of abstraction and attempt to see what Sartre means in terms of ordinary human experience, we find a radical affirmation of human freedom and a view of Self as a value to be pursued rather than either a determining nucleus of possibilities or a hidden nugget to be uncovered. We *are*, in our inmost being, a power of choosing again at each moment the relation which we wish to establish with the world around us and with our own past and future experiences in that world. As a consciousness, each one is individualized by the accumulation of individual acts of consciousness apropos of specific objects just as he is particularized by the constant presence of a definite body as instrument and center of reference. If we may develop the image implied in Sartre's statement that consciousness is the assumption of a point of view, we find that the earlier experiences are always piled up as a necessary part of the landscape into which or beyond which the viewer is looking. They do not imprint their shape or color on the retina.

Recalling that consciousness is nothing at all without an object and yet that it is not the same as its objects, we may understand how consciousness is nothing except its experiences and at the same time not one with them. We may see, too, how every consciousness is never without a personal coloring, yet is not identical with the ego or definable personality.

Sartre's paradoxical description of man as the being who is not what he is and is what he is not finally makes sense. Man is not what he is, for he is free to put everything into question —his past, his present project, the future which he envisions for himself. He is what he is not. Sartre says that as a being-for-itself, man *is*, in the manner of an event. Nobody exists except in a given situation, located in time and space. Thus a person *is*, for example, a man who works on the assembly line for the Ford Motor Company in Michigan in 1966. In the same way he *is* the performer of each one of his acts. Yet the "is" in such statements does not have the same meaning as the "is" in objects where essence precedes existence. Man exists in a situation, but he internalizes that situation and bestows on it a particular meaning and significance. He lives it by transcending it.

In denying that there is any Unconscious, Sartre naturally does not claim that at every moment we are aware of the full significance of our present act as related to all of our past experiences. What he denies is that there are buried experiences or parts of our psyche, on principle out of reach, which are actively participating in our immediate choices while a conscious Ego acts in ignorance of its own motives. Sartre allows that we may will to ignore certain of our own past acts. We may refuse to reflect upon our present motives or even lie to ourselves about them. This is the procedure of a consciousness in bad faith. Sartre differs from Freud in insisting that a consciousness is never totally the dupe of its own lie.

When Sartre discusses the Self, he speaks of it as that which is forever pursued but never attained. This is because man is a self-making process and because the consciousness which man *is* always stands at a distance from what it has experienced. Consciousness *is* freedom. Yet it is consciousness which by its own intention establishes the unity of life as it relates its own past, present, and future acts in a meaningful pattern. For consciousness is nothing without an object. It exists as an awareness of the things in the world, an awareness of its own relation to them, and an awareness of its relation to its own past and future intentions.

We may now return to the Underground Man. In terms of Sartrean psychology, but without committing ourselves to a specific ethics, what are the Underground Man's alternatives as he deliberately sets about choosing against his own self-interest?

On the one side there is the value which we may call ethical in the strict sense. This is the experience of satisfaction, partly aesthetic, partly conceptual, partly more personally psychological, which stems from the conviction that one can rationally defend his life and justify it as a coherent structure. It includes as essential the belief that the pattern of meaning and significance which one has imposed upon his existence is what he wants it to be. This complex of feeling and reflective judgment derives from the fact that we are each one a temporal consciousness in the world. The ethical resides in the unity of the individual's past, present, and future. This is a unity which consciousness itself imposes. As such it is subjective. There is an objective aspect as well. Consciousness is a continued awareness of objects in the world and of its own relations with those objects. Its acts of intention are already a modification of the significance and meaning of the world. The bodily actions which result serve as the objectification of a consciousness' self-projection. As Sartre puts it,

15

man by his projects inscribes himself in Being. Existentialism insists that the individual is free to revise his attitude toward his own past. Insofar as it is correct to say that each man carries his past within him as a part of his present total attitude toward the world, we may add that at every moment, he remakes his past by the attitude which he takes toward it, not only looking reflectively back upon it, but, through his options, *actively* deciding the part it will play in his choice of a future. By the same stroke he acknowledges that he is at this moment forming what will be the past which he will have to remake in the anticipated future. Sartre argues that a consciousness is not identical with the personality. The "I" and the "Me" are but ideal poles of the psychic material in the continuous states of consciousness. Yet although a consciousness may adopt a new point of view on all that has preceded a particular moment and impose upon it a new organization and a totally different significance, it cannot blot out of its awareness the remembrance of its earlier states. My past *is* what I make it; it *was* then what I made it then. My present objective acts and the subjectivity which evokes them become a part of the background for all later intentions of my consciousness. In fact this consciousness is *my* consciousness by virtue of the accumulation of its specific intentions. Temporally a consciousness pursues a Self which is an essence gradually evolved from a self-making existent. This Self is the creation of consciousness. Self-realization here is the rounding off the project, the particular choice of Being. Its value is realized reflectively and in time. From one point of view, any life *is* a self-realization inasmuch as it is inevitably the development of what has been its possibilities. Yet inasmuch as the lived possibilities were but a small fraction of those which might have been chosen, we may, if we like, speak of self-realization in a stricter and more normative way. In this case we would say that self-realization is accomplished only by a consciousness which recognizes and assumes its freedom to choose the life it reflectively finds best. In either case, temporal self-realization is centered on the recognition of the connection between the states or acts of a consciousness. Certainly the idea of the justified life would be impossible for a consciousness which was not temporal.[4] Justification is reflective and demands a coherence between the present judging consciousness and its other intentions—whether they be in the remembered past or in the projected future.

The second kind of self-realization is immediate. It is the direct intuition of freedom. I am not speaking of the reflective and abstract *idea that* one is free. The *experience* of freedom is best realized in the nonreflective spontaneous act in which consciousness' implicit self-awareness of itself as acting takes the form of a nonreflective comprehension that the act is free of any considerations save the immediate willing. I do not mean to say that consciousness is ever for an instant wholly nontemporal. Even the process of reaching out toward a desired object implies a coherence of time. The totally isolated instant is pure imagined abstraction. If we may speak of instants at all, they are not entities but phases of a continued process. Speaking relatively, however, we may say that a consciousness may will itself nontemporal to the extent of refusing to make remembrance or anticipations of its more remote states into a significant aspect of its present choice. In a response which is radically inconsistent with its reflective pursuit of a coherent self-pattern, a consciousness vividly experiences itself as truly being that freedom which it is. As the Underground Man has told us, this spontaneous, nonreflective self-realization is infinitely precious. In a peculiar way it is more immediately identifiable with the sense of one's concrete personal existence than any kind of reflective temporal appraisal can possibly be.

In asserting that at times one positively ought to act contrary to one's own self-interest, the Underground Man is setting up one sort of self-realization against the other. The two realizations represent two aspects of man. He lives by

---

[4] Kierkegaard (especially in *Repetition* and in *Fear and Trembling*) has discussed certain aspects of the relation between temporality and time, though not in the same terms nor from the same point of view as that which I have adopted. Cf. Schragg, pp. 132–42.

17

inscribing himself in Being; that is, he makes himself be. But besides this he lives his nonbeing or his being-as-nothingness, his separation from Being. Or we might say, Man realizes himself both as Being, which he makes, and as Becoming, which he is. Sartre, of course, has presented the view that man is both Being and Nothingness. Man's Being derives from his "facticity," his finite existence in a specific situation in the world. It would not be quite right to say that his consciousness is Nothingness. More accurately, consciousness is a process of effecting a nothingness or separation between itself and its objects, of enfolding each of its objects with a nothingness which thereby introduces differentiation, significance, relations into the world. Sartre has stressed this psychic distance in man as the source of his freedom. He recognizes that it is this which results in man's having to choose what he will be rather than simply being it. Sartre, however, has stressed the idea that a consciousness' recognition of its nothingness and consequent freedom is a moment of anguish and despair. Most people flee from it in bad faith, taking refuge in "the serious world." This is the realm of convention where one unquestioningly accepts as absolutes the prevailing values of the group in which one finds oneself. I do not deny that this is the pattern followed by the majority of people. I think Sartre has failed to realize that the confrontation of freedom may just as well be grasped as a moment of self-realization and that one may cling to it as such, either with an attitude which Sartre, too, would call ethical or by making of it a reason for choosing the nonethical.

In short, the choice is not merely between authenticity and unauthenticity. It is threefold, and those critics arc right who have pointed out that authenticity by itself does not necessarily result in what may properly be called the ethical life. Persons who take refuge in unauthenticity and bad faith do not deliberately choose the nonethical. They recognize a need to justify their lives but are terrified at the thought of trying to do so without some clearly defined, impersonal standard which from outside themselves would guarantee certain absolute rights and wrongs. They want a certainty which they cannot feel so long as they realize that the choice of values derives from their own freedom. We cannot call their position ethical inasmuch as it is based upon self-deception, but it is the very opposite of an open choice of the nonethical. It is in reality a choice of the appearance of the ethical.

The choice to live unauthentically rests upon a refusal to recognize the existence and demands of freedom; it seeks to hide from itself the very fact that it *is* a choice. The choice to be ethical embraces both the recognition that one is free and the acceptance of the responsibility which freedom entails. It is an authentic choice, for it recognizes that the decision to justify one's life derives from one's own spontaneous desire and is not imposed from the outside. There remains a third alternative, which is that of the Underground Man. We cannot call his choice unauthentic, for the Underground Man is fully aware that he and he alone is responsible for what he chooses. Indeed it is freedom itself which he chooses as the value so far beyond all others that he pits it against all possible values which might in the future result from submitting this freedom to any sort of calculated restriction, external or internal. The moment of his recognition of freedom is identified with self-realization and in so far as is possible, the Underground Man severs it entirely from the temporally limited Self. To put it another way, the Underground Man asserts that he prizes his freedom not to be ethical. He does not have to justify himself, he is not obliged to choose happiness or any other self-evident good. He chooses his independence of all regulating value systems. The Underground Man chooses to live this recognition in a deliberate choice of present unhappiness. More often the refusal to justify one's life takes the form of choosing at whim the immediately desirable without concern for being able to defend the choice objectively. In this case, too, there is a deliberate rejection of responsibility for one's own past and future as for that part of one's self-projection which involves others. To reject the temporal is to reject the objective side of oneself; it is to identify oneself solely with the subjective.

That the Underground Man's kind of self-realization in-

19

volves a true apprehension, albeit a partial one, and a value not easily given up is attested in the experience of all of us. In practice an ethical system is lived as a personal value system and moral code. In every person's life, no matter how reflectively self-justifying he may be, there are certain actions which he cannot justify by reference to his moral code. If one always regarded these as moral lapses and failures, they would present no theoretical difficulty. Any normative ideal represents to some degree a goal to be achieved, not something fully and forever attained. The trouble is that sometimes these departures are just those actions and choices which one secretly and genuinely treasures. One may blush or feel slightly ashamed or judge soberly that the risk involved was too great to justify either the anticipated or the actual reward. One may even go so far as to declare that if the opportunity should be offered again, he would act differently. The fact remains that we are still glad to have done as we did and would not cancel it out of our past even if we had the chance. A closely related phenomenon is the Exception. The most ethically determined among us will at times resolve—and feel right about it—to do something mildly illegal, for instance, even if his theoretical position is that one should obey all laws not manifestly unjust. We may choose an action which we would not be willing to have made into a Universal Law. At the same time, we may feel that if there could be another Me acting in just this way for these reasons and just this once, we would approve. I am not satisfied to cut this Gordian knot by merely agreeing that man is prone to rationalize and cannot—without grace—live up to any ethical ideal.

It is fairly easy to give psychological explanations for the inconsistent behavior. Most often probably the Exception, when it is not mere rationalization for failure, represents an incomplete realization that what one reflectively holds to be his value system does not actually represent his true feeling. There is not necessarily bad faith here, rather an as yet only partial comprehension of the significance of one's mode of remaking his past and choosing his future. Even without appeal to an Unconscious, it is obvious that the greater part of our awareness is on the nonreflective level. The Exception may actually represent a step toward an ethical position which is more comprehensive and closely articulated than our present one.

Often the past act which we inconsistently do not regret or the present insistence on the Exception comes closer to what the Underground Man was defending. As free human beings with an infinity of potentialities, we resent even such self-imprisonment as results from our intention to make of ourselves any chosen type of person, developing those capacities rather than certain others. Even the choice of constructive values over destructive involves restriction and a sacrifice. The recollection of having acted "out of character" may easily produce a keener sense of pleasure than of guilt. For it is an enrichment, a reassurance that we are in one sense more than we are. The excluded side of what we might have been has been given a token recognition. What has happened is that a person has for the moment stepped from one value system into another. The contradiction is too sharp to be resolved by modification and enriching of the original code so as to include the exceptional conduct. One feels guilty, senses that he can't go on repeating the act without giving up all aspiration to the ethical. Yet he has no regret. He pays psychologically just as one pays physiologically for overindulgence. A blend of repentance and secret pleasure is characteristic of both kinds of hangovers.

Some of these departures from the ethical are curiously akin to innocence. Perhaps, after all, we should say that the best personal value system is one which allows a moral holiday now and then for a brief sojourn in another climate. The disruptive choice or the choice which carries a risk disproportionate to the probable reward may be justified if the only alternative is psychic starvation. It is a truism that the life with the minimum of acute unhappiness is unlikely to have many peaks of joy. The perfectly coherent, rigidly observed code of ethics may well be maintained at the cost of foregoing all spontaneity. To be perfectly what one has chosen to be will inevitably exclude much that is precious in what he might otherwise have been.

At this point we are admittedly going beyond the point at issue and beginning to talk about requirements for a specific ethics rather than the problem of whether or not one ought to choose to be ethical. I have allowed the slight digression in order to underscore the point that the choice not to be ethical, not only is a real possibility, but seems to offer certain genuine values. We return now to the original question. Have we discovered any reason for saying that one ought to choose the ethical?

There is a peculiar way in which it is the very positing of the question which necessitates an affirmative answer. Furthermore, although we may be able to set up theoretically and abstractly a situation in which the question is not posited, I do not believe that there ever has or could be a human life in which this is the case for very long—certainly not if the life is above that of the imbecile and continued beyond early childhood. Such a person would have to be one for whom there was no appeal whatsoever in harmonious continuity of judgments and conduct, one who felt no interest or even connection with his own past and future, and one who was without any inclination to experience more rather than less of positive value. This theoretical man cannot exist. Since a consciousness cannot be unaware of its temporality, it is forced to choose its own way of living this temporality and to choose the value it will assign to the two possibilities of realizing a Self. Consciousness cannot avoid being reflective, for its past experiences are there as part of the background of every choice. The decision to regard the coherent justification of one's temporal existence as important, or not to do so, is an answer to the question implied, or stated: "What ought I to do?" Consciousness by itself poses the question to itself; the "ought" is there as the motive or reason or criterion in accordance with which the choice is made. The Underground Man declares that he *ought* to choose against his own self-interest; that is, he ought to choose spontaneous realization of himself as freedom rather than temporal realization of his gradually objectified self. By saying "ought" he indicates that he recognizes the need to justify his choice, at least to himself, as somehow the better one.

Yet I have persisted in calling his choice nonethical. This I must myself try to justify. In speaking of "ought," we imply the presence of a compelling factor of such a sort that to recognize it is simultaneously to grant that it sets up a demand which must be filled. Even in the disguised form of "This is better" or "This is preferable," there is set up the idea that one recognizes the requirement to choose the greater value. In the Underground Man's statement that it is better to choose against his own "self-interest" in order to preserve his "life," he makes two value assertions: that it is good to preserve the truly vital self and that the way to do this is to choose against the self which normally serves as the basis for any hedonistic calculation. We may argue against him as follows: (1) By introducing the idea of "ought," he himself has acknowledged the demand for justification, at least in the form of saying that one should choose that which gives the greater positive value. (2) He therefore opens himself to the possibility of the charge that he is mistaken in thinking that his choice is in reality that of the greater value, which if proved, undermines his whole position. (3) The Underground Man's choice of "life" is based on the view that he wants to preserve what he is. We may argue in turn that while he *is* the spontaneous realization of the freedom to be what he will, he *is* also the temporal unity of all such moments. He *is* a projection of his future in the light of what he makes of his past. Of course he is free—if he will—to reject all rational justification, and to limit his sense of satisfaction to the narrow realization that he does not *have* to be happy in any of the multitude of ways open to him. There is nothing to force him to choose the course which will result in a higher degree of value. But if he says, "I ought to choose" or even "I prefer to

23

choose," we have caught him. For in so saying, he declares the value to be greater, and we can show that he is mistaken.

There is no way of persuading a man to accept the challenge to justify his life if he refuses to see justification itself as a good, as a value which he is willing to accept and reach out for. Similarly, if he declares that he rejects all such values as happiness, the sense of being satisfied with his life and finding it worthwhile, of expanded experience—in short, if he chooses pain, misery, half-aware self-deception, inconsistency, and dishonesty, there is nothing to be done. But to say there is nothing to be done is simply to confess failure in persuasion. We need not stop at this point. If one argues purely abstractly that honesty, consistency, feelings of pleasure, and the sense of being happy with one's life are not self-evident goods which one ought to seek, I agree—abstractly—that there is no external, impersonal proof that they are. Yet the person we are postulating exists only theoretically. He is a more appropriate obstacle for the idealist than for the existentialist, who is concerned with living men and women. To adjust everything to him is a bit like trying to form an ethics for a two-year-old child abandoned by chance on a deserted planet. In actual fact the man we are theoretically postulating does not exist. The live man who most closely approximates him is in reality acknowledging and acting in the name of those values which he pretends to reject. The would-be suicide may resist all our arguments that life can be rewarding. The fact remains that if he could be convinced that there were goods worth striving for, he would not kill himself. The man who declares that he does not want to live states implicitly that he cannot find those things which, if attained, would make him want to live. He may be sincere in claiming that the problem is not that he cannot find what he wants but that he cannot find anything to want. Even so he presumes that the feeling of wanting-and-finding is good.

In insisting that one ought to choose to be ethical, we are on sure ground in affirming at least these things: First, the choice not to be ethical is almost wholly a rejection. Its bare minimum of positive value is the true recognition that one is in fact free not to subject himself to any demands whatsoever if he so chooses. Although this realization of the film of nothingness between a consciousness and its own projects may bring dread to most people, it is possible to embrace it in joy and attempt to make it the sole absolute value of a life. The wholly arbitrary excludes any consistent motivation. The purely nonethical life is as impossible to sustain practically as the perfectly ethical one. Insofar as it can be lived, it takes the form of rejecting all rational calculation, all responsibility for others and for one's own past and future—at least in the sense of feeling that one's acts should be governed by such considerations. It places all value on spontaneous self-realization and none on the temporal kind. Thus it is a choice of subjectivity and a rejection of objectivity, not an expansion of life but a reduction. It is a refusal to admit that it is necessary or even desirable that there should be a positive correlation between reality and one's behavior, for it rejects rational justification as being a good which one ought to seek. The choice to be nonethical is not a choice of being or of becoming. It is in truth a choice of Nothingness. In it, consciousness, like the Schopenhauerian Will, seeks to prey on itself. In the name of asserting itself as a free relationship to all things, it denies the importance of all those relations it establishes and of those objects without which it would be nothing at all.

The choice to be ethical affirms the importance of realizing oneself objectively in time. It does not deny or preclude freedom's spontaneous self-realization. This is where the Underground Man was mistaken. Although the nonethical choice embraces the constant possibility of ignoring all demands for imposing a consistent value system on one's life, the ethical choice requires that we recognize all of the truth about man as part of the data on the basis of which we make our decisions.

Once we grant that the choice to be ethical is a commitment to the need to justify one's life, we can fairly rapidly set up certain basic requirements which will have to be met by any system which purports to be an ethics. First of all, if the idea of justification demands that there be a harmony of subjective judgment and objective experience, then our ethics must never knowingly assume a view which conflicts with what is believed to be reality. An ethics must introduce rationality as one of its criteria even though it may at the same time insist that its goal is happiness or satisfaction or some other state which is closer to emotion than to reason. Fidelity to the truth of man and the Universe is essential. Philosophical systems vary as to the degree to which such Truth is thought to be absolute and attainable by everyone, but no ethics may be allowed to act contrary to what it believes to be real and true. Possibly honesty would be the better term here, but I use the word to comprise more than the quality of not deceiving oneself or others. It includes, as well, the determination to know insofar as possible what reality is and never to allow conduct which cannot be justified without denying what one holds to be given. An example is the existentialist belief in human freedom. If one accepts freedom as a fact, then no act is ethical which acts as if men were not free. Rationality involves more than intellectual honesty. It requires as one of its corollary values a respect for consistency.

Here we must be careful. I am not asking for that kind of obedience to the laws of logic which Schopenhauer compared to a man's walking with crutches when he could perfectly well go on two sound legs. Formal logic may very well represent only one partial organization imposed on reality by imperfectly developed thought, in which case any attempt to limit human experience to the logical might be specifically nonethical. Existentialism in particular takes this position, and I think it is right to do so. If logic and what we believe to be reality do not conform, then we must regretfully bid logic adieu or put it aside until it is more adequately developed. Nevertheless, there is a recognizable difference between the process of canceling out all facts which do not fit into an intellectual scheme and cheerfully accepting opposing views at whim as if their opposition were not itself a fact to be taken into consideration.

26

Finally an ethics must meet a certain minimum of pragmatic tests. It must provide clearly discernible ways of attaining the values which it promises. Moreover, if the ethical choice is to have preponderance over the nonethical, it must offer the opportunity of achieving *more* value. The traditional problems of all hedonistic calculations still remain—qualitative distinctions among types of value, diversity versus intensity, immediate satisfactions versus anticipated, and so forth. However it may try to solve these difficulties, a specific ethics must make the individual feel and believe that this way of life offers the highest degree of value experience open to him. Otherwise there is no reason at all for him to choose the ethical. If there is any one universal fact about man, it is the experience of values and disvalues. There is no one who does not experience a sense of reaching out toward some things, of welcoming them when they are grasped, and of shrinking from others, wishing they were not present when they are. If words have any meaning at all, values are good and disvalues are bad—relative to the one establishing the values and disvalues. To say that one would choose a disvalue is nonsense. To say that one always chooses value may be tautological, but it at least recognizes a reality and offers some clarification. The minimum aim of any ethical system is to promote value and to reduce disvalue. The ethical choice differs from choice as such in this way: Any choice is a selection of one value in preference to another. The choice of the nonethical is a resolve to possess certain immediate values, one of which is freedom not to make the effort to determine whether or not one is going to enjoy the highest degree of value possible for him. The ethical choice is the will to live the life which may be reflectively appraised as holding in truth the greatest value.

We may thus argue abstractly that one ought to choose the ethical. One ought to choose what offers the greater value, for value is the only object of choice and its sole motive.

Man is a creature of such a sort that if he once asks himself, "What have I made of myself and how do I appraise what I have become?" then he *must* answer. So far we may

27

say that justification assumes the form of a defense. If at the same time he asks himself, "What do I want to be?" he commits himself to a particular future. The ethical choice derives from our awareness that these two moments are forever repeated and inextricably bound together.

II

Sartre's Choice

At the time of the publication of *Being and Nothingness* in 1943, it was possible to argue that the seeds of a responsible ethics were already present in Sartre's philosophy. He himself promised this development in a later work. In the late fifties I tried to show that the connection between Sartre's fictional examination of ethical choices and his ontology was closer than most critics were willing to admit. Had I been writing the present book before 1960, I should have proceeded immediately at this point to show that those who denied the possibility of an existentialist ethics were both disregarding the positive side of Sartre's work and setting up untenable criteria for what an ethics must be. Now in the mid-sixties, we must first confront another problem. This is the fact that Sartre himself has stated flatly that he no longer has any interest in writing an ethics. More than that, he apparently believes that the project of working out a formal ethics is an irrelevance, an escapism, if not a downright impossibility.

In her autobiography, Simone de Beauvoir states that Sartre arrived at this conclusion in 1950. Quoting from Sartre's own unpublished notes, she says that Sartre gave up the idea of formulating his own philosophical ethics "because he was convinced that 'The ethical attitude appears when technological and social conditions render positive conduct impossible. Ethics is a collection of idealist devices to help you live the life which poverty of resources and lack of techniques impose upon you.' " [1] The date is highly significant. Sartre, who was born in 1905, has declared that he dreamed the first fifty years of his life. *The Words*, the autobiography of his childhood, was first written in 1954. Its theme is an awakened reappraisal after almost fifty years of delusion. Sartre's particular dream had been that it was possible to be saved through literature. In an interview held soon after the publication of *The Words* (1964), Sartre makes clear that he puts literature and formal ethics on the same plane. [2]

As early as the period when I was writing *Nausea*, I wanted to work out an ethics. My development has reached the point where I no longer dream of it. Today I regard *Les Nourritures ter-restres* as a frightening book. "Do not search for God anywhere but everywhere." Go talk about that to a worker, an engineer! Gide can say it to me. It is a writer's ethics which addresses itself only to a few privileged persons. For this reason it does not concern me. It is necessary first for all men to be able to become men through improving the conditions of their existence if they are going to be able to formulate a universal ethics. If I begin by telling them: "Thou shalt not lie," political action is no longer possible. What matters first is the liberation of man.

In answer to a question as to whether he had abandoned the somber view of man presented in *Nausea*, Sartre replied, "No. The universe remains black. We are shipwrecked ani-

---

[1] Simone de Beauvoir: *La Force des choses* (Paris: Gallimard; 1963), p. 218. Here and elsewhere translations from the French are my own unless otherwise indicated.

[2] This idea and much of the rest of the material in this chapter I have discussed in a paper which I read at the annual meeting of the American Catholic Philosophical Association in 1965 and which was later published. "Literature as Salvation in the Work of Jean-Paul Sartre," *Proceedings of the American Catholic Philosophical Association*, Vol. XXXIX (1965), pp. 53–68.

mals. . . . But I discovered suddenly that alienation, the exploitation of men by other men, undernourishment—these make metaphysical unhappiness a luxury and relegate it to second place. Hunger—now that *is* an evil." [3]

There are several remarkable things about Sartre's recent position. It is evident, first of all, that he has not really abandoned ethics. He has chosen to act in accordance with the practical ethics of Marxism (albeit his own version of Marxism) in preference to the task of working out the theoretical ethics of existentialism. He himself does not regard this interim attitude as being in itself ethical. He seems to adopt it more in the mood of Descartes setting a temporary set of regulations for conduct to guide him while he sought the Truth. But Descartes resolved to live moderately and quietly, staying out of trouble until he might find absolutes to justify whatever he might then choose to do. Sartre seems ready to risk everything now for the sake of achieving certain absolute goods which will then create for us a society where we may safely indulge in abstract justifications of our conduct. In short, ethics, which is unimportant anyway and a luxury at best, is to be put on the shelf while we do the hard work of helping men and women attain the condition which will allow them to fulfill themselves as human beings. All of this seems to me quite backward. Sartre's present position is not consistent with his earlier existentialism, and I personally do not think it is defensible. I do believe that it is understandable and that Sartre himself has given us the clues which we need in hunting for an explanation. Why, then, does Sartre reject the idea of an ethics for existentialism *now?*

Sartre's refusal to write an ethics appears to be based on two convictions: First, an existentialist ethics is at present impossible. Second, the act of trying to formulate any theoretical ethics is not at present ethically justified.

Sartre's reason for finding an ethics impossible at this time is not, needless to say, a confession that those critics are right who claim that Sartre's ontology does not allow

[3] "Jean-Paul Sartre s'explique sur 'Les Mots,'" an interview with Jacqueline Piatier published in *Le Monde*, April 18, 1964.

for an ethics. He seems to have two other reasons. First of all, he is convinced of the impossibility of purity of action in an unjust society. Sartre had already developed this idea in his analytical biography of Genet. He has it in mind in his sarcastic reference to the incompatibility of lying and effective political action. De Beauvoir expresses the same despair in the final summing up of her autobiography. "When you inhabit an unjust world, it is useless to hope by any method to be purified of injustice; what would be necessary would be to change the world, and I do not have the power for that. To suffer from these contradictions is of no use; to forget them is to lie to oneself." [4] I confess that I react to these words with a feeling of impatience. Of course the ideal of ethical purity is unattainable as is that of any other perfection. This is not to say that all action is equivalent or that anything short of purity is without ethical significance.

Sartre's second reason for finding an ethics impossible raises more seriously the question of whether he has renounced the most fundamental of all existentialist theses—the belief in man's freedom. The problem is posed by a passage in *Search for a Method*, found at the conclusion of Sartre's discussion of the proper relation between existentialism and Marxism.

We support unreservedly that formulation in *Capital* by which Marx means to define his "materialism": "The mode of production of material life generally dominates the development of social, political, and intellectual life." We cannot conceive of this conditioning in any form except that of a dialectical movement (contradictions, surpassing, totalizations). . . . We are all acquainted with the passage in which Marx alludes to that far-off time: "This reign of freedom does not begin in fact until the time when the work imposed by necessity and external finality shall cease; it is found, therefore, beyond the sphere of material production proper. . . ."
As soon as there will exist *for everyone* a margin of *real* freedom beyond the production of life, Marxism will have lived out its span; a philosophy of freedom will take its place. But we have no

---

[4] De Beauvoir: *La Force des choses*, p. 681.

means, no intellectual instrument, no concrete experience which allows us to conceive of this freedom or of this philosophy.[5]

We should note that this philosophy of freedom is not contemporary existentialism as we know it. Sartre envisions a dialectical movement: First, existentialism will modify Marxism from within by reinserting at its heart the "existential project," thus conferring upon Marxism once more the "human dimension" which the heirs of Marx have all but destroyed. Then, existentialism will cease to exist in its own right but will live on, "absorbed, surpassed and conserved by the totalizing movement" of the revitalized neo-Marxism it has helped bring into being. Finally, when the world's inhabitants have been freed from economic pressures induced by the "problems of production," Marxism itself will be surpassed and conserved in the new "philosophy of freedom."

Starting at the far end, I may say that I have intense admiration for Sartre's ability to envision the transcendence of his own thought (both existentialist and Marxist) in a new philosophical system beyond his present comprehension. This represents a refreshing change from the tendency of most philosophers to view the past history of philosophy as a dialectical process pointing toward them and to anticipate a future world forever filing its events neatly within the categories which they as philosophers have established. Sartre does not, either in an excess of modesty or of cynicism, imply that all philosophical formulations, including his own, have been so tentative that they may be wiped out like the tales of elves and brownies. His attitude is rather that of the space scientist who relies upon the truth and adequacy of his present knowledge and methods to open the door to other possibilities and techniques which he cannot at present grasp even as problems. Sartre's hopeful prediction represents one of the few instances where he takes seriously his own pronouncement that human life is a continuing self-transcendence, that human nature is not fixed, that man is indeed a creature who

[5] Jean-Paul Sartre: *Search for a Method*, tr. Hazel E. Barnes (New York: Alfred A. Knopf; 1963), pp. 33–4.

makes himself by a process of constant change. Humanistic existentialism has always insisted on viewing man as he exists concretely in a specific situation, in a milieu defined as to time and place and human institutions. It would be illogical to expect that the ethics and social philosophy for men and women living in an environment dominated by material scarcity and economic competition would remain the same in a society where the problems of production had been adequately solved. It is akin to attempting to solve beforehand the specific problems of human relationships in a world where extrasensory perception would be the established means of communication. The philosophy of man, whose very existence is a continuing self-transcendence, ought to be itself self-transcending.

What disturbs me, both in this passage and in his declaration that he has abandoned his aspiration to write his own ethics, is Sartre's assumption concerning the first stage when presumably existentialism still has a reason for being—even in the judgment of Sartre as a neo-Marxist. It is one thing to speak of a future philosophy of freedom; it is quite another to hold that there can be no philosophy of freedom now. Does this mean that Sartre's own contemporary existentialism is *not* a philosophy of freedom? Strangely enough, Sartre's theoretical answer here is easier to accept than his practical one. His scornful implication that it will be a long time before more than a few people possess any *real* freedom is not intended as a denial that man is free existentially. Sartre absolutely never falls into the trap of assuming that the coming of the Marxist millennium is inevitable. Its arrival is not guaranteed by any mechanistic functioning of economic laws or by a suprapersonal historical determinism. Sartre has explicitly stated that in his opinion socialism "is the movement of man in process of making himself; other parties believe that man is already made." [6] The dialectical progress of history is carried on by men and women who refuse to live the life which conditions impose on them and who find ways

[6] Jean-Paul Sartre: "Le Fantôme de Staline"; quoted and discussed by Simone de Beauvoir in *La Force des choses*, p. 218.

of changing those conditions. Sartre's form of Marxism could not exist apart from the premise that men are free to choose how they will live the situation in which they find themselves. He has never confused the freedom to choose with the power to do what one would like to choose. In the passage quoted, Sartre implies that psychological freedom is of little value when the practical possibilities are narrowly restricted. His enemies have argued precisely this, and it is discouraging to see Sartre apparently agreeing with them. In fairness, however, we should point out that it is the immeasurability of man's potentials that provides much of the motivating force for Sartre's insistence that all men must be liberated from the factual limitations of their practical freedom. Sartre seems to restate with added psychological overtones Rousseau's political manifesto that "Man is free and everywhere in chains."

Sartre has not made clear to me why there cannot be an ethics, derived from existentialism as *our* philosophy of freedom, which would guide and support this very process of liberation. He postulates the future existence of a philosophy of freedom for persons who know they are free existentially and who have attained the material means for giving scope to this freedom in projects in the world. He rejects the possibility of a philosophy of freedom for those who have recognized that they are existentially free and want to work toward the practical realization of freedom on the part of everyone.

If we look further, it seems to me that Sartre's belief that an ethics of freedom is impossible now depends less on his sense of present restrictions to men's actions than on an implied definition of ethics not consistent with his own philosophy. When he says that ethics is "a collection of idealist devices" to help one endure a life one cannot change, he may be accurately defining certain ethical systems—Stoicism, for example, or Epicureanism, or some of the philosophies of India. Such a quietist ethics would hardly be what one would expect of a philosophy such as existentialism which maintains that each man defines himself through his acts. Yet it is in the name of action that Sartre rejects the idea of an ethics for our period, finding the writing of an ethics to be an irrelevance, a

35

luxury, even going so far as to suggest that it is an escape in bad faith for those who would like to find an excuse to neglect their social responsibilities. Clearly Sartre is thinking here of an ethics which would be little more than an abstract, introspective search for principles to solace our metaphysical unhappiness. In short, Sartre seems to associate ethics with our need for absolute salvation.

I have pointed out that Sartre links formal ethics and literature in the statement that he has given up his intention of "making an ethics." I think that if we look briefly at the evolution of his changing attitude toward the role of the writer, we shall be in a better position to understand his view of what ethics is and to criticize his final rejection. Inasmuch as Sartre himself has discussed his aesthetic development in terms normally used for the religious experience, I think it is appropriate to observe that his view of literature has progressed in three stages: Sartre began by seeing literature as a means of salvation. In a middle period, he continued to feel that through it the writer might be saved, but he emphasized that literature could represent as well a dangerous temptation. Finally he concluded that literature is a damnation.

Sartre presented seriously the idea that literature constitutes a salvation, or is a means of salvation, in his novel *Nausea* (1938); he satirically attacked it in *The Words* (1964). Throughout the novel, Roquentin contrasts the contingent superfluity of existents with the internal necessity of ideal or imagined things. In a circle each segment has its own *raison d'être;* it is guaranteed, so to speak, by the circle as a whole; yet it is not made or determined by anything outside itself any more than the rest of the circle is. Similarly, in an adventure described in a book, the beginning, the end, each separate episode partakes of this same necessity. Any seemingly trivial event or object is loaded with significance. The denouement which is to come has impressed its mark on all that precedes it. Roquentin finds it impossible to live such adventures in his own life. He is imbued with the contingency of all existing things. He is *de trop*, and he is aware constantly of that nausea which accompanies the revelation of his body to his consciousness. The brief moments of respite from the nausea occurred when Roquentin listened to a blues record on the café phonograph. This "glorious little melody" had the necessary perfection of the circle and of the adventure. It existed independent of the particular disk on which it was recorded. Hearing it led one to remember the composer and the singer. The song existed apart from them; yet because of the creative link which brought it into being, they remained essential to it. "To me they are a little like the dead, a little like the heroes of a novel. They have cleansed themselves of the sin of existing. Not completely, of course, but as much as any man can." Roquentin resolved to write a novel so that someone at some time might think of him as he thought of the composer and the singer. "Then perhaps I would be able, through it, to think back on my life without disgust. . . . And I would succeed—in the past, only in the past—in accepting myself." [7] What Roquentin proposes is a personal salvation for the writer by means of a creative objectification of himself. In *The Words* Sartre says that he *was* Roquentin, but he blames himself for having stayed too much aloof from his character and for having cured himself of Roquentin's unhappiness by the act of writing about it. The self-reproach seems unnecessary. Sartre's solution and Roquentin's are the same, and we are led to believe that Roquentin would ultimately find significance and happiness in life by inventing a literary hero. Perhaps this character would in turn suffer as Roquentin had done and find Roquentin's cure. If so, there is an ever-widening circle. The circle, we recall, was the symbol of necessary Being which Roquentin so wistfully desired.

It is natural to imagine that at this period of his life, Sartre looked upon his prospective ethics in much the same way as he regarded the work of fiction. De Beauvoir relates that both she and Sartre in the prewar years held themselves aloof from politics and social action with the excuse that in the unjust bourgeois society in which they lived, no positive choices

[7] Jean-Paul Sartre: *La Nausée* (Paris: Gallimard; 1938), pp. 221–2.

37

were possible. She mentions that upon one occasion Sartre did
not even bother to vote in an election. We can scarcely even
guess what the Sartrean ethics would have been had Sartre
written it out in those days. Utopian, perhaps? Neo-Nietz-
schean? A justification of his own quietism? It seems most
likely that it would have been highly abstract and self-contained, probably more descriptive than normative, its relevance to contemporary issues more implied than specifically
stated. In any case, it seems obvious to me that Sartre's
present attitude suggests that this is the way he thinks now of
the ethics he might have written. It is ironic, too, that so
many years later, his refusal to write an ethics is reminiscent
of his not bothering to vote in the thirties—both based on the
plea that nothing positive can be accomplished in an unjust
society.

De Beauvoir has recorded that during the early stages of
the war, Sartre on furlough informed her that he had decided
his earlier aloofness was wrong. It was necessary to participate directly and immediately in the affairs of the society.
The writer's responsibility followed as a corollary.[8] When
American readers became acquainted with Sartre in the early
forties, he appeared to them as the confirmed proponent of
engaged or committed literature. The great temptation of the
writer is to write for immortality and not for his own time.
The way to do this is to refuse to put anything into question,
to pose purely aesthetic problems with formal solutions,
equally valid for any generation and equally nonchallenging.
Sartre argues that the writer must engage himself. He must
confront the concrete problems of his period. Furthermore, he
must write to promote human freedom, for anything else is to
betray both humanity and literature. For Roquentin the outside world was of value only as material setting; even the
reader was necessary only as a means of securing the Being
of the writer. For an engaged literature, the reader and the
outside world are essential. Literature is action. Its function

[8] De Beauvoir discusses Sartre's gradual development from apolitical theory to political action in the opening pages of *La Force des
choses*.

is to show man his reflection as in a mirror, a magic mirror which images potentiality as well as the actual.

The theory of engaged literature rests upon an implied ethics of responsibility. From one point of view, Sartre is careful not to bestow upon the writer any privileged place. He rejects the slogan of "art for art's sake" as a mere pretense on the part of the author that what he writes has no connection with the world of his contemporaries. The writer's situation is that of everyone. Just as Sartre says of all of us that with each act we choose ourselves, that not to choose is already to have chosen, so we may say that a writer commits himself by the very act of writing. If he creates an imaginary world of such a sort that all of the conventional values of contemporary society are implied or not brought into question, this is to support those values. The choice in good faith is a choice that is fully aware, one in which the chooser recognizes his responsibility in choosing. Most of the criticism directed at Sartre's plea for the writer's commitment claimed that he was asking for a propaganda literature. This was certainly not Sartre's intention. Certainly his own work of this period is not devoted to arguing for any specific political or social platform. Admittedly it presents an existentialist view of the human condition and a portrayal of character consistent with existential psychology. This is merely to say that its psychological and philosophical commitments are not those of naturalism or Freudianism or any of the other world views which have been explicitly or implicitly introduced as the background worlds of fictional beings. For our purposes, what is important is the fact that Sartre at this stage felt that the individual's private dilemmas, his "metaphysical unhappiness," and his attempts to justify his existence in his own eyes were all significant for the writer, for the philosopher, or for the one who lived them. In short, each person had the right and the obligation to create his own value system, to objectify himself by modifying his external situation, and to bestow upon his situation the authentic meaning which he freely chose. At this stage it mattered whether one's life were in good or bad faith, lived authentically or unauthentically. Sartre found it worth his while to investigate the subject-object conflict in *No Exit*, to explore the anguish of newly realized freedom in *The Flies*, the anxieties of conflicting commitments in *Dirty Hands*. In so doing he exemplified perfectly his own notion of the committed writer who in seeking to justify himself as a writer, demonstrated to others the need to assume responsibility for their own lives and for the world. Obviously for Sartre at this time, ethics and literature, while not the same, were inseparable, in the same way that one might say Christianity and literature were for Dante. Sartre as writer, Sartre as philosopher, and Sartre's existentialist heroes all quite obviously sought a way by which one could justify one's life. Everywhere implied was the idea that one must be faithful to the facts of the human condition, and this required both the scrupulous recognition of the absolute subjectivity of every individual freedom and the assumption of one's own responsibility for what he made of his life and for the consequences of his acts in molding the situations within which other freedoms made their choices. Although Sartre did not formulate an abstract system of ethics, one felt everywhere the presence of an implied ethics, whose general outline at least was clear.

Paradoxically it was Sartre's own further developed sense of responsibility for the oppressed of this world which led him to dismiss his own efforts as inadequate. "Literature is crap!" he exclaimed, in fatigued discouragement, contemplating some of the wreckage of the war.[9] Speaking of Goetz, the hero of *The Devil and the Good Lord*, Sartre said, "I had Goetz do what I was unable to do." What Sartre apparently meant was that his hero, within the framework of the play, was able to escape from the realm of metaphysical abstractions, to choose himself freely and ethically in a way which worked directly toward the liberation of all men. Sartre, on the other hand, felt that his own situation involved an irreconcilable contradiction.

The contradiction was not in the ideas. It was in my being. For this freedom which *I was* implied that of all. And all were not

[9] De Beauvoir: *La Force des choses*, p. 333.

free. I could not, without fibbing, submit myself to the discipline of all. And I could not be free alone.[1]

Whatever one may think of such delicacy of conscience, Sartre was unwilling to settle for the sense of personal justification won by the committed writer. What particularly disturbed him was that he considered himself to be still addressing only the privileged few.

To speak to one whom one cannot convince (the Hindu who is dying of starvation), or else all communication is compromise. That is very certainly the meaning of my evolution and of my contradiction.

De Beauvoir adds the comment, "To have given an aesthetic solution to his problem was not enough for him. He sought for a way to do what Goetz had done."

Just as Sartre suffers from being forced to write about the oppressed whom he would help, instead of speaking directly to them, so he has gradually come to disdain all activity which is not immediately involved in the economic and social liberation of man. It is in this spirit that he cynically relegates literature to secondary importance, even as he continues to write it, and seems to regard ethics and indeed all philosophy as leisure activity—except for the socio-political. One feels that only the realistic sense of his own limitations prevents Sartre from renouncing all writing in the interest of direct political candidacy.

In this final stage Sartre sees literature as a species of damnation, a damnation in that it once nourished in him a false hope, one which turned out to be one more particularly subtle and powerful form of bad faith, promising salvation where there was none. "Out of the need to justify my existence, I had made literature into an Absolute. It took thirty years for me to get out of that state of mind." [2] It is my conviction that if, instead of literature, we were to read "formal philosophy," including ethics but not, of course, political

[1] From unpublished notes quoted by Simone de Beauvoir in *La Force des choses*, p. 262.

[2] Interview: "Jean-Paul Sartre s'explique sur 'Les Mots.'"

theory, we should not be distorting Sartre's position and we should be aided in understanding his present attitude toward an ethics. Sartre evidently sees all activity as damnation—if to hold that there is no salvation means that men are damned. For he goes on to say that one is not saved by politics either, nor by anything. "There is no salvation anywhere." The idea of salvation implies an Absolute, Sartre maintains, and the Absolute is not to be found. I feel that we are hearing again, more than twenty years later, a new variation on that theme stated so powerfully in *Being and Nothingness*—that man is a useless passion for a missing God.

Indeed Sartre views his own development as a religious evolution, but it is my belief that his self-appraisal is incomplete. More important, I think the evolution itself has been truncated and that Sartre has neglected to take the final step. As he himself explains things, the inner meaning of his Catholic training was transferred, as it were, from the theological setting to the literary.

Lifted out of Catholicism, the sacred settled in Belles-Lettres, and the man of the pen appeared, an *ersatz* of the Christian that I could not be. His sole concern was salvation; his sojourn here below had no other purpose but to pass all tests by which he might show himself worthy of posthumous beatitude. . . . Earthly immortality was offered as a substitute for eternal life. . . . I thought I was devoting myself to literature when in reality I was entering into Holy Orders.[3]

Sartre relates that one morning when he was about twelve, while waiting for some tardy school friends, he decided to think about the Almighty.

Suddenly he tumbled into the blue and disappeared without offering any explanation. "He doesn't exist," I said to myself with polite surprise, and I believed the matter settled. . . . But the Other remained, the Invisible One, the Holy Ghost, He who guaranteed my mandate and dominated my life with great, anonymous and sacred powers.[4]

[3] Jean-Paul Sartre: *Les Mots* (Paris: Gallimard; 1964), pp. 207–8.
[4] Ibid., p. 209.

42

As one "still of the Church," Sartre sought to "wrest his life from chance," to "save himself by works," to "unveil the silence of Being by a thwarted rustling of words." It is easy to recognize Sartre-Roquentin in this description, and indeed Sartre has said, "I *was* Roquentin." Sartre himself does not recognize as a significant change what I have described as the second stage of the committed writer. Instead he indicates that he continued as priest of Belles-Lettres until his fiftieth year. His description of his awakening is remarkably vivid. "I nabbed the Holy Ghost in the cellar and threw him out. Atheism is a cruel and long-range affair. I believe I have seen it through to the end."

Sartre is wrong. He has not lived out his atheism to its logical conclusion. I believe him when he says that he has given up God and got rid of the Holy Ghost. He still holds on to the Messiah. Naturally I do not mean that he would allot the role of Saviour to an individual—certainly not to himself, not even to his idealized portrait of Marx. But the Messianic message is clear. At the very moment when Sartre claims to have renounced all hope of Absolutes, he introduces the heaviest and most positive Absolute of his career. Everything is judged in relation to the central imperative of hastening that ideal future state of society when the problems of production will have been solved, when the true philosophy of freedom will emerge. Then men and women can afford to speculate about metaphysics, writers may be novelists without feeling guilty at not being politicians, and Sartre—if he lives that long—will feel ethically justified in publishing his Ethics. This gospel is not other-worldly, I suppose, but its concern is definitely with another world. In the meantime Sartre does not seem to me to avoid the particular trap set for all sincere social reformers—that of sacrificing earlier generations to a Utopia to come, decreeing in advance that if some individuals are not expendable, at least their happiness is so. Obviously Sartre does not intend to sacrifice the real to the nonexisting ideal. It is living suffering and specific evils which he wants to cure, and I am with him in this. Like him I am optimistic enough to believe that some approximation to a just society

43

will someday be achieved and that the goal of helping to bring it into existence is sufficiently exhilarating to bestow significance on many an individual life. Yet Sartre seems to overlook the fact that if we insist that no concerns are valid save the socio-political, we establish an empty regression. I am reminded of my childhood puzzlement as to how, if everybody lived only to help others, there was anyone whose simple function it was to enjoy receiving help. It is imperative to provide bread and freedom for all. But unless we whose lives have been preserved and liberated find them worth living, we have an empty goal to offer those we hope to rescue. It is my belief that we must begin now to formulate the philosophy of freedom, of which Sartre speaks, if we do not want to be lost forever in despair.

Sartre's attitude toward the role of ethics in this process is indeed a strange one. Ethics must be universal, he insists, and he seems to imply that for this reason, there can be no ethics until all men's situations are the same. I find in Sartre now a curious mixture of two attitudes: At times he seems to feel that ethics must be a set of absolute commandments, established objectively and imposed regardless of specific situations and the subjective colorations imposed by those who live those situations. (E.g., his use of "Thou shalt not lie.") If this is what ethics is, then no wonder Sartre rejects it. The only question is how he could conceive of there ever being a time when such an ethics would be anything but bad faith. On other occasions he apparently sees ethics as the purely psychological device of managing to feel content with one's life—or as I have been saying, to justify it. Here again his position is ambiguous. In his references to the possibility of universal ethics *after* the liberation of man, he suggests that perhaps such justification is far in the future but still a legitimate goal. Sartre himself, like a Marxist Bodhisattva, refuses to save himself until he can take all mankind with him. More often Sartre seems to associate ethical justification with an ideal Salvation by means of some nonexistent Absolute. Then he declares that nobody is saved, not even by politics. "There is no salvation anywhere." Commenting on the concluding words of de Beauvoir's autobiography, which are "I have been cheated," Sartre says, "When she uses this word [*flouée*], it is to signify that she has demanded of life an Absolute which she cannot find in it. We have the same point of view." [5]

I thought that in *Being and Nothingness* Sartre had come to grips with his "useless passion" and "desire to be God." But the "missing God" still haunts him and molds the very language he speaks.

Are the Absolute and Salvation missing as realities? Or is it just that the terms as Sartre uses them are meaningless in the context which Sartre provides for them? Why, I wonder, does he not realize that the Absolute and Salvation must be redefined for humanistic existentialism? Obviously neither the Absolute nor Absolution exists as an abstract, universal value or guarantee imbedded in the structure of the Universe or coming from any other source than human consciousness. It is from this premise that Sartre's existentialism derives, and we should hardly expect its goal and final discovery to be the contradiction of its point of departure.

Humanistic existentialism does postulate an Absolute. It is precisely the irreducible reality of the free individual consciousness. In one sense, we may even argue that the values which each consciousness creates from its experience are absolute as they are experienced. Sartre pointed out long ago that there are certain absolute evils which cannot be redeemed. He uses as an example the torture which reduces a person to a near-thing and leads him to betray himself and what he has held most sacred. Sartre acknowledges that the opposite, the man who does not break under torture, reaffirms the value of the human. If there are specific absolute evils, it seems that there must be specific absolute goods, and Sartre formerly claimed that this was so. [6]

Whether one is saved or not depends on whether or not his life can be justified. Not by God, of course, and not perfectly.

[5] Interview: "Jean-Paul Sartre s'explique sur 'Les Mots.'"
[6] Jean-Paul Sartre: *Situations*, II (Paris: Gallimard; 1948), p. 248.

Even in Christianity, one's sins are blotted out—as it were—and not held against him. God himself cannot make them not to have been, neither the sins nor their consequences. But in human terms, "a little," as Roquentin said, I believe that one can save one's life. A life is justified if he who lives it can say: First, that he has freely chosen the values by which he has guided and judged his life and that he has found it good; second, that insofar as was in his power, he has willed that each of his acts should keep open the door to such self-justification by other free subjects. This is subjective justification, if you like. If those whose lives have been directly or indirectly touched by his could in good faith support that self-judgment, I personally am willing to say that the life has been objectively justified.

Sartre has said, "The Absolute has departed. There remain innumerable tasks to be done."[7] I agree. But these tasks do not rise up before us labeled in order or priority and with printed instructions. Taking care of the world is a strictly do-it-yourself project, and we are all amateurs together. Sartre pointed out long ago that we must not make the mistake of thinking that things in the world appeared with values already stamped upon them. The time when ethics is most needed is in the period of conflict, struggle, and uncertainty, not when some approximation of Utopia has been achieved.

I should like to conclude this discussion of Sartre's rejection of ethics with two concluding observations. First, it is Sartre himself whom I am opposing to Sartre. Yet I do this without any feeling that there is a genuine philosophical conflict between *Being and Nothingness* and Sartre's writing published since 1950. Both his ontology and his psychology have remained consistent. Man's relation with the Universe is still the same. It is only in his expressed view of formal ethics and of man's immediate obligations that I believe Sartre has made statements which are inconsistent with his own systematic philosophy, whether early or late. Sartre has remarked in *The Words* that he has always made it a habit to think

[7] Interview: "Jean-Paul Sartre s'explique sur 'Les Mots.' "

against himself. I believe that recently he has *chosen* against himself, and that this peculiar choice of self-against-the-self is for all mankind—as Sartre once declared all choices to be. In choosing between the two ways of realizing the self, Sartre has resolved to put spontaneous self-realization in parentheses, to place all value on the side of commitment to a life-plan of recognizing the need to justify his existence by working to realize the practical freedom of others. Insofar as Sartre's choice is for himself, I admire it—one-sided as it may be. If he seeks to impose it on all others, one must remind him that they have the right to find their own way of reconciling the demands of the two self-realizations. Otherwise the freedom he wants to save will be destroyed in the very process of liberation.

Finally, we must not make the mistake, which I think Sartre has made, of assuming that an ethics without God must posit and fulfil the same needs as an ethics which is theologically grounded. We must not let the missing God determine our thought by His very absence. If we replace Absolute Being with a radical human freedom, then some things are irretrievably lost. New values will appear in new forms and cannot be expected to fit comfortably in the old places left empty.

Only Sartre could write *the* ethics of humanistic existentialism, by which I mean the full development of the ethical possibilities of Being-for-itself which Sartre analyzed in *Being and Nothingness*. For my part, I firmly and absolutely disavow any intention or pretense of presuming to do the job for him. My intention is simply to present what seems to me a part of the answer to a question which I have asked myself and which I have often been asked by others: I accept Sartre's description of human consciousness and its relation to the rest of reality. If I want to live a life which appears to me consistent with this philosophy, then to what kind of existence am I committed? If, as a humanistic existentialist, I accept the challenge to try to justify my life, what are the attitudes and the obligations which logically follow upon my acceptance of radical freedom and total responsibility? The ethical choice as such involves a justification of conduct in reference to a definite concept of what reality is. Suppose that we make the Sartrean view our point of departure. Presumably there will be wide variation in the specific ways in which free individuals live out their free choices of Being. Yet there must be an existentialist choice which will try to justify itself as ethical, which will include and to some degree qualify all of these varied and private value systems.

III

The Existentialist Choice

Hostile critics have argued in effect that humanistic existentialism is committed to choosing the nonethical. Their conclusion is based on what they take to be the nature of existentialist freedom. The free individual is restricted factually by his own finitude, the projects of other free individuals, and the stubborn resistance of the outside world; he cannot be subject to ethical principles, for he alone decides whether or not he wills to attach a value to the ethical. I believe that we can partly answer this criticism by pointing out that the initial choice to be ethical always stands outside any particular ethics. It is never possible to take a principle which a philosophical system has established in response to the challenge to be ethical and then seek to use it as a categorical imperative to compel the original choice to be ethical. Existentialism is not unique in this respect. It has merely emphasized what other philosophies have tended to ignore. The more serious problem is whether existentialism can offer anything to the person who has chosen the ethical, or whether the moment of freedom's self-recognition is itself the only absolute value.

49

I am convinced that those who hold that the arbitrary caprice of the Underground Man is the natural corollary of existentialist freedom are wrong. I admit that their position is understandable. In the first place there are those two devastating sentences from *Being and Nothingness:* "Man is a useless passion." And "Thus it amounts to the same thing whether one gets drunk alone or is a leader of nations." It is true that these quotations are derived from a description of life as it is generally lived by persons who seek to avoid the anguish of freedom in bad faith. True, too, that Sartre has expended considerably energy—in fiction, in essays on political philosophy and in direct political action—urging us to commit our freedom in responsible action on behalf of the world's oppressed. Since Sartre has not written a specific work bridging the gap between *Being and Nothingness* and these examples of ethics-in-action, most of Sartre's friends and enemies both have concluded that his concern for others resulted from his personal choice of being and was in no way consequent to his philosophy. Thus Sartre's choice appears to be neither more nor less justified than that of the Underground Man. Drunkard and Leader of Nations remain equivalent.

Besides these statements which, at least when removed from their context, seem to preclude any Sartrean ethics, there are three concepts absolutely fundamental to humanistic existentialism which many persons, without further examination, accept as self-evident proof that any existentialist ethics is impossible. First, there is the idea that values are "created" by the individual who chooses them; they are not discovered. At most we may say that they are revealed and chosen in the way that the sculptor decides to bring into being *these* potentialities of a piece of marble rather than any others. Values are in no sense a priori. They do not fall into any objectively established hierarchy. Second, there is no ultimate independent and impersonal reference point by which to judge human conduct. There is neither a God nor Absolute Mind nor pre-established Human Nature. Third, the Sartrean view of human relations excludes the possibility of a communion between persons which would dissolve the subject-object relationship. Subjects never become each other or directly experience each other's inner life, no matter how great the sympathy or how nearly perfect the communication between them. Subjects may be reciprocally related, they interact, but there is no merging. My oneness with mankind is a metaphor, or it refers merely to our inhabiting the same planet and sharing those biological and other finite characteristics which make up the "human condition." To sum up, the existentialist man is an isolated individual who is not compelled to acknowledge his involvement with others unless he cares to do so. His one certainty is his own freedom. He has no source or origin in any divine Being or rational plan, and no pre-established goals. Without a sure pattern, he makes himself be.

I accept this view of what man is. I deny that it leaves no room for an ethics. What kind of ethics it allows I mean to discuss by gradual development of what seem to me the consequences of the existentialist description of consciousness and the world. A few general observations I think ought first to be established to show the connection between existentialism as Sartre has formulated it and the over-all aims and qualities of the ethical position which I believe can be derived from his premises as its foundation.

First, what about those Sartrean pronouncements which appear to deny any place for an ethics? When Sartre says that man is a useless passion and that it doesn't matter whether a person gets drunk alone or is a leader of nations, he is speaking within a precise context; namely, in reference to man's desire to be the impossible union of Being-in-itself-for-itself, his own Causa Sui, or God. Sartre contends that the ruling passion of most persons, or what might be called their choice of being, is the contradictory desire to realize their freedom and yet at the same time have it supported and guaranteed by something outside itself. To put it another way, they want to feel that they are absolutely free to choose and yet may find outside themselves the directives and guarantees which would enable them to know that their choice is the right one. Thus their freedom would possess an absolute value derived from some other source. Consciousness tries to hide from itself the fact that its own subjectivity is what bring values into the world, and it projects them outward onto objects. This attitude Sartre calls *l'esprit de sérieux*, and he argues that the result of existential psychoanalysis ought to be to make us repudiate this "spirit of seriousness."

The spirit of seriousness has two characteristics: it considers values as transcendent givens independent of human subjectivity, and it transfers the quality of "desirable" from the ontological structure of things to their simple material constitution. For the spirit of seriousness, for example, *bread* is desirable because it is *necessary* to live (a value written in an intelligible heaven) and because bread *is* nourishing. The result of the serious attitude, which as we know rules the world, is to cause the symbolic values of things to be drunk in by their empirical idiosyncrasy as ink by a blotter; it puts forward the opacity of the desired object and posits it in itself as a desirable irreducible. Thus we are already on the moral plane but concurrently on that of bad faith, for it is an ethics which is ashamed of itself and dares not speak its name. It has obscured all its goals in order to free itself from anguish. Man pursues being blindly by hiding from himself the free project which is this pursuit. He makes himself such that he is *waited for* by all the tasks placed along his way. Objects are mute demands, and he is nothing in himself but the possessive obedience to these demands.[1]

Insofar as men and women seek to find their missions written in things, Sartre feels that they are sacrificing man in order that the Self-Cause or God may exist. It is from this point of view that Sartre declares all human activities to be equivalent. They are all alike doomed to failure, for their goal is an impossible contradiction. Man will never become his own Self-Cause. God does not exist. If man is free, he is free all the way. If he tries to say that the value structures which his freedom has brought into being are the absolute Being

[1] Jean-Paul Sartre: *Being and Nothingness*, tr. Hazel E. Barnes (New York: Philosophical Library; 1956), p. 626.

which causes and supports this freedom, the lie to himself is as much self-deception for the leader of nations as it is for the solitary drunkard. What makes their conduct equivalent is the fact that both—and perhaps the leader of nations even more than the lone drinker—feel that a mandate has been bestowed upon them by the world itself.

I feel that Sartre must surely hold other criteria by which he does not find all conduct equivalent. He suggests in the closing pages of *Being and Nothingness* that although ontology cannot by itself impose imperatives, his ontological description of man nevertheless allows us "to catch a glimpse of what sort of ethics will assume its responsibilities when confronted with a *human reality in situation.*" Like a leitmotif appearing and reappearing throughout the whole of *Being and Nothingness* is Sartre's claim that most human beings, in their anguished flight from the confrontation with their own freedom, spend their lives in a vain attempt to become the impossible union of two types of being; they want to be a being-in-itself-for-itself. They wish to realize the freedom which distinguishes them from things and the other creatures in nature and at the same time to possess their absoluteness. This self-contradiction, which we have already met in the form of God or the Self-Cause would be—if it could exist at all—a conscious unself-consciousness, a free life possessed of a fixed being. The problem is how, once we abandon this pursuit, a consciousness may remain a consciousness in-the-world without letting itself be imprisoned by the situation in which it finds itself. For Sartre as for his critics, the crucial question is twofold: First, is it possible for freedom to escape from this haunting desire to be guaranteed in its being? "What will become of freedom if it turns its back upon this value? Will freedom carry this value along with it whatever it does and even in its very turning back upon the in-itself-for-itself? Will freedom be reapprehended from behind by the value it wishes to contemplate?" It seems evident to me that Sartre's answer is that freedom need not be forever "reapprehended from behind." Although he puts his reply in the form

53

of a question, he obviously feels that the alternative to seeking one's being in things is simply freedom's own recognition of itself as the chooser of all values.

Is it possible for freedom to take itself for a value as the source of all value, or must it necessarily be defined in relation to a transcendent value which haunts it? And in case it could will itself as its own possible and its determining value, what would this mean? A freedom which wills itself freedom is in fact a being-which-is-not-what-it-is and which-is-what-it-is-not, and which chooses as the ideal of being, being-what-it-is-not and not-being-what-it-is.[2]

In other words, the ideal which existentialist freedom chooses is the realization of itself as process, as the creator of a nothingness between itself and its objects, between itself and its own continually renewed self-projection. I think it is fair to say that in this choice, a person recognizes that he *is* the Nothingness which cuts him off from the rest of Being.

Sartre's second question, I believe, asks whether freedom's self-apprehension will necessarily recognize that it is a part of Being, that the individual in some sense *is* even if he is-what-he-is-not and is-not-what-he-is. The psychic detachment which consciousness introduces is a *specific detachment from something*. Nothingness exists only in relation to Being. Each nihilating act of consciousness is a nihilating of something. Once again, Sartre's questions seem to posit an obviously affirmative answer on his part.

This freedom chooses then not to recover itself but to flee itself, not to coincide with itself but to be always at a distance from itself. What are we to understand by this being which wills to hold itself in awe, to be at a distance from itself? Is it a question of bad faith or of another fundamental attitude? And can one *live* this new aspect of being? In particular will freedom by taking itself for an end escape all *situation?* Or on the contrary, will it remain situated? Or will it situate itself so much the more precisely and the more individually as it projects itself further in

[2] Ibid., p. 627.

54

anguish as a conditioned freedom and accepts more fully its responsibility as an existent by whom the world comes into being? [3]

There is a paradoxical relation between these two questions, but I do not believe that it is a contradiction. Or if there is a contradiction, then it is one which is resolved in the peculiar form of reality which Sartre calls Being-for-itself— i.e., in human freedom. Sartre concludes first that an individual can constantly maintain in his awareness the realization that he himself establishes his relations with the rest of Being. Sartre asserts immediately afterward that the freedom which wills itself to be its own value and source of value will situate itself (not *be* situated) by recognizing the responsibilities for the structures of the world which it has brought into being. Thus freedom is both absolute and conditioned. Is it responsible for its own conditioning? As freedom, no. But as a particular freedom, yes. That is, the freedom of a finite being (and this is the only kind we can even begin to comprehend) chooses within the area of its own awareness. It cannot do otherwise. It structures this area *as it chooses*, bestowing meaning upon it through the relations set up by each successive choice. In this structuring, it objectifies itself as a past self and outlines the form of a probable future self. If to know that one is free is to realize that he is the source of meaning and value, then this is also to recognize that he is the author of what has been and will be as well as the one who is making the present choice. Sartre suggests that the existentialist in good faith will recognize that at any moment, simultaneously, he *is* and *is not* his situation. He *is not* his situation in the sense of being determined by it and finally identified with it. He *is* his situation in the sense that it is *this* situation and no other which he has already by his past choices constituted as having these particular structures rather than all others and which by his present choice he will reconfirm or transform. If a fully aware freedom must logi-

[3] Ibid., p. 628.

cally admit its capacity to choose as it will, then by the same token it must grant that it *has* chosen as it willed, which is to confess its responsibility for what it has chosen.

The tantalizing comments at the end of *Being and Nothingness* suggest that in the ethical choice, a freedom must choose itself both as Being and as Nothingness. Whether or not such was actually Sartre's intention, this is at any rate the starting point for an ethics which seems to me to be logically derived from Sartre's existentialist description of what man is. Obviously I have anticipated this conclusion in my discussion of the two kinds of self-realization.

If a person has chosen to be ethical, then an existentialist ethics—like any other kind—must provide its own justification as a way of achieving the highest possible degree of value consistent with its view of all reality, including the human. Fundamental to an existentialist ethics will be the recognition of the importance of both kinds of self-realization. Theoretically an ethics need not give equal weight to all aspects of man. Christianity, for instance, is perfectly logical in preaching bodily mortification inasmuch as its basic premise is the infinitely greater importance of the eternal soul. So, too, Aristotelian ethics, despite its emphasis on the golden mean, rightly gives the greater weight to the rational side of man inasmuch as reason is not only the gateway to the highest truth and purest happiness, but the sure guide to the maximum of success and enjoyment even on the lower levels. Existentialism has no magic formula whereby it can mathematically weigh the relative value of the two self-realizations and determine a priori the part to be played by each in any specific choice. Existentialism resists the temptation to argue that there is any objective hierarchy of values which must be the same for everyone. To do so would be to make values into objective entities or to attach them to things; we would fall back at once into the spirit of seriousness. What is necessary is that neither the temporal nor the spontaneous aspect of human reality should ever be totally excluded from any choice. Commitment to the value system one has chosen should never be so complete as to suppress one's awareness that one has chosen it and that one is always free to effect a totally new orientation to Being and one's relation to the world. On the other side, freedom cannot ethically prolong the enjoyment of its own withdrawal from Being, certainly not to the extent of denying its dependence on its own situation and its responsibility for the way it has and will structure its own lived environment. Being and Nothingness are not only two aspects of human reality. They represent the limits beyond which the self cannot be pursued. If an individual tries to find himself wholly in Being, he tries in vain to make himself one with the things of the world; or—as Sartre says— he denies himself as Man in order that the missing Self-Cause might exist. But if he seeks to identify himself only as the abstract possibility of nihilating Being, he forgets that freedom itself does not exist, but only particular freedoms. Without external objects, there can be no self-consciousness, for consciousness is only an awareness *of* its objects plus an implicit or reflective awareness of that awareness. Freedom can value itself only indirectly via the Being to which it relates itself. Without some recognition of its temporality, freedom is nothing at all.

Once we have recognized this interplay of Being and Nothingness in the spontaneous and reflective pursuit of self, we may quickly outline the external form, as it were, of an existentialist ethics before we set about trying to determine more specifically what, if any, normative principles it has to offer and what relevance it possesses for our contemporary situation.

First of all, a word concerning this freedom which I have been postulating as the heart—the essence, if you will—of the human person. Sartre has continually argued the case for man's psychological freedom, against Behaviorists, Freudians, and all sociologists or academic Marxists who attempt to reduce man to the status of a passive reactor to hereditary and environmental pressures, whether biological, social, or economic, conscious or unconscious. Among the many who have discussed Sartre's psychology of freedom, I have been one of the comparatively few who have supported his radical claim.

I will not repeat here either his arguments or my own defense of them. Yet one or two explanatory comments are in order.

That man is free is the absolute starting point of an existentialist ethics. At no point will we admit the validity of any position which either denies the reality of this freedom or deliberately ignores it. To do so would be the equivalent of a present-day scientist's assuming that the earth does not move in space. Furthermore, it is my view that no ethics, qua ethics, can exist without presupposing freedom. It may, like Stoicism, rest upon a doctrine of ultimate necessity and determinism. Yet when the Stoics speak of the individual's attempt to live the best life, they make it perfectly clear that the will is free to choose its own attitude, its personal mode of relating to the predetermined world events. The Stoic discussion of the justification of suicide to avoid incurable disease or madness would be unintelligible unless supported by a belief in free rational choice. It is true that most ethical systems suppose a limited freedom. Inevitably they address those who are free and insofar as they are free. Even so thoroughgoing a determinist as B. F. Skinner attempts to arouse a sense of moral obligation in the minds of those who are free to see the advantages of achieving an improved society by means of a program of better conditioning. Yet while "ought" implies the possibility of genuine choice, we must be wary of adopting, with all its implications, Kant's *I ought* implies *I can.* "I ought" implies "I have a choice." This is safe and sure. "I ought" implies "I can" is too often misinterpreted as claiming that the sense of what should be entails its realistic possibility. Existentialist freedom of choice emphatically does not mean that a person can do whatever he chooses or that all persons are born with equivalent potentialities.

We may use the analogy of a group of painters who have been provided with different kinds of painting materials. The one who has been given only water colors obviously will not produce an oil landscape. Yet what will ultimately determine the quality of the picture is more significantly the painter himself than his materials. It is in some such fashion as this that existentialism can declare both that man is free and that all men ought to be free. It is possible to argue theoretically that sometimes the painter who is allotted a limited and difficult medium may achieve heights within it which he would never have attained without this restriction. Generally speaking, however, an artist will develop his full potentialities only if the materials at his disposal are adequate and varied. If he is kept in an unheated cell and deprived of all paper and canvas, the drawings he scratches on the wall will be but poor reflections of what might have been. Recognition of these two dimensions to man's freedom is what impels Sartre in *Search for a Method* to dismiss scornfully the freedom he has been at such pains to establish in *Being and Nothingness* and to speak hopefully of the day when there will be "real freedom" for everybody. There must *be* a freedom of choice in order for practical freedom from factual limitations to have any value. Once again, the two kinds of self-realization are relevant. Realizing oneself as free in relation to all of Being is always open to man. He may at any time in a spontaneous act refuse to recognize any of the contingent obligations of his situation by embracing his own nothingness. Self-realization in Being is the harder thing, for my choices here are inevitably intertwined with those of others.

This brings us to a second point. Some critics of existentialism have argued that its famous authenticity and good faith refer solely to structures within the individual consciousness and need not include any consideration of other people. If a person acts always in accordance with what he actually feels, and if he never pretends that anything but his own choice is responsible for what he has done and become, then it seems we must acknowledge that he is authentic and in good faith, regardless of what sort of life he has chosen. Authenticity guarantees neither rational self-interest nor concern for others. It is possible to carry the argument even further. Suppose we do grant that the concepts of authenticity and good faith might be extended so as to include responsibilities for others, do we have any basis for the claim that one ought to choose these ideals in preference to unauthenticity and bad faith?

Suppose one authentically resolves that henceforth he will live unauthentically?

This second question we have already discussed. To choose to live unauthentically in bad faith is to choose the nonethical and to abandon all pretense of wanting to justify one's life. Once the decision to be ethical has been made, the unauthentic life is ruled out. Bad faith, a lie to oneself, is on principle excluded from the ethical, which as we have seen comprises as a minimum requirement the intent to present a true picture of reality and not a falsification. The unauthentic is forbidden inasmuch as it involves the refusal to confront one's freedom, the necessity of which is the very cornerstone of an existentialist ethics. Even without going beyond Sartre's preliminary suggestions, it is possible to go one step further and to establish that the authentic choice in good faith *must* include respect and concern for other freedoms. Authenticity, good faith, and the original choice to be ethical all demand that one not knowingly shut his eyes to the data on the basis of which the choice is made, that the choice be reflectively (i.e., objectively) defensible. Sartre has put it in terms of good faith, which in this context is practically the same as honesty.

One can judge (and this is perhaps not a value judgment but a logical judgment), that certain choices are based on error and others on truth. One can judge a man, saying that he is in bad faith. If we have defined man's situation as a free choice, without excuses or recourse, then every man who takes refuge behind the excuse of his passions, every man who trumps up a determinism is a man in bad faith. Someone might object, "But why shouldn't he choose himself in bad faith?" I reply that I do not have to pass a moral judgment upon him, but I define his bad faith as an error. Here one cannot escape from a judgment of truth. Bad faith is obviously a lie, because it conceals the total freedom of the commitment. On the same grounds, I shall say that there is also bad faith if I choose to declare that there are certain a priori values. I am self-contradictory if at one and the same time I will them and declare that they are imposed on me. If someone says to me, "And suppose I want to be in bad faith?" I shall answer, "There is no reason for you not to be. But I assert that you are and that the strictly coherent attitude is the attitude in good faith." [4]

Once I have accepted honesty with regard to all the facts as a necessary ingredient of the ethical decision, Sartre argues that I am in a position to make moral judgments.

Thus in the name of that wish for freedom which freedom itself implies, I can pass judgments on those who seek to hide from themselves the total gratuity of their existence and its total freedom. Those who, either in the spirit of seriousness or by deterministic excuses hide from themselves their total freedom, I shall call cowards. Those others who try to show that their existence was necessary, whereas it is the very contingency of man's appearance on earth, I shall call stinkers. But cowards or stinkers can be judged only by a strictly authentic criterion. [5]

So far so good. When it comes to the proposition that to value and try to promote the scope of my own freedom demands that I simultaneously affirm the value of others' freedom, too, Sartre's position is positive and definite.

Freedom as the definition of man does not depend on others; but as soon as there is engagement, I am obliged to want the freedom of others at the same time that I want my own freedom. I can take my freedom as a goal only if I take that of others for a goal as well. [6]

This is a fine assertion, but I wish Sartre had spelled out the inevitable progression from my choice of my own freedom to that of others. I myself would put it like this: Since I recognize that freedom is my essence, both as myself and as a human being, I cannot truthfully deny that the same is true for all other persons. Their freedom is as much a part of the data as my own. Therefore, if I declare that the development of my own free projects is the goal and good of my life, I must—if I am in good faith—allow simultaneously that my freedom holds no privileged place over this assertion when it

---

[4] Jean-Paul Sartre: *L'Existentialisme est un humanisme* (Paris: Editions Nagel; 1946), pp. 80–2.
[5] Ibid., pp. 84–5.
[6] Ibid., p. 83.

is made by someone else. If the ethical choice includes acknowledging my responsibility for the way in which my consciousness has objectified itself in the world, then part of this objectification has resulted from my being the author of acts which have structured in a particular way the situation in which the other has made his choices. If the ethical choice is a resolve to justify one's life, my relations with others cannot be ignored. As de Beauvoir expresses it, any individual may choose to leave his life a pure contingency. But a life "is permitted to wish to give itself a meaning and a truth, and it then meets rigorous demands within its own heart." [7]

The choice to be ethical and to realize oneself both as Being and as Nothingness demands that a freedom willingly subject itself (Sartre's word is "engage") to a self-imposed value system and code without ever forgetting that at any time it is free to choose another way of being. There is certainly an interplay of reason and emotion in this process. I do not think, however, that we would be accurate if we tried to equate spontaneous self-realization with emotion and to identify temporal self-realization with reason. The interweaving of rational and irrational are far more complex than this. Regardless of which we feel ought to be given the higher place ultimately, we must grant that in the living person they are inextricably linked. We see this to be true from whatever point of view we attempt to approach the question. [8]

First of all, if the aim of reason is to account for all the facts, then it must include irrational behavior and attitudes among its data. If, for example, one wants to draw up a rational plan for finding the most satisfactory kind of life for himself, he must weigh the emotional factors involved in producing the satisfaction. If one wants to plan for a perfectly happy society patterned on rational lines, he must take into account the question of how to deal with the irrational reac-

[7] Simone de Beauvoir: *The Ethics of Ambiguity*, tr. Bernard Frechtman (New York: Philosophical Library; 1948), p. 16.

[8] The following two paragraphs are taken with slight modifications from an article of mine: "The New Humanism in Education," *The Colorado Quarterly*, Vol. V (1956), pp. 201–3.

tions of those who are to be the new society's citizens. If the psychologist or philosopher wants to account for all of human behavior, he must include or explain away the data of mystic experience. We find that in any of the traditional defenses of either reason or the irrational, there is always an implicit or explicit appeal to the opposite of what one is defending. In recent times Santayana has perhaps presented the best case for reason by an open appeal to animal faith. It has been suggested also that we could give extra support to Santayana's position by adding that reason alone meets the test of consistency (thus not requiring constant readjustment of all basic positions) and that it passes the pragmatic test by enabling life to be lived with more ease than by any other method.[9] Yet each one of these arguments involves an appeal to the emotions. Faith is a feeling. If we did not choose to be guided by this feeling, and if we did not value consistency, and if we did not want to have life conducted smoothly with a minimum of obstacles and forced readjustments, then none of these arguments would carry any weight. We encounter this same sort of curious reversal if we start at the other end. Suppose that we admit that Nietzsche was right in saying that ethical systems are but the sign languages of emotion? Even if it is by emotion that we establish our basic goals or values, it is by reason that we set up our plans and estimate our chances for attaining these goals. Reason enters into our evaluative comparisons of one goal with another. It is by reason as well as emotion that we judge goals as constituting dead ends or, on the contrary, as likely to lead to other possibles; it is by reason that we calculate the wisdom of earlier choices as having produced what they promised, as to be repeated, to be avoided, etc.

What, pragmatically, do we mean when we speak of the rational and the irrational? Reason is consciousness' perception of those organizations and relations which the universe is

[9] George Santayana: *Scepticism and Animal Faith* (New York: Scribners; 1923). See also Gardner Williams: "On Our Lack of Certainty as to the Truth of Any and All Propositions," *The Philosophical Review*, Vol. XLVIII (1939), pp. 623–37.

capable of sustaining, and it is the perception of relations established in human products (language, etc.) of such a sort that any human being may recognize them. It is also the will to confine oneself within these limits. The irrational or emotional is consciousness' personal relation to the universe. Sartre has shown that we *choose* whether we will live on the rational, deliberative level or on an emotional one. The choice, of course, is not made once and for all but at each moment renewed (or changed). This basic choice is man's personal relation to being—to unconscious matter and to other people as well as to that combination of body and psychic states, present and remembered, which contribute to the making of the sense of self. The individual consciousness must choose whether it prefers to live primarily within the sustaining limits of universalizing reason or amidst the evanescent, flickering disconnections with external reality which are produced by the emotions. This is the fundamental paradox of human reality—that by a pre-rational choice it must decide whether or not to accept the responsibility of being rational.

Religious existentialism, like almost all religious philosophy, postulates a higher Being or Truth which is beyond reason as we know it. Although not to be identified with ordinary emotions, it is grasped by means of them much more surely than through intellectual concepts. Thus for the New Theologian one may see God in human love whereas the Reason which would seek to prove or to disprove His existence is dismissed as irrelevant. Unamuno, in the face of all the logical reasons against the possibility of individual immortality, argues that we should hearken rather to the desperate intensity of man's universal longing. Kierkegaard, too, contends that a rationally comprehensible God would be no greater than the constructs of the human mind. Only the irrational is commensurate with the grandeur of man's need.

There is a group of existentialists, strongly influenced by Husserl's phenomenology, who have tried to maintain a position midway between theism and atheism. I am inclined to call them Being Philosophers. Foremost among them is Martin Heidegger, whose influence upon existential psychology is perhaps even more important than his impact on philosophy —if we except his recalcitrant pupil Sartre. Heidegger's "listening to Being" or "standing in the openness of the Truth of Being," clearly points to something more than conceptual knowledge though I, for one, have never been quite sure what it is. Heidegger does not, however, advocate the validity of purely individual emotional responses in reckless disregard of objective reality. Some of the psychologists of Being come dangerously close to doing so. I think the explanation is that they misuse one of the most valuable contributions of Husserl and Heidegger. This is the distinction between the scientfiic world and the life-world (*Lebenswelt*). The world of science is never comprehended as a thing-in-itself independent of the intellectual structures imposed upon it. It is the contention of phenomenologists and existentialists alike that even if we could know that the latest scientific field theory was the final and absolutely accurate interpretation of the Universe, the scientific world would still not be the world that anybody lives in. We may make use of it as the stuff of our projects, but it remains only part of the furniture of the life-world in which we truly reside. The life-world is the world as it appears to each one of us with its "horizon of meanings," its values, its organization in relation to ourselves as vantage point and center of reference. In the life-world, objects are not portions of matter but instruments and possibilities. Social institutions may include material buildings and impersonally formulated constitutions; they, like all of human culture, are colored with variegated tones of approval and disapproval, smiling invitations, and threatening prohibitions. The life-world is both objective and subjective, just as consciousness is always outside in its objects and yet—as a point of view upon these objects—is never identical with them. Similarly, the life-world is both public and private. In communication with others, I not only establish common reference points and meanings. I find that my own attitudes toward the external environment and toward myself change as the result of the "views" which other persons disclose to me. Nevertheless my life-world, while it opens into the common world in which others and I can sustain communication, maintains its irreducible areas of privacy where nobody else can enter in, no matter how much he and I may wish it. Kant's noumenal world is approachable only through the categories, which stand as the lenses everyone must look through. In viewing the life-world, one adds to these the special lenses of his period and the colored glass of his own temperament and personal history. We all *look at* the same world; we *do not see* the same world. The life-world concept was anticipated in William James's description of a *fact*.

A conscious field *plus* its object as felt or thought of *plus* an attitude towards the object *plus* the sense of a self to whom the attitude belongs—such a concrete bit of personal experience may be a small bit, but it is a solid bit as long as it lasts; not hollow, not a mere abstract element of experience, such as the "object" is when taken all alone. It is a *full* fact, even though it be an insignificant fact; it is of the *kind* to which all realities whatsoever must belong; the motor currents of the world run through the like of it; it is on the line connecting real events with real events. That unsharable feeling which each one of us has of the pinch of his individual destiny as he privately feels it rolling out on fortune's wheel may be disparaged for its egotism, may be sneered at as unscientific, but it is the one thing that fills up the measure of our concrete actuality, and any would-be existent that should lack such a feeling, or its analogue, would be a piece of reality only half made up.[1]

If those who plead with us to recognize that the life-world is as real as the world of science and just as much to be reckoned with were content to leave matters at that, I should have no disagreement. Unfortunately, some people jump too quickly from the conclusion that the worlds of science and of logic are only partial interpretations of reality to the conclusion that any particular emotional assertion, if it be sufficiently intense, can outweigh the claims of science and logic

[1] William James: *The Varieties of Religious Experience* (New York: Modern Library; 1937), pp. 489–90.

in their own spheres. Sartrean existentialism does not make this mistake. Sartre, for example, has traced explicitly the movement in bad faith which jumps from the assertion that my strongest "knowledge" is really only "belief" to the conclusion that I am, therefore, justified in holding any belief whatsoever. He at no time advocates holding a position which is in open contradiction with what today appear to be the facts of science or the demands of logical consistency. He resists the idea that science or logic has or can establish a hierarchy of values within which the individual ought to choose his way of being. Sartre is acutely aware of those ultimate choices which are prior to all science and all logic. At the same time, the Sartrean position allows us to maintain that once a person has chosen to be ethical—i.e., to try to justify his life—he has in effect committed himself to establishing a harmony between the subjective and the objective. He pledges himself to act in such a way that he would still approve of his conduct even if it were that of another. More accurately, he is prepared to assume toward the objectified part of himself a point of view in which consciousness assumes, as best it can, the role of the other while still acknowledging that this role is freely chosen.

Sartre in *Being and Nothingness* emphasizes that the Self, like Being, is that which is always pursued but never attained. In this respect it is like the Future; it is always present as the meaning and the ideal goal of each act, but we never coincide with it. Any psychologist, I suppose, would agree that the Self is not complete until the moment of death. Sartre would argue that I am still pursuing my Self even then. There is always the enfolding shell of Nothingness between the reflecting consciousness and the consciousness reflected-on, and it is not correct to identify the Self as exclusively one or the other. Perhaps the most fundamental reality in this Being-for-itself, which I am, is the reflecting consciousness, but this is nothing at all without an object—neither an "I" nor a "Me." Thus "my" being-for-myself is indeed both the reflecting consciousness and the consciousness reflected-on, but the union is never one of identity. The ethical goal for existentialism is a harmony of the two, not a suppression of either or a total subordination of one to the other.

Humanistic existentialism sees man as a creature of inner distances who lives in a world into which he introduces his own spaces. It is a psychology eminently appropriate to a space-age. More than anything else, this existentialism projects an open future for the individual and for mankind collectively. Each person will make himself, men and women together will make their history by freely chosen projects. Every man is responsible for the future. The ethical choice is the decision to live this responsibility in a way which one can justify. This justification will include the two questions which have always been the proper concerns of ethics: the problem of the normative with respect to right and wrong; the problem of how to find meaning and a personally satisfying life. Traditionally, in the Western world, both these answers have been provided by a personal God who has revealed himself or by an impersonal First Cause, the steps of whose plan lay clearly imprinted in the Universe itself. Existentialism rejects both hypotheses. We must consider now whether this philosophy which sets man radically free but leaves him abandoned in his forlornness can provide either regulative principles or motives for living. If God is dead, is everything allowed? Is life worth living if there is no higher meaning?

IV

Sin without God

The notion of "Sin," the very word itself, exerts a strange
fascination. Asocial, selfish acts hold no appeal. *Sin* conjures
up visions of loveliness, dancing there tantalizingly, just beyond the "No Trespassing" signs. Sin is dangerous, we are
told, but terribly attractive since it is, after all, a Temptation.
Perhaps to Billy Graham, Sin is still as real as the Devil, and
I am sure that there are some members of his vast audiences
who fear and manage to abhor it. For most of us, the idea of
Sin speaks softly from yesterday—like saloons and shivarees
and the cancan. The acts it connotes are vaguely glamorous
and not in the least connected with our own Saturday nights.
"The sinful" is more luridly intense than "the naughty," but
it is almost as outmoded.

"Guilt" is not the same. It seems to belong to us whether
we choose it or not. Yet we are not quite sure of its existential
status. At times a sense of guilt seems to be like a bad cold, to
be suffered through and got rid of as quickly as possible, or
like a poison-ivy rash which one should have had the sense to
avoid in the first place. We are ashamed to feel guilty. Then

69

again it seems that guilt is so inseparable a part of the human condition that not to recognize one's guilt is in itself a moral lapse. We feel guilty if our sense of guilt is less acute than we are told it ought to be.

The most interesting question in all of this concerns the relation between guilty feelings and actual guilt. Speaking very broadly, we may say that those who think about the problem at all fall into two distinct groups. There are the relativistic sociological view and the absolute theological one. The first is held not only by sociologists, but by most psychologists and probably by the majority of the population, at least in the West. It maintains that a sense of guilt is always relative to a pronounced prohibition against the conduct inducing the guilty feeling. Both the conduct and the prohibition are viewed objectively—i.e., neutrally—by the psychiatrist or the sociologist. Particularly in the Freudian context, the aim of the therapist frequently is accomplished exactly at that point when the patient renounces his guilt feelings, understanding them to be without foundation in anything which the mature individual would pronounce wrong. For both psychologist and sociologist, guilt feelings stem from an awareness of having failed to meet the prescribed or implicit requirements of authority. The commands of parents or internalized super-ego, the laws and pressures of a given society may be cruel or humane, destructive or sincerely directed toward fostering the individual's personal growth. In any case, the sense of guilt is considered to be relative to the code by which a person has learned to judge himself. Here we seem perhaps to have guilt feelings without guilt. Still it is not accurate to say that real guilt does not enter in. The truth is that it is implicitly defined as the breaking of the code. Thus we may say that one not only *feels* guilty but *is* guilty when one has acted contrary to the standards of those around him. As for the standards themselves, the psychologist and sociologist remain theoretically neutral. In practice, this relativism is somewhat modified. The psychiatrist certainly posits the mental health of his patient as a self-evident goal and value by which he may judge the patient's own self-judgments to be damaging and wrong. It is unfair to accuse all psychiatrists and counselors of setting up "adjustment" as a sacred absolute. Most of them, if pressed, would probably say that the happiness or creative living of their patients was the aim and that the ability to achieve these in the real world is what is meant by adjustment. Nevertheless, good mental health and adjustment, even in this broader sense, are usually interpreted well within the prevailing norms of contemporary society. Most psychiatrists would consider it unprofessional to suggest a code of ethics to the patient even if they themselves believed in one. The sociologist, for his part, does some evaluating too. Usually this involves an internal relationship, a judgment, for example, as to whether or not institutions and customs contribute to the stability of a given society. At other times, as for example in the work of David Riesman or of Vance Packard, considerations of human dignity and happiness are certainly included as part of the data. Even here relativism is not abandoned. There is seldom, if ever, an attempt to find an "ought" or to offer a description of man which is more fundamental than the sociological. The sociological view of guilt does not point to anything beyond man. In a curious way, one may say that within its perspective, guilt feelings and guilt are both ethically neutral. They may be good or bad, harmful or protectively fostering. There is no definite point of view from which to judge them. They are comparable to any other human emotion, to be judged only in context.

The theological attitude is altogether different. It claims that man's specific feelings of guilt may or may not be mistaken. But beyond these contingent feelings of failure in definite circumstances, it postulates an over-all awareness of imperfection. Man's dissatisfaction with what he is, both individually and collectively, and the very existence of his sense of shortcoming derive from our intuitive realization of our own inadequacy. For some, it appears that the realization of human imperfection leads inexorably to the belief that there is a suprahuman solution to make man whole and perfect. Thus, when Camus's hero of *The Fall* seemed to prove

71

that no human act is wholly altruistic, certain critics concluded that the author's next move would be in the direction of the Catholic Church. Despair of man's perfection leaves only the recourse of appeal for Grace from a perfect Being.

Here then is our problem. Is guilt a purely social phenomenon relative to a code which is ethically indeterminate? Or is guilt an existential structure of the human being? If so, need we conclude that this structure would not exist if there were not some suprahuman Being toward whom or which man's aspirations are directed? Let us consider first the nature of guilt feelings, taken phenomenologically; that is, just as they appear without, for the moment, raising the questions as to whether or not this *sense* of guilt is based on objectively real guilt.

My thesis is that even without God or neurosis, guilt feelings are inevitable. Since we are speaking here of *feelings*, I suppose we could call them psychological phenomena. Nevertheless, I believe them not to be a purely social manifestation but to constitute an existential structure derived from the very nature of consciousness and its relation with the outside world. There is probably no human situation which is not a possible source for the sense of guilt. The subjective variations are similarly infinite. Yet without doing violence to the psychic complexities, and speaking very generally, I believe we may say that most guilt feelings derive from these existential situations:

First, and the most evident, I suppose, is the inner discomfort which arises when we are aware that we are not what another thinks we are—or what we think he thinks we are. There is an everyday sense in which this experience is so self-evidently universal as to need no discussion. It may occur if the other mistakenly trusts us or believes that he has our sympathy or admiration when he does not. It may exist because he gives us credit for doing what we have not done, for cherishing attitudes which we do not hold. The possibilities are as many as they are obvious. Although society as we know it would disintegrate if we were not willing to put up with large amounts of such discomfort, sincerity is the ideal cure for this kind of guilt feelings. Thus, theoretically, they are not inevitable.

There are two other ways in which this sense of discrepancy manifests itself, and these are not avoidable. In the first place, my judgment of the other—like his of me—is necessarily based on outward signs. Yet my appraisal of my own acts and words is accompanied by a complexity of mixed motivations and marginal awarenesses which considerably color its appearance to me but are not included in the overt expression. We may use a trivial sort of example. If a friend and I are together when a third person solicits contributions to a worthy cause, we may respond outwardly with equally cheerful alacrity. I approve his prompt generosity and am uncomfortably aware that there was in me a momentary shamefaced wish that I had been elsewhere when the solicitor happened to come round. It is not necessary that there should be so obvious a contradiction. Even with all the time in the world, and even if the other had the patience to hear me to the end, I could never quite convey all the nuances of an emotion which I try to express or the precise balance of motivations for my acts. The inner and outer points of view are never the same.

I *am not* my "Self-for-others," to use Sartre's expression. This statement is true in two ways. In the first place, only the surface of my act, as it were, appears to the other. He must guess at its "inner horizon," its depths and shadings. Moreover, I *am not* the role I play. It is not only that my potentialities cannot all be manifested at one and the same time. Whereas the things I say and do have an objective being, my own consciousness is a process, a becoming. Therefore I am always a bit beyond myself if by "self" here we refer to something already brought into existence. As for discernible personality traits, cowardice, selfishness, avarice, compassion —these may have belonged to what has become my past, but they are no longer mine unless I choose anew to re-create them. Thus I am doomed not to be what I seem. There is a quartet of personalities in even the most intimate of human relations—the other as he is for himself, his self for me, my self for him, and my self in my own eyes, or the self I want to project.

A second origin of a sense of guilt stems from the very nature of emotion. Once again, we find a discrepancy between an experience as it is lived and as it is expressed. Here there is no need to bring in the Self-for-others. The feeling that there is something wrong or lacking may arise in a person's relations with himself. Generations of poets and novelists have accustomed us to the idea that emotions may be mixed. Still it is one thing to sympathize with a hero who both loves and hates an attractive but unworthy woman—wife, mistress, or mother—and quite another to accept the confused medley of irritation, resentment, boredom, and attachment which we feel toward those we admire and honestly believe ourselves to love. Despite all that has been written and our own inner evidence, society—like the Jury in Camus's *The Stranger*—still maintains the fiction that proper emotions should attend on appropriate events and that they must be recognizably pure and classifiable. What disturbs us most, perhaps, is not the necessity of learning to call a collection of contradictory feelings by the name of the one which dominates, and to act by this. It is rather the disquieting extent to which we realize that these seemingly opaque states which settle down over us are willed, or at least consented to. We must work at our emotions if we are to keep them alive. Somehow the fiction writers had never prepared us for this. Sartre has commented on this sense of lack apropos of suffering. If in the midst of my unhappiness I see a statue of "Grief," it stands before me almost as a reproach. The figure there is suffering totally, is nothing but suffering. In comparison, my own sorrow appears somehow thin and incomplete. It is not quite commensurate with that which I have told myself that I feel, with the causal event as I have analyzed it. Looking at this frozen anguish which the sculptor has created, I judge myself lacking. I suffer from not suffering enough.[1] What is involved here is the sense of being sincere with ourselves, and we have

[1] Sartre, *Being and Nothingness*, pp. 91–2.

74

an internal equivalent to the situation first described in connection with my Self-for-others. Confronting the other, I discovered a sense of guilt derived from the fact that the inner complexity of my acts prevented me from being my Self-for-him. Similarly, I never quite coincide with my own idea of myself. Ideas—even of oneself—necessarily serve to abstract and highlight. Whether I introspectively analyze my emotions or simply appraise them nonreflectively in order to act, in either case I end up labeling them by the dominant coloring, disregarding splotches which would not fit into the picture. There need not be an actual lie here, not even to oneself, but there is usually an uncomfortable sense of an unharmonious state. We recognize it, for example, in situations where pity or fear or horror, as the prevailing emotion, is subtly underlined with a personal enjoyment of the unusual intensity, of the dramatic, or even of a sense of self-importance. We feel no sense of guilt when we complain of extreme heat and secretly hope that the thermometer will go three degrees higher and break all local records. It is more disconcerting to find ourselves enjoying the drama of the hurricane which spared our house but took our neighbor's. Many a person, if given a chance, would have the generosity to take over part of his friend's pain if he could. This fact does not prevent him from having some sense of pleased superiority that a fate beyond his control has spared him this disaster. Just as our sensory perception or our mental concentration, no matter how sharply focused, is always accompanied by a multitude of peripheral sensations and reflections, so no single emotion ever overwhelms us completely, at least not when we reflect upon it.

Basic to any ethical system, and another obvious source of guilt feelings, is the problem of conflicting demands. Once again, the drama is played out both in our relations with others and in the arena of the individual psyche. At the moment, I am not raising the question as to what our responsibilities toward self and others ought to be. I am merely noting the obvious fact that innumerable situations arise in which we are unable to satisfy all of the claims which we recognize as legitimate. The supplications of two people appealing to us may be mutually exclusive, or we may face the dilemma of having to weigh the needs of another against our own. The feeling of guilt will be more or less intense, depending on the degree to which we feel confident that we have as objectively as possible decided in favor of the stronger appeal. But aside from the question of just how one evaluates the strength of such demands, the feeling of guilt at not having satisfied the rejected side is inevitable. To the extent that one acknowledges any claim as valid, one feels impelled to satisfy it.

Within a single person, there are just as evidently conflicting demands. These arise partly as the result of the complex emotional situation discussed earlier. More than this, there is the problem of the manifold potentialities of the human being. Contemporary psychologists, both existentialists and others, have placed new emphasis on the need for self-realization. But the process of realizing one's potentialities is—like every other human activity—one of exclusion as well as a reaching out. To become the self which at this moment I am means that I have renounced being that self which I might have been. The denied potentialities fall into the same position as the rejected claim of another person. One might argue, of course, that many of these possibilities would have been destructive and that no sense of guilt could be attached to an awareness of having denied them. This is probably true sometimes though I believe the point is debatable in more instances than one might think. Even a destructive potentiality may have exerted some claim which one has had to deny in the interests of one with more far-reaching possibilities. Let us exclude those which our rational appraisal tells us ought never, under any circumstances, to have been satisfied. There still remains a myriad of unexploited opportunities, facets of ourselves, rich experiences which we have forever missed. It might have been better or worse, but at any event something which craved fulfillment has been pushed aside and has left a haunted emptiness. I believe that this sense of carrying within us the unsubstantial shadows of these other

might-have-been-lived existences is one of the roots of the
reasons for the myth of reincarnation, which perpetually exerts its fascination even upon those of us who cannot finally
accept it. A secret fear that one has not chosen the best
combines with the hidden wish to have been also what one
has most rejected, and the feeling of guilt is inescapable.

Finally, there is the question of our own evaluative judgments, approvals and disapprovals. Let us assume that we
have learned to pay very little attention to our awareness that
we are not what the other thinks we are, that we have accepted with a minimum of discomfort the contradictions in
our emotions, and that we have become at least resigned to
the particular selection of potentialities which we have made.
There still remains one psychic factor which is bound to
subject us to self-judgment and resulting guilty discontent.
This is my realization that I am subject to the same kind of
judgment that I pass upon the other. Once more there is an
outer interpersonal aspect and an intrapersonal one. If I know
that the other approves or disapproves of me, this evaluation
forms part of the data which I am forced to recognize as
being in some way attached to me. If I genuinely believe the
other to be mistaken in his disapproval, or if I honestly feel
that he condemns what I admire and deliberately embrace,
the feeling of guilt may become mere discomfort or a sense of
alienation. If I recognize his favorable or unfavorable judgment to be valid, then, of course, I praise or condemn myself.
Possibly his judgment is pinned to a specific event in my past,
one which I feel that I have left far behind, which is no longer
me. Still the pronouncement that I *have been* a coward or a
liar rests fixed in my own self-portrait. I find it difficult to
exclude this trait from my self-evaluation when for him it has
been and perhaps still is a part of me.

Most important of all for ethics is the appraisal which I
myself make of human behavior. No matter how unformulated or flexible the standard of judgment may be, there is
nobody who does not approve or disapprove of the specific
conduct and personality of others. Self-deception may blur
the accuracy with which I apply these standards to myself,

but it can never entirely hide the fact that if I blame another for doing a specific thing, I myself am blameworthy if I perform the same act. Perhaps this quality of our psychic structure is the one absolute starting point for a humanistic ethics. Those holding the sociological view of guilt have given too little attention to the true nature of this inner judgment. I do not deny that our appraisals of others are influenced by theirs of one another and of us. But the really vital point is the fact that my own judgments cannot move outward without an accompanying inward movement. Consequently, I am always before the Bench. The eye of Judgment is ever there. Sartre has evolved the idea of the "Medusa concept" to signify the exaggerated fear of being petrified as an object before the look of the Other. The implied image is an apt one, for the Self-for-others called forth by any actions does indeed maintain a kind of objective existence over which I no longer have any control—even though it remains in a peculiar sense myself. I believe that this sense of never being free from Judgment—even when alone—is personified in the Evil Eye of ancient Mediterranean lore and in the stern Eye of God which looks down upon us from the dome of the Byzantine Church. It is not solely the introjection of Society. The uneasy awareness that the Other is always there looking on is literally true. It is I myself who am constantly watching and passing sentence. Admittedly, the split is not complete. Although a consciousness is always theoretically able to make a new choice of Being and to establish an entirely different value-orientation, our consciousness, in most situations, chooses within a structure already set up. Even so, and for this very reason, there is a continuity and consistency in the judgments which I pass on the acts of others and on my own. At any given moment there is a psychic separation between the consciousness which has just chosen a particular act and the consciousness which adopts a point of view upon that act. Yet this second consciousness is nothing more than this awareness of its objectified past and its projected future. Thus the image of Judge and Defendant is accurate enough, for consciousness does, indeed, hold within itself this strange couple. In this instance alone the god and his creation never become independent of one another.

A special manifestation of this inward drama occurs in what psychologists call the Ego Ideal. Although my concept of what I want to be may be open to a number of objections from almost any responsible system of ethics, I, who hold it, must meet its requirements or pay the consequences by suffering guilt feelings. Here, as earlier, we find that the highly complex character of the human person will never allow a one hundred per cent conformance to any such ideal. Consequently, the lapses from it will be psychically painful regardless of whether an outsider would call them crimes or moments of an awakened social conscience.

Considering these various sorts of guilt feelings, we find that they have one thing in common; that is, a sense that there is a discrepancy between a governing idea and an existing state of consciousness. In some cases the disproportion lies in the difference between what is there and what someone else believes to be there. In others there is a feeling of lack, an expectance of fulfillment where something is left uncompleted. In others we find a more definite sense of "ought." Always there is a gap between a demand, or what is expected and what actually exists.

Such a state of affairs is possible for man because he carries within himself the capacity to effect a kind of nonbeing, because he is—as Sartre has demonstrated—both Being and Nothingness. This Nothingness is naturally not restricted to guilt feelings. Its presence is essential to all consciousness. There is a nothingness between man's present awareness and his past, between what he is now and what he will be in the future. There is a nothingness between consciousness and its objects, between a man and himself. More accurately, it is this nothingness which renders man forever incapable of *being* himself and condemns him to being the perpetual pursuit of himself. From this nothingness stems man's freedom; here if anywhere are the possibilities for his guilt.

So far we have merely indicated that an awareness of

certain types of discrepancies gives rise to uncomfortable feelings which we may call a sense of guilt. We have not yet raised the question as to whether there are any criteria by which to judge these feelings legitimate or mistaken, nor have we established that the existing discrepancy is in fact the essence of guilt as such. Is it possible that this split in man is itself a guilty imperfection? Is it in this sense that the old catechism was right in saying that we sin every day in thought, word, and deed? In theological terms we might be content with some such conclusion, for the function of Grace in Christianity (like Love in Plato's *Symposium*) is to make divided man whole again. Does such a concept make any sense in humanistic terms? It seems that if we are to identify guilt or sin with man's existential nothingness, we are lost at the start so far as an ethics is concerned. We would be in the position of those Christian philosophers who argue that man is incapable of saving himself, but we would be without hope of Grace to deliver him. Would it be correct to say simply that with no wholeness and perfection against which we may measure this creature of splits and gaps, the moral imperative cannot arise? We come face to face finally with the basic question, Can there be sin without God?

In attempting to find an answer, I should like to begin by examining the typical view of sin which has been prevalent in our Western culture. I will use religious terminology because I believe that an ethics of humanistic existentialism must make meaningful use of these concepts if it is going to offer a valuable alternative to the religious life.

There have been two kinds of sin in our Judaeo-Christian tradition, both of which involve the existence of a discrepancy between what is and what ought to be, a failure to meet a demand. There is sin as transgression or trespass, and there is Original Sin. Sin as transgression is a deliberate breaking of God's commands—usually as interpreted by the rules of a specific church. We are morally responsible for sin as transgression, and we can, by resolute perseverance bolstered by prayer for assistance, avoid it. If out of human weakness we fail now and then, we can wash sin away by repentance and atonement, by a heartfelt "I'm sorry." We are saved from sin as transgression both negatively, by avoiding acts of disobedience, and positively, by carrying out the prescriptions for righteous living—in short, by works.

Original Sin is the more interesting kind. This is what we are born in. We have no choice. The only way to get out of it is to admit that we can't do it by ourselves. If we confess that we are abysmally unworthy of God's Grace and appeal to His Mercy, then we are promised that He will bestow it on us. The confession must be sincere, not a calculated acknowledgment for the sake of gaining a reprieve. One must simultaneously hold that Grace is not merited and trust that it will be given. Thus man is saved from Original Sin by Faith— though, curiously, faith consists in the hope that he will be given what he has decided he does not deserve.

Since humanistic existentialism rejects belief in God or any kind of impersonal Absolute, and since it throws into question most of our social structures, we might suppose, as many persons have done, that its only concept of sin would be, at most, a relativistic version of sin as transgression. In this case, sin and guilt would be regarded as the infringement of such rules as humanity might arbitrarily choose to set up. Always in the background there would be the thought that new ideals, with appropriately modified regulations, might at any time replace the current ones. I do not hold this conclusion to be valid or necessary. I believe that within the framework of humanistic existentialism, one may speak meaningfully of both types of sin and that in each instance sin or guilt is something more than merely breaking the rules of the game.

Starting with the concept of sin as transgression, I think that the existentialist equivalent to the Christian idea of disobedience or the broken bargain is found in the Sartrean concept of "bad faith." Much has been written about "bad faith"; there has been a wealth of discussion concerning its place in Sartre's philosophy, its relevance in understanding the psychology of characters in existentialist fiction, and its connection with the Freudian notion of self-deception. I do

81

not believe, however, that the implications of bad faith for an ethics have been fully investigated. Certainly those of its correlate, "good faith," have not been, not even by Sartre himself except indirectly in working out the specific dilemmas of his literary protagonists.[2]

To put it briefly, bad faith is a particular kind of lie to oneself. It involves an illicit shifting back and forth between identifying oneself with his situation and conduct and dissociating himself from them. Bad faith is revealed in one's attitude toward himself and in relations with others—both the personal and the social. It is easier to begin with the personal.

We may see an exemplification of Sartrean bad faith and at the same time distinguish it from ordinary self-deception if we will consider an example from Eugene O'Neill's *The Iceman Cometh*. Freud's idea of self-deception is probably sufficient to encompass O'Neill's overt intention. Sartre's concept includes but goes beyond it. In the play we find a certain Rocky, a bartender, and two girls closely involved with him. The girls collect money for going to bed with strangers and give part of their profits to Rocky, who keeps a protective eye on them and steers trade in their direction. The trio are reasonably happy, thanks to the scrupulous care with which each one avoids "calling things by their true names." Rocky, all insist, is not a pimp but a bartender since he does, after all, earn wages by serving drinks. The girls are "tarts" but not "whores." As developments in the plot force them to recognize that their way of life does indeed merit the pejorative labels conventionally applied, everything collapses. Rocky aggressively demands more money and threatens to beat the girls up. They taunt him with openly expressed contempt, put on a new cynical toughness in their dealing

[2] I have discussed in considerable detail Sartre's analysis of bad faith and examples of both bad faith and good faith in existentialist fiction in *The Literature of Possibility* (Lincoln: University of Nebraska Press; 1959), reprinted in paperback with new Afterword under the title *Humanistic Existentialism* (1962). I have gone beyond Sartre in extending the concept of bad faith to include my relations with others as well as with myself.

with customers. In short, all make themselves thoroughly
miserable by deciding to live up to the names they now accept
for themselves.

In this episode there is a two-step progression into bad
faith. Obviously there is self-deception involved in the first
stage. At this time Rocky and the girls regard themselves as
somehow separated from their own conduct, not to be identified with it. The falsity lies in the fact that they are unwilling
to realize that their past actions, once they have been objectified in the world, are subject to precisely the same impersonal appraisal as those of anyone else. The three may *feel*
that they are different from the typical image of pimps and
whores. Insofar as pimps are defined as men who live off the
sexual enterprises of women, and whores are females who sell
sex, Rocky and the girls *have been* pimp and whores.

But *are* they pimp and whores? It is here that O'Neill's
traditional concept of self-deception reaches its limit and the
Sartrean comes into play. For a Behaviorist or Freudian psychology, the three *are in fact* pimp and whores, for their
nature has been adequately displayed in the past and may
surely be counted on to remain so in the future. O'Neill's play
is intended to demonstrate the impossibility of their continuing to exist with this true picture of themselves, and it shows
the trio rapidly retreating again into the relative content of
mutually sustained self-deception. Existentialism would argue that the conduct displayed at the supposed moment of
self-enlightenment and confession was just as deeply rooted
in bad faith as the earlier stage had been. At first the three
had tried to deny the objective side of themselves. Now they
are denying their subjective side. When they decide to *be*
pimp and whores since they *are* pimp and whores, they make
two false assumptions: first, that they are fully identified with
the role they play as this is conventionally defined by the
words applied; second, that they must continue to be in the
future what they have been in the past because this is their
nature. It would have been artistically disastrous for O'Neill
at this point to have made them into existential hero and
heroines. For that matter, O'Neill with his Freudian commit-

83

ment would not admit that a new choice of being would be even theoretically possible for them. Yet if we forget the play as such and consider Rocky and the girls simply as people, existentialism would say that their decision to *be* what they *are* is not sincerity but bad faith. Good faith would allow at least two different possibilities. The three might admit that as words are used, the terms "pimp" and "whores" technically apply; realizing that such words do not fully exhaust or fully describe the being of the person, they might choose to make of these roles what they pleased. In other words, they would refuse to accept the usual subjective connotations of the terms, and would make their own evaluative appraisals of their way of life. As a second possibility, the three might resolve that since they genuinely shared the feeling of opprobrium which the roles of pimp and whores connoted, they would *no longer be* pimp and whores. In this case, they would defy not society, but their own former selves, making a new choice of being. In neither case would the retreat into bad faith be inevitable; existentialism, which relentlessly refuses to allow anyone to avoid responsibility for what he has been, is less despairing than determinism. Its vision of what one is reveals no fixed nature but rather the necessity of choosing one's future and the possibility of choosing a future which will be altogether different from one's past.

Someone may object at this point that retreat into self-deception would be easier for Rocky and the girls—or for anyone—than either defiance of society's values or the choice of a new way of life. True, and this is exactly Sartre's point. Bad faith, like most forms of sin, is always easier than the bleak path of virtue; that is why so few of us are saved. Bad faith involves a discrepancy as all sin does, and this discrepancy is an actual falsification. Fundamentally it is a lie about one's freedom. Bad faith is a way of declaring that one is not responsible for what he has been or not free to choose what he will be. It seeks refuge in the idea that man may either cut himself off completely from his situation or that he *is* identical with his situation and *determined by* it. Good faith, as the existentialist sees it, lies in accepting the truth about man's being—namely, that one is always *in* a situation but that he lives and makes himself by constantly transcending it. Perhaps it would be more nearly accurate to say that man always exists *in relation to* a given situation and that he is perpetually in process of choosing what his specific relation will be. Bad faith denies the inextricable union of freedom and responsibility which is the very essence of human reality. It is a lie based on cowardice and fear of the human condition. At the risk of seeming overfanciful, I would suggest that while it offers no substitute for a God against whom this transgression is committed (only the pure datum of man's existence *as freedom*), existentialism does have its triune Devil, its Unholy Trinity. The three Persons, I suggest, are these: first, those psychologists (Behaviorist and Freudian) who insinuatingly whisper to man that he is not free and cannot change himself; second, such sociologists as proclaim to us that we are, each of us, one with the roles we play; finally, those cynical manipulators, often collectively termed Madison Avenue, who publicly and subliminally coerce us into fitting their own commercial image. All of these weaken man's resistance to temptation, the first two sinning in ignorance and the third in deliberate, willed wickedness.

In our relations with others, we find Bad Faith manifested in either or both of two related ways. Either there is an identification of the Other and of oneself with the accidents of our social situations, or there is an illicit postulating of one's own freedom as being intrinsically more important than the Other's. In either case there is usually involved also a surreptitious treating of the person (either Self or Other) as if he were only an object or only a subject, whereas in fact everyone is always both. Later we may examine in more detail certain aspects of a society in bad faith and consider possibilities for an endeavor toward more of good faith in our social relations. At present, we may simply note how quickly we can detect a mispresentation of the facts of the human condition, a lie in bad faith, as an essential structure of certain forms of social injustice.

Obviously any hereditary caste system, any discrimination

based on race, religion, national origin, or sex, any exploitation of primitive peoples are condemned at the start. All are founded upon the myth that men and women are determined by some accident of birth or that (in the case of religious prejudice) the whole person is adequately expressed in a single aspect. All deny that a person is what he or she makes himself. All cut off the possibility of an open future. Usually such attitudes attempt to support themselves by an appeal to biology, which not only existentialists recognize to be false, or they grant to the individual only such traits as have been abstracted out as typical culture traits of his nation. The most cynically honest and chauvinistic nationalist might conceivably go so far as to admit that he opposes minority groups simply because they are other than his own. Even he is classifying people by traits which are partial and accidental; furthermore, his actions declare that one small group contains the sole free subjects, using others as if they were objects only. I call bad faith "sin as transgression" because it introduces deliberately a discrepancy between human actions and the facts of the human condition as one knows them to be.

A second over-all manifestation of bad faith in society parallels still more closely what happens within the sphere of the individual's inner relations with himself. One of the most ubiquitous forms of bad faith on the personal level is the cluster of devices to escape responsibility for what one has done and has made of oneself. This involves among other things the fiction that the standards and values of what Sartre calls "the serious world" are absolute, supported by some impersonal guarantee. Such a lie is profoundly reassuring to the majority, who would rather believe almost anything rather than that it is up to them as individuals to choose and to be responsible for the value system by which they live. On the social level we find a parallel in the attitude that a given social structure is not to be questioned. Even more firmly established is the supposition that the existing laws or customs are equated with absolute standards of right and wrong so that one may regard the one who breaks them as being evil

86

through and through. Similarly, of course, *les honnêtes gens* may complacently congratulate themselves on their righteousness.

The varieties of bad faith are infinite; the essential structure, whether within the person or in interpersonal relations, remains the same. It always involves the suppression of the fact of freedom and responsibility. It introduces a willed discrepancy between what exists and what one postulates. Just as with the sin of transgression in the religious context, one may save oneself by works. Here obedience is not to any external authority but to the logic impelled by the honest recognition of the demands of human freedom. There is no God to help. Instead one accepts with anguish the realization that one can look only within. What one finds there is freedom and responsibility.

If we hunt for a possible basis for the idea of Original Sin in humanistic existentialism, we discover that Sartre has already defined it in *Being and Nothingness*. "My original fall is the existence of the Other," he says.[3] And later, "Original Sin is my upsurge in a world where there are others"; "whatever may be my further relations with others, these relations will be only variations on the original theme of my guilt."[4] Sartre has devoted very little space to the direct discussion of this original guilt though it might be argued that its implicit presence is part of the tension of all those specific ethical dilemmas portrayed in his fiction. In the passages from which I have quoted, he explains that there are two ways in which I am guilty before the Other. In the first place, I bestow upon him a new dimension of Being, which he experiences as an alienation. By my look, by my very existence as a consciousness, I make him realize that he has an outside, that he is—to me—an object. Even his subject-being as a freedom becomes—for me—an objectified subjectivity, a nature with such and such potentialities. Sartre feels that this Self-for-others, this object side, may be experienced in shame or in pride. In either case, the Other is alienated from that

[3] Sartre: *Being and Nothingness*, p. 263.
[4] Ibid., p. 410.

which is in some sense himself, for he can never grasp this self which he is for me.

In the second place, I am guilty because even while I try to acknowledge the Other as a freedom and as a subject, I make of his freedom the instrument of my own project. To use Sartre's term, my awareness of him constitutes him as a "transcendence-transcended." I make of him a thing even as I may declare him to possess the possibility of making me a thing in turn. Try as I will, I never arrive at meeting him as subject.

Fundamentally Original Sin derives from this existential paradox: consciousness is always consciousness of something as well as a self-consciousness; yet while consciousnesses may be aware of the same object, they never become one with that object, nor do they merge. Thus I know *that* the Other is a subject, but I know *him* only as object. I may—in good faith —regulate my conduct by the postulate that he *is* a subject, but my very resolve to do so is positing him as object. It is *I* as subject who determine the conduct which is appropriate.

Put abstractly in this way, existentialist Original Sin seems a poor colorless reflection of the theological variety and hardly worth the trouble of feeling guilty over. Nevertheless its existence is demonstrably real, which I have never personally felt to be true of the Christian variety. One need not take it on faith. As lived, it may be a source of anguish and despair though the sinner can, of course, harden his heart to its presence.

Original Sin manifests itself in our relations with others as we live by obviously false "as-if" fictions. We live as if there were one world, whereas there are as many worlds as there are individual persons. This is not to deny the existence of a world of matter external to those consciousnesses which are aware of it. But this world is never experienced as one and the same world or even as a total world by those who live in it. The world of science is impersonal and objective insofar as it provides data for conscious beings to work with. It is only a partial world. At most it is the most firmly structured organization which has been superimposed upon Being and the one which is most steadfast. It is not all-inclusive even for the practicing scientist, not even at that moment when he is most engrossed in it. The world in which each one lives is the "life world." Even the so-called "physical world" varies extremely in its structured appearance according to the private interests, intentions, projects, and emotional outlook of those perceiving it. When we are concerned with the interpretation of human events, then the nucleus of common experience is narrow indeed as compared with the subjective variations introduced by all the experiencing consciousnesses.

Guilt or sin enters in when there is a necessity of judgment. Both privately and publicly we spend our lives passing judgment—selecting our friends and our senators, disagreeing with our parents, rewarding a child, condemning a murderer, or signing petitions for the impeachment of a public official. Is it the acts we approve and condemn, or is it the actor? Insofar as it is the acts only, there is a minimum of guilt—provided we judge by criteria we really believe to be adequate and which we would be willing to apply toward our own conduct. Yet the old injunction to hate the sin and love the sinner, pronounced in the interests of compassion and understanding, contains a kernel of bad faith. Possibly in some purely private relations, one may, out of love for the malefactor, condemn his overt acts without letting the person feel the ill effects of the judgment. More often my sentence severs him, as well as his acts, from my approval. In the public sphere there is seldom, if ever, any such separation. To the criminal sentenced to die, it means very little that some of the jurors felt sympathy for him as they judged him guilty. It is the man or woman or child who is judged. Our consideration of the motives involved may lead us to plead extenuation; this is itself a demonstration that it is the person and not the objective conduct which we are judging.

It is at this point that we stop halfway. We claim to judge an act in the light of all its inner structure of motivations and intent—in other words, by the way it appeared to be the one who performed it. But there are two things wrong here. First, we can never really see how the act appeared to him, for to abstract the motive and purpose of the particular act from the total context of the life-world of the performer is to distort and falsify. Second, many a crime, when seen from the point of view of the one who performed it, is innocent. Either it seemed best to do at the time, or it was performed under intolerable pressures. Within its proper life-world it *was* the right act.[5] It may still be so in the eyes of the one responsible. Or, if not, then how can he be condemned for willing what he disowns?

Thus the social structure is based on a contradiction which involves a certain dishonesty. Claiming to be objective, we hypothesize an impersonal world, but it is a world which nobody inhabits. For purposes of expediency, for sheer self-protection, we are forced to pass sentence externally, giving the label of impersonal justice to the fiction that the acts as committed and the acts as judged exist in the same milieu. Since I am speaking here of Original Sin, I will not mention those devices whereby we prevent ourselves from attaining higher degrees of understanding and greater humanity than we have been content to put up with. Such tricks fall within the purview of Bad Faith. All these aside, there will always be some residue of guilt, no matter how liberal and enlightened the society. To some degree the majority will always live at the expense of the minority. Yet there is no arithmetic by which one may justifiably add up and subtract human souls, no more than there exists a system of mathematical transformations enabling us to move from one private world to another—like those scientific fantasies which would allow a person to travel back and forth among the temporal dimensions of past, present, and future. We may grant, for the sake of argument, that we might at least come perceptibly closer to Utopia, might wipe out presently existing forms of oppression and economic injustices. We could certainly eliminate capital punishment and transform corrective imprisonment into a genuine program of rehabilitation. There would remain the problem of a criminal group as such, however treated,

[5] I do not mean to say that the criminal may not act in bad faith or that what seemed to be the best act was objectively so.

and of the dangerously abnormal and insane, of the substandard. The majority would still treat them as things, as objects to be dealt with instrumentally in order that they might not stand as obstacles to the projects of the world's free subjects.

There are other ways in which our existence involves a false "as-if." For one thing, even apart from the question of passing judgment, we are forced to use some people as objects, no matter how firmly we are resolved to respect their subjectivity. One cannot in every single contact with those one encounters take time to be intimately concerned with the subjective personality of the Other. The guilt here is relatively slight except in the case where one does not limit himself to a formal and provisional acceptance of the Other as his role—waiter, delivery boy, etc.—but behaves as if he were in reality a thing. (There is a difference between bracketing the Other's personal subjectivity and acting as if it were nonexistent.) More serious is the conflict of subjectivities. Sartre has pointed out that one limit of freedom is the existence of other freedoms. In the fulfillment of my own projects or in helping certain others to fulfill theirs, I will necessarily use some people as means, as instruments, as objects. Although each Other *is* a process of becoming, a continual self-creation, I inevitably, in my own inner world, make use of him as a being, an entity, an object. Suppose I set up the Other's freedom as a prime value, eagerly wishing to sacrifice my own in his interest as many a parent has done for a child. I am faced immediately with the recognition that whatever I do, I am choosing for his freedom. If I attempt deliberately to mold him for his own good, I am trying to create him into an object after my own image—to nail down this freedom. If I resolve to stay out of his way entirely, neither preventing him in anything nor offering him anything, then I again infringe upon his freedom by failing to open up to him those visions of dangerous and constructive possibilities which would widen the scope of his choice.

With perfect wisdom, I might hit the proper Aristotelian mean—providing the maximum of free opportunity with the minimum of protective restriction. But how can I ever know? Here we meet with another set of "as-ifs." By my actions I objectify myself or—as Sartre puts it—I inscribe myself in the world of matter. But "the world steals my action from me." I am responsible for the consequences of my act insofar as I am the author of it. I never possess sufficient knowledge of all the factors in either past or future to enable me to foresee these consequences. The rock I throw to kill a poisonous snake may be deflected against the forehead of my friend, who rushes to my rescue with a stick. The people's government which I help to put in power may prove to be a ruthless dictatorship. I commit myself wholly and responsibly but never with full knowledge nor with the power to guarantee the particular future which I have projected.

So far we have been considering Original Sin in the context of one's relations with others. Can we find Original Sin within the structure of the Self and its own inner relations? I think that we can and do in the way that we have already examined in connection with guilt feelings. I am guilty in that I fulfill some of my potentialities at the expense of others. I am guilty if I prevent myself from responding to new possibilities of growth, but this willingness to change to meet the demands of my freedom may involve me in infidelity to my old emotions, to my old commitments to an ideal self.

Someone might object here that we cannot avoid this kind of guilt, and this is true. That is why I call it Original Sin— because one cannot escape it. Sartre has pointed out in so many words that I am helpless before this guilt but that this helplessness never succeeds in cleansing me of it. For Original Sin, humanistic existentialism provides no salvation. Furthermore, just as the Christian theologian declares that the ultimate sin is that pride which leads the believer to think he can save himself from sin by his own efforts, so there is for humanistic existentialism, too, a comparable final temptation. This is the temptation of pure Sainthood. There are no saints without God if one means by "Saint" a person who is cleansed of the sin of existence and washed clean. All action is, at least to some slight degree, guilty action. So is a life of retreat and quietism, for to refuse to act is to support by default those things which one might have prevented, to blight forever the potentialities of what one might have brought into being. Just as much to be condemned is the opposite reaction. Camus in *The Fall* has portrayed the cynical preoccupation with human imperfection, reveling in hatred of self and mankind, which renders futile all human endeavor, which is content to dwell with the worst of what man is since it cannot achieve a perfection which would be no longer human.

Camus's hero confuses the two kinds of sin. Because he finds some self-seeking in everyone, which he interprets as an Original Sin which prevents any truly moral position, he refrains from all effort to remove avoidable evil, a procedure which is one of the more subtle procedures of bad faith. Confusing the two kinds of guilt is frequently an excuse. For example, to recognize, as we have done, that some "inequity" apropos of criminals, etc. is unavoidable may easily pass into the attitude that our present system may as well be accepted. Fromm has commented on this kind of thinking when he pointed out that we are prone to confuse what he terms existential and historical dichotomies.[6] To accept the fact that man is mortal in his concrete experiences and infinite in his projects is comparable to recognizing that man always contains a germ of Original Sin. To take literally the statement that the poor are always with us is to assert that an avoidable social evil is an existential structure of the human condition. This last claim is false; it is a device in bad faith.

If there is to be an existentialist saint, he will resemble, not Camus's self-lacerating Clamence but the "picaresque saint" described by R. W. B. Lewis.[7] The existentialist, saint or otherwise, confronts the problem of what to do with those attributes formerly ascribed to the "missing God." It is easy —at least for most of us—to realize that omniscience and

[6] Erich Fromm: *Man for Himself* (New York: Rinehart; 1947), pp. 40–50.
[7] R. W. B. Lewis: *The Picaresque Saint: Representative Figures in Contemporary Fiction* (Philadelphia and New York: Lippincott; 1959).

omnipresence are not for us. The temptation of taking over God's prerogative of Judgment and of being as stern and absolute as He has been represented is all too easy for us to succumb to—as Camus's "Judge-penitent" proves. The existentialist saint will strive rather to take over two other qualities of the divine attributes—forgiveness and the will, harder for man than for God, to look at the subjective heart within. Like the priest in Graham Greene's *The Power and the Glory*, baptized in the sins of the world, he accepts the guilty as well as the virtuous, understands and tries to help without condemning. Original Sin cannot be got rid of either by the quest for purity or by accepting the sinful state, with easy, forgetful resignation, as inevitable. If there is partial salvation, one is, once more, saved by faith—faith in the lovability of mankind.

In examining the kinds of guilt and of guilt feelings, we have found that they are always centered around a discrepancy—as is true of sin in the traditional sense. One way or another, the manifestations seem to involve one or more of three things. First, as process, not entity, man is free and responsible. Sin, guilt, or evil involves denying this fact, either in oneself or in another person. Second, there is no merging of the private worlds although the object side of man's being and experience necessitate a sphere of selves-for-others, which we posit as being neutral, impersonal, and objective—though nobody ever really experiences it as such. Third, everyone *is* a subject but appears as an object to others (and reflectively to himself). Our actions affect the Other in his being though all we ever know of him is his appearing. Of his being we can only form hypotheses to which, at most, he may give assent.

Existentialist ethics, like any ethics, may be said to have both an unattainable ideal of perfection, which serves as regulating Idea or principle, and a set of broad practical directives. The perfection is on principle impossible. There is no way by which every freedom might have full scope to actualize all of its potentialities. So long as human beings remain individual consciousnesses, there can be no hope of completely knowing another's private world. Even extrasensory perception would not reveal that inner context *as the other sees it*. Finally, there is no method by which to transform our present relations of subjects and objects into one in which the Other and myself might be considered solely as subjects in a relation of pure subjects. If these ideals could be achieved, the human being as we know him would not exist, and there would be no need for an ethics. As de Beauvoir has said, one does not offer ethics to a God. Only a Being-who-lacks is free and, faced with the necessity of choosing, has need for standards and justifications for his choices.

A more practical ethical ideal may be defined as the achievement of the closest possible approximation to this imaginary perfection. Here we must be careful to avoid a misunderstanding. Although I have stressed the importance of recognizing the absolute quality of the Other's freedom, his private life-world, and his subjectivity, the same is true for myself. Obligations toward myself are at least as important as toward others. Sin against myself is fully as much a temptation and a crime. The ideal is not that sort of merging in which either I or the Other would be reduced—or even raised —to some common denominator. Sin is the prevention of the free and responsible development of a unique self.

One may wonder to what degree this negative formulation of what is contrary to an ethical imperative may be said to parallel the positive imperative of Kantian ethics. Certainly the emphasis on respecting the Other as subject suggests the Kantian Kingdom of Ends. De Beauvoir's *The Ethics of Ambiguity* has been labeled a neo-Kantian commentary—not justly, I think, if one means that it is only that; yet the appellation is not without some reason. That existentialism is closer to Kant than to Plato or Aristotle or Leibniz or to innumerable other philosophers one might mention is certainly true—both in its ethics and in its epistemology. I suppose this might be said of almost any post-Kantian philosopher, just as one might make a comparable statement concerning any post-Copernican scientist. Sartre's rejection of the distinction between noumenal and phenomenal worlds

95

makes it impossible to call his theory of knowledge Kantian in any significant sense, despite Sartre's heavy emphasis on the function of consciousness in assigning distinction and meaning to an otherwise undifferentiated universe. In the same way, the parallel with Kant's ethics is limited and partial. To acknowledge everyone as a free subject and not make of him a mere thing or object is admittedly so close as to seem almost a translation of "Treat everyone in his own person as an end and never as a means only." The settings, so to speak, are altogether distinct. The very condition for an ethics is different in the two philosophies. Kant holds that man is completely determined within this phenomenal world, which means that he is determined insofar as we can observe and interpret him empirically. He may be transcendentally free, to be sure, but the movement from the idea that man *may* be free as noumenon to the idea that he ought to act as if he knew himself to be free, involves for Kant all sorts of unprovable hypotheses: the existence of God, immortality and the goal of eternal happiness, and the claim that we may take as self-evident the inner sense of duty (the moral law within like the order of the starry firmament above). Granted that Kant does not establish these conclusions in the same way that he sets up the a priori forms of thought by the process of pure reason. Their authority is that of Regulative Ideas. Nevertheless, Kant clearly holds to a certain absoluteness in establishing that "I ought" implies "I can," the moral quality of the Good Will, and the relation of the whole ethical system to the transcendent noumenal world. Where Kant's freedom is hypothetical, Sartre's is a fundamental given. Kant emphasizes the importance of duty performed for its own sake alone. Sartre says that man *is* his actions. Kant presupposes an impersonal absolute to which all conduct is ultimately referred; Sartre denies it. For the existentialist, man has no future eternal life in which to reap the desserts of his present performance. Kant's categorical imperative to universalize our behavior, to act as if our act were to be made a universal law is not precisely opposed to the existentialist position. Yet everything about it is somehow not quite in line.

Most fundamentally, Kant states it as a *categorical* imperative. To the existentialist, all imperatives are hypothetical, beginning with the principle that it is only when one *wants* to justify oneself, that the question of ought or good faith or ethics arises.

V

The Far Side of
Despair

Among the accusing adjectives which hostile critics have attached to humanistic existentialism, one of the most frequently heard is "nihilistic." Existentialists, it appears, believe in *nothing;* hence nothing stands to block their destructive impulses, and we may expect *anything* from them. Whether spoken naïvely or formulated with philosophical sophistication, this attitude contains an important assumption: that there is a logical connection between what one believes about ultimate reality, one's sense of purpose, one's values, and one's concrete action.

The interrelation of all of these and their bearing on the question of nihilism has been posed in a particularly subtle and provocative manner by Friedrich Duerrenmatt in his novel *The Quarry.* The hero, Barlach, a retired police commissioner, is aware that he has terminal cancer and arranges to have himself put into a clinic run by Dr. Emmenberger. The police commissioner knows that the doctor had worked under another name with the Nazis, and Barlach suspects that he has secretly continued his practice of operating without anesthesia and killing his patient-victims. Emmenberger recognizes Barlach, prepares to operate on him, and cynically reveals all the truth about himself. Barlach calls him a nihilist, but Emmenberger says that it is not he who is the nihilist. He himself believes fervently and absolutely in his own existence in a world of matter and in his freedom to enjoy the act of torture. It is the decent people who are the real nihilists, for they really believe in nothing. Emmenberger then proposes a wager. He will let Barlach go if the police commissioner can state that he believes in anything as absolutely as the doctor holds to his creed.

"I shall concede my defeat if you, Commissioner, can prove to me that you have a faith as great, as unconditional as mine."

The old man was silent.

"Say something," Emmenberger continued. . . . "Give me an answer. You're a Christian. You were baptized. Say, 'I believe with a certainty, with a power that overshadows the belief of a shameless murderer in matter like a sun of light overshadows a pitiful winter moon.' Or say at least, 'I believe with a power that equals his, in Christ, who is God's son.'

The clock ticked in the background.

"Maybe this belief is too difficult," said Emmenberger. . . . "Maybe you have an easier, more popular belief. Say, 'I believe in justice and in the humanity this justice is to serve. . . .' Say it, it is an easy, decent belief, which we can still demand of today's belief. . . . And when you say it, I will think that you have a belief as great as mine."

The old man was silent.

"Maybe you don't believe that I will let you go?" asked Emmenberger.

No answer.

"Say it anyway," the doctor ordered the old man. "Confess your belief even if you do not trust my words. . . . I bind your escape to a silly joke, to a childishly simple condition, that you can show me a faith as great as mine. Show it! The belief in goodness ought to be as strong as the belief in evil! . . ."

Only the clock could be heard.

"Your faith!" screamed the doctor. "Show me your faith. . . ."

The old man was silent.

Then Emmenberger's face—which had been greedy for an

99

answer—became cold and relaxed. . . . It was as if disgust shook
him when he turned away from the sick man, tired and indifferent.[1]

On the surface and verbally, Emmenberger has won. But
who is the Nihilist? Can either one justly be said to represent
the existentialist position? I would say that there are two
reasons why Barlach is unable to respond to the challenge.
One is the fact that he (and probably Duerrenmatt, too)
acknowledges that the traditional objects of belief have lost
their power. Even for the majority of nominal Christians,
religious faith is scarcely more than a wishful "Maybe there's
something beyond it all that makes sense." Second, Barlach's
silence stems from a disillusion still greater than lack of
religious faith. The novel as a whole, with its background of
Nazi concentration camps and contemporary oppressions,
stresses the never-ending existence of injustice and cruelty
and the impossibility of ever setting things right on the big
scale. Looking at mankind as a whole, Barlach feels only
disillusion for past and present; he can find no reason for faith
in the triumph of justice in the future. Yet against this setting
of social corruption, the individual may fight to wipe out
particular evils. Barlach's presence in this room of death is
overwhelming proof that he was willing to face extreme torture in order to win justice in this one instance over what
seemed to him a crime against humanity. Thus concern for
justice and mankind both live in him to the point of inspiring
an unassuming but genuine heroism.

There is another point of view from which we should look
at this scene. Traditionally the abstract principles which govern ethical decisions are supported by some claim to universality attached to a particular metaphysical view. Interestingly enough, Emmenberger's position is in this sense more
orthodox than Barlach's. It is *because* he feels that the Universe is wholly material and amoral that Emmenberger, who
is a distorted version of Nietzsche's Overman, defends his
position, not as an arbitrary caprice, but as the sort of con-

[1] Friedrich Duerrenmatt: *The Quarry* (New York: Grove Press;
1961), pp. 117–19.

duct which is in keeping with this kind of world. Abstractly, Emmenberger's argument might be put like this: (1) The Universe is composed of matter, which in no way reflects or supports those values customarily called spiritual or moral or specifically human. (2) Man, too, is matter and holds no privileged place. (3) Therefore, since man is of no importance, I am justified in treating him like any other material object. Possibly we are going too far in stating this so-called justification as something positive. Perhaps it would be more accurate to express it negatively: The nonhuman nature of the material Universe precludes there being anything which might legitimately oppose the doctor's positive pleasure in torturing.

Emmenberger's belief, strong though it may be, remains a nihilism. Its essence is a twofold denial. It rejects the idea that anything in the over-all structure of the universe should stand in the way of the immediate impulse. At the same time, it refuses to admit that something new is introduced by the human. At least it does in so far as the victims are concerned. But the doctor is, of course, in bad faith. His desire to torture is based on the realization that human beings are not *only* matter. His "belief in his own existence" is valued as the recognition of something more than mere bodily existence. Even as he appeals to the world of matter to defend his rejection of human values, he asserts their reality. He is a nihilist, not because he believes in nothing, but because what he believes in is the idea that there is no reason why one should not regard all human claims as nothing and reduce all human beings to nothing. Implied is the conviction that because the material universe is not human, it renders all that is human worthless.

Clearly Emmenberger's position is nihilistic and not existentialist. What of Barlach's? In his case, he attaches so high a value to justice and to human beings that he risks his life in their behalf. Yet he cannot justify his heroism by an abstract statement of wholehearted allegiance to any faith or belief. Unlike Emmenberger's, Barlach's code is unsupported by a metaphysical framework. Neither the universe nor mankind as a whole displays an already existing purpose or positive value. In a sense Barlach's act is against the world, not with it. He finds no overarching or imminent purpose in the structure of things, no intrinsically good essence in human nature. By his action, he chooses to bestow value upon a human attitude, to create justice where there had been none. His goal means enough to him so that he is willing to die for it. In comparison with Emmenberger's disgusted disillusion when his challenge is not met, Barlach's agony in the face of expected torture seems preferable. At least it bestows on his life a significance and a meaning. Barlach in this scene seems to me to be a dramatic representation of the existentialist who *creates* values by his action.

It is generally assumed that a lack of higher meaning or over-all purpose in the Universe is a terribly bad thing. Even Sartre has remarked that it would be much better if God the Father existed. Our forlornness is due to our discovery that He is not there. It is worthwhile to ask ourselves just what this hypothesis of higher meaning and purpose really does and has meant to man and why he has felt the necessity to project it. Most of the time I believe it has been bound up with the hope for immortality. Certainly in traditional Christianity, as in any religion which promises a personal afterlife, the significant part of the idea of historical development is not that God and His Universe are infinitely good and eternal but that the individual shares in this destiny. Most important of all for our present selves is the thought that the specific role we play in this far future is determined by the way we conduct ourselves here and now. This life on earth is our trial and test, and the grade we receive indicates the eternal class we go into. The undeniable positive element here is the conviction that what we do matters forever. If taken literally—or as near to literally as today's fundamentalist is willing to take it—the pragmatic value of this doctrine is overwhelming. Meaning, purpose, and progress toward some definite destination are clearly defined and omnipresent. The catch is that the more concrete and specific the positive promise, the darker the negative side. The Medieval Heaven gains part of its shining light from the contrast with the smoky darkness of the Hell which lies below it. "Here pity or here piety must die," says Dante; and I, for one, would at this point bid piety a hasty adieu. A God who would for eternity subject even one person to horrors surpassing those of Buchenwald, a Creator who would create souls capable of deserving such punishment seems to me to echo man's ignoble desire for vengeance more than his aspirations for an understanding Justice. Of course very few people today believe in everlasting punishment, and it is easy to see why. Only the most hardened sinner could bear to live with this sort of anticipation for any of his acquaintances—let alone the fear of being condemned himself.

In a more acceptable form, Christianity for today's average believer stresses the mercy of God. Although it may not be put in quite this way, the idea seems to be that since God views each life from within, He sees each man's good intentions. *"Tout comprendre, c'est tout pardonner."* Hell isn't left quite empty, but like the Greeks' realm of Hades, it is reserved for the really great sinners—like Hitler, perhaps—who are condemned by almost everybody and sufficiently remote so as not to concern us. Heaven and Hell are less concrete and precisely located than they used to be. If one gets liberal enough in his Christian commitment, he may think of Heaven as simply the eternal consciousness of God's presence and Hell as the painful awareness of His absence. At this point, even if individual immortality is not lost, we are in danger of floating off into a vague pantheism which is no longer specifically Christian. In itself, this makes no difference for our present discussion. The issue is not specifically between existentialism and Christianity. Yet we may note that the more the old idea of Heaven and Hell is subjected to ethical purification and intellectual criticism, the feebler becomes any specific hypothesis as to the meaning and ultimate goal of the individual life. If Christianity reaches the point of no longer postulating any afterlife for the specific person, then we may well ask what remains of what centuries have found most valuable—the infinite value of every human soul, its eternal existence, and its freedom of choice to determine the quality of that existence.

Not all hypotheses of the existence of a higher meaning necessarily postulate eternal life for the individual consciousness, whether separate or absorbed in some ultimate Unity. Aristotelianism does not—despite the First Cause, the Unmoved Mover which thinks itself and by its very presence draws all other forms upward toward pure Thought. The Hebrew prophets, too, speak of no future life for man. It is in the present that man must walk humbly and righteously in the sight of the Just God, who will champion those whose cause is right. These interpretations of reality are not oriented toward any eternal Future, but they do serve as some sort of absolute guarantee and point of reference. If the Universe is rationally organized, whether ordered by a Deist Creator, or simply sustained by an Unmoved Mover, it at least serves as a mirror for man wherein he can find himself and his proper place. If the order of the Universe both corresponds to human reason and exists independently of it, one may conclude, at the very least, that Reason is our essence and guide, that to develop it to its greatest extent is our highest good. It is an easy step from there to the notion that Reason may discover absolutes in the ethical sphere as well and that the ultimate attainment of rationality will be a culmination of all that is best in ourselves and a steadfast bond between us and the outside world. Similarly, the belief that the structure of things is permeated with the spirit of Justice offers a sustenance and guarantee to man which come from outside himself. Not only will God reward the Just. He furnishes the assurance that we *ought* to be just and that we may know what Justice is.

Existentialism rejects all of these blandishments. In the early writing of French existentialists, man's recognition that he stood alone in an irrational world without God was expressed in an attitude in which revolt and despair were equally mingled. Things ought not to be this way, was the cry. We will never accept our fate with resignation, but we will live it —in our own way—against the Universe. At the end of *The*

Flies, Orestes declares: "On the far side of despair, life begins." But the life which was to start involved no change in the view of things which precipitated Orestes' self-chosen exile. Camus said that his thought had gone beyond what he formulated early in *The Myth of Sisyphus*, but he added that he had never renounced the vision of the absurd which led him to ask, "Can I live without appeal? Can Thought live in this desert?" It is important not to forget this tragic vision of man against the Universe. Humanistic existentialism finds no divine presence, no ingrained higher meaning, no reassuring Absolute. At the same time, no humanistic existentialist will allow that the only alternative is despair and irresponsibility. Camus has pointed out the fallacy involved in leaping from the premise "The Universe has no higher meaning" to the conclusion, "Therefore my life is not worth living." The individual life may have an intrinsic value, both to the one who lives it and to those in the sphere of his influence, whether the Universe knows what it is doing or not.

Merleau Ponty has remarked, "Life makes no sense, but it is ours to make sense of." In a popular lecture, Sartre expressed somewhat the same idea, explaining in simple terms both what he means by creating or "inventing" values and by value itself.

To say that we invent values means nothing except this: life has no meaning a priori. Before you live it, life is nothing, but it is for you to give it a meaning. Value is nothing other than this meaning which you choose.[2]

In *Being and Nothingness* Sartre defined the ontological status of value as "beyond being" and as "the lacked." "Value is the self insofar as the self haunts the heart of the for-itself as that for which the for-itself is."[3] This definition sounds more negative, but it is not really so. Or if it is negative, it is the same sort of negativity which allowed Plato to describe love as the reaching out toward what one does not possess—even if the desire is only for the continued future

[2] Sartre: *L'Existentialisme est un humanisme*, pp. 89–90.
[3] Sartre: *Being and Nothingness*, p. 93.

possession of what is already within one's grasp. Value for Sartre corresponds to the ideal full moon by which one judges the present form of light to be only a crescent. Value is "the missing totality toward which a being makes itself be." [4] Sartre in these passages makes no clear distinction between "meaning" and "value." In other contexts, it seems that he would have to do so. When it comes to the reasons and motives for living, he is probably right in recognizing that value and meaning become inextricable. Both are included in our word "significance." Value and meaning are subjective structures which one imposes upon the world. They cannot, of course, exist independently of the world.

In contrasting traditional and existentialist attitudes toward the question of the meaning of life, I should like to use a homely example as an illustration. Let us imagine reality to have the shape of a gigantic Chinese checkerboard—without even the logically arranged spacing of the regularly shaped holes as in the usual game board, and with various-sized marbles, only some of which will fit into the spaces provided. The traditional attitude of religion and philosophy has been that we faced two alternatives. Theological and rational positions have assumed that there exists some correct pattern, impressed into the board itself, which can be discovered and which will then show us how we may satisfactorily and correctly arrange the piles of marbles near us. They have assumed—and so have the Nihilists—that if there is no such pattern, then there is no reason to play at all. If there is no motive for making a particular pattern, they have concluded that one might as well destroy the patterns set up by others or commit suicide. Existentialism holds that there is a third possibility. There is no pre-existing pattern. No amount of delving into the structure of the board will reveal one inscribed there in matter. Nor is it sensible to hope for some nonmaterial force which might magnetically draw the marbles into their correct position if we put ourselves in touch with such a power by prayer or drugs or any other device

[4] Ibid., p. 94.

which man might think of. But while this lack deprives man of guide and certain goal, it leaves him free to create his own pattern. It is true that there is no external model according to which one may pronounce the new pattern good or bad, better or worse. There are only the individual judgments by him who makes it and by those who behold it, and these need not agree. If the maker finds value in his own creation, if the process of making is satisfying, if the end result compares sufficiently favorably with the intention, then the pattern *has* value and the individual life has been worthwhile. I must quickly add that no such pattern exists alone. Although its unique form and color remain distinctly perceptible, it is intermeshed with the edges of the patterns of others—like the design of a paisley print. The satisfaction in a life may well result in large part from the sense that these intermeshings have positive significance for the individual pattern. There is another kind of satisfaction—that which comes from the knowledge that other persons have declared one's pattern good. Still a third derives from the realization that what one has done has helped make it easier for others to live patterns intrinsically satisfying to them.

That a positive value is present in experiencing a delight in what one has created and in the approval of others cannot be denied. For many people this is not enough. The sense that there is something missing is sufficient to undermine any quiet content with what one has. We hear most frequently three basic complaints, and these refer respectively to (1) the starting point, (2) the here and now, and (3) the farther on. First, there is the feeling that we need some sort of eternal archetype or measuring stick. Existentialism admits that there is nothing of the sort and that life is harder without it. Yet we may well ask whether the privilege of having such an authority would not come at too high a price, and cost more than it is worth. Pragmatically, the over-all destiny and purpose of the Universe play a small part in the daily projects of Western man—with the possible exception of those remaining fundamentalists who still take the promise of Heaven and Hell quite literally. Mostly it is there as a kind of consolation at moments of failure, cheering our discouragement with the idea that things may be better sometime in a way that we cannot begin to comprehend. I do not deny the psychic refreshment of such comfort. But if the belief in any such authority and plan is sufficiently specific to be more than a proud hope, it must be restrictive as well. If man can be sure that he is right by any nonhuman standard, then his humanity is strictly confined by the nonhuman. He is not free to bring anything new into the world. His possibilities are those of the slave or the well-bred child. Higher meaning is itself a limitation for a being-who-is-a-process. Such a future is not open but prescribed. Man as a tiny being in an impersonal world may be without importance from the theoretical but nonexistent point of view of an omniscient objective observer. Man in the theological framework of the medieval man-centered Universe has only the dignity of the child, who must regulate his life by the rules laid down by adults. The human adventure becomes a conducted tour. It is in this sense that I seriously question the sincerity or the wisdom of Sartre's statement that it would be better if God the Father existed. The time has come for man to leave his parents and to live in his own right by his own judgments.

The second disturbing aspect of a life of self-created patterns emerges when we compare ourselves with our fellow man. Obviously some people are satisfied with patterns which others regard as deplorable. Can we allow this chaos of judgments and still cling to the belief in the positive value of whatever patterns we ourselves have made? Is the result not such an anarchy of the arbitrary that to speak of pattern at all is nonsense? Here existentialism begins by saying that up to a point, arbitrariness, inconsistency, and the simultaneous existence of divergent value systems are not to be lamented but welcomed. The creative freedom to choose and structure one's own pattern would be worthless if we were to agree that we would all work in the same way toward the same end. Just as we expect persons to differ in their specific projects, so we should allow for those individual over-all orientations which bestow upon the project its significance and which are, in turn, colored by it. Sartre has declared that the creation of a value system by which one is willing to live and to judge one's life is man's most important creative enterprise. This means more than the working out of standards of right and wrong and the regulation of one's own demands in the light of our relations with others. It involves the whole context of what we might call "the style" of a life—not just the moral but the aesthetic, the temperamental—everything which goes to make up the personality which continues, with varying degrees of modification, until death and which even then will leave behind it an objectified "Self for Others." Every such life is unique, no matter how hard the one who lives it may have tried to mold himself after the pattern of his contemporaries. Existentialism prizes this uniqueness and resists all attempts to reduce it to the lowest possible minimum. Existentialism recognizes and exults in the fact that since everyone *is* a point of view, there is no more possibility of all persons becoming the same than there is of reducing to one perspective the views of two people looking at a landscape from different spots.

Someone will object that this is exactly what is wrong with existentialism—that it is nothing but a chaos of arbitrary outlooks and that if uniqueness is cherished and justified, then no ethics or supraindividual value system can exist. This book is, of course, an attempt to show that chaotic relativism is not the only alternative. Let us admit, however, that an existentialist ethics is chosen, that it is not a priori. Is this any reason for finding it untenable? As we have seen, any ethics is hypothetical, not categorical. So are most human activities. The man who values freedom of movement does not insist that everyone must go where he goes. It is the possibility of choice which he holds as the absolute, not the specific choice itself.

The most difficult aspect of the problem comes when we ask whether this conclusion justifies our waiving those fundamental principles which we have discovered to be the conditions of an existentialist ethics. Could our ethics, for example, allow the choice of an individual value system which attached positive values to bad faith? Or action based on the premise that we are not free and responsible? Or that we may consider and treat the Other as being merely object, not subject? Or that people *are* to be identified with the accidents of their situations?

No. No, quite simply because both types of self-realization, which must be the culminating value embracing all values, depend upon the recognition that man is a free consciousness. The other premises follow as corollaries. At first thought there might appear to be one exception. I don't think that we need to argue again the claim that an existentialist ethics cannot accept bad faith or the attempt to deny one's responsibility for one's own life. Is the same true with regard to our attitude toward others? In the chapter on guilt, I tried to show that respectful acknowledgment for other people as free subjects and recognition of our responsibility for them is an inevitable part of good faith and that guilt stems from the attempt to deny it. In that discussion, I associated ethical responsibility with self-realization in the over-all pattern of a life, i.e., with self-realization in being. It seems, however, that in the spontaneous realization of oneself as free consciousness there might easily be an assertion which would affront this Other's freedom as the result of a deliberate realization that one did not have to be ethical, that one was free not to act by any regulative, temporal demand. Even more probably, one's fullest realization of freedom might involve the deliberate choice to demonstrate its power over the Other taken as object. One cannot deny that there is a positive immediate value for the acting consciousness at this point. Can the ethical category apply at all in an experience which involves a separation from the usual temporal considerations? Moreover, if we allow that this kind of bad faith may still be called ethical, we seem to undermine the entire structure of an ethics in good faith.

Depending on the situation, we find either an easy answer or a hard one. In some instances there is merely a conflict of ethical principles such as we are used to encounter in any traditional ethics. We may find an analogy in the lie. I do not see how any ethics could—abstractly and universally—classify a lie as anything but a disvalue. Ethical systems always claim to have some firm connection with reality (regardless of what, specifically, reality is taken to be). The lie tends to undermine such connections. To lie is wrong because it is calculated to promote a disvalue which undermines the ethical system itself. Yet we are all aware that there are innumerable occasions when the lie, even if it does blur connections with reality, is nevertheless the ethical choice; for in certain special cases, the lie results in promoting other and more intense vital values. I would maintain here that some sort of hedonistic calculus is inevitable. The lie retains its minus quality as disvalue. The sum of the resulting value may pragmatically be possible only because of the lie. It would be greater if it could be effected by a method not involving the lie.

We have observed already that some degree of Original Sin is inevitable in human relations. Even in a clear ethical choice, there may be a conflict of values which can be resolved only by acting against the freedom of someone else. Obviously there are many instances when one's own freedom seems to exert the greater claim. In these situations there is no bad faith. One does not pretend that the Other is not a free subject or that one is not responsible for one's own actions. One realizes only that in pursuing the greater good, lesser values are sacrificed. The choice is impure ethically but justifiable. An example would be the killing of a guard in order to save a dozen prisoners condemned by an enemy tribunal in wartime. Such ethical choices involve what Camus called "calculated culpability." The term suggests that it would find a place only in reflective self-realization, but I believe that such acts can be performed nonreflectively; it is the later judgment of them which is reflective.

When Sartre says that we cannot describe the authentic man inasmuch as he freely makes himself, we can agree only with reservations. It is true that we cannot predict in advance the unique style of his life or the specific ordering of his freely created hierarchy of values. Yet we can declare in advance certain limits within which he must choose if his life is to remain authentic. We are on still firmer ground if we move from "authentic" to "ethical."

Despite these qualifications, I do not want to play down the dangerous aspect of the existentialist view that each one is a creator as he is a chooser of values. It is perilous as is any resolve to venture upon new ways of thinking and acting. To put everything into question is always a risk, no matter how firmly we determine that our answers will be responsible ones. It may be interesting to note that the New Theologians have arrived at a position which, while radically different in its foundation, places fully as much emphasis on the unpredictable uniqueness of each moral decision which the individual must make and on the necessity of choosing without objective rules or guarantees. Bishop Robinson says of his "theonomous" ethics (in contrast to "heteronomous" or "autonomous"), "It is, of course, a highly dangerous ethic and the representative of supranaturalist legalism will, like the Pharisees, always fear it. Yet I believe it is the only ethic for 'man come of age.' "[5] Theonomous ethics takes its point of departure from St. Augustine's directive, "Love God, and do as you will." As Robinson points out, these words "were never safe." Tillich speaks of an "ethics of kairos," an "existential" or "situational" ethics, in which a person, secure in that external Love which is his relation to Being, mediates "the meeting with the eternal in the temporal." The New Theologians are in complete harmony with humanistic existentialism in declaring that there are no rules, codes, or commandments which may not be set aside by the authentic choice of an individual who judges in the light of his vision of new and greater possibilities for human freedom in-the-world. The New Theologian's reliance on Love and man's ability to *know* that this love is of God purports to introduce an assurance that one is right, albeit a subjective one. To my mind it is even more open to self-deception than the humanis-

[5] John A. T. Robinson: *Honest to God* (Philadelphia: Westminster Press; 1963), p. 117.

tic appeal to the authentic ethical choice without God. The New Theologian's choice is certainly no more objective, and it seems to rest finally on an irrationalism which makes its own claim to being absolute.

The absence of any discernible higher meaning in the Universe takes on a new and special significance when we confront the future, not merely my own but that of the world as a whole. What difference does it make, some will ask, whether I fashion one kind of pattern rather than another or none at all? All patterns will be blotted out as though they had never been. If this world is all, how can one attach any significance whatsoever to the individual life in the face of the immensity of space, the staggering infinity of Time? "We are sick with space!" cries Robert Frost. The French keep reminding us of the futility of all endeavor "from the point of view of Sirius." Again, I feel that we suffer still from Christianity's insistence that all of us together and the Universe with us are going somewhere definite and that the destination bestows its meaning on the present mile of the journey. Deprived of this forward voyaging, we find no delight in the nonpurposeful development of an impersonal cosmos which has no prearranged destination. Whether this drifting Universe will eventually become cold and lifeless, or whether there will occur once again—or many times—the coming together of organized matter and the appearance of other forms of consciousness, it seems unlikely that man will be remembered any more than we have reason to think that all of this present world of matter was put here for his express benefit.

Is there any reason *why* we should try to adopt the point of view of Sirius? We should realize that observation of a dead planet through a telescope is neither more nor less true as a vision of the Universe than is the examination of living organisms through a microscope. To see the big without the small is to exclude much of reality just as surely as to stay within the limits of the microscopic. If there is a falsification of boundaries at the one end, there is a blurring of details and elimination of foreground at the other. William James has commented that inasmuch as death comes at the end to cut off all human projects, every life is finally a failure. The point of view of Sirius reveals the same message on the cosmic scale. Yet if it were possible for one to stand on Sirius at the instant before the final disappearance of all life, that moment of conclusion would be no more real or significant than any one of the moments preceding it. If there is an absolute negative quality in the absence of what will not be, then there is a corresponding positive value in what will have been. This last awareness might just as well take pride in what had been there as despair in the knowledge that it will no longer be. One does not choose to eat something bitter today simply because tomorrow it will make no difference which food one has chosen. The addition of positive moments does not add up to zero even if the time arrives when nothing more is added to the series. One might say that there is never any adding up of the sum, but this is not quite true. The new digits carry the weight of those which have gone before.

It is illogical to conclude that human values and meanings are unreal and of no importance simply because they do not originate in the structure of the nonhuman Universe. It is enough that the world serves to support these subjective structures for the consciousness which lives them. At the same time it is only natural that an individual man, whose being is a self-projection, should rebel at the prospect of seeing his projects suddenly brought to a stop. If the patterns and meanings which a consciousness creates were restricted to those experiences which we can live directly, then despair would in truth seem to be our only proper response. But man's being is that of a creature who is always about-to-be. In a peculiar sense also, he is, in his being, always outside or beyond himself, out there in the objects of his intentions or—more accurately—in his projects in the world. An impersonal Universe cannot sustain these subjective structures. But we do not exist in an impersonal Universe. We live in a human world where multitudes of other consciousnesses are ceaselessly imposing their meanings upon Being-in-itself and confronting the projects which I have introduced. It is in the future of these intermeshed human activities that I most fully transcend myself. In so far as "I" have carved out my being in this human world, "I" go on existing in its future.

What sort of world future does humanistic existentialism envision as the framework of its projections? Confronting the present scientific interpretations of the Universe, an existentialism which will not appeal to God may consistently follow either of two alternatives. Each rests upon a hypothesis. While the distant future may confirm one or the other, contemporary man must recognize that his rational choice is necessarily accompanied by some degree of faith or what William James calls "over-belief." We must live by a view of things which goes beyond our confirmable knowledge since our choice involves to some degree an attempt to predict the future.

The first alternative assumes that the human condition will not be significantly altered. By "human condition" I refer to those circumstances of man's being which—at least at this stage of the evolution of *Homo sapiens*—are inseparable from any human existence: man's finiteness and his mortality, the fact that his mind is dependent upon a body, that his nervous system responds to stimuli in terms of both physical and mental pain and pleasure. These are but a few of the obvious factors. On this hypothesis, we would include certain things which perhaps are more debatable: that the possibilities of communication between consciousnesses are forever fixed, that the quantity of man's knowledge will increase but not the definition of what we call "knowing." To call the human condition immutable is to state that man will undergo no further existential changes. Its corollary is the view that while science may be expected to continue to develop both theoretically and technologically, future discoveries will not essentially alter our appraisal of the Universe so far as man's relations with it are concerned. This is the position which until now existentialist philosophers have all assumed, at least implicitly. We must be careful not to restrict it too narrowly or make it too wholly negative. For while the *human condition* will never change, the view still holds that there is no fixed *human nature*. Sartre and de Beauvoir explicitly deny the existence of any human nature. Camus, to be sure, suggests in a passage to which critics have attached undue importance, that perhaps, after all, the Greeks may have been right in ascribing reality to some sort of underlying idea of man. But aside from the tentative and incomplete quality of this remark, Camus makes no use of the concept of human nature in any way which would constitute of it a determining force. For him it is an idea of what "humanity" is which serves to explain why men will revolt, placing a higher value on an ideal to be attained than on life itself. It is the basis also for the sense of human solidarity. To my mind, this is only another way of saying that man transcends himself in his projects—or, more accurately, man *is* his projects. Be that as it may, neither Camus nor any other existentialist philosopher holds that man's moral traits are predetermined or determining. Such a position means that we must give up both the belief in inevitable progress and the gloomy predictions of decline. Along with the latter must go those old saws which claim that war is inevitable, that human life is and always will be merely a more subtle manifestation of the tooth-and-claw struggle for survival, that man is essentially selfish, lawless, and cruel—in short, that "you can't change human nature."

None of the existentialists seem to me to have made even a fair beginning at developing the positive implications of this position. De Beauvoir in her novel *All Men Are Mortal* affirms her belief in the continuing sameness of man and his institutions, an attitude which I find to be inconsistent with her basic philosophy. Incredibly she uses the moon as a symbol for the futility of human aspirations, assuming that man can never reach that cold and shining sphere. Camus, who employs almost the same moon symbolism in his play *Caligula*, does not, any more than de Beauvoir, envision any significant changes in human attitudes. Friedrich Duerrenmatt, admittedly neither a philosopher nor an avowed existentialist, nevertheless writes fiction in which the existentialist view of man seems omnipresent. He, too, in *Traps* and in *The*

Visit, appears bent on demonstrating the cynical notion that everyone is guilty and has his price, and that this is the way things always have been and will be. Only Sartre, as I have shown in his prediction of the "philosophy of freedom" which is to come, allows for the possibility of there being a society so far in advance of anything we have known that we cannot now imagine its "open spaces." Sartre himself has so far limited himself primarily to explanation of the failures of historical Marxism and to the philosophical analysis of the emersion and collapse of a We-Group as it has been observed in France, in the Soviet Union, and in North Africa. His efforts toward a future have been cast in terms of direct political action or in sketching out a "progressive-regressive method" to be used in interpreting events in history and in the biographies of famous individuals. But Sartre is at least theoretically aware that both the social structure and the so-called "human character" are open to such willed modification that the life of man in the future may well be as different from that of our contemporary as ours is from that of the Neolithic inhabitants. It will not necessarily be better or worse. What it will be and the extent to which it develops beyond our present concepts depends on us. Thus, in choosing for ourselves, we are indeed choosing for mankind.

The second alternative goes further. It envisions not only a life for creatures like ourselves which satisfies in ways we have never known or thought possible. It proffers the hypothesis that future human beings may be very much unlike ourselves. Without going so far as to postulate the evolution of a creature one could no longer call human, we may accept the idea that there may be thrusts forward as significant as the discovery of writing or even the development of language. And of course there is no reason to exclude the further development of man as a species as the result of a consciously controlled evolution such as has certainly never happened before on earth. For this view, the future is not only open but unlimited. Space exploration, for instance, may be allowed, at least hypothetically, to change life essentially, not merely to increase the geographical scope of familiar conflicts.

There are, then, two possible ways in which to respond to the challenge to create meaning in a Universe where we have found none already inscribed. The first looks toward founding a society in good faith, to changing the external life of man in such a way as to give the fullest possible scope to his creative freedom. The second is more profoundly a self-creative process. It seeks self-transcendence of a kind which might well transform the very concept of meaning and purpose and the possible ways of satisfying our demand for them.

PART TWO

EXISTENTIALISM
AND
OTHER REBELS

LIKE MAN HIMSELF, philosophy is always "in situation." Existentialism in particular, which goes so far as to define man as "a point of view," is acutely aware of its own position in the specific world order of the twentieth century. It can envision its own transcendence. It lays no claim to being a final statement. But it insists absolutely upon its relevance to the society within which it has been formulated even as it directs itself toward a future which it strives to mold and determine.

It is not my purpose here to consider the academic affiliations of existentialism with other philosophies past or present; nor am I concerned with discussing its sociological origins and influences. In so far as existentialism holds itself aloof from the prevailing attitudes of positivism and from Freudian and behavioristic psychology, I am content to consider what it is rather than what it is not, what it offers rather than what it opposes. Its connections with earlier writers such as Nietzsche and Dostoevski, the parallels, where they exist, between Kierkegaardian and Sartrean existentialism, points of view shared by existentialism and pragmatism—such influences are not denied, but I am not interested here in exploring them.

In the contemporary American scene there are certain specific writers, movements, and attitudes which an existentialist ethics should confront for other than academic reasons. Existentialism is not alone in challenging the ensconced traditions. In fact, if we examine the motives back of these rebellions, we may find them remarkably similar, in explicit formulation as well as implicitly. In some cases the solutions are widely divergent and offer a challenge which I believe an existentialist ethics must try to meet. At other times, the positions are close enough so that one may well ask whether existentialism might not profit by adapting some of these insights to its own purposes.

I have in mind three trends—it would be inaccurate to call them schools—which seem to me to stand in significant relation to existentialism, whether as opponents or fellow travelers. First, there is Ayn Rand's Objectivism, which its author and her followers believe to be a systematic philosophy. Second, there are those whom I am going to call the Negative Rebels. These fall into two groups which are not always sharply differentiated. On the one side are those who are labeled variously Beatnik or Hipster and the authors who write sympathetically about them. Here we find persons who have deliberately cut themselves off from the mainstream of American culture, not by claiming to be above it, like the heroes of *Atlas Shrugged*, but because their sympathies are with the outcasts, the derelicts, those whom the middle class would rather forget. The most articulate of these writers (philosophically speaking) is Norman Mailer although, despite his frequent manifestoes and programs for social reform, he is certainly not a recognized spokesman for this group in the way that Ayn Rand may be said almost to *be* Objectivism. Distinct from these primarily hostile rebels, yet in some ways deriving their impetus from the same initial need to protest, are the activists emerging from discontented, rebellious college and university students—particularly the New Radicals. Finally, there is the recent swing to an American version of Oriental philosophy, especially Zen Buddhism.

Obviously existentialism is not to be identified with any of these. Neither is it accurate to make any of them a tributary of existentialism or vice versa—although Norman Mailer has called himself the first American existentialist and although a large number of scholars have attempted to draw parallels between existentialism and Oriental philosophies. Diverse as these three trends are, they all—and existentialism too—are significantly related as contemporary forms of rebellion. All three groups are made up of persons who believe that man has somehow lost his proper center and concept of selfhood. In one way or another, they feel that man must rediscover himself. They proclaim that life as lived by the average man is not satisfying and that a more positive experience in living is possible. All oppose the narrow Judaeo-Christian tradition which has dominated the Western world for nearly twenty centuries, and none is willing to settle for merely a liberalized restatement of Christianity or for the New Theology. To varying degrees and from different points of view, all criticize our society as it is presently set up, reject its popular ideals as inadequate, despise its tendency to settle for easy and comfortable conformism. All are suspect in the eyes of the Middle Class—if in fact, the vast bulk of the population does not simply shift its eyes away from them. The views represented exert a special appeal to the more daring intellectuals, but none of these movements is without its lunatic fringe (hate groups, delinquents, crackpots).

Perhaps the most important thing about them is the fact that all of these rebels believe that man is able to change. They refuse to accept the idea that he is essentially an automaton or the mere result of sociological conditioning. This is probably the answer to the fact that they seem to open the door, to invite each individual man to assert himself and to lay claim to new dignity, perhaps to joy, possibly even to salvation. Still we must not forget that while any newly discovered path comes as a relief to a person lost in the woods, not all will take him where he wants to go. Some may, even by a circuitous route, bring him back close to his point of departure. Looking down these roads as far as we can see, what directions do they appear to follow and into what landscape do they seem to lead? In other words, what are the premises of these rebels, and what do they promise?

VI

Egoistic Humanism: Ayn Rand's Objectivism

The very name "Objectivism" suggests that this philosophy would be the antithesis of existentialism, which is generally thought of as a philosophy of extreme subjectivity. That the two are natural opposites seems borne out by the association of Objectivism with conservative capitalism and of existentialism (at least in the case of Sartre and de Beauvoir) with socialism or Marxism. Ayn Rand has made her own position on existentialism very clear. In her essay, "For the New Intellectual," she writes, "The majority of those who posture as intellectuals today are frightened zombies, posturing in a vacuum of their own making, who admit their abdication from the realm of the intellect by embracing such doctrines as Existentialism and Zen Buddhism."[1] Despite all this, the popular images of the Rand hero and the Existentialist have something in common. Both are commonly held to be totally selfish and solitary individuals who acknowledge no authority save their own arbitrary whims, whose human relationships are motivated solely by immediate self-interest, who recog-

[1] Ayn Rand: *For the New Intellectual* (New York: New American Library; 1963), p. 12.

nize no responsibilities. If we forget about these popular distortions and leave the level of overgeneralization, we find that the task of comparing the two is surprisingly complex. There are a few precise similarities; there are some obvious sharp divergences. There are many instances where the task of balancing application against the formulated theory so as to arrive at some fair appraisal is extremely difficult.

Phrasing it very carefully and yet remaining scrupulously honest, one could sum up in a few sentences the essence of these two philosophical revolts. It would not be a distortion to say that both Objectivism and existentialism call for the assertion of the free individual against those theologies and those oppressively conformist societies which seek to make him deny his unique self in the interests of ready-made social molds and values. Both oppose a psychology which would reduce man to the animal level or to a mechanistic pattern of stimulus and response. They are equally opposed to the soul-body dichotomy of traditional theology. Objectivists and existentialists argue that every person is responsible for what he has made of his life. Each man is ultimately a free choice. In so far as they claim that man himself is his own end and purpose, both may properly be called humanistic. This is an impressive list of parallels. One might easily suppose that with the sympathetic sharing of such fundamental premises, the general similarity in their over-all positions would outweigh any differences in detail.

Only what emerges is not a common point of view. It is not merely that Rand and Sartre differ as to how the individual should go about engaging his freedom and asserting his newly discovered self. One discovers that somehow words have not meant the same things in these descriptions. The self and its freedom do not mean for Rand what they mean for Sartre. If we examine these basic premises and starting points closely, we find that only one is left standing as a common landmark. That is the rejection of God or of any form of belief in an eternal spiritual world beyond the human. Man remains the author of his own destiny, the creator of his own values.

At least, so it is stated. But Objectivist Man and Existentialist Man are not the same species even though each may lay claim to being *Homo sapiens* himself. Ayn Rand has rejected the Behaviorists' animal-mechanism and the sociologists' statistical average, but the creature who replaces them boasts Aristotle as his ancestor. Rand claims to get rid of false absolutes; she replaces them with new ones and declares that those she has established are eternal. Since they are easily discerned and clearly labeled, anguish is evidently out of place.

In claiming that man needs an ethics, Rand writes:

A human being cannot live his life moment by moment; a human consciousness preserves a certain continuity and demands a certain degree of integration whether a man seeks it or not. A human being needs a frame of reference, a comprehensive view of existence, no matter how rudimentary, and, since his consciousness *is* volitional, a sense of being *right*, a moral justification of his actions, which means: a philosophical code of values.[2]

This statement is something with which Sartrean existentialism can agree. Man's consciousness is fundamentally a reaching out toward, a volition, a desire, a choice. Since a choice is the same as a declaration of a desire or a want, it is equivalent to an evaluation. It implicitly says, "This is better than that." As such, it carries with it the necessity of justification. If by my choice I declare that one thing is better than another and then later decide that it was not better, I pass judgment not only upon the object in question but upon the earlier choice as well. In simplest terms, one may say that one's value system is a coherent method of relating past, present, and future choices in such a way that one's present choice is not undermined by an awareness of chaotic inconsistency with what was or is yet to come. Choice is both a way of making oneself and relating oneself to the outside world. Rand, like Sartre

[2] Ibid., pp. 16–17.

and the phenomenologists, recognizes that consciousness is always consciousness *of* something.[3] Thus man *is* choice, but he makes himself by what he chooses.

But what is this consciousness which chooses? What are its objects in that outside world? And what is the status of this sense of being right? It is in their answers to these statements that Objectivism and existentialism part company forever.

Nathaniel Branden, in a passage which has surely been approved by Rand, encapsulates Objectivism in three sentences.

In metaphysics, it is the principle that reality is objective and absolute, that it exists independent of anyone's consciousness, perceptions, beliefs, wishes, hopes or fears—that that which is, is what it is—that "existence is identity," that A is A. In epistemology, it is the principle that man's mind is competent to achieve objectively valid knowledge of that which exists. In ethics, it is the principle that the values proper to man are objectively demonstrable.[4]

Branden does not state explicitly what man is, according to Ayn Rand, but her work makes it easy to fill in the blank. A man is what he is. His essence is Reason. His values are rational. In short, every man, insofar as he fulfills his potential essence as Reason, *knows* what is right and what is wrong—absolutely. On this basis, Rand's fictional spokesman, John Galt, finds no difficulty in proclaiming to his audience, "Accept, as your moral ideal, the task of becoming a man."[5]

If we were to prepare a comparable formulation for exis-

[3] "A consciousness with nothing to be conscious of is a contradiction in terms. A consciousness conscious of nothing but itself is a contradiction in terms: before it could identify itself as consciousness, it had to be conscious of something." Ayn Rand: *Atlas Shrugged* (New York: New American Library; 1959), p. 942.

[4] Nathaniel Branden: *Who Is Ayn Rand? An Analysis of the Novels of Ayn Rand*, with a *Bibliographical Essay* by Barbara Branden (New York: Random House; 1962), p. 56.

[5] Rand: *Atlas Shrugged*, p. 982.

tentialism, it might run something like this: Man is a being who is what he is not and is not what he is. In him existence precedes his essence. Or better, man's essence is freedom itself, the choice of making his essence what he will. For himself he decides what is right and what is wrong, from his own point of view. His task is to make himself and to help prepare the definition of what man will have been.

"Existence is identity." "Existence precedes essence." *There* is the heart of the difference. Rand's view of man retains the old acorn theory. Man's potentialities may be hidden, but they resemble the embryo oak tree. The question is simply whether the individual will be, as it were, a bigger, stronger oak or a more feeble one. Everyone knows what a good oak tree ought to be and how to judge it. Oak tree nature and human nature are equally limiting. Sartre has pointed out that it is precisely this ideal pattern which is in question. Being a man means deciding what man will be. Reason, instead of being essence and self-evident guiding principle, is but one part of man. Rand, like Aristotle, sees man as differentiated from other animals by his reason and so concludes that reason, being the essentially human, is that which mankind should most develop. Without quibbling as to whether animals in reality do or do not possess a rudimentary reason, we may point out that reason is not the only distinguishing factor of the human. It seems equally clear that human emotions are not all or always the same as animal emotions. The primary difference appears to be the emergence of self-consciousness in the human being, but to equate self-consciousness with reason is simply wrong.

There is a concealed anarchy even within Rand's own presentation of objective Reason.

Rationality is the recognition of the fact that existence exists, that nothing can alter the truth and nothing can take precedence over that act of perceiving it, which is thinking—that the mind is one's only judge of values and one's only guide of action—that reason is an absolute that permits no compromise.[6]

[6] Ibid., p. 945.

All of this presupposes an impersonal and self-evident criterion of truth, an ultimate reference point to serve as a sort of fulcrum for reason. Indeed this official standard is reality itself.

Reality is that which exists; the unreal does not exist; the unreal is merely that negation of existence which is the content of a human consciousness when it attempts to abandon reason. Truth is the recognition of reality; reason, man's only means of knowledge, is his only standard of truth.[7]

All this is very hopeful, suggesting that reason is like a public door which, when opened, leads to the outside world directly. Then there follows immediately another paragraph to remind us that each one goes through his *own* door.

The most depraved sentence you can now utter is to ask: *Whose* reason? The answer is: *Yours.* No matter how vast your knowledge or how modest, it is your own mind that has to acquire it. . . . It is only your own knowledge that you can claim to possess or ask others to consider. Your mind is your only judge of truth—and if others dissent from your verdict, reality is the court of final appeal.

There are two pitfalls in this passage. One's grasp of truth depends on one's rational ability and on one's information as well as one's honest devotion to Reason. Verdicts may differ and what then? Rand's final appeal to Reality sounds fine, but it is exactly Reality which is in question. If one *could* get to Reality directly, then individuals' reasons could not disagree. I hold with Rand that there are millions of experiences of reality where we needlessly create trouble if we refuse to accept a practical certainty. These are the areas where disagreement is rarely or never found. Where individual rational conclusions do not agree, the appeal cannot be to something beyond Reason or to Reason and Truth as if they were tangible entities. One must choose between various beliefs or propositions, each one of which claims to be Reason or Truth.

This is never more completely the case than in the matter

[7] Ibid., p. 943.

of values or in the realm of human relations. One would think that surely here Rand would have to allow an appeal to emotions. She does not. In her definitions of "value" and of "love," it might appear that she does. Of value, she says, " 'Value' is that which one acts to gain and keep, 'virtue' is the action by which one gains and keeps it." [8] And of love, "As there can be no causeless wealth, so there can be no causeless love or any sort of causeless emotion. An emotion is a response to a fact of reality, an estimate dictated by your standards. To love is to *value*." [9]

Here there seems to be a recognition of value as simply the object of desire; emotion is close to being the same as an evaluation, a reaction of acceptance or withdrawal, depending on the individual value system. Rand is willing to say that "man chooses his values," [1] but she goes on to classify these chosen values objectively as rational or irrational—which for her means "true" or "false," "right" or "wrong," "real" or "unreal." "Emotions," she flatly states, "are not tools of cognition." [2]

What Rand ignores is that there is a wrong, avoidable manner of employing emotions *instead* of reason and a necessary and proper way in which emotions must come to the aid of reason in all fully conscious and significant living. One must, for example, choose between a life which offers richer rewards and more intense happiness, but almost certainly, too, more anxiety and suffering. One must somehow balance a short-time peak of happiness against a longer-term possession of more subdued content. One may be obliged to choose between a higher salary with greater prestige in an unattractive location against less money and fame in a place one loves. Reason cannot decide here. Even if someone claims that the qualitative may somehow be transformed into a quantitative calculation, the process of deciding is not a mathematical one.

[8] Ibid., p. 939.
[9] Ibid., p. 959.
[1] Ayn Rand: "The Objectivist Ethics" in *The Virtue of Selfishness: A New Concept of Egoism* (New York: New American Library; 1964), p. 28.
[2] Rand: *For the New Intellectual*, p. 55.

Rand holds that the ultimate goal of life is joy or happiness. She qualifies her hedonistic approach by saying that while happiness is the purpose of life, it is not the standard. In the same way, Branden points out that what one thinks is one's self-interest is not necessarily so. Obviously reason must serve both to enable one to achieve the emotional state of happiness and to determine when happiness is allowed (i.e., when it is rational) and to decide what one's true self-interest is. But whose reason and when? I may decide today that I was wrong in what I called my self-interest yesterday. What judgment will I have next week? Is an uninvolved third person's appraisal necessarily the truly rational one? There is always in Rand's work an implicit reference to an absolute judgment which stands outside the immediate involvements of the individual life, which remains human and yet is never caught up in human affairs. The truth is that her system needs Aristotle's Unmoved Mover. John Galt cannot replace him.

The assumption that the totally objective point of view exists and is accessible for everyone is only wishful thinking. It is the same sort of wish which underlies Rand's breathtaking statement that if businessmen lived in a perfectly laissez-faire society and followed pure self-interest, there would never arise any conflict among them. Rand yearns so nostalgically for a world of simple absolutes, where black is black and white is white and nobody color blind that she is willing to live recklessly by the assumption that reality (including human reality) is in fact this simple. Thus with perfect equanimity, she writes, "There are two sides to every issue: one side is right and the other is wrong, but the middle is always evil." [3] To her this is the same as saying—which she does a few sentences later—"In any compromise between food and poison, it is only death that can win. In any compromise between good and evil, it is only evil that can profit." Existentialism, too, asks for commitment and proposes an either/or. But this refers to one's basic choice of Being.

[3] Rand: *Atlas Shrugged*, p. 978.

When it comes to specific choices in the real world, existentialists are aware that the complexity of life is such that almost no action is pure and that still we must choose as best we can.

The either/or which Rand presents as man's basic choice is "to think or not to think." She adds that "to think = to be." This is, of course, a natural conclusion for her neo-Aristotelian insistence that man's essence is rational. We will agree with Rand that thinking is hard, that it demands intelligence, constant effort, and the strength to recognize something as true when it would be more convenient to believe otherwise. The charge to be rational, which, at the very least, urges one to avoid self-deception and to see things as clearly as possible, is hardly something one would seriously oppose. But what does it mean? For Aristotle, it led to the Golden Mean in ethics and to intellectual contemplation as the ultimate goal of life, neither of which suits Objectivism. At the very least, we need a corollary or a definition. For Rand, to think means to see things as they are. For A is A, and man can know what A is. If one is speaking about physical objects, I see no objection here. If one identifies a table as a table, knows its typical function and the molecular structure of its material, one does indeed know what a table is. Even if Sartre is right in insisting on a certain transphenomenality of Being, claiming that after one has performed a host of examinations of an object, there is still something left over—even so one knows what a table is. It *is* those things I have discovered about it even if it is something more too. Stating that one never knows absolutely is not to deny all knowledge as such. Rand is right in insisting that we have certainty about many specific things even if absolute certainty is lacking.

Rand goes much farther than this. For her, values and morals are subject to the same sort of rational appraisal as tables are. In many ways, it would be a great relief if this were so. It would all be so easy. The stakes are as clearly outlined as the First National Bank. The rules are laid down and written out. Best of all, one need never ask whether the game is really worth playing or what constitutes good sportsmanship. The existentialist, on the other hand, confronts his freedom in anguish. What he sees is not a twofold choice as definite as the old one which Christianity proffered. He realizes that all is open. His freedom is not just the choice between thinking and not thinking, between seeing what is right or refusing to see it. He knows that being free means creating standards of right and wrong. It means that there is no right pattern for man, but many possible patterns to be discovered and invented. God Almighty has not been deposed merely in order that Mother Nature—or Daddy Warbucks—might sit there, passing out the blueprints.

Rather than continuing to discuss abstractly the nature and function of human reason as seen by Objectivists and existentialists, we may proceed by looking at their respective portraits of man as he is and as he ought to be.

By either standard, most men are condemned as living lives of evasion. Interestingly enough, both Sartre and Rand in their classic descriptions have pinpointed an all-pervasive desire to escape responsibility, which results in a loss of authenticity. The relevant passage for Objectivism is from *The Fountainhead*, Howard Roark's portrait of the "second-hander." In some ways the "second-hander" is reminiscent of Erich Fromm's "Market Personality." He values himself according to his worth in the eyes of others and models himself after what he thinks will win their approval. In Sartrean terms, he puts the self-for-others above the authentic consciousness. Roark says, "It's what I couldn't understand about people for a long time. They have no self. They live within others." Roark goes on to explain that because such people will do anything for fame, prestige, public admiration, their ambition is labeled selfish. Actually they are almost totally selfless. Their achievements are imitations or borrowings from others. Their habits, their beliefs, attitudes, values are all derived.

If any man stopped and asked himself whether he's ever held a truly personal desire, he'd find the answer. He'd see that all his wishes, his efforts, his dreams, his ambitions are motivated by other men. He's not really struggling even for material wealth, but for the second-hander's delusion—prestige. A stamp of approval, not his own. He can find no joy in the struggle and no joy when he has succeeded. He can't say about a single thing: "This is what I wanted because *I* wanted it, not because it made my neighbors gape at me." Then he wonders why he's unhappy.[4]

The second-hander has modeled a pseudo-self, one which seems to be unique but which is so only in the way that most political speeches differ from one another in the arrangement of their clichés.

The "second-hander" is cousin germane to Sartre's man in bad faith, dwelling in the "Serious World." The emphasis is different. Sartre is concerned less specifically with the social climber and more with the smugly content bourgeois. But the "serious man," too, lacks any authentic self. He identifies himself with his social role as it has been defined by others. The idea that he might be the originator or even the chooser of his values and code of behavior would horrify him. He regards them as absolute entities, self-evident, and too sacred to be questioned. Values are fixed and clearly defined. The world is like a bargain table with each article presented with its proper price tag.

I could continue with this comparison to the point of being tedious. Moreover, the picture could be extended to include the definition of aggravating conditions. Such sub-men, Rand and Sartre would agree, are encouraged in their illness by prevailing doctrines teaching that people are the helpless victims of psychological and social pressures, that nobody is really free and responsible, no matter how much he may cherish the illusion of being a free agent. They would agree that "second-handers" and "serious men," out of mingled hate and fear, make it their duty to oppose and push down the individualist (Rand's term) or the authentic man in good faith (Heidegger's and Sartre's terms).

The description of symptoms is, for all practical purposes, the same. Diagnosis and therapeutic treatment are radically different. The blight of the "second-hander," Rand states, is

[4] Ayn Rand: *The Fountainhead* (New York: New American Library; 1952), p. 600.

due to the doctrine of altruism. Centuries of teaching that one must live for others and not for self have resulted in making man lose all sense of self-esteem. He feels that any action motivated by self-interest is wrong in itself. Moreover, since the ideal of living wholly for others is impossible to attain, men are presented with an inhuman yardstick by which to measure themselves. Hopelessness and guilt feelings are the inevitable result. Self-hatred prevents a person from developing an authentic self-center which can support a self one can respect. Yet since nobody can bear life without some sense of approval, the "second-hander" cultivates a pseudo-self-esteem through the good opinion of others.

After centuries of being pounded with the doctrine that altruism is the ultimate ideal, men have accepted it in the only way it could be accepted. By seeking self-esteem through others. By living second-hand. . . . And now, to cure a world perishing from selflessness, we're asked to destroy the self.[5]

If one has, as I have, the double feeling here that Rand's argument has a seeming logic and that, nevertheless, altruism is not an adequate nor even a correct explanation of sterile conformism and unauthenticity, I think it is because Rand is using the term "altruism" in a way peculiar to her. *Webster's Seventh New Collegiate Dictionary* defines the term as meaning "regard for or devotion to the interests of others." One can be concerned for and attach value to what pleases others without thereby giving up all interest in oneself. Rand uses "altruism" as though it always and only meant preferring another's good at the expense of one's own. Rand, in denouncing altruists, includes such diverse groups as the early Christians, the Medieval Church, nineteenth-century Utilitarians, and the Democratic proponents of the New Deal. (For the Kennedy administration, she adds the epithet "Fascist.") When she uses "altruism" in argumentative passages like the one just referred to, Rand presents altruism as a concept closely related to the Christian idea of Original Sin. I agree that to say that man should love only others and not

[5] Ibid.

himself and to condemn him as evil because he cannot do so is a diabolical doctrine which has possibly caused more needless mental anguish than any other single factor. It is probably true that a man cannot really love others unless he can honestly love himself and admit it. It is also true that he will not be able to love himself if he has no love for any other.

Furthermore, the man whom Rand's hero, Roark, uses as an example of the second-hander, Peter Keating, is in no way whatsoever an example of an altruist. As Rand portrays him, he has no self in the sense of developing a genuine set of values to live by. But he is certainly a *self-seeker*. Even if he goes about it in the wrong way, it is his own happiness which he sets as a goal. At no time does he deliberately aim at the welfare of anyone but himself. The same is true of every one of her "altruistic" heroes. Rand, of course, argues that such mistaken self-seeking is the inevitable result of altruism because of the inherent falsity of the doctrine. But the cynical use of altruism as a cover by her villains is in no way an application of the doctrine, not even a mistaken one. What motivates Peter Keating is not the desire to win the approval of others because he can't live up to the Christian (or Utilitarian) command to sacrifice himself to the good of others. Restricting ourselves solely to what Rand herself has told us of him, we see that Keating was dominated from the beginning by desire for a fame which his slim talent could not achieve and which he was, in any case, too lazy and soft to try to work for honestly. His contempt for himself was based on his recognition that he did not have inwardly what it took to be the kind of man he admired. Roark's attempt to attach such personality patterns to the doctrine of altruism is after-the-event and without root in the psychology of the character he is trying to explain.

It is in the theory of human relations that we best see the inadequacy of Rand's two premises—"A is A," and "Man can know what A is." We meet a difficulty immediately when we attempt to judge another's action. It is nonsense to say that the concrete external action, the "objective," is all that should be considered. An act, if it is to be thought of as in any way different from a bolt of lightning, contains an inner structure of motive and intention as well as overt motion. In short, it includes the whole context of the individual's private world. This is what the Objectivists would like to leave out in their judgments. They would, of course, allow for a broad, gross distinction between accident and premeditation. Motive would not be left out entirely. Yet they are unwilling to grant any ultimate validity to the subjective world within which the act has been performed. Once again, the assumption is that the road from the subjective to the objective is always open and that nobody is to be pardoned for not taking it.

Objectivism proposes the ideal of an atomistic society, which has often been falsely attributed to existentialism. The irony is that this world of isolated self-centers is supported by the notion of a common objectivity. The latter, of course, is lacking in existentialism, which nevertheless proposes an ethics of positive responsibility. It is the interplay of the doctrine of absolute standards of judgment and absolute individualism which makes Objectivism unique. It simultaneously declares that nobody has any responsibility for others and yet retains the right to judge others.

For Objectivism, the impersonal objective world is the real world, and access to it is ready at hand. In this common world every person proves his value. There are the men of the mind, and there are the parasites, the rotters, those who would substitute *feelings* (spoken with utmost disdain) for thought. The rational are the productive, and this demonstrates their value. For they produce that which others want. The others, needless to say, want these things because they are worth wanting, and they give what is wanted and worth wanting in return. He who contributes more—i.e., produces more—gets more. Those who produce little or nothing get little or nothing; since they are worth little or nothing, one need not worry about them. They have what they deserve, and what could be more logical and rational than that?

It is easy for men of the mind (and these, after all, are the only *real* men) to find joy and rational happiness in such a world. Being rational and intelligent, they will quickly recog-

nize, commit to memory, and practice the one absolute Truth
—that each man must live only for himself and never for
others. Also—for we must be fair—there is a corollary. Not
living *for* others means also not living *against* them—that is,
not initiating force against them. One must be careful to
interpret this only negatively. For as Howard Roark has said,
"The only good which men can do to one another and the
only statement of their proper relationship is—Hands off!" [6]

This doctrine is unabashedly egoistic. Rand does not reject
such adjectives as "self-centered" and "selfish." She embraces them and strives to demonstrate their rational beauty.
Her chosen term for the guiding moral principle of Objectivist ethics is "rational self-interest." Neither the term nor the
fact is in itself any reason for rejecting Objectivism. On the
face of it, I do not see why anyone should be convinced that
he ought to choose something completely contrary to his self-
interest as he sees it. No matter what the ethical system, no
matter what specific choice of action is involved, a person
chooses it because it in some way satisfies the chooser. Even
"self-sacrifice" is, strictly speaking, a self-contradictory
term, for the man who chooses to suffer or die for another
does so in order to satisfy something in him which finds a
value in the act. If the Underground Man tries to choose
against his obvious self-interest, he does so because he values
his independent freedom to choose something opposed to his
self-interest, as conventionally appraised, more highly than
he values any other apparently self-evident interest. If we
were to speak of pursuing one's self-interest in the narrow
sense of choosing only that which in one way or another
relates back ultimately to satisfying the desire of the chooser,
then one cannot act except out of self-interest. But in this
case, not only does the word "selfish" lose all pejorative
significance. We are in danger of rendering the term simply
meaningless. What is involved here is the question as to
whether there are significantly different ways of satisfying
the interests of the self so that we may restore meaning to

[6] Ibid., p. 676.

expressions like "selfish" and "unselfish." And we may as well, at this point, raise another inevitable and related question: Is there a distinction between Rand's "rational self-interest" and the old "enlightened self-interest" of Utilitarians and other altruistic Liberals?

The answer, I believe, lies in the question of the breadth of the horizon of the personality, the compass of the self-concept. If one can satisfy oneself only by the kind of outward impulse which returns directly, as in the case of eating, for example, then the horizons of the Self are restricted. The adjective "selfish" is applicable because the circle of self-interests is confined narrowly to its original center. The "unselfish" personality has extended its circumference to include the spheres of others so that what happens to them refers back its joy and suffering just as certainly as the impulse which includes no other center. Rand understands this idea better in working out the relations of her fictional characters than in the abstract theory. Thus John Galt cautions Dagny Taggert not to let his opponents know that she is in any way connected with him.

"If they get the slightest suspicion of what we are to each other, they will have you on a torture rack—I mean, physical torture—before my eyes, in less than a week. I am not going to wait for that. At the first mention of a threat to you, I will kill myself and stop them right there. . . . I don't have to tell you . . . that if I do it, it won't be an act of self-sacrifice. I do not care to live on their terms. I do not care to obey them and I do not care to see you enduring a drawn out murder. There will be no values for me to seek after that—and I do not care to exist without values." [7]

It is amusing to see Galt defending himself against the suspicion of altruism with the same sort of rationalizing that most people employ to convince themselves that they are not really selfish. And no more successfully. No matter how Rand tries to disguise the fact, Galt is willing to die rather than to know that he is indirectly responsible for the suffering of another. His love for Dagny transcends the pleasure which she offers

[7] Rand: *Atlas Shrugged*, p. 1013.

him directly. If it were only the latter, then clearly the rational and selfish thing to do would be to lose the part and not the whole. But the pain which would come to her is something which Galt makes a part of his own consciousness. He can and does endure the torture inflicted on his own body. He prefers the loss of all existence to the awareness of Dagny's suffering. All this in the name of a philosophy which takes life (the individual's own life) as the source of all value and morality! In the narrow sense, Galt's conduct is "selfish," because he wants to do that which he himself prefers. In the only meaningful sense of the term, he is "unselfish" since he has attached to another's consciousness a value higher than any other part of his existence. Dagny and her life have become a part of him, if you like. It would be more accurate to say that he has expanded his Self to include them.

Any ethics, I am convinced, sooner or later makes some sort of appeal to the need and desirability of the expanded self. I do not think we need defend ourselves here against any charge of "the naturalistic fallacy." We are not simply saying that something which happens to be true ought to be true, as one might argue that because people and other animals *do* generally want to avoid physical pain, therefore the avoidance of physical pain is a self-evident value and starting point. Surely, if an ethical system is anything, it is a way of appraising and directing the growth of a self which seeks to enjoy more and more of the feeling of value.

I reject Objectivism, not because it is self-centered or because it seeks self-aggrandizement. I criticize it for being selfish in the pejorative sense of restricting the horizons of the Self so as to leave the self-center, not enriched but impoverished, not blown up but withered and blighted. The Self of the Objectivists runs the risk of the only child—it is not unloved, but it is likely to be spoiled, ailing, and fretful, due to overprotection and the too close attention which prevents the growth of responsible freedom.

Objectivism claims to be a humanism and to reaffirm the essential worth and dignity of the human being. In reality it is one more form of evasion, seeking to escape the vision of what it really means to be human. Objectivism declares that every man is an end in himself and that it respects the right of every person to seek his own self-interest. Yet its basic ethics is a refusal to acknowledge any positive responsibility for others. Objectivism proclaims that individual freedom is its starting point and goal. But for the Objectivist, this freedom does not direct itself toward the creation of a unique self. Free enterprise is its *summum bonum*, not the free choice of values.

"We do not live or work with any form of the non-objective," John Galt says of himself and his companions.[8] That is true for Rand as well, and it is what is fundamentally wrong with her Objectivist ethics. In turning her eyes away from whatever cannot be reduced to the objective, she cancels out vast areas of human experience. Subtly a new conformism is introduced. Those who approve of this portrait of man and who have the best ability to liken themselves unto it form a distinct elite at the top. Those with less talent but who accept the validity of the model have smaller rewards but dwell in relative content lower down in the pyramid. Anyone else lives as discarded rubble on the surface. He is not incorporated into the structure of things. He is tolerated and ignored—so long as he does not interfere.

Objectivism proposes two categorical imperatives. Every man should seek his own self-interest. One should never use force against another to prevent him from seeking his self-interest. Rand interprets this as a simple "Hands Off." I think we must go further than that if we are to open our eyes to things as they are.

Let us take as an example what Rand has written apropos of the Negro struggle for civil rights. In an article called "Racism," she begins by condemning racism in the strongest terms.[9] The points she makes are not new, but she states them forcefully, and they are certainly sound. Briefly, she

[8] Ibid., p. 987.
[9] Ayn Rand: "Racism," *The New Conservative*, Vol. II (October 16, 1963), pp. 11–14. Originally published in the September 1963 issue of *The Objectivist Newsletter*.

protests against judging the individual by the group and treating race as if it were a biological determinant. She correctly attributes the origin of racism to "a quest for *an automatic self-esteem*," the need to cover over one's feeling of inferiority by identification with a group proclaimed to be superior. I think she is right in saying that racism is a form of collectivist thinking. Given her definition of "collectivism," however, equated with "statism" and applied indiscriminately to Nazi Germany, the Soviet Union, and any liberal government which does not definitely eschew the concept of the Welfare State, then Rand's statement that "historically racism has always risen or fallen with the rise or fall of collectivism" is not supported by the evidence. This was not the case with the ancient Graeco-Roman world. The thesis is particularly hard to sustain for the United States. Rand attempts it by stating, "It is the capitalist North that destroyed the slavery of the agrarian-feudal South in the United States." It is true that the North, because of its greater industrialization, had less need for slaves, but it was not the capitalist leaders of industry who became fervent abolitionists. It was the liberal intellectuals and religious idealists. Nor should one equate the near-feudalism of the South with collectivism. Rand entirely ignores the fact that, in the twentieth century, it has been the Liberals who have consistently spearheaded the pressure for civil rights and nondiscriminatory legislation. But then Rand, as we find out later in this same article, is not in favor of strong legislation to correct the racism which she so deplores. She condemns the South for its oppression of Negroes.

Racial discrimination, imposed and enforced by law, is so blatantly inexcusable an infringement of individual rights that the racist statutes of the South should have been declared unconstitutional long ago.

Well and good. But then she goes on to condemn the federal government for using "the racial issue to enlarge its own power and to set a precedent of encroachment upon the legitimate rights of the states, in an unnecessary and unconstitutional manner." I do not know what Rand means here unless she refers to the federalizing of the National Guard, sending troops to Little Rock, Arkansas, and to Oxford, Mississippi, and other comparable measures to enforce the U.S. Supreme Court's decision against segregation. But was not that judgment precisely for the purpose of declaring the states' racist laws unconstitutional? Would Rand have the Court pass the law and the government make no attempt to enforce it?

Rand goes on to criticize the Negro leaders for asking for a quota system in hiring. The wisdom of this request is certainly questionable. In view of the existing injustice which it was designed to correct, I think it hardly fair to call the proposal "racist," as Rand does. Again, one may debate the desirability of transporting children to schools in distant neighborhoods as a way to fight de facto segregation. Rand, however, reduces this complex issue to an emotional outburst, "The mere idea of using children as pawns in a political game should outrage all parents, of any race, creed or color." Are the Negro children simply being used? Is there no honest effort anywhere to better their condition? It comes now as no surprise when Rand calls the Civil Rights Bill "another example of a gross infringement of individual rights" and "the worst breach of property rights in the sorry record of American history in respect to that subject." By two arguments she attempts to justify this interpretation of the bill as injuring the rights of the white individual rather than protecting those of the Negro. First, nobody has the right to lay claim to the property of another, whereas "A man's rights are not violated by a private individual's refusal to deal with him." On this basis a Negro might be refused service in any restaurant, the privilege of owning or renting a house, the right to use any but publicly owned conveniences. If he insisted on his rights to any of these, his act would be considered an effort to lay claim to property not his own.

Rand's other point is a familiar one. Racism is an evil doctrine, but we must protect the racist's right in the "disposal of his own property" just as we allow Communists to have freedom of speech. For "private racism is not a legal, but

a moral issue—and can be fought only by private means."
Thus the essay which began by attacking racism as "a doctrine of, by and for brutes" ends by concluding that the only
hope for the Negro is to wait patiently until state governments and private individuals grow sufficiently enlightened to
decide to change their ways. Presumably the Negro may
express verbally his discontent. He must not ask for positive
legislation. Furthermore, he, like the rest of the world cannot
demand his rights. John Galt has said, "As a basic step of
self-esteem, learn to treat as the mark of a cannibal any man's
demand for your help." [1]

I have introduced this article of Rand's because it demonstrates several things. In the first place, it is an important
clue to her real intent. Some of her statements, such as the
prohibition against initiating force against another and the
precept to remember that every man is an end to himself, as
well as the general proclamation in favor of individual freedom—these, if kept on the level of abstraction, could easily be
given a Kantian turn. "Rational self-interest" conceivably
might be little different from the "enlightened self-interest,"
which has been associated with Utilitarians and other altruis-
tically oriented philosophies and social theories. Such is not
the case. When Rand says she wants to do away with altruism, she really means it. Her ideal of the perfect government is, in very fact, a perfect laissez-faire, approached but
not quite fully attained in American capitalism of the nineteenth century. Such a society would inevitably tend to give
still further protection to the strong, who least need it. This
fact we see neatly illustrated in the article on racism.

Second, the essay demonstrates Rand's naïve confidence in
the fact that the way to solve existing injustice is simply to
trust in the eventual decision of the in-group to alter the
situation. This is comparable to her confident statement that
among untrammeled industrial leaders pursuing their own
rational self-interest there will be no conflict.

The theory of "Hands Off" has merit only insofar as it

---

[1] Rand: *Atlas Shrugged*, p. 984.

forbids interfering with something which is noninjurious. Suppose, however, that I refrain from helping the victim of a hold-up. No ethics would *demand* that I give my own life in place of the victim's though some (not Objectivism) would say that a Self inclusive enough to want to do so would indicate the attainment of a valid ideal. If I do not intervene to help the victim when the danger to myself is nonexistent or minor, then it seems to me that I am guilty of helping to force another to act contrary to his own self-interest, even by Objectivist standards. In many respects our position in society resembles that of a person witnessing a hold-up. Objectivism is not intentionally on the side of the hold-up man, and it will certainly use all its resources to avoid being an unarmed victim. Through no choice of its own, it *is* in the position of the onlooker. Does the prohibition against initiating force against another extend to coming to his aid when such force is being applied? Logically it might do so, but in the writing of the Objectivists, I don't think that it does. Some time ago, a large number of people in a New York apartment house watched while a man attacked and killed a woman on the sidewalk. In such a situation, an Objectivist in that apartment might have come to the woman's aid either because he valued her or because he was righteously indignant over the violation of a principle which he valued. Nothing in his philosophy would make him feel guilty if he did not decide that intervention ministered to his own self-interest. He might simply pull the drapes and complain of the inadequacy of the police force and the faulty education system. If we allow this incident to symbolize the broader social environment, we must say that Objectivism goes beyond nonintervention. It comes dangerously close to defending the right of the attacker to act in the light of his own mistaken doctrine. This fact I insist upon despite the fact that one of the frequent Objectivist laments is directed toward our leniency toward the criminal.

Finally, the article on racism shows what Rand means when she states that one must not compromise. She does not compromise on her most basic principle: that the government must never interfere with the self-interest of employers or property owners. Another principle, that nobody is to be prevented from the fair chance to pursue his self-interest is, of course, sacrificed. To sacrifice some individuals to the interests of the majority is against Rand's principles too. But when principles clash, the lesser must give way to the more important.

In theory, Objectivism, like Plato's *Republic*, simply gives to every individual the opportunity to advance as far as his ability will take him and to enjoy proportionate rewards. Unlike Plato, it assumes that the mere lack of restrictive legislation will bring about this happy state of affairs. A free mind requires a free market, Galt declares. There is no way to insure that a free market will actually foster the potentialities of all free minds. Since the family structure is left intact, Objectivism certainly makes no provision for equal opportunity for all children. The intellectual elite, whose superior talents and rational morality will have won their place at the top, will owe a large part of their success to chance. Rand's rejection of the *demand* to love and look after the worthless members of one's family might reduce nepotism a bit; it seems unlikely that leading industrialists will try hard to seek out and develop those who can't make it in their given circumstances but who might if help were given.

In her discussion of love, Rand says that there must be a relation of two free beings in which each values the other for what he is and respects his independence. As Sartre would put it, this is the relation of two subjects in good faith. The indifference with which Objectivist heroes regard all who do not minister to their own self-interest amounts finally to regarding them as objects. Rand and Branden may caution us to remember that the other is an end *in himself;* somehow he never becomes an end *to* anyone except himself. Existentialism, like Christianity, proclaims the infinite value of every human soul or person. In Christianity this value is handled a little roughly, for the soul which does not measure up to expectations is rejected for eternity—like a pot that failed to come right in the firing. In this respect Christianity proves finally to have something in common with Objectivism after all. "Infinite value" seems to mean only that souls are equally divine in essence—in the way that an acorn is in essence an oak tree. At least while a person is still alive, Christianity can logically maintain that he is infinitely precious and must not be injured. For existentialism, the "infinite value" refers to the immeasurability of the person, actually as well as potentially. This immeasurability derives from the absoluteness of the private world within which each one makes himself and his life. Existentialism realizes that we must keep separate our levels of judgment. One forms one's individual estimate of a person, in accordance with one's own value system. This purely private point of view predominates in all personal relations, whether one is considering the other as possible lover, spouse, friend, business associate, political representative, author whose books one will buy, etc. Then there is the socially necessary legal judgment by which society declares whether or not a given person may safely be allowed free range in a society. Here existentialism would modify existing concepts but would agree that something in the nature of a social contract must stand and that preventive (if not punitive) measures must be taken against transgressors. There still remains a third level—the "worth" or quality of the person measured, against the background of his inner life, and here the existentialist knows that he cannot pass judgment.

Rand argues that in all human relations one must give justice, not mercy. A man's success is measured by the objective value of what he has produced. Clearly implied here is the idea that the man himself is measured, that he *has* his objective value. It is on this basis only that any absolute justice or absolute judgment can be based. Such absolute judgments could be defended only if acts were in themselves tangible entities which could be weighed without reference to their inner subjective environment. This the existentialist denies while Objectivism surreptitiously assumes it to be true. Existentialism recognizes a kind of Original Sin in the universe inasmuch as people are forever being treated as if all lived within the same frame of reference as objects, whereas all are subjects in private worlds. Acting upon the fiction of one impersonal world, the Objectivist may classify and ignore the need of another and reject any demand that we see things from his point of view. Existentialism refuses this easy fiction. As the existentialist asks for tolerance of his own authentic value system, he grants the same to others.

Finally we see that existentialism and not Objectivism is really in favor of an open society to foster the growth of unique self-centers, each one pursuing its genuine self-interest and allowing every other to do the same. Objectivism is for free enterprise but not for the free creation of values. It equates creativity with productivity. The businessman and the intellectual are its heroes, and Rand suggests that it would be fruitful to have exchange scholarships for the two groups, replacing the "ludicrous" arrangement whereby American and Russian students visit each other's countries and try to understand one another.[2] In truth I do not see the need for such a program in the proposed Objectivist society. The ideals of the two groups are already almost identical. Only the material products are different.

Objectivist Man is both an ideal and a reality. He represents only one of the possibilities for the human species. Existentialism rejects Objectivism because it ignores the two sources of existentialist despair instead of seeking some way to overcome them. Objectivism hides the fact that to be free to become what one chooses means also that one must choose what one feels one ought to become. Objectivism tries to evade the knowledge that to exist means not only to be-in-the-world but to-be-with-others. John Galt said in his radio speech that men have secretly hated the doctrines of altruism and of living for others. Existentialists, too, confess to a horror at the knowledge that one must face these unchosen responsibilities. But it refuses to evade them. Rand attacks those who say that we can have no absolute certainty. Existentialists, too, oppose those who use the inadequacy of knowledge to defend irresponsible action or to refuse to en-

[2] Rand: *For the New Intellectual*, p. 52.

gage themselves. But existentialism never seeks to clothe its commitment with the false certainty of authoritative guarantee.

To the existentialist, Objectivism appears to be based on wish-fulfillment. Barbara Branden's biographical sketch of Ayn Rand treats as significant Rand's early decision to create a life which would resemble the world of the operetta rather than the given reality of the Soviet Union in the early twenties.[3] And we are told that while Rand loves the theater, she does not care for tragedy. Joy and happiness are possible in this life, and I think they are legitimate goals. I do not think one can win them legitimately by denying the essence of the tragic vision. The cross, like the hemlock, is an ambivalent symbol, one which reminds us of the failures of the majority at the same time that it speaks to us of the heroic self-transcendence in self-fulfillment on the part of a few. We may feel as Rand does, and as I do, that the cross as a symbol of self-sacrifice is not an adequate measure of human aspiration. I do not think we will improve things by replacing it with the dollar sign. That is all too good an emblem for Objectivism, suggesting that happiness is for those who have the wherewithal to pay and in the currency set by those who are in power. Existentialism seeks something less subject to the arbitrary whims of the market.

[3] Nathaniel and Barbara Branden: *Who Is Ayn Rand?*, pp. 149–50.

VII

The Negative Rebels

The Apolitical Left

In 1955 Robert Lindner made a statement which is even more obviously true today than it was then.

Throughout all levels of our Western society there may be observed a wry and amused sufferance of the rebellious adolescent, and an almost pitifully conscientious attempt to "understand"—and so forgive—his disquieting behavior. . . . Until quite recently the rebellion of youth in the West could be viewed with the detachment usually accorded anything so common and natural. . . . As adults, we have even come to view it, despite its attendant personal and social distresses, with nostalgia. Unhappily, however, such an attitude of benevolent forbearance and, in some instances, secret complicity, is no longer appropriate. *For the brute fact of today is that our youth is no longer in rebellion, but in a condition of downright active and hostile mutiny.*[1]

I think most persons in the West would grant that Lindner's judgment applies to a significantly large proportion of the younger generation. Furthermore, the revolt is by no

[1] Robert Lindner: *Must You Conform?* (New York: Holt, Rinehart and Winston; 1955), pp. 4–5.

means confined to adolescents. Teenagers and undergraduates may make up the bulk of the rebellious; the leaders are frequently young adults in their middle or late twenties, sometimes even older. Although there is a feeling of youth about it all, one senses that those who protest now are not simply waiting for their diplomas before they settle down in the Establishment, at least not without cracking the framework of things first and imposing certain conditions.

It would be inappropriate for me to make this chapter into a sociological treatise; I do not claim in any case to have discovered either a new explanation as to how it all started or a magic formula for solving the problems raised. I have two reasons for including this aspect of the American scene in a discussion of existentialist ethics. First, in two instances where there has been some attempt to arrive at a philosophical formulation, a link with existentialism is openly recognized. Norman Mailer states flatly that "Hip is an American existentialism." He says that his *Barbary Shore* was the first existentialist novel in America. His political proposals he calls "existential politics." The New Radicals, who emerged in the course of the student revolt at Berkeley, disavow any commitment to any specific ideology. They have used the word "existential" to describe their approach to social action. Naturally the word does not in itself indicate an affiliation with existentialism as a specific philosophy. I hope to show, however, that the term is aptly chosen and that there are certain genuine connections between Sartrean existentialism and the activism of the New Radicals. My second reason for considering this amorphous group of negative rebels is the fact that they all represent a search for new values as well as a rejection of the way of life which has become most typical of our society. Whether or not this break with the Serious World is genuine and existentially pure, the young rebel deliberately chooses what he believes to be authenticity and seeks to become a new kind of person. At this stage of our discussion, I prefer to leave the question open as to whether this "mutiny of the young" springs from a genuine ethical concern or resembles the nonethical stance of the Underground Man.

Our conclusion may depend on which particular corner of this vast area we choose to locate ourselves in. Certainly there is no one uniform and definite attitude which we can pinpoint and analyze as the kernel of all youthful protest—unless it is the bare fact of hostility to the status quo.

If I am to speak of negative rebels in terms that are at all meaningful, I must start by excluding those who may indeed be manifestations of the general spirit of unrest but who do not seem to me to represent a search for new values or to be rebelling against anything except the particular limitations which define their personal situation. Thus I exclude those ultraconservative groups who simply want to protect or to reassert what they hold to be both eternal values and true Americanism. (The Objectivist brand of conservatism I have already discussed.) I am not concerned with any of the established, well-disciplined ideological parties, whose methods are now traditional, however radical their platforms. I exclude too those delinquents and criminals who simply resort to violence and illegal methods in order to get an unearned share of the material goods of our society. After this sifting process, there remain those whose revolt seems to me significant philosophically and of legitimate concern to anyone interested in an existentialist ethics.

Without making the mistake of assuming that these negative rebels belong to a well-defined group, I think we may legitimately isolate, if not a common essence, at least constantly recurring themes. Even here I believe that we ought to differentiate. The distinction I would make is based in part on recent historical developments; partly the revolt seems to me to have assumed two different forms according to the temperament of those involved. On the one hand, we have the Beatniks and Hipsters of the fifties, who were mostly apolitical and antisocial. On the other side, there are the New Radicals of the sixties, who are tirelessly active in making specific demands of all sorts: civil rights, a new policy in Vietnam, pacifism, suppression of censorship, changes in university policies—the list is a very long one and varies with the local setting of the protesters. We must be careful not to make too sharp a dichotomy or to postulate too obvious a rational progression from one type to the other. I grant that a Hegelian dialectical movement is dimly perceptible: Thesis, an unjust conformist society; antithesis, the hostile with-drawal of some of its members; synthesis, action by the disaffected to correct specific abuses in the society. In general outline this three-step pattern is as true to the facts as most such historical generalizations are. In detail, of course, things are not quite so neat. Besides the fact that old-style liberals were working via traditional methods for such causes as civil rights through all three periods, it is not strictly accurate to limit all activism and social concern to the politically oriented rebels of the sixties. Norman Mailer, who quite early and self-consciously elected to be a spokesman for the Hipster, was writing political commentary for *The Village Voice* long before he announced in 1960 that he would run for Mayor of New York. On the other hand, not all the rebels of the sixties joined in the marches and demonstrations for civil rights and peace in Vietnam. Hal Draper, writing of the student revolt at Berkeley, has commented that the "non-ideological radi-cals" were hampered and embarrassed as the result of their being confused with the nihilist disaffiliates. Draper points out that not all of the disaffiliated remained wholly aloof. Some demonstrated actively their contempt for society and for all efforts to improve or correct it.

Je pisse sur tout is a kind of social program, with a primitive ideology of its own, which provides a simulacrum of social radi-calism, since among other things it rejects also the going social system and its authorities. But it is only a simulacrum, for it has no real social vision or even moral vision of its own. These types want to disaffiliate from society, not to transform it. . . . They propose their own version of "militant tactics" mainly to scandal-ize that Beast, the Public (*épater la bourgeoisie*) and not to win, for winning involves taking responsibility. Their salute is not the clenched fist but the thumb to nose. They actually achieve their personal program of disaffiliation from society only by opting out

153

the real world with marijuana or LSD, which is their personal "revolution." [2]

Although the Beats and Hipsters may have "opted out of society," as Draper puts it, they asserted loudly and clearly the reasons for their discontent and the kinds of values they sought in their withdrawal. In most instances the New Radicals are against the same things. There exists a genuine and interesting question as to how great a change there has been in the values sought.

For purposes of this discussion, I should like for the moment to proceed as if the two groups were more easily separated than they actually are. I want to begin by concentrating on Norman Mailer and his Hipster existentialism. Although I mean to use Mailer's work as a guiding thread, my intention is not to restrict myself to Mailer. Without wanting to play down his originality as an artist, we may recognize that the world Mailer portrays and his own attitude toward it have much in common with those of John Rechy, William Burroughs, Jack Kerouac, James Baldwin, Edward Albee, and the cluster of writers whose work appears in the *Evergreen Review*. Or if we look abroad, we may name Jean Genet, or Samuel Beckett, or Harold Pinter. Artistically these writers may be worlds apart. They do have at least two things in common. They all express a revolt against society and against the human condition; they all are sympathetically concerned with those who, from choice or necessity, live as outcasts on the fringes of society. The public, which would like to ignore this semi-underworld, complains that contemporary literature is concerned only with homosexuals, dopesters, criminals, sex maniacs, perverts, all so far removed from the life of the average person. When the junior executive looks up to see a Beatnik son or confronts the policeman who has come to tell him that his boy is involved in a narcotics ring, he blames the literature, along with the comic books, for their pernicious influence—as though a dose of *McGuffey's Readers* and Ho-

[2] Hal Draper: *Berkeley: The New Student Revolt* (New York: Grove Press; 1965), p. 165.

ratio Alger would have changed everything, and as if writers were inventing contemporary life and not reflecting it.

Mailer is perhaps no more articulate in expressing this hostile protest than several other authors. I find him unique in his ability to retain side by side the feeling of belonging with the disaffected and the detachment which enables him to analyze and formulate as an observer. He both embraces the individual's revolt against contemporary society and seeks a method to integrate the disaffiliated once more in a society which they will help to establish. His is a view of life which stresses emotion and disdains systematization; yet he feels the need to form an intellectual appraisal, to work out a program, and to attempt a coherent statement of his philosophical position.

Inasmuch as Mailer calls his proposals "existential" and declares that "Hip is an American existentialism," his relation to European existentialist philosophers proves to be somewhat surprising. Heidegger he classifies as "Hip" in contrast to Sartre, who is "Square." But Mailer confesses that he cannot understand Heidegger, and he has no patience with Heidegger's brand of philosophical abstractions. He is at pains to let us know his disagreements with both Heidegger and Sartre in important areas—the problems of religion, of death, of irrationality and the unconscious. Yet Mailer's insistence on maintaining a place for religious values does not lead him in the direction of such non-Hip existentialists as Kierkegaard, Tillich, or Jaspers, whom he ignores completely. It is in the left wing that he belongs if he belongs anywhere in the existentialist camp. In a loose sort of way, I think he does have a claim though perhaps it is more that of second cousin than of direct heir. Mailer makes no pretense of being a philosopher. If it were only for academic reasons, I should have no interest in arriving at a decision as to whether his point of view may rightly be called existentialist or not. His importance, from my point of view, lies in the fact that he tries (I think successfully) to set forth in his Hipster philosophy the values, goals, and attitudes by which large numbers of the new rebels are actually living. Some critics have ar-

gued that existentialism is so peculiarly European in its outlook that in America it must remain an unabsorbable foreign
import. Mailer believes that he has formulated a way of life
which is both indigenously American and existentialist. I
should like to consider these questions: What kind of rebels
are these for whom Mailer wants to be spokesman? What
does this Hipster existentialism have to offer? Is our humanistic existentialism enriched by this look at the American
scene? Can it accept Mailer's solutions? Is it equipped to meet
these rebellious utterances on its own terms?

The prevailing mood of the nonpolitical rebels is contempt
for the American way of life, not as it is formulated in the
Constitution but as they have known it. They are not unpa-
triotic in the sense of preferring another country to their own.
Their great fear is that the values and concept of "the human" which are dominant here will shortly become those of
the whole world. Their revolt, strictly speaking, is neither
political nor economic in origin. Their attitude is perhaps
best typified by the despairing cry of Osborne's hero in *Look
Back in Anger*—"There aren't any good, brave causes left."
They do not join movements because of a conviction that man
is capable of something better. They remain aloof, ashamed
of what he has considered success. Their sympathies are with
minority groups but always with the unsuccessful members
of those groups. Why work to improve the conditions of the
migrant workers or to provide better housing and jobs for
unemployed Negroes if this would result in making them
indistinguishable from the despised Middle Class?

The average citizen is frankly bewildered by this contemptuous hostility. Understandably so. Traditionally the
violence of rebellion is proportionate to the force of the op-
pressive authority. Now everything seems backward. Authority was never more permissive, or so it believes. Admittedly
there is some pressure to conform. Children are occasionally
sent home from school because of their hair styles or the fit of
their jeans. High school teachers sometimes lose their jobs
because of political or religious heresies, and so less frequently do university professors. Young executives advance

156

more rapidly if they are appropriately married and not known to have dangerous or peculiar ideas. Yet on the whole, we are coaxed into being sensible and content not to raise a fuss, we are not violently coerced. We have nothing quite so inflexible and ungentle as the Inquisition. Even in the McCarthy era, the supposed witches were not literally burned at the stake. Today's unhappy parent would find his son or daughter easier to understand if only there were some definite areas of disagreement. He cannot comprehend why the child should object so vehemently to the prospect of having the sort of life which his parents have been happy and proud to achieve, particularly since he is leaving it in the name of nothing save his chosen hostility. Why should the boy or girl prefer the life of the underprivileged, steal what his father would gladly pay for, and escape via narcotics—from what? Lindner is right in saying that the mutiny of today's youth cannot be explained as simply the age-old effort of a new generation to assert its independent maturity. Both sociologically and existentially, a further explanation is needed.

The cause most commonly cited is the atom bomb. Is it *fear* of the bomb? Possibly, to some slight degree. So long as there is any feeling at all that maniacs or myopic politicians might destroy all or most of us, lurking doubts as to the meaning or worthwhileness of life may poison the springs of all endeavor. Children and adults too will sometimes destroy a loved object which they know is going to be taken away from them. Even so, I cannot believe that the threat of losing the life we have is the primary motive for rejecting it. Delight in destruction, danger, and violence is so great a part of the lives of this group of rebels that I would entrust the bomb to their tutelage with even more trepidation than I watch it balanced in the nervous hands of the military.

There is another way in which I think the bomb figures much more importantly, although here it is but one of a number of factors contributing to a single attitude. Fear is not the only natural reaction to the bombing of Hiroshima and Nagasaki. There are also indignation and a sense of outrage. For too many reasons, we have a weak case if we try to persuade the disaffected that contemporary society deserves their support. I believe that disgust with the injustice, hypocrisy, and cruelty which are every day displayed as regular ingredients of our way of life plays a large part in motivating the rebellious refusal to cooperate with society. I am not speaking of abuses which would offend only the ultrasensitive soul of a saint or Utopian perfectionist. I refer to evils which no reasonably moral person would even try to justify save, at best, by calling them necessary or unavoidable or temporary. One does not have to go back so far as the concentration camps and bombings of World War II. There is our own destruction of the rice crop in Vietnam, indefensible even if we generously waive the question of whether our military aggression is justified in the first place. There is our willingness to restrict our food production when millions of the world's population are hungry. Despite the progress recently made in civil rights, the majority of white Americans is still reluctant to accept Negroes as not constituting a special and lower class. Rights, yes, but not acceptance of the Negroes as neighbors, doctors, or in-law relatives. Prejudice against most minorities is admitted at the breakfast table even if not in the office. And of course there are still churches where Negroes are not welcome to worship. Dishonesty and corruption are occasionally punished when they become too flagrant and too careless. Mostly we take it for granted that public officials will take bribes, that advertisers will falsify and politicians lie, that big-time gambling operators and some police officers will make deals with the Mafia, that houses of prostitution will flourish outside the law. The father who is genuinely shocked when his child is caught shoplifting makes no secret of the fact that he himself brings home office supplies and hunts for ways to cheat on his income tax. If we simply acknowledged that all commercial relations were a game in which each man would do whatever he could get by with and the rest of us be constantly on our guard against him, things might or might not be noticeably worse. There would at least be a refreshing absence of hypocrisy. It is possible, I think, to see a parallel between the reaction of some of the young rebels and that of the hero of Camus's play *Caligula*. The embittered Emperor resolved to take to their logical conclusion the truths of the Universe and the values by which men live. His atrocities were but a grim *reductio ad absurdum* of the reverence for wealth, the idea that the end justifies the means, the acceptance of cruelty, starvation, suffering, and death as inevitably part of the structure of things. Comparably the Beat and Hipster, brushing aside the veneer of conventional morality, live openly and to excess the surreptitious conduct of their elders. In place of petty chiseling, they steal; extramarital "playing around" becomes openly acknowledged sexual liaison and shared promiscuity; tranquilizers give place to marijuana and LSD. Violence and unjust treatment of other people is excused on the plea that this rotten world and the people in it deserve no better.

The rebels' rejection of society is not always (I doubt that it is usually) the result of moral indignation alone. Often it is due simply to a feeling of emptiness and boredom. Some of the Beat writers have tried to see the conflict as one between materialism and spiritual values—or at least the values of "really living." The television set has been made a symbol of easy contentment with the mediocre. A typical passage is this from Kerouac's *The Dharma Bums*.

Everything was fine with the Zen Lunatics, the nut wagon was too far away to hear us. But there was a wisdom in it all, as you'll see if you take a walk some night on a surburban street and pass house after house on both sides of the street each with the lamplight of the living room, shining golden, and inside the little blue square of the television, each living family riveting its attention on probably one show; nobody talking; silence in the yards; dogs barking at you because you pass on human feet instead of on wheels. You'll see what I mean, when it begins to appear like everybody in the world is soon going to be thinking the same way and the Zen Lunatics have long joined dust, laughter on their dust lips.[3]

[3] Jack Kerouac: *The Dharma Bums* (New York: Viking Press; 1958), p. 104.

The real objection here is not to materialism as such but to the low level of satisfaction for which the average American is willing to settle. The trouble is not that he works too hard for money, but that he doesn't know how to get his money's worth when he spends it.

There is nothing radical in all of this. Scarcely a school day goes by when there are not hundreds of American teachers paying lip service to the need for independent thought and self-questioning. On the weekends one may hear the same message from the pulpit. The trouble is that the audience, and frequently the speaker, too, find it all so boring. One somehow senses that to think for oneself means choosing between voting for liberal Republicans and middle-of-the-road Democrats, that to be an individual means not looking at TV except for news programs, that to be socially responsible involves contributing to United Appeal, the American Indian Fund, and just possibly the Americans for Democratic Action. The search for excitement in living may lead one to take the trip to Europe a year earlier than the budget warrants or even to go daringly alone instead of with a tour. For too many liberals these pious exercises are a species of bad faith, a verbal assurance that one is living creatively—just as effective a cure for the tension headache as aspirin, martinis, and tranquilizers.

The literature of protest is written by those who find anything more acceptable than the boredom of most American life. Being bored, or the fear of being bored, carried to the borderline of the pathological, is probably the most important single factor back of the excesses of youthful offenders and their retreat into the near criminal underworld, and responsible too for the apathy of so many high school and college students who do not get into overt trouble. In the long run the last group may well be a greater loss to society in terms of human happiness, and even in more conventional terms, than the Beats and the Hipsters and out-and-out delinquents. Paul Goodman in his book *Growing Up Absurd*, a convincing demonstration that the genesis of the "organization man" and the new-style delinquents are one and the same, goes one step further. "My thought is that the average adjusted boy is, if anything, more humanly wasted than the disaffected." [4]

Norman Mailer declares that life in America becomes more economically prosperous and more psychically impoverished each year. Mailer, too, has hard words to say about the low level of the average TV program, and he considers boredom "the national disease." Speaking of the causes of juvenile delinquency, Mailer writes: "For all the talk of broken homes, submarginal housing, overcrowding in the schools and cultural starvation, the other root is more alive, and one kills it at one's peril. It is the root for which our tongues once found the older words of courage, loyalty, honor and the urge for adventure. . . . Yes, there is a place for everybody now in the American scene except for those who want to find the limits of their growth by a life which is ready to welcome a little danger as part of the Divine Cocktail." [5]

At this point, the negative rebel's revolt appears strikingly similar to that of the Underground Man. Both choose against themselves, on the reflective level, in order to preserve some sense of free spontaneity—"life" rather than "square roots," intensity of any sort in preference to psychic starvation. Only the violent act of wrenching oneself away completely can break through the strangling Lilliputian cords. If we realize that this hostile withdrawal is a desperate attempt at self-preservation, then we can understand the willingness to risk everything for a seemingly trivial thrill. It must be admitted that the conduct associated with the mutinous young is frequently both destructive and self-destructive. Drag races, insane speed, daring thefts, vandalism, experimenting with narcotics—these are not creative acts. That they may—for a brief moment—seem meaningful to the one who performs them is possible because of their double motivation of self-hatred and the desire to preserve the self at all costs. If one is

[4] Paul Goodman: *Growing Up Absurd: Problems of Youth in the Organized System* (New York: Random House; 1956), p. 70.
[5] Norman Mailer: *The Presidential Papers* (New York: G. P. Putnam's Sons; 1963), p. 21.

unable to find any satisfying way of realizing oneself in a life of sustained meaning, then there may indeed be a wildly exultant joy in asserting that one renounces all wish to do so. The New Testament idea that one finds one's life by losing it has bearing even here.

We must recognize, however, that not all the behavior of the Beats and Hipsters is a flirtation with self-destruction or a cynical willingness to ignore the rights of others. We must face the question whether at times "delinquent" conduct is not relative to the particular view of those who so define it. Furthermore, even in those instances where we may decide that we as observers are unwilling to call the behavior ethical, it nevertheless constitutes a search for genuine values, based on the conviction that life can be joyously rewarding. One feels this even in Kerouac's delinquent heroes. Kerouac says of one of them, "His 'criminality' was not something that sulked and sneered; it was a wild yea-saying overburst of American joy." [6]

The thrust toward positive values is generally expressed in one or more of four separate but related manifestations. First, there is absolute insistence on everyone's right to a fuller and freer sexual experience, combined with a naïvely sentimental faith in the power of sex to dissolve all other problems. Second, there is a desire to value each person for his uniqueness, to let him be himself. This ideal is in no way opposed to another which at first might seem to be inconsistent with it, the claim that human relations ought to be based on a more authentic sort of communication. Third, there is a drive for more intense experience, usually sought either by deliberately courting danger or by trying to expand the consciousness by means of drugs. Fourth, there is a longing for some sort of noninstitutionalized religious value, which may on occasion turn to Eastern philosophy but which more often expresses itself in a species of neo-primitivism. All of this could perhaps be summed up as a thirst for total experience, Kerouac's Yea-saying; it is pre-eminently for an experience which is not

[6] Jack Kerouac: *On the Road* (New York: Viking Press; 1957), p. 10.

subjected to rational control. Is this set of attitudes anything which conceivably might be made the basis of a positive program? However unpromising the task appears, I should like to take up briefly each of the points mentioned.

We may start with the question of sex. There have been amusing, somewhat pompous articles debating whether or not sex among the Beats is more or less satisfying than sex in Suburbia. Goodman, for example, assures us solemnly that his "impression is that—leaving out their artists, who have the kind of sex that artists have—Beat sexuality in general is pretty good, unlike delinquent sexuality, which seems, on the evidence, to be wretched." [7] With due respect to all concerned, I do not think that a manual of Beat sex techniques would help the world more than the *Kama Sutra*. Nor do I believe that Victorian inhibitions still remain a serious threat to sexual enjoyment between partners who are addicted to television, books, or even the stock market. Self-deception, artificiality, neurosis, and rigid personality structures impede sexuality as they impair all human relations. If the withdrawal from ordinary society is accomplished in the name of authentically chosen positive values, then the individual is probably better able to sustain meaningful relations of all sorts than one who lives discontentedly in a "neurosis of chronic boredom." (The expression is Goodman's.) If his retreat is wholly hostile, an escape rather than a free choice, then it seems unlikely that he will not cast the blight of his own shadow on all of his projects.

I question whether there is any more obsession with sex among the Beats, Hipsters, and other negative rebels than can be found in any other social stratum in this country. There is less hypocrisy among these voluntary exiles, more openness in discussing sex in something other than clinical or psychoanalytical terms. Whether or not there is actually any more promiscuity I do not know. It is certainly more openly practiced and defended. Homosexuality is accepted by the majority as a legitimate sexual choice—though this does not

[7] Goodman: *Growing Up Absurd*, p. 185.

mean that most rebels become homosexuals. Miscegenation is common and often is idealized and sentimentalized as being somehow on a higher plane than any other relation. There is certainly something to be said for this refreshing declaration that human sex organs were not designed with the express purpose that they be employed solely in matrimonial monogamy between partners of one color, religion, and social class. Promiscuity is as likely to prevent a person from establishing a meaningful love relationship as to aid in the search for it. On the other hand, if casual sexual relations are open and honest, they are probably less psychologically damaging than the guilt-ridden evenings which businessmen away from home spend with call girls; they are no more "animal" than the fraternity and sorority couplings in parked cars. Temporary liaisons of couples who share the same "pad" strike me as less offensive than the dreary unions of pairs who "go steady" in order to be sure of not being left without dates for school dances.

Nevertheless, too much is claimed for this liberated sexuality. Mailer, with overtones of Lawrence and Reich, speaks of the search for "the apocalyptic orgasm" as a struggle to come closer to the Life Force, to God. Admitting that Hip is still a passive philosophy of the defeated and despairing, Mailer proclaims that there may emerge from it "a philosophy which may be imbedded some day in a four-letter word so famous and infamous that this newspaper would be destroyed if I were to put it into print." [8] But—thanks partly to the pressure of Mailer and others of like persuasion—this four-letter word has been appearing with boring regularity in a great deal of recent writing, and almost any publisher will print it: fuck. Once it is said—and done—then what? I do not mean to speak disdainfully either of sex itself or of the importance of doing everything possible to allow and aid all persons to work out their own problems of love and sex in the best way possible. Much of what passes for metaphysical malaise and social discontent is a disguised and generalized unhappiness

[8] Norman Mailer: *Advertisements for Myself* (New York: G. P. Putnam's Sons; 1959), pp. 314–15.

over one's personal situation. In societies where few are hungry, I suspect that sexual-erotic problems are among the most common and the most keenly suffered. Mailer's story "The Time of Her Time" reveals, in spite of its grotesque details, much more tenderness and understanding than the *Reader's Digest* article that advised frigid women not to worry over their inability to have an orgasm. In so far as Mailer or the Hipster or anyone else can point the way to more significant sexual experience, he merits our approbation and our gratitude. The extravagant hope that a revitalized sexuality will bring about man's salvation seems to me incredibly naïve. In the first place, as Mailer himself admits, the solution is not simply more sex. If sex is important, then one must not take it for granted as being necessary but ordinary—like bread and water. Mailer finally rediscovers the old-fashioned truth that what is precious must not be treated as trivial, that maybe "sex is worth waiting for." Obviously the mere lifting of restraints and the lack of inhibitions, while they may give fuller play to immediate pleasurable sensations, are not enough in themselves to guarantee either personal fulfillment or perfect human relations. Yabyum games at the United Nations would not be much improvement over the Profumo affair.

Finally, of course, the problem of significant sexuality becomes that of the intermeshing of personalities and cannot be separated from the general question of our attitude toward other people. Here our appraisal of the negative rebels will inevitably be mixed. On the one hand we seem to find less sense of responsibility for others than in any other group one could mention. Not all of the increased crime in the country can be attributed to them. Some of it must be. Mailer sees violence as a necessary ingredient of his interim Hipster philosophy. Kerouac's heroes usually do no physical injury to others, but they regard personal betrayal of trust as quite to be expected. (This same sort of treachery toward those closest to one is a favorite theme of Genet.) In all of these writers as in the behavior of rebellious youth everywhere—and not solely among those who are out-and-out delinquent—

there is a particular delight in disregarding property rights. Kerouac's *On The Road* is all too typical with its description of shoplifting for sport, stealing cars for joyriding, and senseless destruction. One of the best passages, aesthetically, is Kerouac's description of the pointless wrecking of a new Cadillac. With American writers the motivation for all this is mostly a search for thrills, but it involves too the intent, more fully developed by Genet, of undermining all that is necessary to keep even a corrupt society going.

Side by side with this attitude which not only disdains material possessions but puts other people on a level no higher than that of things, there is a desperate search for closer communication between two persons within a small group. Here I believe the negative rebels have made some advance. Perhaps in part they have learned anew the old lessons of the past—giving of oneself, accepting the other in spite of his fallibility, discovering in one another a meaning which the world refuses, the value expressed so poignantly in Matthew Arnold's line, "Ah, love, let us be true to one another." What I think is new, or at least more genuine, in the Beat or Hipster is the honest conviction—not merely a pious assertion—that it is the uniqueness of the person that must be valued and protected at all cost. One finds in Beat writing an aesthetic delight in the other's personalizing eccentricities. Within the small group of those who are "with it," we find at least the beginnings of the relation in good faith of two subjects, neither of which tries or even wants to make an object of the other or to be lost with him in a common self.

Two particular problems in human relations deserve special attention. The first is that of the attitude toward the male and female as such. The second is that toward racial minorities. Toward women, behavior and theory are simultaneously liberal and regressive. One thing can certainly be said. In the code of sexual behavior, there is an almost total absence of the double standard. Let no one remark cynically that this is but natural in a situation where promiscuity is the rule. Prostitutes and courtesans flourished under Queen Victoria and even in Puritan United States. In the Western world they have never been accompanied by the general acceptance of equal sexual freedom for men and women. Among today's rebels, we find no trace of that particular duplicity which by placing so high a value on feminine virginity subtly implies that the female who has tasted sex is slightly stained, like a used vessel. Whether practiced casually for the joy of the particular moment or reverenced as the foundation of the lasting union of two against the world, the sexual act is a shared experience of equal partners. The girl has no reason to feel that she is cheapened by her willingness to give.

This is only one side of the coin. Unfortunately the Beats and the Hipsters seldom attain to and live with the full recognition of women as people. We find instead something comparable to the magic process by which the Age of Chivalry elevated woman as symbol while imprisoning her more tightly than ever in her role as the representative of a species. The exaggerated view of the liberating potency of sex tends to see in women simply the vehicle and instrument of this mysterious power. The woman becomes an Earth Mother in the eyes of her lover and in her own eyes. Losing herself in this role, she is prevented from ever becoming an authentic individual. In the light of the prevailing tendency in this group of rebels to stress feeling and the irrational, it is not surprising to meet a neo-primitive, Lawrentian concept of sexual relations. What is more surprising is to find an antediluvian view of femininity expressed in such perceptive writers as Norman Mailer and Paul Goodman.

Mailer states flatly: "The fact of the matter is that the prime responsibility of a woman probably is to be on earth long enough to find the best mate possible for herself, and conceive children who will improve the species." [9]

Goodman is greatly admired by the more active wing of the negative rebels. Although he writes with some understanding of the quietly Beatnik or nihilist type of rebel, he clearly feels that they represent failures as completely as the

[9] Mailer: *The Presidential Papers*, p. 130.

overadjusted man in the gray flannel suit. In trying to explain the curiously passive roles of the girls in these circles, Goodman resorts to a pat, narrow Freudian interpretation strangely at variance with his open perspective upon the broader scene. Early in his discussion Goodman states that when he speaks of the problems of young people, he means "young men and boys" because they are the ones who have difficulty in finding a way to be useful and make something of themselves. "A girl does not *have* to, she is not expected to 'make something' of herself. Her career does not have to be self-justifying, for she will have children, which is absolutely self-justifying, like any other natural or creative act." [1] Why then do girls rebel? Goodman himself is a bit puzzled and can only point to the special attraction which the young Beats exert over the girls.

These young fellows are sweet, independent, free-thinking, affectionate, perhaps faithful, probably sexy—these are grand virtues, some of them not equally available among American men on the average. But Beats are not responsible husbands and fathers of children.[2]

The girl may adopt a maternal attitude. "She devotes herself to helping him find himself and become a man, presumably so that he can then marry her." Or she may seek the age-old role of serving as inspiration for his genius.

Another possible relation is Muse or Model; her Beat is her poet and artist and makes her feel important. This is a satisfaction for her feminine narcissism or penis envy. But it comes, often, to ludicrously overestimating the young man's finger painting and laying on him an impossible burden to become the artist that he is not.

Goodman seems for a moment to sense the waste and the destructive quality of a life doomed to exist parasitically through another. His remedy is more of the same.

One sometimes sees a pathetic scene in a bar. Some decent square young workingmen are there, lonely, looking for girls or even for

[1] Goodman: *Growing Up Absurd*, p. 13.
[2] Ibid., p. 185.

a friendly word. They feel that they are "nobodies"; they are not Beats, they are not artists. They have nothing to "contribute" to the conversation. The girls, meantime, give their attention only to the Beats, who are sounding off so interestingly. But these Beats will not make any life for the girls, whereas the others might make husbands and fathers. If a square fellow finally plucks up his courage to talk to a girl, she turns away insultingly.

Although I cannot accept Goodman's appraisal, I agree with him that these girls live a singularly derivative life. The heroines of Beatnik literature are almost wholly void of individuality, scarcely distinguishable from one another save in age or nationality and social background. They are flat types. One of Kerouac's wandering heroes makes a revealing remark. "I suddenly realized that all these women were spending months of loneliness and womanliness together, chatting about the madness of the men." [3]

I think it is significant that we do not have any women novelists tied closely to this group in the way that Burroughs, Mailer, and Rechy, for example, are. Françoise Sagan in France possibly comes closest, but her total preoccupation with the nuances of the erotic makes one feel that she belongs rather in the tradition of Colette. She is not even remotely a feminine Genet. One reason for this lack may be the fact that a woman's decision to embark upon a full-fledged career involves even today a certain element of revolt and considerable self-understanding. Consequently the woman who wishes to develop her abilities will not be found in this group of negative rebels. She will be among the activists. Yet I believe that the peculiar, almost mystic concept of sex as a way of regaining a lost primitive oneness with the source of life tends to imprison a woman in her femininity and perhaps cuts off many a feminine revolt halfway.

Although it is sometimes tainted by a bit of this same sort of mystification and role-playing, generally the attitude and practice of the negative rebels in the field of racial relations and apropos of minority groups is a magnificently positive

[3] Kerouac: *On the Road*, p. 187.

contribution to the American scene. What is new here, in contrast to the outlook of sincere liberals of an older generation, is the fact that these rebels are not merely *for* the Negro and other minority groups; they are *with* them. In the past there has been an unspoken assumption that equality for all meant that everyone should be allowed and encouraged to demonstrate that those differences which set some men apart from others are only superficial and can be easily transcended. The belief that every person is "as good" as anyone else was hardly distinguishable from the idea that "all men are alike under the skin." Tolerance was extended to continued differences in religious belief but not to the perpetuation of distinctions due to varied cultural heritage. At the same time, while the equality of all was postulated, it was tacitly assumed that at least in the case of Negroes and whites, there would be no true merging—friendship but not marriage, coexistence with aloofness. In answer to Southern fears of miscegenation, the liberal thought he was being honest when, instead of limiting himself to the obvious reply that no man's sister would be forced to marry a Negro, he responded in all sincerity that neither the sister nor the Negro would wish to marry each other. Thus well-intentioned reformers, simultaneously and inconsistently, demanded a superficial sameness rooted in deeper differentiations which would express themselves in voluntary segregation. The name given to this process when put into effect is assimilation. A passage from Mailer points up the contrast between the old and the new ideals. Mailer rejects assimilation, believing it to be a disaster for all parties.

The problem in a democracy is not to assimilate minorities but to avoid stifling them as they attain their equality. If the Jews and Negroes attain a brilliant equality with the white Anglo-Saxon Protestant and the Irish Catholic, then America will be different. Whatever it will become, it will be different from anything we can conceive. Whereas if the Negro and Jew are assimilated into the muted unimaginative level of present-day American life, then America will be very much like it is now, only worse.[4]

[4] Mailer: *The Presidential Papers*, p. 188.

Again Mailer writes,

The argument of existential politics might be that one never understands a people or a time by contemplating a common denominator, for the average man in a minority group is no longer a member of that minority—he is instead a social paste which has been compounded out of the grinding stone of the society which contains him. He is not his own authentic expression. By this logic, the average Negro or Jew is not so much a black man or a Semite as a mediocre ersatz Protestant.[5]

There is a paradox inherent in Mailer's statement. On first thought, we might seem to have the same inconsistency, but in reverse, which I indicated in the position of the older liberal. In the passages quoted, Mailer obviously wants the negro never to forget those things which enable him to be different. At the same time, as we see throughout all his work, Mailer desires a genuine merging of races and cultures. Indeed the Hipster, who is for Mailer a forerunner of that better time to come, has emerged as a fusion of race and class. Mailer says,

In such places as Greenwich Village, a ménage-à-trois was completed—the bohemian and the juvenile delinquent came face-to-face with the Negro, and the hipster was a fact in American life. If marijuana was the wedding ring, the child was the language of Hip for its argot gave expression to abstract states of feeling which all could share, at least all who were Hip. And in this wedding of the white and the black it was the Negro who brought the cultural dowry. Any Negro who wishes to live must live with danger from his first day, and no experience can ever be casual to him. . . . The Negro has the simplest of alternatives: live a life of constant humility or ever-threatening danger.[6]

The truth is that if Mailer and the Beats and the Hipsters want it both ways, if they want members of minorities to be conscious of differences, yet to marry and otherwise intermingle, it is because they demand also a change in the relation between the individual and his society. However mud-

[5] Ibid., p. 189.
[6] Mailer: *Advertisements for Myself*, pp. 340–1.

171

died the ideal may become in practice, it remains in theory a pure example of the existentialist goal of human relations in good faith. Where the individual is valued for his uniqueness and is encouraged to live his particular situation in line with his own authentic choice, then cultural distinctions and biological differences deriving from race become merely part of the material out of which each freedom makes itself individual. If we refrain from setting up any one type as a yardstick, then the variations among human types is not a limitation but an invitation for enrichment. The fault with the Serious World is not that it offers varied values but that each item in it has its price tag affixed. Even in interracial liaisons and marriages, the rebel's aim is neither a least common denominator nor the absorption of one partner into the world of the other. His goal is the union in difference of two individuals who remain themselves even as their lives are enriched by the new ways of living which the other offers. The right to choose one's own style of life is the foundation stone of this revolt. It does not preclude the recognition that in the world in which one finds oneself, there are already established groups with traditional patterns which are not the same as those prevailing in the social setting in which one has been born. To their everlasting credit, the members of the "Beat Generation" have made it clear from the beginning that minority patterns were not deviations from the "human," but merely so many more variations on a theme which appears only in its variations. They have insisted that the individual has a right to play his own harmonies, picking and choosing where he will.

Naturally there have been distortions and failures. They have generally resulted from the same sort of mystification which we observed apropos of sexuality. Just as those rebelling against sexual inhibitions have tried to make unrestrained sexuality solve too many things, have tended to reduce all meaning in life to the erotic and to see in each woman all of femininity but nothing of herself, so there has been a tendency to find in each Negro—or even in each Spanish-American—the embodiment of a primitive life force which will save decadent civilization. Norman Mailer has linked both of these mystifications in a statement which elicited vehement protests from segregationists, friends of the Negroes, and the Negroes themselves.

> Can't we have some honesty about what's going on now in the South? Everybody who knows the South knows that the white man fears the sexual potency of the Negro. And in turn the Negro has been storing his hatred and yet growing stronger, carrying with him the painful wound that he was usually powerless to keep from being cuckolded.
>
> For the white, symbolically and materially, has possessed Negro womanhood for two centuries. Which is what all the literary critics mean when they talk about the blood guilt of the South.
>
> The comedy is that the white loathes the idea of the Negro attaining equality in the classroom because the white feels that the Negro already enjoys sensual superiority. So the white unconsciously feels that the balance has been kept, that the old arrangement was fair. The Negro had his sexual supremacy and the white had his white supremacy.[7]

Although this is presented as an explanation of Southern prejudice, Mailer quite clearly feels that the feeling on the part of whites is more widely spread and that half of it is justified. When James Baldwin protested against the "myth of the sexuality of Negroes which Norman, like so many others, refuses to give up," [8] Mailer countered with the claim that not only he himself but the average white man and perhaps Baldwin himself, secretly, believed in the more profound sexuality of the Negro.

> Baldwin's buried point is that I shouldn't talk this way because it's bad for the Negro people, it's going to slow them up, going to hurt them: talk about Negro sexuality hurts their progress because it makes the white man nervous and unhappy and miserable.[9]

Surely it is Baldwin who is right in regarding this as a dangerous fantasy. In the first place, although intended as a

[7] Ibid., p. 332.

[8] James Baldwin: *Nobody Knows My Name: More Notes of a Native Son* (New York: Dell Publishing Co.; 1962), p. 220.

[9] Mailer: *The Presidential Papers*, p. 146.

tribute to the Negro, it tends to reduce him to the level of being only a primitive near-animal. Baldwin says,

I was also baffled by the passion with which Norman appeared to be imitating so many people inferior to himself, i.e., Kerouac, and all the other Suzuki rhythm boys. From them, indeed, I expected nothing more than their pablum-clogged cries of *Kicks!* and *Holy!* It seemed very clear to me that their glorification of the orgasm was but a way of avoiding all the terrors of life and love. But Norman knew better, had to know better. *The Naked and the Dead*, *Barbary Shore*, and *The Deer Park*, proved it.[1]

The "myth" turns out to be one more manifestation of a strange and dangerous tendency to solve civilization's problems by a regressive neo-primitivism. It holds another trap as well. In the sentimental heroization of Negroes and Mexicans, Kerouac, Mailer, and countless lesser writers have blurred over any realistic grasp of the actual situation of oppressed and underprivileged minorities; they risk falling back into the very position they despise—of seeing the individual only as a member of his race. No matter how glorified, the Negro who feels or is made to feel that he is The Negro Race or Quintessential Virility has not found himself as a free person any more than the Earth Mother has.

The possibilities of either good or bad faith in human relations are clearly delineated in established liaisons and marriages between whites and Negroes. From the existentialist point of view, such relations are judged by the same criteria as any other. Ultimately the test is whether each one appreciates and respects the other person for what he is as a free subject. At the same time we recognize that there are even more than the usual temptations to fall into bad faith— aside from all the obvious difficulties resulting from an unsympathetic society. If both partners enter into the union simply as a gesture of defiance of conventions, the relation is unlikely to endure; it is not necessarily in bad faith. If one of the pair exploits the love of the other as a way of manifesting his own rebellion, if either claims love as a pretext for what is

[1] Baldwin: *Nobody Knows My Name*, pp. 228–9.

really an atonement for guilt feelings or a symbol of achievement, this is to treat the other as an object. It is as immoral
an act as any other affront to human freedom. Less objectionable, perhaps, but just as mistaken is the attempt to form a
lasting relationship based upon pure fascination with those
traits which mark the other as being of a different race (or
nationality). If one learns to love this otherness as it has been
internalized and individually lived by the beloved, then such
an attachment may perhaps endure in good faith. Otherwise
one of two things is almost certain to happen. Either the lover
is frustrated upon learning that the beloved is by no means
the *type* he hoped to possess. Or the beloved tries to deny all
free individuality in order to pretend to *be* the racial essence
which the lover is seeking. In both cases the positing of the
species as an ideal denies the reality of the free individual.

The last two motifs or demands which I have indicated as
typical of the negative rebels reveal once again both a positive
and a negative aspect. Despite my awareness that to say so
marks me forever as "Square" and not "Hip," I must conclude that here the negative far outweighs the positive. I refer
to the thirst for enlarged experience, either by the expansion
of consciousness or through acts which court danger and are
expressed in violence. The initial impulse is all to the good.
An alertness to new experience, a willingness to give up the
ease and comfort which so many Americans find indispen-
sable, and simple courage—these, if I may use so old-fashioned a word, are noble traits. Furthermore, there is no denying the fact that they are often accompanied by a greater
openness to new forms of art and thought and to new solutions of social problems. Among those who are quietists or
even nihilists, so far as political activity is concerned, we still
find the conviction that one can cultivate a quiet corner of
personally ordered authentic contentment as a retreat from a
hostile world. The belief that individual happiness is worth
pursuing tirelessly and in hitherto untried ways is a source of
hope for a society which has settled chiefly for either a dull
routine or the competitive rat race and tranquilizers. Yet
while there are exceptions, I think it has to be admitted that

this impulse has mostly turned in directions which lead to a dead end—if they are not downright destructive. Mailer's remark that the Hipster has emerged from the sympathetic meeting of Negro, bohemian, and juvenile delinquent contains an important truth; so does his indication of marijuana as the bond holding them together. The desire to expand consciousness has too often manifested itself merely in smoking marijuana or in experimenting more perilously with the true narcotics. The thirst for experience has taken the form of a search for thrills, either in personal risk, e.g., drag racing, or in deliberate lawlessness—stealing or destruction of public property—or in acts of violence against others. It would be all too easy to exclude these extremists among the rebels, to label them as the criminal fringe which accompanies all movements of social protest and so dismiss them. I do not think we can rightly do so. Unless we are to apply the term "delinquent" to everybody who has ever smoked a reefer or engaged in a drag race, we must recognize that participation in this kind of illegality is fairly common in nondelinquent groups. Mailer himself goes so far as to include violence as a necessary component of his socio-philosophical, semi-prophetic prescription for our recovery.

I may say at the start that to identify the expansion of consciousness with the use of drugs or to restrict intense experience to extreme physical sensation and the turbulent emotions aroused by violent aggression is primarily a negative choice rather than a positive one. It is a choice of the nonrational and thereby precludes those vast areas of human possibilities in which the rational plays the dominating role. In its extreme form, it is almost certainly a choice of spontaneous over reflective self-realization. If it goes so far as to refuse to consider any claim that the rights of other freedoms must be respected, then it is recognized finally as the choice of the nonethical life. On the level of abstraction, an existentialist must reject it on principle as we did with the choice of the Underground Man. Yet I believe we ought to consider briefly whether there is any specific demand in these protests which might be made part of a legitimate existentialist choice.

The use of drugs for the purpose of expanding consciousness raises two quite separate questions. The first is the issue of religion, or at least of metaphysics. It involves the possibilities of mysticism, of union with some cosmic power or the discovery of a higher Self. This problem I wish to reserve for a later discussion. The second question does not pertain to the revelation of any more profound Truth. It asks whether there are limits (legal or as the logical consequence of our initial choice to be ethical) which should be placed on the individual's freedom to manipulate his own sensations and bodily reactions.

Waiving for the moment the question of legality, we may begin with a few obvious points. First, the greatest stretch of imagination could hardly make the use of drugs into an imperative. At most one might say that not to exploit their possibilities was to miss the opportunity of enjoying a particular kind of value, like that of drinking or smoking or any of the unquestioned pleasures such as listening to music or looking at paintings. The difficult question is whether or not drugs provide a positive value which is not as self-evidently outweighed by negative consequences as eating poison is, or torturing a child, and whether each person has the right to make his own evaluation of value and disvalue and to act accordingly.

It seems to me obvious that addiction to narcotics is not compatible with the ethical choice. I would not go through the ritual of arguing toward what I consider a foregone conclusion if it were not that I recall a seminar discussion in which several of my students insisted that the choice of living in a continually drugged state was as defensible as any choice so long as the individual honestly found it to be more satisfying than any life he was able to attain without drugs. Implicit in their defense was the old argument that from the outside one could not be sure that Socrates' discontent was better than the state of the satisfied pig. As I see it, even the most scrupulous weighing of theoretical possibilities does not oblige us to grant more to this argument than the same sort of grudging acknowledgment we allot to the contention that suicide or killing a person might under extreme circumstances be defended as the lesser of two evils. To affirm the right to kill in self-defense or to defend others is not to claim that murder as such is a good. I would not hold that the prisoner's resolve to kill himself rather than risk giving information under torture is a nonethical choice. I am unwilling to condemn the suicide of the hopeless cancer victim, much as we would hate to see our loved ones make such a decision. Keeping the incurably ill under narcotic sedation is something we condone even though the addiction in this case is imposed and not chosen. None of these examples justifies either suicide or drug addiction when other positive choices are possible. The choice of drugs as a way of life is open to still more objections than the Underground Man's decision to choose against himself. However mistakenly, he at least was trying to assert his spontaneous freedom and to preserve his sense of intense personal life. The drug addict forswears his own freedom completely, putting it under a yoke of necessity from which it is harder to escape unaided than from any prison. He cuts himself off from reality and from all human contact. He makes himself into a near mechanism, one capable of registering certain sensations of delight but never enough to outweigh the anguish. William Burroughs, who can certainly not be accused of merely expressing the Puritan's prejudice against physical pleasure, has summed up this grim indictment in a brief description of his own awakening from "The Sickness." Two passages are especially pertinent.

I lived in one room in the Native Quarter of Tangier. I had not taken a bath in a year nor changed my clothes or removed them except to stick a needle every hour in the fibrous grey wooden flesh of terminal addiction. I never cleaned or dusted the room. Empty ampule boxes and garbage piled to the ceiling. Light and water long since turned off for non-payment. I did absolutely nothing. I could look at the end of my shoe for eight hours. I was only roused to action when the hourglass of junk ran out. If a

178

friend came to visit—and they rarely did since who or what was left to visit—I sat there not caring that he had entered my field of vision—a grey screen always blanker and fainter—and not caring when he walked out of it. If he had died on the spot I would have sat there looking at my shoe waiting to go through his pockets. Wouldn't you? Because I never had enough junk—no one ever does.[2]

Junk yields a basic formula of "evil" virus: *The Algebra of Need*. The face of "evil" is always the face of total need. A dope fiend is a man in total need of dope. Beyond a certain frequency need knows absolutely no limit or control. In the words of total need: *"Wouldn't you?"* Yes you would. You would lie, cheat inform on your friends, steal, do *anything* to satisfy total need. Because you would be in a state of total sickness, total possession, and not in a position to act in any other way.[3]

I think we need not spend more words in showing that the choice of addiction is not an ethical choice. Nevertheless a closely related problem remains. Reminding ourselves again of the parallel with suicide (for both suicide and addiction are forms of self-destruction), we may ask whether or not a person has the right to destroy himself. Here the questions of ethics and of legality come together. We may say that except for the kind of extreme cases already mentioned, suicide and addiction are never an ethical choice. Does a person have the right to choose not to be ethical? So far as the law is concerned and in the case of suicide, I think that he does. The law which would punish attempted suicide proclaims itself pure vengeance. It certainly is no preventive. What threat is meaningful to the man resolved on death? If we wanted to carry such logic to its absurd conclusion, we could, I suppose, promise all unsuccessful suicides a death by slow torture. But this, instead of deterring them, would inspire them to be more efficient. We ought individually and collectively (1) to do all in our power to insure that individuals will not find themselves in a situation where suicide is the preferable alter-

[2] William S. Burroughs: *Naked Lunch* (New York: Grove Press; 1959), p. ix.
[3] Ibid., p. vii.

native and (2) to help prevent persons from carrying out suicides if there is any hope at all of their finding a life which is better than death. On the strict ethical plane we might argue that self-destruction in many cases (e.g., the only supporting parent of young children) injures other freedoms for whose well-being one is responsible. This is one more reason why we cannot call the decision for suicide an ethical choice. Even here I do not think that any law which purports to be based on anything more than revenge ought to intervene. Public stigma attached to the dead man harms only the innocent survivors. If the would-be suicide is rescued, the knowledge that he is pronounced a criminal will hardly aid him in making his life a success.

The parallel with drug addiction is closer than might at first thought be believed. There is some difference of course. The fear of being caught, of being imprisoned, or of losing one's reputation or one's job may possibly discourage a few people from experimenting with drugs, and a small number of such persons may consequently avoid being hooked who otherwise would have succumbed. I do not believe that these are nearly so many as those who have been perpetrators or victims of crime as the result of the singularly obtuse policy of the American method of combating narcotics. Obviously the solution is not to allow companies to advertise narcotics and sell them in the grocery stores and at the same time warn the public against using them—which has been our compromise policy with cigarettes. Unless we assume the position of extreme conservatism and maintain that it is not our business to interfere with any man's deterioration so long as he doesn't harm others, we must endeavor to do something to prevent addiction. The present policy is clearly wrong. It obviously is not effective since federal agents are the first to say that the use of narcotics is on the increase and that many types of criminality are directly linked with the desire to get possession of drugs illegally or to profit by selling them. Moreover, we find ourselves in the peculiar position of objecting to narcotics on the ground that they render a man no longer a free agent and at the same time punishing him when he fails to obey our injunction to stop using them. Burroughs pinpoints the error and makes a suggestion which increasing numbers of psychologists and sociologists are publicly supporting.

If we wish to annihilate the junk pyramid, we must start with the bottom of the pyramid: the *Addict in the Street*, and stop tilting quixotically for the "higher ups" so called, all of whom are immediately replaceable. *The addict in the street who must have junk to live is the one irreplaceable factor in the junk equation. . . .*
Addicts can be cured or quarantined—that is, allowed a morphine ration under minimal supervision like typhoid carriers. When this is done, junk pyramids of the world will collapse. So far as I know, England is the only country to apply this method to the junk problem. They have about five hundred quarantined addicts in the U. K. In another generation when the quarantined addicts die off and pain killers operating on a non-junk principle are discovered, the junk virus will be like smallpox, a closed chapter, a medical curiosity.[4]

If someone less experienced than Burroughs had written that last sentence, we might be tempted to call it naïvely unrealistic. Burroughs, it seems to me, has reason to know the truth of what he is saying. He and others have attested to the efficacy of the British prescription of apomorphine as both a more humane cure and lasting one. I see no reason to doubt his confidence that in a more understanding society no man with the capacity to find an undrugged life endurable would voluntarily slip back into the addict's world of illusory pleasures and torments all too real. Someone may argue that there will always remain some denizens of the derelict fringe who, having once realized that a way of escape is possible, will pay any price rather than be forced to confront themselves and

[4] Ibid., p. viii. Attorney General Nicholas Katzenbach has joined the ranks of those advocating legislation to provide for more humane treatment and a federal rehabilitation program for addicts. He is quoted as saying: "The real question is how much longer we can allow the public safety to be endangered by continuing the primitive, strictly punitive, approach to addiction." Denver *Post*, January 25, 1966.

the world around them. Let us waive the argument that nobody is beyond salvaging. We must admit that some persons have not managed to come to terms with the human condition or their own situation and that we have not found the means to help them. We have two alternatives. We may continue to hound them, imprisoning those we can catch and leaving the others to perpetuate the criminal couple of addict and pusher and all their hangers-on. Or we can benevolently allow the addict to live out his half-life in peace as we do with the incurably ill and psychotic—though there too we might do so more humanely.

Both in life and in literature the group of rebels whom I have been discussing have displayed a fascination with the subterranean existence of the addict. Mostly this interest seems to be motivated by the same mixture of sympathy and envy which they feel toward all those who live as outcasts in a conformist society. They are quick to champion anyone they feel to be a victim of prejudice, injustice, or inhumanity. They are prone to glamorize any who express their defiance by living outside the law. Yet as Goodman points out, the more quiet among the negative rebels are not deliberately self-destructive. For themselves the aim is "to heighten experience and get out of one's usual self." But "in taking drugs for the new experience, they largely steer clear of being hooked by an addiction." Goodman goes on to explain that this elementary caution does not go so far as to reintroduce the dull, safe routine from which the rebels seek to escape. 'If the aim is to get out of this world, one can hardly play it safe. So it is not surprising if they push their stimulants, sleeplessness, and rhythmic and hallucinatory exercises to the point of having temporary psychotic fugues, or flipping." [5]

If once again we exclude those experiences which border on mysticism, it is obvious that the real point at issue is marijuana. Mailer spoke of marijuana as the bond uniting Negro, bohemian, and delinquent. He might have included the university campus where it finds admission into fraternity

[5] Goodman: *Growing Up Absurd*, p. 180.

and sorority houses as well as into the ranks of left-wing nonconformists. Marijuana is perhaps the best symbol we can find of the conflict between rebellious youth and the rest of society and of the peculiar difficulty we encounter if we try to arrive at any simple appraisal. There is, of course, no question that the smoking of marijuana is illegal or that many of those who use it feel themselves to be morally in the right in disregarding what they feel to be an unjust law. In the eyes of the law-abiding, marijuana is the visible proof of the criminality of the rebellious. On the other side, the prohibition against it symbolizes society's unwillingness to let the individual do what he will with his private life; it represents our fear of opening ourselves to any new and intense experience; it stems from a timid rationality, fearful of what it does not understand; it is a holdover of our traditional Puritanism which begrudges all purely sensory delights. Law officials feel they must protect us from the dreaded danger of drug addiction. The rebels fight to preserve their right to feel more vitally alive.

If the truth about marijuana and its effects were more solidly established, we would be on firmer ground though the problem would still not be a simple one. Certainly something can be said on the side of the rebels. Marijuana is not habit-forming. It is not a narcotic, and its physiological effects are altogether different from those of the addictive drugs. Whatever else we may conclude concerning it, we ought to admit that there is no justification whatsoever for making no legal distinction between marijuana and heroin. Those who use marijuana insist that it is less damaging to the health than alcohol, that it leaves no hangover. They will admit that they are talking about moderate usage, but they hasten to add that alcohol too has its abuses. Burroughs seems to me to have summed up both the pros and cons in a concise description.

Cannabis Indica (hashish, marijuana)—The effects of this drug have been frequently and luridly described: disturbance of space-time perception, acute sensitivity to impressions, flight of ideas, laughing jags, silliness. Marijuana is a sensitizer, and the results are not always pleasant. It makes a bad situation worse. Depression becomes despair; anxiety, panic. . . .

An especially unnerving feature of marijuana intoxication is a disturbance of the affective orientation. You do not know whether you like something or not, whether a sensation is pleasant or unpleasant. . . .

The ill effects of marijuana have been grossly exaggerated in the U. S. Our national drug is alcohol. We tend to regard the use of any other drug with special horror. Anyone given over to these alien vices deserves the complete ruin of his mind and body. People believe what they want to believe without regard for the facts. Marijuana is not habit forming. I have never seen evidence of any ill effects from moderate use. Drug psychosis may result from prolonged and excessive use.[6]

Norman Mailer concluded still more briefly that "marijuana opens the senses and weakens the mind."[7] Mezz Mezzrow has written the most impassioned defense of marijuana, declaring that it enables jazz musicians to achieve new heights in controlled improvisation. He maintains that neither addiction nor hangovers are consequences, insisting "I have yet to find any bad after-effects, outside of a twenty-month jail sentence." Yet Mezzrow's description of his first experience with marijuana sounds like an account of something a little more intense than the traditional Saturday night drunk.

All of a sudden the world is stripped of its dirty gray shrouds and becomes one big bellyful of giggles, a spherical laugh, bathed in brilliant, sparkling colors that hit you like a heatwave. Nothing leaves you cold any more; there's a humorous tickle and great meaning in the least little thing. . . . All your pores open like funnels, your nerve-ends stretch their mouths wide, hungry and thirsty for new sights and sounds and sensations; and every sensation, when it comes, is the most exciting one you've ever had. You can't get enough of anything—you want to gobble up the whole goddamned universe just for an appetizer. . . .

Suppose you're the critical and analytical type, always ripping things to pieces, tearing the covers off and being disgusted by what you find under the sheet. Well, under the influence of muta

[6] Burroughs: *Naked Lunch*, pp. 250–1.
[7] Mailer: *Advertisements for Myself*, p. 234.

you don't lose your surgical touch exactly, but you don't come up evil and grimy about it. . . . Everything is good for a laugh; the wrinkles get ironed out of your face and you forget what a frown is, you just want to hold on to your belly and roar till the tears come. Some women especially, instead of being nasty and mean, just go off bellowing until hysteria comes on. All the larceny kind of dissolves out of them—they relax and grin from ear to ear, and get right on the ground floor with you.[8]

I do not know what the solution should be concerning marijuana. I cannot see that the prolonged or immoderate use of it has any place in the ethically responsible life. Aside from the danger of drug psychosis, of which Burroughs speaks, the pleasures of marijuana strike me as being those of escape from freedom rather than of commitment to intense living. In reading student papers which I had reason to believe were written under the drug's influence, it was apparent to me that what to the writer seemed to be a heightened sense of reality was a confused and chaotic mixture of intense sensation, falsified perception, and abortive attempts to interpret it all rationally. Clearly the life which is dominated by marijuana cannot be defended any more than that of the alcoholic and for much the same reasons. Still society does not prohibit alcohol, despite the dangers it opens up for those who use it unwisely. We are free to smoke cigarettes at our own risk. We are not in an easy position from which to argue that the person who wants to indulge himself occasionally with marijuana should be immediately subject to long-term imprisonment if, as occasionally happens, officials enforce existing laws against the user as they constantly do against the seller of the drug. Some would argue that one thing at least is sure: the law forbids the use of marijuana; therefore to use it is indefensible ethically whether or not it is harmful otherwise. This is to beg the question. Or at least it is to raise another one. The strictly ethical person will not be content to evade an

[8] Mezz Mezzrow. This passage is from Mezzrow's autobiography, *Really the Blues*, excerpts from which have been reprinted in *The Drug Experience: First-person Accounts of Addicts, Writers, Scientists, and Others*, ed. David Ebin (New York: Orion Press; 1961), p. 88.

issue in this way. Is or is not the law a just and wise one? In repealing the Eighteenth Amendment, citizens decided that each individual or local communities might decide for themselves where pleasure became folly; they repealed a law already more honored and more profitable in the breach than in the observance.

I personally still need to be convinced that Mary Jane can be as easily domesticated as Dionysus. Since increasing numbers seem determined to invite her as a guest, I would like to see these things happen: First, a genuine, unprejudiced investigation of marijuana and other borderline nonaddictive drugs—research, the results of which would be intelligently interpreted and widely publicized. Such research should have a double aim. On the one hand, it should attempt to establish once and for all the risk of physiological or psychological damage impendent on occasional or continued use of the drugs, under varying circumstances. Second, there should be an open-minded inquiry into the positive claims made, particularly concerning their efficacy in expanding consciousness, with or without religious overtones. It is entirely probable that more research in these areas would aid us in understanding, not only the distortions of the mentally ill, but the potentialities of the strong mind. It is at least possible that we might learn ways of expanding the capabilities of consciousness as we now know it, and I do not mean by that a relapse into the irrational, but rather a genuine increase in mental powers. To decide how freely the individual should be allowed or encouraged to experiment by himself in these areas is difficult when the sort of investigation I have in mind is still in its infancy, still surrounded with the aura of the seance on one side and suspicions of witch-hunters on the other. On the whole, I should be inclined to let people make the dangerous choice if they so desire, providing we might at the same time institute certain safeguards. If we were to adopt a policy comparable to that of England with regard to narcotics, and if our laws properly distinguished between addictive narcotics and other drugs, we would make it less likely that the user of marijuana would progress to heroin. That this step is inevitable or at least very frequent is the constant theme of the Narcotics Squad. If it is, the reason is not that experience with one artificial stimulant leads naturally to the desire to experiment with another. By this line of argument we would expect the cocktail party to have given way to the opium den long since. What has made it so easy to move from marijuana and peyote to heroin or cocaine has been precisely the fact that the law inadequately distinguishes between them. One is outside the law in either case, must resort to the same illegal methods—in some instances to the same pushers—in order to obtain the drugs. The wonder is that so many have set up their own distinctions and boundaries and stayed within the limits. Despite the obvious risks, I think more good than harm would be accomplished if the severe laws against non-addictive drugs were rescinded or greatly modified. I do not believe that the number of people who would use them would be greatly increased, not so long as we refrain from allowing the same sort of deceptive advertising which we tolerate for cigarettes. Naturally there should be concern on all sides to publicize the truth about the risks involved. The final solution, whatever we do legally, depends on our finding a way to enable more persons to find an excitement in living which derives from sources not artificially induced and which offer challenges, not escapes from reality.

If I am willing to go so far as to urge that we allow more freedom to the individual to make the dangerous choice where his own safety is involved, this is not because I am advocating a Rand doctrine of "Hands Off" as a refusal to accept responsibility for others. Quite the contrary. Both prudentially and in strict observance of justice, I think we must make room for more chance of spontaneous self-realization if we do not want more and more examples of Underground Men choosing against themselves, believing this to be the only way to save themselves.

Although he has used different terms, Mailer has recognized this problem in his discussion of what has brought the Hipster into being and in what he calls the "existential legislation" which is needed. Both in descriptive analysis and in

187

prescription, Mailer seems to alternate between the sociological approach and what, for lack of a better term, I will call metaphysical. It is the sociological Mailer who, distressed over the growing rate of delinquency, seeks to locate and correct the causes. We have seen that he blames chiefly the boredom which blights the lives of American youngsters, deprived of any sense of adventure, forbidden to take risks. Mailer deserves credit here for moving on from explanations to a search for solutions. On a television show he argued that "the best way to combat juvenile delinquency was to give artistic outlet to the violence, creativity, and sense of pageantry which drives the average wild adolescent into disaster." Mailer suggested specifically the idea of holding medieval jousting tournaments in Central Park. He made further proposals in "Postscript to the Second Presidential Paper."

Why couldn't there be horse races through the downtown streets of Little Italy similar to the great horse race in Siena, or a municipal circus which would train young acrobats, trapeze artists, lion tamers, and high-wire acts? Once a year there might be drag races down Broadway from 205th Street to the Battery and back. Mountaineers could even be trained in New York. They would learn to make the ascent of difficult skyscrapers. One could build a pool one hundred feet deep and train juveniles in skin diving, one could erect a great ski jump in Central Park. And one might also have boxing and judo and karate and free-style fighting societies. . . .
Existential politics is simple. It has a basic argument: if there is a strong ineradicable strain in human nature, one must not try to suppress it or anomaly, cancer, and plague will follow. Instead one must find an art into which it can grow. So a word to the ear of the President: a Peace Corps is not enough. Start an Adventurer's Corps as well.[9]

I am not prepared to argue the practicality and efficacy of each of these proposed measures, nor would I claim—any more than Mailer would—that such programs would by themselves transform all potential delinquents into creative, happy citizens. I do believe he is on the right track. There is

[9] Mailer: *The Presidential Papers*, pp. 22–3.

an interesting parallel between Mailer's desire to reinstate risk and danger as counterirritants to life-destroying ennui, and William James's desire to divert mankind's aggressive tendencies into "the moral equivalent of war."

In his controversial and disturbing essay, "The White Negro," Mailer presents his portrait of the Hipster as a "philosophical psychopath." Mailer's position vis-à-vis the Hipster is ambivalent, ranging from clinical detachment to a thinly disguised desire for identification.

It was Robert Lindner who first warned that psychopathy may become "a matter no longer of individuals but of groups, nations, peoples, and continents," and who defined the psychopath as "a rebel without a cause, an agitator without a slogan, a revolutionary without a program." Mailer quotes Lindner's description approvingly, picking up in particular two points of Lindner's: (1) That as a result of the psychological injuries done to him in childhood, the psychopath's "rebelliousness is aimed to achieve goals satisfactory to himself alone; he is incapable of exertions for the sake of others"; (2) that "the psychopath, like the child, cannot delay the pleasures of gratification." Lindner's brilliant analysis in *Rebel Without a Cause* was of a criminal psychopath. Certainly not all the negative rebels whom I have been discussing have gone so far as outright criminality. Yet the egoistic insistence on one's own immediate satisfaction to the exclusion of consideration of either others or one's own future is something which I have increasingly observed even among many of my own students, often the most gifted and interesting, though seldom those with the best grades.

Mailer himself goes beyond Lindner in seeing the psychopath as the necessary negative moment in a positive development. He writes:

Even Lindner who was the most imaginative and most sympathetic of the psychoanalysts who have studied the psychopathic personality was not ready to project himself into the essential sympathy—which is that the psychopath may indeed be the perverted and dangerous front-runner of a new kind of personality

189

which could become the central expression of human nature before the twentieth century is over.[1]

Mailer's description of the psychopath and his relation to the Hipster is not as clear as one might wish. He starts out by seeming to make a distinction.

It may be fruitful to consider the hipster a philosophical psychopath, a man interested not only in the dangerous imperatives of his psychopathy but in codifying, at least for himself, the suppositions on which his inner universe is constructed. By this premise the hipster is a psychopath, and yet not a psychopath but the negation of the psychopath, for he possesses the narcissistic detachment of the philosopher, that absorption in the recessive nuances of one's own motive which is so alien to the unreasoning drive of the psychopath.[2]

Mailer adds that the Hipster has "converted his unconscious experience into much conscious knowledge" and "shifted the focus of his desire from immediate gratification toward that wider passion for future power which is the mark of civilized man." Mailer appears, during the discussion which follows, not to separate philosophical psychopathy from nonphilosophical. I see no point in tracing all the ramifications of his discussion. The ideas which seem to me pertinent and significant for our discussion are these.

First, the psychopath seeks to "create a new nervous system for himself." He looks for a chance to grow up a second time and finds it in an act of violence which breaks through the old contradictions and frustrations of childhood. He "knows instinctively that to express a forbidden impulse actively is far more beneficial to him than merely to confess the desire in the safety of a doctor's room." To drain an old cowardice, for example, he will participate in a new act of danger. "The psychopath murders—if he has the courage— out of the necessity to purge his violence, for if he cannot empty his hatred then he cannot love, his being is frozen with implacable self-hatred for his cowardice," The psychopath

[1] Mailer: *Advertisements for Myself*, p. 345.
[2] Ibid., p. 343.

seeks love, not a mate but the "apocalyptic orgasm," which because of all the hatreds and violence inherent in human relations frequently remains "as remote as the Holy Grail." In seeking "to be with it," the Hipster craves to feel himself working together with a Life Force. There is a sense of truth involved too. But truth "is no more nor less than what one feels at each instant in the perpetual climax of the present." Finally, Hip morality "is to do what one feels whenever and wherever it is possible." The Hipster ethic is reduced to "Know Thyself and Be Thyself," but it is in no way to be confused with the Socratic precept. It is "immoderation, childlike in its adoration of the present."

It is at this point that I find Mailer's own attitude most puzzling and most perplexing. He speaks of the "nihilism" of Hip, which proposes the removal of every "social restraint and category." Yet Mailer holds that this proposal is an implicit affirmation of faith, based on the conviction that man thus set free "would then prove to be more creative than murderous and so would not destroy himself." Mailer is willing to call this the "affirmation of the barbarian." He believes that only "a primitive passion about human nature" would feel "that individual acts of violence are always to be preferred to the collective violence of the State." Nevertheless, Mailer makes it clear that all of today's authoritarian philosophies, whether conservative or liberal, would "restrain us from ourselves." Only Hip would "return us to ourselves."

This position is parallel to that of the Underground Man except that it is less clear-sighted. The Underground Man realized that even as he was conserving what he felt to be his essential life, he was also in some way choosing against himself. The Hipster's choice (at least as Mailer sets it up) is just as much an exclusive choice of spontaneous self-realization over temporal self-realization, of the nonethical against the ethical. The difference is that Mailer (I'm not so sure about the Hipster) assumes that in the narrow moment of realizing our immediate freedom, we *are* our essential selves without connections with past or future projects. Thus he simultaneously cuts off our temporality and turns realization of ourselves as nothingness into some sort of being-entity.

We can understand and sympathize with the Underground Man's choice, even if we will not approve of it as ethical, inasmuch as he was capable of seeing only two alternatives— to assert his individual freedom by choosing against himself or to lose all sense of individual life. Quite obviously Mailer feels that the Hipster confronts precisely this grim dilemma. In presenting his views on the Hipster (1957), Mailer admitted that either of two sorts of futures was possible. It seemed to him that, within the social sphere, we faced either quick death by the bomb or slow death by a conformity which stifles man's every creative impulse. Deciding in self-defense to become a "psychic outlaw" by encouraging the psychopath in himself, the Hipster might lend himself to the most radical or the most reactionary of those movements which would destroy a free society. It was Mailer's hope that instead the Hipster would learn that if one man was to be free, all must be free, and would find in his heart the courage to realize that life could and must be more and better than it has been. Put in this way, Mailer's tentative hope is hardly distinguishable from the existentialist's commitment. On the other hand, Mailer in the late fifties succumbed to the pessimistic view that before things improved, they must get much worse, that only the violent abuse of freedom could achieve the purge of hatred which must come first if all men are finally to be liberated so as to become themselves. "Given such hatred, it must either vent itself nihilistically or become turned into the cold murderous liquidations of the totalitarian state." Such fatalism is not existentialist. Despite the occasional riots and individual acts of violence in the sixties, I believe there are already signs that Mailer's pessimism was not prophetic.

The more I read of Mailer and of other writers who either belong to the Hipster or Beatnik groups or describe their worlds sympathetically, the more convinced I become that there is a strange paradox inherent in this withdrawal from society. The motivating force is the individual's desire to think and feel for himself, to *be* himself. At the outset, what is prized is all that individualizes and makes the person unique. It is his awareness whose lucidity he is reluctant to see dulled by the unthinking routine of the people around him. I do not claim that this impulse is wholly toward rationality. Feeling may be involved more than thinking. Nevertheless, there is an insistence on wanting to maintain an unclouded consciousness of one's free being and one's choices. Among these negative rebels the revolt once launched almost inevitably takes the form of retreat into the irrational. We have seen two aspects of this already in the Lawrentian-Reichian view of sex and in the passionate defense of one's right to stimulate the senses with mind-deadening drugs. Ultimately this search for depths of feeling experience leads to a regressive neo-primitivism in which the individual seeks to evade the differentiating potentialities of rational consciousness and to take refuge in an instinctual life of the senses where the individual no longer need decide on his own but is guided by certainties coming from outside his conscious knowledge.

Mailer as always affixes his personal stamp in expressing this Hip metaphysics, but I believe that his point of view is fairly representative of the less clearly formulated attitudes of many in these circles. What he writes is of particular interest to us because it so clearly distinguishes what Mailer wants to call American existentialism from a humanistic existentialism based on Sartrean premises.

Mailer starts out by declaring that "Hip is an American existentialism, profoundly different from French existentialism because Hip is based on a mysticism of the flesh," and it derives from the "undercurrents and underworlds of American life." [3] Mailer loudly proclaims his divergence from Sartre.

To be a real existentialist (Sartre admittedly to the contrary) one must be religious, one must have one's sense of the "purpose" —whatever the purpose may be—but a life which is directed by one's faith in the necessity of action is a life committed to the notion that the substratum of existence is the search, the end

[3] Ibid., p. 314.

193

meaningful but mysterious; it is impossible to live such a life unless one's emotions provide their profound conviction. Only the French, alienated beyond alienation from their unconscious, could welcome an existential philosophy without ever feeling it at all; indeed only a Frenchman by declaring that the unconscious did not exist could then proceed to explore the delicate involutions of consciousness, the microscopically sensuous and all but ineffable *frissons* of mental becoming, in order finally to create the theology of atheism and so submit that in a world of absurdities the existential absurdity is most coherent.[4]

Mailer's use of the concepts of the Unconscious, death, religion, and God are contrary to that of any writer associated with existentialism. We find that he must have his metaphysical and cosmological certainties after all. He feels that the Unconscious is teleological. It is moving toward a goal and knows at any given moment what is happening to one's being. Possibly it is divine or, if finite, its vast complexity is like that of the ocean. It turns out that the Hipster's choice to live with danger and death is not just a deliberate confrontation of annihilation but a more complicated game of Winner Takes All. In a strange blend of old with new Christianity and a bit of Eastern mysticism, Mailer suggests that the way in which one dies makes a difference. He even expresses a tentative hypothesis that possibilities of rewards and disappointments are ingrained in the very structure of things.

The reluctance of modern European existentialism to take on the logical continuation of the existential vision (that there is a life after death which can be as existential as life itself) has brought French and German existentialism to a halt on this uninhabitable terrain of the absurd—to wit, man must lead his life as if death is meaningful even when man *knows* that death is meaningless. . . . Existentialism is rootless unless one dares the hypothesis that death is an existential continuation of life, that the soul may either pass through migrations, or cease to exist in the continuum of nature (which is the unspoken intimation of cancer). But accepting this hypothesis, authenticity and commitment return to the center of ethics, for man then faces no peril so huge

[4] Ibid., pp. 341–2.

as alienation from his own soul, a death which is other than death, a disappearance in nothingness rather than into Eternity.[5]

There are other suggestions in Mailer of a flirtation with ideas derived from Oriental philosophy, but he has never allowed them to become essential to his world outlook. More personal and more puzzling are his suggestions of a limited Deity, of a God who may be in danger of dying, of a God who "is like Me, only more so." This hypothesis leads Mailer to postulate an existential antagonist to God, a Devil or principle of Evil, and we find ourselves squarely in the midst of a neo-Manichaean interpretation of history. Mailer has never fully developed these ideas, which is probably just as well. He himself admits that he is not altogether happy to be in this "no-man's-land between mysticism and rationalism."

There is a particular paragraph in *Advertisements for Myself* that encapsulates both the positive potentiality which existed in Mailer's Hipster and the clear indication of its failure to develop. Mailer has pointed out that Hip is unwilling to judge human nature by a priori standards or by any criteria handed down from the past. It continually sees new alternatives, regards every situation as unique, finds complexity everywhere, and distrusts simple answers which would reduce everything to the general case. Then comes the surprising and disappointing conclusion. "Given its emphasis on complexity, Hip abdicates from any conventional moral responsibility because it would argue that the results of our actions are unforeseeable, and so we cannot know if we do good or bad." [6] One of the sources of existentialist anguish and despair is our realization that we cannot control the future of those present acts *for which we are responsible*. The Hipster flees from anguish by denying his responsibility, a perfect exemplification of bad faith. The quotation epitomizes the legitmacy of the Beatnik-Hipster protest, its initial insight, and the bankruptcy of its ultimate commitment. Philosophical psychopathology is not the way out for the Under-

[5] Mailer: *The Presidential Papers*, pp. 213–14.
[6] Mailer: *Advertisements for Myself*, p. 353.

ground Man. Even if a return to the primitive certainties of the jungle were possible, it would be a regression, not an advance to greater complexity and to individual fulfillment.

Nevertheless it is possible that this negative moment of protest has been historically a necessary step. Sartre claims that revolutions take place when men suddenly realize the impossiblity of their existence. The first hostile withdrawal from society resulted from the individual's sense that his personal life was being suffocated, that the discrepancy between what society professed and what it practiced was too great to be endured. For a time the rebels limited themselves to a reversal of values, to living *against* rather than *for*. Or else they retreated into new games of role-playing, just as artificial and confining as those against which they revolted. Gradually some of them came to recognize that if a person is to realize himself as a free existence in the world, he must change the world, not merely maintain a hostile distance between the world and himself. The Beats and Hipsters did not altogether vanish from the scene, but the stage was soon dominated by an actor with a totally different style—the New Radical.

The New Radicals

When Paul Goodman wrote *Growing Up Absurd* in the middle 1950s, he claimed that the majority of young Americans perceived only two alternative ways of life, represented respectively by the man in the gray flannel suit and by the Beatnik, both shockingly wasteful of human resources. By implication Goodman allowed a few exceptions—writers who, like himself, used their talents to protest against our warped, conformist society and other creative individuals who had quietly made it against the system. Although I think that Goodman even then underestimated the potentialities of those who passed for Beatniks, he was certainly right in pointing out that at that time the negative and delinquent quality of the revolt was uppermost and that there was no clear third position which called for positive action. By the mid-sixties the situation is radically transformed. Side by side with the civil rights revolution, there is a broader youth-dominated movement for social and political action on college and university campuses. Students may concern themselves with protests against the university's assumption of authority *in loco parentis;* they may hold political "teach-ins," join the civil rights marches in Alabama, or participate in pacifist demonstrations outside the fence of the White House. The walls of the Ivory Tower have collapsed almost as suddenly as those of Jericho. What Hal Draper has said of the student conflict with the administration at Berkeley may be applied to American students everywhere:

The mainsprings of the rebellion are an optimistic idealism about the type of society which can be shaped by the new generation, and an unwillingness to allow the paternalism endemic to college campuses to extend its coverage to the activities necessary for the furtherance of those ideals.[1]

Teachers can no longer complain that students as a whole are apathetic and show no interest in the world around them. After years of exhorting activism and preaching the importance of social responsibility, many a professor longs secretly for the days when he could feel that he was ahead of his students instead of dragging along in the rear. He is embarrassed at finding himself in the position of Katie Lee singing "I can't get adjusted to the You who got adjusted to Me." [2] We ought to welcome the change. Of this I am convinced even though I recognize that this change, like any other, is fraught with its own peculiar dangers. I can understand the consternation of the professors. I have felt it myself. One doesn't make an omelet without breaking eggs. What is being cracked in this case often seems to the Liberal to be precisely those structures which allow progress without the

[1] Draper: *Berkeley: The New Student Revolt,* p. 155.
[2] "Songs of Couch and Consultation," Commentary Record (CNT–01).

upheaval of revolution. He feels like a playwright told that the drama he is hopefully writing will in fact be produced—today.

The New Radicals have found their own way out of the despair expressed in Osborne's lament for the demise of all "good brave causes." We are in a later act. It is still the same play.

In trying to grasp this protest movement as a whole, I am struck by the fact that although it is easy to pick out the component groups by analysis, no true synthesis exists. At one point we find a specific aim uniting in common action groups whose general religious or ideological positions would not meet even at the fringes. In civil rights demonstrations clergymen and atheists, university trustees and high school dropouts, lawyers and anarchists march side by side. The Free Speech Movement at Berkeley showed such diverse groups as New Conservatives, Young Socialists, anti-bomb and pacifist organizations, civil rights workers of all types (NAACP, SNCC, and CORE), and supporters of the right to pornography not only joining forces to demand free expression of opinions but utilizing precisely the same methods to further their entirely separate goals. Buttons saying "Legalize marijuana," "Sack HUAC," "Get Out of Vietnam," and "A Free University in a Free Society" appeared on the same sweater. What makes it possible for us to bring together this conglomerate even for a few minutes of discussion is a common attitude, one which immediately reveals both reassuring and disturbing characteristics. On the one hand, we may note with approval that everyone involved has given the lie to those commentators on the American scene who have complained for so long now that nobody here cares for anything but security. Over and over students and nonstudents, adolescents and adults, too, have attested their conviction that specific wrongs exist which they personally are trying to set right.

On numerous occasions they have proved their willingness to submit to physical discomfort and to risk position, reputation, and even their lives for the sake of a cause they believe in. They have exhibited the same sort of determined energy which we observed in the case of the self-destructive rebel, but they have directed it toward positive goals; they have acted with and for others, not against them. Destructive violence is replaced by a firm commitment to nonviolence in programs calling for passive resistance. All this is very much to the good, but it has its underside. Even if we except those groups whose efforts are not genuinely on behalf of the freedom and rights of everybody, there remains some cause for uneasiness. It is an exhilarating feeling to throw off the usual trammels and to defy Authority and the Law. If one is convinced he is justified in doing so, self-righteousness reinforces defiance. The sense of one's own power is a heady thing. Some of the young leaders of the student revolt at Berkeley were honest enough to admit that delight in fomenting trouble and undermining democratic institutions were occasionally motives for some of the specific actions taken.[3] Sheer love of excitement and the unconfessed desire to get away from the burdensome responsibilities of the daily routine undoubtedly played a part in motivating some of those trips to Alabama and Washington. Not every student was above using a "teach-in" as an excuse for failing a test in a course which did not interest him. The decision to say "No" and "Right now" is justified after a hundred years of bad faith in racial relations. The discovery that recalcitrance will work where negotiation will not is a precious key; the door that it unlocks opens onto a hallway which may take one either to Utopia or to anarchy.

Out of these diverse groups, I should like to single out for discussion those who may properly be called the "New Radicals." Although the name originated as a designation of certain student leaders on the University of California campus, it is a descriptive term that applies equally well to students on other campuses. Whether they will continue to be New Radicals once they have left the campus is a question which genuinely worries them. In singling out the New Radicals, I

[3] Calvin Trillin: "Letter from Berkeley," *The New Yorker* (March 13, 1965), pp. 52–107. See especially p. 96.

distinguish them from members of various ideological clubs who may, as at Berkeley, have temporarily borrowed their methods or joined in the campaign for free speech. I am separating them also from the civil rights workers as such, although action to further the freedom of members of minorities is of prime importance to any New Radical. Although many of them participated actively in various types of protests against segregation, their position on other matters would often not win sympathy from the majority of their fellow demonstrators. Moreover, all civil rights defenders have one important fact on their side. In disobeying local laws, they are acting in the name of a position endorsed by the federal law and violated by the very authorities whom they oppose. So long as nonviolence is scrupulously observed, their position is ethically pure. The case is far more complex when defiance involves the infringement of national regulations as, for example, burning one's draft card or refusing to pay income tax.

Very few, either of the New Radicals whom I have known personally or of those concerning whom I have read in journalistic reports, have seemed to me to live consistently by what I am willing to call an existentialist ethics. Yet despite my many reservations concerning them, I believe that as a group they have come closer to exemplifying an existentialist social and political ethics than any other collection of individuals whom I can think of. I will go further than that. In their better manifestations, the New Radicals have bridged the gap that separated Sartre from Camus. They have refused to sacrifice purity of principle to ideological commitments. But not even Sartre could justly accuse them of quietism or of standing aloof from history.

If I include the New Radicals in a chapter on Negative Rebels, this is partly because of the way in which they have defined themselves. While not without a program they are, as Hal Draper carefully explains, "non-ideological."

These "new radicals" are non-ideological in the sense that they refuse to, or are disinclined to, generalize their ideas and positions. They fight shy of any systematization of their political and social views. They think of this approach as "pragmatic." They are inclined to substitute a moral approach—indeed, a dogmatic moral approach—for political and social analysis as much as possible. They like the description "existential" because it offers a non-political label.[4]

The thinking of the New Radicals is closer to some form of socialism than to any other ideology, but they are unwilling to identify themselves with any existing Socialist party. They are emphatically not Communists. That some Communists were present at Berkeley and elsewhere and may on occasion have sought to profit in some way by the general unrest is entirely probable. Nobody has been able to prove that any student protest has been either inspired or directed by Communists. The New Radicals' resistance to all ideologies would, on principle, make them particularly nonsusceptible to Communist propaganda; their reluctance to submit to any sort of party discipline would seem to mark them as not even desirable members. In large numbers they might be more dangerous to the party's health than the host of infiltrating FBI agents. These non-ideologists are not even Marxists. There are apparently two principal causes for their rejecting political parties and also political theories. One is simple disillusion. On one side, they see the totalitarian governments and loss of individual freedom in states which have supposedly been founded on Marxist principles. On the other, they witness in their parents' generation the disappointed ex-radicals of the brave thirties, now either bitter reactionaries or quiescent, disappointed Liberals. From the point of view of the New Radicals, the Old Left has either sold out or failed. Another factor is the suspicion that any organization or even any formal presentation of an over-all commitment which goes beyond what is needed for the immediate project threatens to impede the goals it is set up to promote. This is partly a strategic calculation. It is much easier to get the support of members of various factions in a particular drive if they do

[4] Draper: *Berkeley: The New Student Revolt*, p. 158.

not believe they are supporting a total position or group of which they largely disapprove. More than this, the New Radicals fear that their own independence of thought and action will be impeded if they commit themselves ahead of time to an all-inclusive formulation of goals and acceptable methods. They are afraid of finding themselves imprisoned within the structures of their own crystallized thought. There is one other thing. Although eager to correct what seem to them unjust economic equities, the motive for the New Radicals' protest is not exclusively or even primarily economic. Consequently they don't think in Marxist terms. Mario Savio has expressed this very clearly.

We're talking about the same objective reality, but it's a question of being more tentative. I don't know if all our problems would vanish if we had a state monopoly on production and distribution. I don't have a Utopia in mind. I know it has to be a good deal more egalitarian than it is now. Maybe the classic Marxist models and the classic Adam Smith models don't apply anymore. There are a lot of people who have enough to eat but who are incredibly resentful because their lives are meaningless. They're psychologically dispossessed. There's a feeling that they have nothing to do; the bureaucracy runs itself. Why are we so alienated? I would say for three reasons: depersonalization, hypocrisy, and the unearned privilege that comes with great wealth. The country's forms aren't so bad, if we would take them seriously, if somebody were willing to say the Emperor had no clothes.[5]

The claim that what the New Radicals are trying to accomplish is simply the realization of the ideals to which we all pay lip service appears again and again. As one student expressed it, "It's really a strange kind of naïveté. What we learned in grammar school about democracy and freedom nobody takes seriously, but we do. We really believe it." [6] Calvin Trillin, in an article in *The New Yorker*, stresses this same idea, pointing out that "the New Radicals often engage in a kind of *ad hoc* activism directed at specific problems

[5] Mario Savio, quoted by Calvin Trillin in "Letter from Berkeley," *The New Yorker* (March 13, 1965), pp. 90 and 93.
[6] Suzanne Goldberg, quoted by Calvin Trillin in ibid., p. 89.

whose solutions are no more than the stated goals of American democracy." Trillin adds that we may see in this fact one of the explanations of the New Radicals' impatience and recalcitrance. "Since they take the position of demanding only what society claims to be giving in the first place, they tend to be contemptuous of gradualism or of a compromise in negotiations." [7]

We must not be deceived into thinking that the New Radicals are nothing but younger, not yet disillusioned Liberals. It may be true that the special bitterness which appears in criticism directed toward Liberalism is of the sort which generally emerges when sharp differences come to separate those who are side by side in the broader spectrum. The distinction is nevertheless clearly discernible and decisive. One of the strongest statements comes from another of the Berkeley students. " 'Liberal' is a dirty word here. Liberalism is a trap. It's the impotence of having principles that make you opposed to something and other principles that keep you from doing anything about it." [8] Hal Draper explains that the New Radicals and Liberals are separated by their respective choices of "two alternative modes of operation: *permeation or left opposition*."

The former seeks to adapt to the ruling powers and infiltrate their centers of influence with the aim of (some day) getting to the very levers of decision-making—becoming a part of the Establishment in order to manipulate the reins to the left. The latter wish to stand outside the Establishment as an open opposition, achieving even short-term changes by the pressure of a bold alternative, while seeking roads to fundamental transformations. [9]

The Liberal, whose bête noire is revolution, will put up with gradualism and token segregation and even seek to see in them signs of peaceful progress. The New Radical is con-

[7] Ibid., pp. 89–90.

[8] Jack Weinberg, quoted by Calvin Trillin in ibid., p. 90.

[9] Draper: *Berkeley: The New Student Revolt*, p. 170. In this connection it is interesting to compare Sartre's concern to distinguish the humanistic outlook of existentialism from the old style of liberal, somewhat sentimental Humanism.

vinced that frequently what passes for democratic process is a disguised form of appeasement of the forces of reaction. Thus while there are many New Radicals, there is no New Radicalism. Instead, we find countless *ad hoc* committees laboriously searching for new methods to correct what appear to be specific self-evident evils. Nonideological radicals are "problem-oriented," working in terms of issues rather than theories. They view the Liberal as a person so preoccupied with the abstract justification of his means that the end is indefinitely postponed and in danger of being lost in Utopian unreality. The New Radicals resort to means which are admittedly dangerous from the theoretical point of view—as is any form of civil disobedience. What saves them, at least in intention, is a combination of three things: (1) the absolute commitment to nonviolence; (2) the specific, immediate character of the goal or issue, which allows for a constant rechecking and reconfirmation of all the aspects and implications of the particular project; (3) the fact that all goals proposed are in the interests of promoting human freedom and dignity.

It is totally impossible to predict, with any degree of assurance, the future of the movement launched by the New Radicals. If we are to reject, as I myself do, the idea that it represents nothing more than a particularly vivid exemplification of the never-ending struggle between the generations, then I think that any or all of three possibilities are obvious. First, the New Radicals in addition to accomplishing certain specific projects which they have undertaken or will undertake in the near future, have already reawakened many a close to dormant Liberal. If nothing more, they will have served as a catalyst to precipitate social action and not let worthwhile goals lie buried forever in the minutes of committees. If a revitalized Liberalism rises to challenge the consensus politics now dominating both of our major political parties, this will be no mean achievement—though it would be a result not without irony and certainly not one which would satisfy the New Radical leaders. The second possibility would be the emergence of a New Radicalism. This would

not be the first time that a movement based upon the individual's protest against the system had evolved into a new
theory or institution designed to protect the values aimed at in
the original protest. We may think of Martin Luther as one
of many obvious examples. I do not mean that a New Radical
ideology would necessarily betray its origins, although it
would need to be constantly vigilant against such ever present
danger. It is entirely possible that a New Radical program
might become the foundation of another political party which
would exert pressure upon the major parties or conceivably
bring about some new alignment. Finally, regardless of the
New Radicals' influence upon other political groups and
whether or not their ideas ever evolve into a coherent theory
or platform, they will in all probability continue for some
time to serve as a stimulus and irritant to the American
conscience. In a paradoxical fashion, the New Radicals who
have, with some reason, been referred to as young revolutionists, come closer to filling the role which Camus assigned
to the Rebel, as contrasted with the Revolutionary. There is
this difference, of course, that Camus presented his Rebel as a
man constantly reaffirming the pure principle of revolt and in
the light of it acknowledging the necessity to justify the
means employed, whereas the New Radical is impatient with
abstract principles and willing to adapt for specific ends a
method which would be disastrous if applied universally. The
difference strikes me as chiefly verbal. Camus did not intend
to advocate quietism, however his opponents may have interpreted him. Camus's Rebel and the New Radical both seek to
free individuals and groups from existing oppression and
injustice without becoming entangled in ideological commitments which risk smothering the spark of freedom they are
pledged to foster. The New Radicals may appear to be closer
to Sartre in their insistence on immediate action and on the
importance of thinking in terms of specific tasks to be done.
Perhaps they are. But they distrust the accumulated weight
of Marxist doctrine which Sartre persists on carrying with
him even though he would transform it with the leaven of the
existentialist project. It is in their opposition to working

closely within the framework of any existing ideology that I find the New Radicals most truly existentialist. They are willing to throw everything into question except the premises most fundamental to humanistic existentialism: that we are all responsible for the situations within which men must make themselves; that no human being may claim, by right of birth or nature, a position above that of another; that equality does not mean conformity but rather the right of each person to work out his own values and way of life freely so long as he does not infringe upon the same right on the part of others. The New Radicals are realistic enough to recognize that there is some inevitable conflict of freedoms; they are quicker and keener than most of us in discerning the line between that inevitable violence to freedom which I have called Original Sin and the devices of a society in bad faith.

I have said already that I am not identifying the attitude of the New Radicals with an existentialist ethics. Nor am I saying that New Radicals should all be called existentialists. There is great diversity among them when it comes to their individual metaphysical and religious commitments. Furthermore, I am sometimes disturbed by what seem to me traces of the anti-intellectualism and irresponsibility which I find to be characteristic of the apolitical, more nihilistic rebels. Resistance to ideological formulation may on occasion be a mere cover-up for refusal to think through all the implications and consequences of a decision. I admire those students who resent the pedantic academicism of our graduate schools and search for ways to develop themselves creatively in spite of those of us who work tirelessly to frustrate them. I deplore the numbers of those whose unwillingness to acquire the self-discipline which any productive life requires is disguised as a proud refusal to play the game. Not all who have displayed so admirable an eagerness to correct blatant social evils have shown equal integrity in recognizing their responsibilities in personal relations and commitments. Impulsive, generous, and warm feelings have indeed a certain intrinsic worth; they are inadequate, even dangerous, if they substitute for thinking instead of corroborating it. Yet with all these things in mind, I believe that I can discern in the New Radicals more hope for a positive moral rebirth in American society than in any other sector of today's world.

If simple justice and ethically responsible action are values which we are honestly striving to achieve, then there are certain stringent requirements laid upon those who participate in active forms of social protest (particularly acts involving civil disobedience) and upon the society that judges them. Martyrs are never widely honored until the cause for which they died has been absorbed as part of an established social pattern. In their lifetime they have usually been regarded as traitors or heretics. Today they are explained away as exhibitionists or masochists. Both of these sorts of martyrs have existed even in the past, and perhaps the lions in the Colosseum could detect their distinctive flavor. We do wrong to attribute a "martyr complex" to all those who brave the wrath of authority or public opinion; we are unjust if we attach the label "subversive" to every disturber of the peace. In the United States we have gradually developed a somewhat more humane attitude toward those who are conscientious objectors on religious grounds. The case is harder for the nonreligious pacifist, but his right to refuse to fight is finally recognized by the law. We still have no official tolerance for the individual whose conscience refuses to let him support a particular war. It seems to me that he should at least be granted the alternatives we allow to the conscientious objector.

If the man who burns his draft card or performs some other act of civil disobedience is concerned with the ethical purity of his action, or if he expects sympathetic understanding and tolerance for his position on the part of those who do not share his specific commitment, then he ought to recognize that he is bound by certain obligations. Sincerity is essential but not sufficient. As in the case of lying, disobedience to the laws of a state whose existence one has supported as a guaranteed protection of individual freedom is *ipso facto* a disvalue. Anyone who contemplates it is in a position comparable to that of a man about to engage in armed revolution. Extreme conduct is justified only in extreme situations. Knowing that some negative consequences are certain, one must be very sure of the positive value to be gained. One must calculate his culpability, as Camus says. Let us take the example of the young man on the verge of burning his draft card, one who feels a need to justify the ethical purity of his act. It is not enough for him to feel vaguely that war is a bad thing or that the United States has no business interfering in the internal affairs of Vietnam. If he decides to defy the law and to impede, insofar as he is able, the course of action which the nation is following, then he is obliged to do everything in his power to learn all the facts of the situation and to weigh them as objectively as possible. He ought also to have in mind some clear alternative to war which he would be willing to have the government adopt. Moreover, he should be ready to accept the situation that would result if all the country's draftees were to burn their draft cards. I am sure that there are many thoughtful, responsible pacifists and opponents of our Vietnam policy who meet these conditions. These are the true martyrs. They deserve our admiration even if we believe them to be mistaken. I suspect they are in the minority. At any rate I have known some among these pacifists who have admitted that, at the present state of affairs, they do not see how we could pull out of Vietnam and that it would be disastrous if wholesale resistance should suddenly paralyze the nation's military endeavor. To my mind, their decision to resist the draft is not defensible. They demand ethical purity for themselves while relying on others to sustain the situation they overtly oppose. Some might offer the excuse that their dramatic protest helps to keep the question alive, hence may open up possibilities of solutions not now perceived. I am unwilling to accept this argument as sufficient justification. In this case it seems to me that another kind of activity is called for, not the refusal to participate in a war one regards as presently necessary although one holds that it is unjust and should not have come about.

Whatever one's own opinion may be, it is easy to understand why the majority of citizens are against those who overtly defy the federal law. The angry cries of outrage against other forms of protest are harder to comprehend, particularly when they come from those whose over-all outlook is fairly liberal. "Teach-ins" are not always impersonal quests for knowledge; mass demonstrations almost never are. Neither are political conventions. So long as the purpose of any gathering is criticism of governmental policy and exhortation to modify it or to replace it with some nonviolent alternative, I cannot see that the right of free speech should be revoked or that the demonstrators are abusing that privilege simply because their ideas are contrary to the majority opinion. Someone might object that more is involved here than speech. Some of the protesters call attention to themselves by bizarre behavior. They sleep in public places or go on hunger strikes or even, in rare instances, set fire to themselves. In the opinion of many, these self-inflicted hardships, instead of being a convincing indication that only a worthwhile cause could elicit such wholehearted devotion from its determined followers, are interpreted as clear proof that crackpots, unstable conduct, and dubious programs suit one another perfectly.

I would not defend everything that is done in the name of social justice any more than I would maintain that all the motives of all who demonstrate are one hundred per cent pure. I confess that I cannot myself accept gratuitous public suicide as a legitimate ethical choice. Violence against oneself is an affront to human freedom just as political murder is. I do not feel that there is a comparable reason to condemn the other novel forms of protest. In the first place, the conduct which may appear to be pointless and senseless is not without point, and it has its own very shrewd sense. It is by their refusal to accept existing situations calmly and sensibly that the protesters keep an issue open in the mind of the public. If problems are relegated to the pages of liberal journals or even to the newspaper columns of "Letters to the Editor," it is possible to regard them as academic or at least not urgent. Many Americans are not happy about segregation or about our war policies (warm and cold), or about the threats attendant on our stockpiling of nuclear weapons. But having found no solution to these problems, they prefer to ignore them as if they had been somehow settled. I am convinced that much of the public's irritation with the demonstrators is not primarily based on objections to the goal proposed or even on well-grounded serious disapproval of the method employed. It is resentment against those who are unwilling to accept evil and injustice as inevitable, and who consequently compel us to recognize how easily we ourselves have grown accustomed to do so. The New Radicals have cracked the Serious World wide open.

VIII

The Temptation
of Eastern Philosophy

Sartre has pointed out that every negation is a particular negation; even as a negation it is—negatively—qualified by that which it negates. When Nietzsche said "God is dead," it was the God of our Judaeo-Christian tradition whose death he announced, of God the Father, the legislator of the Ten Commandments, the source of moral principles, the fount of values. The object of Sartre's atheistic criticism is pre-eminently the Self-Cause of Aquinas, the origin of rational Nature and Human Nature, whose existence, if He were really there, would at once relieve Man of his anguish and deprive him of his freedom. Camus's rejected God is the self-contradictory Scandal, that all-righteous Omnipotence who could have prevented injustice had He so willed and who ought to have willed it if He is as just as the creatures whom He condemns.

I believe that in America today, much of people's feeling of meaninglessness and moral chaos derives in large part from the sense of a missing God, that personal Father-Judge who

211

for so many centuries assigned our tasks and goal, rewarded our efforts, punished and forgave our mistakes. I have deliberately contrasted the ethical positions of humanistic existentialism with a fundamentalist or at least a conservatively traditional view of Christianity. I have done so partly because this has been the focus of the attacks by existentialist writers. In addition, I believe that, regardless of the degree of naïveté or sophistication in the Christian faith of our ancestors, the essence of what is now felt as a lack remains the same; that is, the belief in a transcendent Deity, who in some way guaranteed that the Universe was ordered and purposeful and who served as final reference point for standards of human conduct. This personal, separate Father-Creator is, of course, already outmoded in liberal Christianity and in the New Theology. He is in any case strictly, almost provincially, Western.

That a Westerner would reject Yahweh and the Trinity in order to embrace any other named Deity and Mover in History is hardly conceivable. For humanistic existentialism, the option is out on principle. What about a significantly changed concept of God and the religious? Here there are, I believe, two hypotheses which are living—to use James's term—in the sense that they at least offer themselves as serious possibilities for our belief, whether we choose ultimately to reject them as inconsistent with the premises of humanistic existentialism or to adopt them, possibly with some modification. These are: First, the philosophies of Being—either the New Theology which somewhat defensively still calls itself Christian, or the ambiguous existentialism of Heidegger, which is certainly not religious in any traditional sense but which nevertheless holds on to such concepts as the Holy and speaks of "Being" in a language hardly discernible from that of the New Theologians. For several reasons the consideration of these views of Being is not appropriate in the context of the discussion of "Existentialism and Other Rebels." We will return to this problem later on. Second, there is the challenge of Eastern philosophies, which quite clearly have furnished new kinds of religious hopes and aspirations to many Westerners for whom the Judaeo-Christian theologies no longer exerted any appeal. We have seen that Mailer, self-styled American existentialist, suggested, along with his own peculiar concept of immanent deity, an immortality through reincarnation. Jack Kerouac expressed a feeling of kinship with existentialism before turning decidedly Eastward in *The Dharma Bums.* Zen Buddhism has been associated frequently, though not exclusively, with the group I have called the Negative Rebels. The question of how an existentialist might respond to the claims of Eastern philosophers seems to me an entirely suitable subject for our present investigation.

It is not only novelists like Kerouac and Mailer and Beatniks of the West Coast who have felt akin to both existentialism and Asian philosophy. Eastern and Western scholars, whose discovery of each other scarcely began with the century, have been particularly anxious to point to ideas they hold in common.[1] This eagerness has been intensified in the case of existentialism, probably because existentialists (along with phenomenologists) and Oriental philosophers have been the only ones to offer a serious challenge to philosophy since the analytic philosophers took over.

Martin Heidegger has acknowledged an affinity between his more recent work and the intentions of Zen Buddhists. Even if the ultimate impact of the essential message is the same, the over-all setting and approach are radically different. But at least here the comparison is between the work of one existentialist and a single Eastern system; moreover, it is the final aim and impact which are declared to be one and the same. Too many of these scholarly discussions, even those by reputable writers, employ two equally misleading methods of comparison. Either they point to similarities so broad as to be meaningless—as if one should say "An elephant and a fly are alike in that neither is a plant." Or else, these critics

---

[1] I have discussed this subject more briefly in an article, "The Optimism of World Denial," *The Colorado Quarterly*, Vol. XII (1963), pp. 5–26. Some paragraphs, with certain modifications, have been incorporated in this chapter.

choose such small details of resemblance that they miss the greater dissimilarity. As if, "An elephant is like a fly in that each has two eyes." I realize that there is a danger of falling into the opposite extreme by insisting too much on minute distinctions. It is no help to maintain, "These two objects you call eggs are completely unlike, for one is brown, and one white and they came out of different chickens."

All the same, one finds too often a quite reckless lack of discrimination. For some examples: K. Guru Dutt, in his book *Existentialism and Indian Thought*, gives the impression that existentialism in all its branches is amazingly parallel to all of Indian thought, despite the existence of many different schools of Indian philosophy. Haridas Chaudhuri in an article, "Existentialism and Vedanta," [2] delimits the Indian side of the question but picks and chooses quite recklessly among existentialists, playing up superficial resemblances, putting whole chasms of differences between parentheses. Like Dutt he concludes that existentialism and Vedanta are remarkably similar. Van Meter Ames in an essay, "America, Existentialism, and Zen," shows that existentialism, Zen, and pragmatism have much in common, and many of his points of comparison are undoubtedly correct.[3] His book, *Zen and American Thought* weakens the significance of these parallels by revealing that the author finds Zen in the writing of almost every American philosopher. Among the works of Erich Fromm, I know of none which deals specifically with the relation between existentialism and Oriental philosophy. Fromm does, however, find marked resemblances between Marx and the existentialists and a strong affinity between Western psychoanalysis and Zen Buddhism; he is hopeful that Marx and a psychoanalysis enriched by Zen may significantly improve the lot of mankind. After reading these authors, I am left with the uneasy feeling that every-

[2] Haridas Chaudhuri: "Existentialism and Vedanta," *Philosophy East and West*, Vol. XII (1962), pp. 3–17.

[3] Van Meter Ames: "American, Existentialism, and Zen," *Anthology of Zen*, ed. William A. Briggs (New York: Grove Press; 1961), pp. 238–51.

thing is the same as everything else. There seems to be little point in studying the philosophy of the East since it has all been expressed already by Western philosophers and in languages in which we can at least recognize the alphabet.

My intention is not to attempt still another comparison between Sartrean existentialism and possible parallels in Eastern philosophy. What seems to me more important is to understand what Americans think they are finding in these philosophies which they embrace as promises of liberation and a way of life, then to see how far they may be compatible with the existentialist outlook and, on the other hand, what reasons existentialism might have to reject them, wholly or in part. Inasmuch as any ethics must be closely articulated with a metaphysics, this comparative appraisal may furnish further opportunity for us to study more fully the relation between an existentialist ethics and its own metaphysical commitments.

Most of those Westerners who have adopted some form of Oriental philosophy as a way of life, rather than as subject matter for scholarly inquiry, have encountered the teachings of the East in either (or sometimes inconsistently both) of two forms. There is Vedanta, which, speaking broadly, is the Indian tradition derived from the Vedas and the Upanishads, reformulated and expanded by Sankara in the ninth century. The earlier part of our century learned of it from the Theosophical Society, which has never quite managed to achieve a status much above that of Spiritualism in the mind of the average American. The same ideas have acquired more respectability in recent publications of the Vedanta Society of Southern California. Perhaps the majority of Americans know them best as they have been presented and somewhat modified in the essays and novels of Aldous Huxley. The second influence is Zen Buddhism, particularly as taught by D. T. Suzuki, from Japan, and as interpreted by the Englishman Alan Watts, now resident in the United States. Vedanta is much closer to an important though minor part of the Western tradition. Zen Buddhism, as I hope to show, is more easily related in a meaningful way to existentialism.

Nirvana and Unity

Vedanta seems to me to offer a clear either/or in relation to any kind of existentialism. What is essential in it appears absolutely opposed to that small but significant least common denominator which serves to link all existentialists from Kierkegaard through Heidegger to Sartre. Existentialism has already confronted and rejected a parallel way of thinking in the setting of Western philosophy. This is what Huxley calls "the perennial philosophy," which he feels has been most adequately expressed by Vedanta but which has appeared and reappeared intermittently throughout the world in the myths and dogmas of many religions for some three thousand years. It was present in Plato, fully formulated by Plotinus, restated by Schopenhauer. We find it in the mystic experiences of a number of slightly heretical Christians.

Reduced to its bare skeleton and stripped of its myths of incarnate deities, Vedanta comprises these things: There exists a Divine Ground (the godhead, the one, or Brahman) which is immanent in all things and yet transcendent, a nonmaterial unmanifested principle behind all manifestation. The individual consciousness is only superficially separated from this Eternal Reality, and it may, even in this life, realize its union-in-identity through an experience transcending conceptual knowledge or ordinary sensory perception. The realization that the true self-center, Atman, *is* ultimately in impersonal Brahman ought to be the goal and purpose of every person, for it alone satisfies and liberates. Only this is Truth. The phenomenal world of separated entities is as ephemeral and superficial as the individual personality. The illusion of separate substantiality is maintained for as long as the individual willfully clings to his sense of separation in a series of reincarnations. "To know ourselves is to know our source," as Plotinus said. To exist eternally as all, we must refuse to live separately as ourselves. For the more there is of Ego, the less there is of the Divine Ground.

216

Sartrean existentialism can no more accept this doctrine than it can reconcile itself with a fundamentalist Christian eschatology. There is no need (even if it were profitable) to argue the question as to whether reincarnation and ultimate salvation by absorption can be proved or disproved either scientifically or by logical argument. The Sartrean theory of consciousness, of the self, and of the outside world simply will not fit.

Writing within the tradition of Western theism, Sartre has stated that generally we decide on emotional grounds whether or not to accept the hypothesis of God and then proceed to hunt for reasons to justify our faith or our atheism. Sartre's formal arguments against the notion of theism have always seemed to me less impressive than the passages scattered throughout *Being and Nothingness* where he describes and explains religious attitudes and experiences on the basis of his own existential psychology—much as Freud tried to do with the idea of God as a Father image and conscience as the Super-Ego. Inasmuch as the central doctrines of Eastern philosophies are offered to us as serious hypotheses for our belief and as ways of liberation, I think it is worthwhile to examine them and to formulate an answer to two questions. Why are these doctrines incompatible with humanistic existentialism? Why should we reject them in favor of existentialism?

There is a tendency today to embrace too readily the Hindu assertion that there is one goal but many pathways. Brahman is one, but the dharmas are many and equally good so long as each is appropriate to the personality of the seeker. Contemporary Christians, anxious to compensate for the intolerant and arrogant exclusiveness of earlier missionaries, have understandably moved in the direction of emphasizing the oneness of God by whatever name He is known, blurring distinctions and playing up the Universality of compassion, asceticism, purity, dependence on an ultimate more-than-rational Absolute, and all the other manifestations of religious experience in contrast to the scientific or material. Tolerance for others' ideas and the recognition that not all knowledge

217

and insight are the invention and property of the West are values I strongly uphold. But there is a danger here. It is one thing to realize that in matters involving the ultimate "why" of things, there is always a certain measure of uncertainty, of risk—of faith, if you like. It is quite another to say that all hypotheses are of equal validity; it is going even further to argue that they are fundamentally the same. To maintain that in metaphysics any one hypothesis may be wrong is by no means the same as to declare that they may all be right. The Hindu can quite consistently accept everything in Christianity, except its exclusiveness, and incorporate it into his own framework. It is quite possible for a Christian in all good faith to decide that what is significant to him in his religious experiences may be retained and enlarged within the framework of one of the philosophies of India. But he must realize what he is doing. If he views historical Yahweh and Jesus as but two manifestations of Deity, or if he replaces the Day of Judgment with the doctrine of reincarnation, he may, to be sure, retain a Christian coloration. He has, at most, made Christianity an enclave within a broader and less structured theology. He has not incorporated Vedanta or Buddhism within Christianity. If God is not personal, if we are not His specially created creatures, if the Jews were not a chosen people and Jesus the only manifest son of God, then Christianity in its essential form as the Gospel has been transcended and absorbed in something else.

The three central concepts of Vedanta which increasing numbers of Westerners are finding meaningful are these: reincarnation and gradual salvation, Enlightenment, and the ultimate oneness of all consciousness. In the West until very recently, reincarnation has hardly made more claim on our belief than ghosts and haunted houses. Yet it has existed on the fringes of Western philosophy since the time of the Orphics and Pythagoras. I am convinced that Plato believed in it with some literalness. So did Plotinus. And Schopenhauer found in it the "myth standing closest to philosophical truth." Existentialism, of course, finds it incompatible for two reasons. First, the doctrine demands the recognition that the human being is something quite other than what he seems, either to others or to himself. The essence of the person is a definite psychic entity which is on principle separate from everyday consciousness, unknown to it, and unmodified by its experiences. Vedanta, for all its dependence on the ultimate undifferentiated oneness of all consciousness, offers us a view of man that is more complex in its structure than even the Freudian. The phenomenal ego (atman) of waking consciousness has no ultimate reality but exists as a network of relations of awareness connecting the body and the outside world. One might be tempted to equate the atman with the Sartrean consciousness, but such a comparison is misleading if carried very far. The Atman is definitely rooted in a true self far below the level of empirical consciousness. Coming closer to the *true* consciousness which is not knowing but being, one encounters first the consciousness of dreams, which for Vedanta as for Freud is in a curious sense closer to the truth of things. Then there is the consciousness of dreamless sleep. This seems to common sense a contradiction in terms. Interestingly enough, Socrates seems to have been attributing some form of consciousness to dreamless sleep in the passage in the *Apology* where he stated that a night of untroubled slumber would be preferable to all but a few of the waking days of even the supposedly fortunate great king of Persia. For Sartre, the dreaming consciousness is but an intensification of the imagining consciousness. As for a consciousness asleep and without dreams, one must, within the Sartrean context, say either that consciousness has continued to imagine its dreams but so nonreflectively that it cannot later remember them (which certain recent experiments would suggest to be the case) or that for brief moments in human existence consciousness intends no objects whatsoever. In this case, we should have to say that at this point the particular consciousness does not exist at all. Such a statement may seem at first to be preposterous, but it is no more so than the trite assertion that there is no seeing when the eyes are closed. Sight is not the eyes, and consciousness is not the brain cells. For Vedanta, however, that which a man *is* comes into its own precisely when the separation from empirical experience ends. The fourth state of consciousness is the realization by the Atman (the true self) that it is not separate from Brahman, that it *is* Brahman. The more subtle of Indian philosophers do not stop until even the individual's experience of union is surpassed, when instead of saying that Atman is Brahman, one would have to say (only there would be no one to say it) simply that Brahman is Brahman.

For humanistic existentialism, consciousness is nothing but an awareness of its objects, an awareness which always includes an implicit self-awareness of not being the object. Neither in sleep nor in death is there anything left that may withdraw and depart—either to Brahman or into another body. Clearly the doctrine of reincarnation demands that the individual consciousness is a being even if a separated, partial one; it cannot be the translucent process which is the Sartrean consciousness. One must choose here between humanistic existentialism and Vedanta. No amount of modification can reconcile them to one another without destroying what is essential to each. Existentialism, if it is to hold consistently to its own description of consciousness, must reject the theory of reincarnation even if empirical evidence is on principle unobtainable. Yet any myth that lives so long and appears in so many different settings as reincarnation must satisfy some kind of human demand. Kierkegaard and Unamuno have both had the courage—or the recklessness—to argue that the grandeur of man's need and the persistence of the longing for God and immortality are surer guides for men to live by than the Reason, which says No. Here humanistic existentialism sides rather with Freud, not hesitating to label vast areas of human aspirations as centered on nothing more than wish fulfillment. Sartre in *Being and Nothingness* views almost all of human enterprise as the mistaken attempt to be God as *Causa Sui*, at once necessary and contingent, free and yet secured. Christian immortality and reincarnation are similarly gigantic self-contradictory wish fulfillments.

It is easy to see how reincarnation satisfies the same demands as Christianity and in some ways does an even better job of it. In fact it answers so many difficulties that one might say, paraphrasing Voltaire on God, that if reincarnation did not exist, it would have to be invented. Like Christianity it affirms that this life is not all, and it satisfies our craving for ontological justice. At the end of all, there is ultimate Bliss for him who works to attain it. Moreover, unlike what happens in fundamentalist Christianity, Paradise awaits everyone. Each person is given as many chances as he needs. Ignorance and error may postpone the victory, but nobody ultimately loses. In addition, Eastern doctrine satisfies as well our desire for social justice. Obviously this world is unjust. The wicked prosper and the good die young—or wish they had. Christianity can console its faithful sufferers only with the thought that it will soon all be over, at which point the tables will be turned. The Indian doctrine of reincarnation holds that each man's status is one which his previous incarnation has merited. The myth consoles the unfortunate and soothes the guilt feelings of the prosperous, thus serving as one explanation as to how the rigid caste system could endure for so many generations. Here we have a metaphysics which would completely justify that strong feeling of Sartre's Serious Man and *les Salauds*—that some people come into the world with certain natural rights of superiority over others and are born into a preordained social niche. The reincarnation theory has fringe benefits as well. It reinstates us at the heart of nature, for we have been and may still be one with the rest of the animals. Possibly it ought to placate any lingering sense of guilt we may feel for our exploitation of the animal world. In India it has frequently resulted in an exaggerated reluctance to destroy any life, even that which is hostile to man. Theoretically, reincarnation offers to man a chance to have more and more of life, to which in general he clings as though he finds it good. Historically the doctrine has always been associated with world-weariness; future lives were to be avoided by getting off "the weary wheel of being." The actor grows tired of playing role after role and retires to his well-earned rest. To sum up, this wish-fulfilling myth declares that life and the world are not what they seem.

There is a way to leave them for something better and eternal. Best of all, our getting there depends on our own effort. While the thought of the reward bids us haste, we may have as much time as we require.

One need not be an existentialist or even a psychologist to arrive at the conclusion that reincarnation, like any other concept of immortality, has been invented to satisfy human longings. Existentialist psychology may add something more in the way of its own explanation for the rise and endurance of the theory. In part it appears to explain a fairly frequent phenomenon, the feeling of "having been through it all before" which occasionally comes to all of us. The ordinary explanation here is that the memory at this point is actually less accurate than usual, blurred rather than far-penetrating. Perhaps one small component of the scene is indeed repetitive, but we are unable to isolate and identify it. The feeling of familiarity is dislocated from its proper focus and falsely extended to the broader environment. Doubtless this frequently happens. It is possible also that on some occasions the explanation moves, as it were, from the other end. It may be that the attitude which consciousness is adopting toward its objects, its particular way of organizing the environment of its attention, is what is the familiar aspect and that one falsely assigns the feeling to the surrounding objects.

More important than the question of this sort of abnormal feeling for something unnatural is the relation between consciousness and its own past and future. E. R. Dodds in *The Greeks and the Irrational* argues, from a Freudian point of view, that the presence of the Unconscious may have been back of the development of the reincarnation myth. Since a person dimly but inadequately senses that he once experienced events and feelings which now are on principle cut off from him, which in a peculiar way have been a part of him, still influence him, yet are not *he*, he tries to express his sense of this mystery in the story that once he *was* another person in another life. Existentialism cannot rely on the concept of the Unconscious, but it may adopt Dodds's thesis to its own needs and premises. In bad faith a person represses those impulses which he prefers not to acknowledge and denies to himself the truth of his own intuitions. The unacknowledged awareness remains alive on the non-reflective level. We might go further. The Sartrean consciousness is always aware of not being its objects. Its emotions and actions are only its way of living its particular situation. Nevertheless if I am angry, I am not at that moment anything other than my anger. Thus although I never *am* my anger in the sense that my eyes are blue, still I *was* this anger. I *was* whatever state my consciousness has in the past become. Moreover, these outlived moments have not vanished. They live on as the psychic residue which forms the background for my new constitution of my situation and way of living it. Particularly, since I can never intend all of this psychic material at once and as a totality, there is a sense in which I carry the traces of my own avatars within me without ever being able to grasp them fully. If we accept the affirmation that man is free, then as a person projects what he chooses to become, he is aware of all of the other selves he might create if he were to choose differently. In *Steppenwolf*, Hermann Hesse has developed, in an imaginative experience strangely resembling reincarnation, this idea of all the potential selves which might have been and which might still be if a person were to satisfy all the demands clamoring for attention within him. Perhaps this realization that we mold our lives by a constant process of selection and exclusion may be back of the myth that, given infinite time, the same "Self" might take on various roles and destinies. The Sartrean consciousness, too, is not permanently one with the roles it plays. But, of course, there is no actor who remains when all the plays have been laid aside.

Possibly if we could have the Universe be whatever we wanted, some version of reincarnation would be the best thing to settle for. Yet even as a wish fulfillment, the theory involves an insurmountable contradiction. Once the chain of memory is broken, it is meaningless to speak of the *same* self as living in a succession of bodies. Even if it could be established that the same psychic—but not personal—entity had in actual fact dwelt in the body of Cleopatra and my own, we still cannot say that "I" was Cleopatra. The consciousness with the personality known as Cleopatra existed in psychic isolation as I do myself—in exactly the same way whether there has been reincarnation or not. Reincarnation and Christianity share the same difficulty. Immortality for us as we are now, with all our differentiating restrictions, would be intolerable. But if I am changed beyond recognition, then in what sense would it be "I" who would be present to enjoy either absorption or blissful contemplation of the presence of God? If it is simply consciousness as such which I prize, then I may be content to know that others will exist after my death— without any doctrine of immortality. But if it is I as myself who want to live on, the truth is that neither Christianity nor Vedanta can fulfill its promise of immortality. One may as well speak of the continued existence of the nitrogen in my body or of the indestructibility of its energy particles.

As compared with the Christian eschatology, reincarnation strikes me as more gentle and compassionate. I should think too, that it would find self-sacrifice easier. Without wanting to detract from the nobility of Gandhi and his followers, I am inclined to believe that nonresistance is less difficult when the prevailing thought is that one will have a chance at another life. By the same token, it leaves life less heroic. Christianity, of course, promises immediate bliss for the martyr, but it is harder to be sure that one will be among the Elect. I cannot see, however, that belief in reincarnation is intellectually any easier than Christian immortality for a person in our scientific age—or any harder. Both demand the supreme degree of faith and willingness to renounce the rational, scientific approach which has certainly been responsible for what we all call the positive achievements of civilization.

Here, of course, is exactly the point at which the Eastern philosopher presses his strongest claim. The personal experience of Enlightenment, attested by innumerable mystics all over the world and theoretically open to all who will honestly seek it, seems to stand as irrefutable proof—for those who have had it—that the rational approach is not the right one.

To argue against the empirical validity of an experience in which, say these witnesses, one *knows* and *is* the Truth absolutely and blissfully, seems hopeless. To accept it as evidence secondhand is equally difficult. The cleavage between mystics and nonmystics is possibly the most unbridgeable of all human dichotomies. Nevertheless, if we are resolved not to spend our lives seeking a revelation which those who have found it declare to be the only thing of true value, we ought to have some justification for our refusal—especially if we can offer no blissful certainties of our own.

Acknowledging that most claims of Enlightenment are not deliberately fraudulent and without dismissing them as obvious hallucinations, we may fairly ask just what the experience is and what it proves. William James took us a long way in *The Varieties of Religious Experience*. James demonstrated unequivocally that there is a common essence of all mystic experiences, whether they involve a sense that the individual consciousness is lost in a greater union or whether, more simply, there is merely the sense of the presence of, and one's own presence to, the supernatural. All involve an ineffable noetic quality. All appear to be something which happens to a person, to which he opens himself, not something which he actively effects. James adds other observations: Enlightenment is not limited to any particular religion or philosophy; what happens and the explanation of what happens are two different things. This statement would in no way disturb Indian Vedanta, which admits that there are many approaches to ultimate Reality, some more nearly adequate than others, and that any conceptualization of it is necessarily fragmentary and, at most, approximate. James's second restriction is more important, and I think that even he failed to see all of its consequences. After examining hundreds of testimonies, James concluded that the vast majority were of the optimistic, dynamogenic, expansive, pantheistic sort. There was a significant minority of exceptions. These were experiences of demonic possession or of desolation. Yet these too bore the same noetic stamp, the sense that "this is it and nothing else is as real or true." When noetic certainties contradict one another, what is the basis for asserting the validity of one against another?

In the decades since James wrote, there have been attempts to investigate the mystic experience scientifically by the use of hallucinogenic drugs. One may smile at the inevitability of this—that the West, too impatient to reach Nirvana by ascetic contemplation and a lifetime of seeking, would attempt to do it quickly with synthetic chemicals. Nevertheless, one cannot fairly dismiss the results as not being relevant to the study of Oriental attainment of Nirvana or Satori without drugs. On the whole, it is the believers in the validity of the mystic experience who have hastened to claim the evidence for their side. Aldous Huxley, one of many, argues in *The Doors of Perception* that peyote or mescaline may "open the sluices" to a realm of consciousness normally inaccessible. For Huxley, mescaline simply performs more effectively the ancillary services traditionally rendered by fasting and other self-disciplinary devices to prepare one for the expansion of consciousness. American Indians have used both peyote and sacred mushrooms in religious services. Laboratory scientists have produced a comparable but far more powerful drug in LSD (lysergic acid diethylamide) which both psychologists and lay public have experimented with for their separate purposes.

In reading the accounts of those who have taken the hallucinogenic drugs I am impressed by two things. First, the subject tends to find in the experience that which he expects to find; more accurately, what he experiences is harmonious with, even a crystallization of, the metaphysical hypothesis, formulated or unformulated, by which he lives his daily life. Those whose basic orientation may properly be described as religious will ultimately, if they try long enough, achieve a sense of union or oneness or expansion or presence which qualifies as a religious experience. Sceptics who resolve to take the drugs as a kind of scientific experiment usually have one of two reactions. Either with mingled feelings of disappointment and "I told you so," they experience nothing at all out of the ordinary; or frequently they do testify to the feeling of being far removed from familiar reality, but they are possessed by a sort of ecstatic hilarity, finding everything inexplicably funny. Here I cannot help feeling that the response is dictated by the subject's private belief that he is engaged in an absurdity by his very decision to partake in the experiment. Many people seem to encounter simply an intensification of their immediate psychological difficulties, living in an acute form experiences of alienation, depersonalization, depression, paranoia—in short, the whole gamut of the pathological. In rare cases the aftereffects of LSD have been to precipitate schizophrenia, which apparently had been latent before the taking of the drug. From this point of view, the conclusion seems inescapable that the "truth" of the experience is the truth of the experiencer. As a self-revelation it has some value, and this is probably one of the reasons why hallucinogenic drugs have been helpful in psychotherapy.

The second thing that impresses me is that, regardless of the extravagant claims of believers, and aside from the question of why the abnormal states of consciousness occur, they seem, when carefully examined, to have very little to do with any significant revelation of external truth. Peyote indisputably plays tricks on the nervous system. However interesting the visual and olfactory hallucinations may be, they remain illusions. The bursts of color, the strange shadows, are not revelations of an objective reality either material or nonmaterial. At most, one learns to see the beauty of color and form in common objects usually ignored, a lesson which the artist may give us in a different way. Often under the drug's influence, the person is aware of the subjective quality of what he perceives. Sometimes the illusion is altogether compelling. These flights of fancy are not the important part of the experience for persons who eat their peyote with religious intent. Those who are convinced that a higher truth is actually attained in such nonrational experiments will, of course, argue that the hallucinations are but the side effects of the peyote. Yet I can see no reason for attributing ultimate truth to the accompanying attitudes—the sense of euphoria, the benign, nonerotic love and concern for others, or the less common feeling that one is in a significant way closer to truth and God. The nausea, the loss of motor control, the total relaxation, and the somewhat frightening feeling that one is in some way overcome by a stronger force are physical. One's imagination may enter in to bestow on them a spiritual value, but I cannot believe that this is intrinsic to the experience. A heightened sense of reality is not the same as the revelation of a higher truth. Laboratory tests have indicated that subjects who thought they were seeing colors more intensely were actually below their own average in distinguishing gradations of color. Accounts written under the influence of the hallucinogens may have glowed with lyric intensity in the minds of the authors engaged in writing them. To the sober reader they were chaotic, unoriginal, void of intellectual insight, and undistinguished artistically.

Takers of hallucinogenic drugs and mystics who have attained enlightenment without artificial aids are alike in insisting that the essential quality of the significant experience cannot be conveyed accurately in words or even reconstructed precisely by the recollecting imagination. This is true to a degree, of course, of any sensation or feeling. Too often, however, I think that those who report the experience confuse the remembered sense of value and intensity of feeling with self-evident objective truth or reality. But intensity of pleasure and a sense of fulfillment do not of necessity point to anything beyond themselves. Take as an example these quotations from a passage in which Huxley is describing his reactions to mescaline.

Confronted by a chair which looked like the Last Judgement—or, to be more accurate, by a Last Judgement which, after a long time and with considerable difficulty, I recognized as a chair—I found myself all at once on the brink of panic. This, I suddenly felt, was going too far. Too far, even though the going was into intenser beauty, deeper significance. The fear, as I analyze it in retrospect, was of being overwhelmed, of disintegration under a pressure of reality greater than a mind, accustomed to living most of the time in a cozy world of symbols could possibly bear. . . .

228

None too soon, I was steered away from the disquieting splendours of my garden chair. Drooping in green parabolas from the hedge, the ivy fronds shone with a kind of glassy, jade-like radiance. A moment later a clump of Red Hot Pokers, in full bloom, had exploded into my field of vision. So passionately alive that they seemed to be standing on the very brink of utterance, the flowers strained upwards into the blue. Like the chair under the laths, they protested too much. I looked down at the leaves and discovered a cavernous intricacy of the most delicate green lights and shadows, pulsing with undecipherable mystery. . . .

We walked out into the street. A large pale blue automobile was standing at the curb. At the sight of it, I was suddenly overcome by enormous merriment. What complacency, what an absurd self-satisfaction beamed from those bulging surfaces of glossiest enamel! Man had created the thing in his own image—or rather in the image of his favorite character in fiction. I laughed till the tears ran down my cheeks.[4]

Some time later, Huxley reports, he "returned to that reassuring but profoundly unsatisfactory state known as 'being in one's right mind.' "

The scorn of the concluding sentence attests to the value which Huxley placed on the extraordinary state of mind. To be sure, this is not the ultimate ecstasy of final union. Yet clearly Huxley regards it as a revelation of truth or an encounter with reality which is on an entirely different level from the self-indulgent dreams of the man who eats hashish. If we look at the passage carefully, I think we can distinguish two components in the experience—although obviously there was no awareness of any such separation as Huxley lived it. First, there is clearly distinguishable an overlay of Huxley's recognizable individual personality, interpreting his perceptions and sensations; beneath this we can detect a direct confrontation by consciousness with the world, independent of the more personal subjectivity. The perception of the car, however pleasant the merriment it evoked, is comfortably within the world of symbols and of Huxley's own concepts. The object is in no way seen for itself; it is all but lost in the

[4] Aldous Huxley: *The Doors of Perception* (New York: Harper and Brothers; 1954), pp. 55 and 59–60.

idea which Huxley wraps around it. Significantly this episode occurred fairly late when the effects of the mescaline were beginning to wear off. In describing the earlier encounter with the chair and the flowers, Huxley attempts to distinguish between the direct experience and his later explanation of what he was feeling. I think we may grant the existence of a certain quality of revelation in Huxley's new perception of objects. Due to the drug, things are not seen in their usual relations, subordinated to our habitual patterns of perceiving objects always in relation to our own purposes. Things appear now in their otherness, their quality of simply being there, independent of our presence, forever non-unabsorbable and not fully comprehended. As such, they threaten the habitual attitudes of consciousness. Since these ordinary ways of seeing are felt to be so much a part of us, the personalized everyday consciousness feels threatened with disintegration. This seems to be a common ingredient of such ecstasies, whether drug-induced or not. This part of the experience Huxley conveys to us so that we can grasp its reality separate from his interpretation. Just barely. The peculiarly Huxleyan attitude colors the description in recollection, and clearly the immediate experience too was not entirely unqualified by Huxley's predispositions. He is perhaps right in analyzing the fear he had felt, and at this point he recognizes what is after the event. But the seeing of the chair as a "Last Judgement," the over-all sense of beauty and mystery, in particular the expression "they [the flowers] seemed to be standing on the very brink of utterance"—these point to the inward subjective side of the moment's realization. In short, whether we choose to say that the perceptions of chair and flowers were more or less objective than usual, they still retain a subjective side.

I think it is fair at this point to make use of the account of Jean-Paul Sartre's experiment with mescaline. Sartre took the drug at the suggestion of a psychiatrist friend who knew of Sartre's interest in anomolies of perception. At the time, Sartre had been feeling somewhat depressed about his situation as a teacher at Havre and his status as a still unrecognized writer. His friend had warned him that the experience might be somewhat disagreeable. It was. De Beauvoir has described the episode.[5] Sartre did not have hallucinations of the sort which claimed to be objectively real. He was aware that what he seemed to see was without materiality, was not "really there." Yet he was not able to prevent the pseudo-perceptions from appearing, nor could he banish them at will. It seemed to him that objects turned into monstrous shapes—umbrellas into vultures, shoes into skeletons, while roundabout swarmed crabs and octopuses. For some months afterward, Sartre found himself frequently troubled by such visions —by houses with grimacing faces, covered with eyes and open jaws, by a black spot dancing in the air before him, by marine creatures that seemed to follow him. So vivid were they that Sartre was terrified lest someday he would suddenly believe in them at last and fall hopelessly insane. In this account, I am sure that nobody would claim that there is an encounter with any reality other than that of Sartre's inner psyche. The obnoxious images were vivid projections in symbolic form of Sartre's anxious sense of being engulfed in the trappings of the bourgeois world, the situation he has described so vividly in his autobiographical novel *Nausea*. Apparently Sartre's experience was fully as intense as Huxley's, more hallucinatory, and still more completely personalized by the subject's own outlook. We find in it no trace of a nonpersonal encounter with objects simply as they are.

If we look at *Nausea*, which Sartre had begun writing at the time he took the mescaline, we may discover several reminiscences of that event. Sartre has, of course, adapted them to his own novelistic purpose, and most of them are interesting primarily as indicating the literary genesis of the book. Such, for instance, is the description of Roquentin looking at the configuration of his own hand, finding it strange and inexplicable, feeling it might suddenly turn into something else—into a crab, for instance. Roquentin's "horrible ecstasy" in the park is more significant, and I believe that it

[5] Simone de Beauvoir: *La Force de l'âge* (Paris: Gallimard; 1960), pp. 216 ff.

echoes rather specifically the mescaline experience. Since this scene is of obvious importance in the expression of Sartre's view of the world and of consciousness, the parallel means something. Certainly we find in it that common ingredient which I mentioned in connection with the Huxley passage. Its essence is a confrontation with existing things—directly, not in the usual conceptual framework where things are only instruments, obstacles, or neutral background for our projects.

Roquentin begins this entry in his diary by remarking that, like most people, he habitually spoke of things as existing without ever fully realizing what such existence meant. When he thought of things as *being*, he implicitly thought of them as belonging. "I told myself that the sea belonged to the class of green objects or that green was part of the qualities of the sea." Sitting in the park, Roquentin encountered existents stripped of the veneer with which words and usage had cloaked them. Like Huxley, he finds their existence too forceful, too specific, too unclassifiable. Was the root "a serpent or a claw or a root or a vulture's talon"? In any case it hardly mattered.

It was useless to repeat, 'This is a root.' It wouldn't do any longer. I saw clearly that you couldn't move from its function as a root, as a suction pump, *to that*—to that hard, tight seal skin, to that oily, horny, stubborn look. Function didn't explain anything, it allowed you to understand in general that it was a root but not *this*.

And again:

I didn't simply *see* it as black. Sight is an abstract invention, a stripped simplified idea, a human idea. That black there, an amorphous flabby presence, overflowed far beyond the boundaries of sight, smell, and taste. But this richness turned into confusion, and finally it wasn't anything any longer because it was too much.[6]

[6] Sartre: *Nausea*, pp. 164 and 166.

We remember Huxley's "they protested too much." A bit later we find a kind of fear at this encounter, not quite like the fear which Huxley reported, but reminiscent of it.

How long will this fascination last? I *was* the root of the chestnut tree. Or rather, I was entirely a consciousness of its existence. Still detached from it, since I was conscious of it and yet lost in it, nothing else but it. An uneasy consciousness, which yet let itself go to hang with all its weight over this piece of inert wood. Time had stopped—a little black pool at my feet. It was impossible for anything to come *after* that moment. I would have liked to tear myself away from that atrocious agonizing possession, but I did not even imagine that this was possible. I was inside. The black trunk *did not pass on*, it stayed there in my eyes, like a large lump caught in my throat. I could neither accept nor reject it.[7]

Where does all this lead us? To begin with, we have another example of the point made earlier—that the quality and significance of the abnormal state of consciousness depends on the subject, that any immediate revelation of truth is the truth of the perceiver. One is entitled to prefer Huxley's gaiety to Sartre's horror—or Roquentin's. This does not by itself justify Huxley's metaphysics. What interests me more is the fact of the common ingredient and the probable reason for it.

I do not pretend to know the physiological explanation of the mescaline visions though I suspect that dilated pupils, by altering the usual visual process, have something to do with it. There may be also some disturbance of habitual brain synapses as there is certainly interference with ordinary motor connections. The important point is that because one's usual responses do not rush to prevent it, the original encounter of consciousness with the world takes place, stripped of the overlay of associations—or at least more nearly so than is normally possible. (This escape from conceptual habits may come about as the result of fasting, systematic contemplation, exercises in concentration, or a number of other causes as

[7] Ibid., p. 167.

well as through drugs.) Sartre and Huxley are alike in emphasizing two aspects of this encounter. First there is the realization that the object somehow overflows all that we can grasp of it whether through the senses or by mental concept. Something is always left over and is forever not absorbed by our consciousness. It remains alien, heavy. Because it resists our attempts to make it part of us, its reality seems greater than our own. Both men emphasize, too, the sense of a threat to consciousness, that consciousness might in some way disintegrate or be annihilated if it fully acknowledged this real Outside. At this point the explanations differ as do the respective philosophies and psychologies.

For Huxley—and for Vedanta—it is all a matter of levels of truth. One could almost say layers. Our ordinary view of things is a limitation and thereby to some degree a falsification. The Being of things is something more and other than they seem. Transcendent to them as well as immanent in them is an eternal nonmaterial reality, manifesting itself in cosmic play. What impedes our coming closer to it is our individualized consciousness, which we falsely take to be an ultimate center, without which we feel we would be nothing at all. Thus the fear Huxley explains in the passage quoted is, from his standpoint, both justified and mistaken. Consciousness, as the individual knows it, might in fact disintegrate if one opened oneself freely to Reality. But the disintegration would be a transformation into something much greater, which would include the individual consciousness but without its personalizing restrictions. Borrowing from Tibetan metaphors, Huxley often speaks of ultimate Reality as a bright light and of the individual consciousness as a self-restricting clot, refusing participation in the light.

Sartrean existentialism, although still in the Cartesian tradition, offers no reassuring theory of rational spirit confronting clearly delineated portions of material extension. In fact, a superficial reading of Sartre's "Introduction" in *Being and Nothingness* might easily seem to put him closer to the idealistic Eastern doctrine of Maya than to Descartes's dualism. Existentialism, if it is to explain abnormal states, whether or not we call them mystic, and if it rejects the explanation offered by the Perennial Philosophy, must ground both explanation and refusal on its theory of the nature of consciousness and the outside world and their relation to each other. We have touched on this problem on several occasions. It is time now for us to confront it head-on.

Sartre himself, of course, believes that his theory of Being and Nothingness strikes the proper balance between realism and idealism, avoiding the difficulties of both views. Critics have accused him of falling over on one side or the other. A. J. Ayer amusingly criticizes him for being on both sides of the fence. Ayer says that Sartre's theory is really (apparently without Sartre's knowing it) a kind of realism comparable to that of Bertrand Russell. Objects are groups of sensibilia existing independently of any actual perceiver. Then he claims that Sartre goes too far in the direction of idealism. Sartre, in Ayer's view, confuses the *discovery* of relations between outside objects with the *existence* of these relations. To discover them is the proper function of a consciousness, to create or bring them into existence is not. There is an obvious inconsistency in Ayer's attack. If Sartre's theory really postulates the separate and independent existence of groups of sensibilia, then he is not sustaining a view which makes objective existence depend on consciousness. I will grant, however, that Sartre's philosophical language varies, depending on the purpose he has in mind when he discusses the outside world. Here, I believe, lies the explanation of Ayer's contention, although in all fairness I do not think that Ayer was making any great effort to understand what Sartre really did mean.[8]

When Sartre writes abstractly on the fundamentals of his ontology, he states definitely that Being-in-itself is a plenitude, is undifferentiated mass. When he discusses man's concrete existence in the world, he implies the independent existence of separate portions of Being—e.g., the sun and moon—to which we attach a purely human significance via our pro-

[8] A. J. Ayer: "Novelist-Philosophers V: Jean-Paul Sartre," *Horizon*, Vol. XII (1945), pp. 12–26 and 101–10.

jects. If the two kinds of statements are reconcilable, we must find our point of departure in the abstract formulation.

Everything hinges on Sartre's concept of "the transphenomenality of Being." Sartre is faithful to phenomenology when he insists that whatever becomes the object of a consciousness is exactly what it appears to be; that is, there is no underlying substance or anything hidden which supports its apparent qualities. Yet as we are aware of the outside world, we are aware that it *is*, we are aware of its being. In other words, there is a phenomenon or appearance of Being itself to consciousness, which causes us to postulate the transphenomenality of Being. By this obscure term, Sartre refers to the inexhaustibility of the appearances of the object. Perception does not use up an object. There is always something left over. Neither any one awareness nor any sum of awarenesses, however large, could take in all of an object. Furthermore, consciousness of the object or of Being always implies a separation. Consciousness is not the object. Consciousness never becomes Being-in-itself.

We can easily see how Sartre's view suggests and yet is different from Kant's. As with Kant, there is no objective knowledge or perception unmodified by the consciousness of the knower or perceiver. The thing-in-itself is outside our awareness of it. Kant, however, in speaking of the thing-in-itself, constantly implies that if the human mind were perfect, there *could* be a knowledge of what a thing *is* in itself. Something is there which the limited forms of our mind prevent us from grasping without alteration. Knowledge is what is limited. Thus the world of appearances is to some extent a world of illusions even though the illusions are shared by all humanity. The true world exists and may be legitimately introduced as the subject matter of our regulative hypotheses. Sartrean existentialism rejects the idea that an object is *anything other* than it appears. Nevertheless we do not absorb its appearances, and in this way it is something more than any of its appearances-to-date. It points beyond them. Sartre states that the lemon is the yellow color, the roundness, the acid taste, etc. We might say that Being *is* its own transphenomenality.

Practically, the transphenomenality of Being is experienced as a consciousness's awareness of the existence of something outside which is not itself and which it can neither create nor annihilate. A consciousness may, through the body, effect modifications in that which is outside, but it cannot prevent there being an outside. Nor can it prevent itself from being in a definite position relative to that which is outside.

But if things *are* their appearances, how can Sartre insist as he does, that without consciousness, Being-in-itself is as undifferentiated as it is without significance? Certainly this is what one would assume Sartre means when he says that all one can truthfully say of Being-in-itself is that it is and that it is itself.

The dangerous step here is to conclude that Sartre's refusal to ascribe original differentiation and significance to Being-in-itself is equivalent to saying that Being-in-itself is all one and all the same. To introduce concepts of unity and sameness is to do violence to what Being-in-itself is, fully as much as notions of multiplicity and variation do. If we do not guard against taking this step, then in truth the borderline between Sartre's thought and Eastern idealism is tenuous indeed, if not altogether nonexistent. The doctrine that everyday reality is "Maya" does not, as has been popularly supposed in the West, mean that the world of matter is unreal as we might say that a mirage is unreal—i.e., nonexistent. Maya, the root meaning of which denotes "making" and is closely related to the word for "measure," refers to the superficial organization of a reality which is primarily, ultimately, and more significantly, something else. One may think of a blackboard on which someone has drawn chalk patterns. What is the board? The board is not the patterns although it supports them and they could not exist without such support. One may, of course, become interested in the patterns to the exclusion of the board, but this is to lose sight of the question, to invert the idealist view of the order of importance and of reality both. Although any analogy might break down, perhaps a metaphor for Sartrean Being-in-itself might be a many-textured, stained, cracked wall. Anyone contemplating it might form relations and patterns of many kinds—mentally or by using chalk. One could with equal accuracy state either that the cracks, the variations in texture or color existed by themselves prior to and independent of a perceiver, or that the wall was a meaningless, undefined expanse until a perceiver (or perceivers) selected and defined the particular connections which the variegated surface allowed. There is a world of difference between the two positions which I have roughly tried to contrast in these crude figures. The first (the Eastern) suggests the placing of a fragile cut-out pattern or a play of lights over a smooth, undifferentiated expanse; it claims that the expanse alone is enduring and fundamental. The second suggests a resistant but still malleable material which allows an infinity of patterns to be traced upon it but which is never anything other than the actuality of present patterns and the potentiality for others. Even in *Being and Nothingness*, Sartre speaks of the material world as offering a "coefficient of resistance" to consciousness. In the section on "Transcendence" he points out that only a temporal consciousness can see the half moon as a *half* moon—i.e., as a lack rather than as a full mass of matter of a certain shape. Sartre does not deny that the perception of this solid piece of matter rather than some other —or nothing at all—depends on something more than the subjective intention of consciousness. At the same time, we may acknowledge that a conscious species with mental and sensory capacities might effect totally different organizations which would be neither more true nor more false than our own, although they might be more or less effective in furthering the purposes of those responsible for them. The world of science is still a product of consciousness even though it is—at least in intention—the product of a consciousness which holds itself solely within the reflective mode rather than the imaginary. Different organizations are always possible. What seems fixed may be due to the material "coefficient of resistance." Possibly all that is needed is hitherto untried synapses in the brain. It is for this reason that Sartre claims that existentialism offers the most thoroughgoing atheism that the world has known—because the order of the Universe is the pattern which man has put there as his mind has worked with the meaningless chaos around him.

Being and Nothingness stressed particularly the part played by consciousness in ordering experience. In the *Critique of Dialectical Reason*, published almost twenty years later, Sartre gave more emphasis to the world of which we are conscious. In this book Being-in-itself and Being-for-itself are barely mentioned. They are replaced by two other terms, "praxis" and the "pratico-inerte," which, while not synonyms, perform much the same function. "Praxis" refers to any purposeful human activity and is closely related to the "project" which held so important a place in *Being and Nothingness*. The chief difference is that (in the second work) Sartre is particularly concerned to show the way in which individual praxis is continually blocked, frustrated, and deviated by the structures of the outside world. It is here that we meet the "pratico-inerte." "Hell is the pratico-inerte," Sartre declares, a remarkable departure from the early statement in *No Exit*, that "Hell is others." The pratico-inerte includes those human structures in which one's free project is entrapped—institutions, communication systems, the formal rules of language, contemporary connotations of words, etc. Sartre gives full weight, too, to the natural world —to physical space and the terrain, to climate, to the presence or absence of natural resources. He suggests surprisingly that it is even possible that there exists some sort of dialectic in nature though at present we do not have enough knowledge to support either a strong affirmation or a denial. On one point he is emphatic. The world "steals my action from me." As I act to carry out my project, it is as though I "inscribed myself in matter." Matter may evoke from my action a "counter finality," as a result for which I am responsible but which I had neither intended nor wanted.

In *Being and Nothingness* Sartre argued that "destruction" is a human concept and would have no meaning, could not even exist without consciousness. In the *Critique* he says that it is legitimate to speak of minerals (e.g., the presence or absence of coal) as provoking or demanding certain historical events. Superficial reading might see in this a shift from extreme idealism to an almost naïve anthropomorphism endowing inorganic nature with life and purpose. Yet if we read carefully, we find that Sartre is quite consistent, and I think that the *Critique* bolsters and clarifies the interpretation of Being-in-itself which I believe to be the correct one in all of Sartre's writing on that subject.

Sartre begins the discussion of destruction with a passage which many have taken as proof of the idealistic character of his ontology.

In a sense, certainly, man is the only being by whom a destruction can be accomplished. A geographical plication, a storm do not destroy—or at least they do not destroy *directly;* they merely modify the distribution of masses of beings. There is no *less* after the storm than before. There is *something else.* Even this expression is improper, for to posit otherness there must be a witness who can retain the past in some manner and compare it to the present in the form of *no longer.* In the absence of this witness, there is being before as after the storm—that is all.[9]

I have never been able to understand how people could interpret this passage as indicating that nothing occurs without a consciousness or that consciousness is responsible for the existence of natural phenomena. Sartre states explicitly that there is a modification in "the distribution of masses of beings." Mere movement or change does not constitute the breaking or destroying of a form unless someone has established the form as such. The flow of water or the movement of clouds do not involve destruction until someone has isolated patterns of ripples or cloud shapes. If what was declared to look like a bull is seen to disappear and give way to the form of an octopus, then, I suppose, one may say that the bull has been destroyed. Later in the same paragraph, Sartre

[9] Sartre, *Being and Nothingness,* p. 8.

states in so many words that "destruction, although coming into being through man, is an *objective fact* and not a thought." What he seems to mean is that, strictly speaking, there cannot be destruction without negation and temporality, both of which depend on consciousness. Yet the possibility of eliciting a negation must be inherent in the object. There is, Sartre adds, "a transphenomenality of non-being as of being." It seems obvious to me that even here where Sartre is arguing that the activity of consciousness must be present before there is meaning or significance or ordered discrimination, he does not postulate homogeneous matter as the proper description of a world without consciousness.

That this is the correct interpretation seems to me borne out by examination of the *Critique*. Our problem here is the reverse of that suggested by "destruction." If the presence of gold "provokes," or if the lack of rain "demands" certain human action, this is a realistic recognition that specific aspects or parts of "Being-in-itself" exist independently of any consciousness. Yet clearly, too, the yellow metal could never by itself "provoke action." It is only when it has been wrapped with human significations that its presence or absence becomes distinguishable from that of ordinary rocks. We never, Sartre says, encounter matter as matter except by artificial mental abstraction. "Consciousness is always consciousness *of* something." If that of which it is conscious were homogeneous unity, then where would consciousness derive its own experience? For there is nothing *in* consciousness.

I think there is no concept in Sartre's philosophy more difficult than that of a consciousness which bestows meaning and significance on a chaotic world, a consciousness which is absolutely free and unique, which is separated (psychically) from all that of which it is conscious, and which is finally defined as distinguished from the rest of reality precisely by Nothing! Just *what* is consciousness and *where* is it?

The question of just *what* consciousness is remains hard to answer—even if we resolve to accept Sartre as final authority and have read all that he has written. Consciousness cannot, I believe (Sartre has never said so specifically), be identified with simple awareness; in that case, we could not distinguish between human and other animals. It is imperative that we do so, for otherwise the assertion that consciousness is free and that for this reason human nature is not fixed would fall by weight of common-sense observation. Animal consciousness is clearly not free, and there seems to be every reason to associate instinctual living with fixed characteristics of the species. Can we then define Sartrean consciousness as an awareness which necessarily includes an element of self-awareness? This is true to Sartre's intention and distinguishes man from the rest of Nature in so far as we know it. We cannot stop here. What is the relation between human being, consciousness, and Being-for-itself? At times Sartre writes of them as if they were identical. Certainly they are so inextricably united that to use any one of the terms implies the presence of the other two. I do not think they are synonyms. Being-for-itself may be equated with the human person, which—to paraphrase the description applied to the Stoic Universe—may be equally well described as body infused with consciousness or consciousness invested with body. We must remind ourselves that it is as important in connection with Sartre as it was with the Stoics to avoid all suspicion of dualism. The human being, as a For-itself, is still a part of Being, but he is that part which is characterized by the peculiar quality of being able to effect a psychic withdrawal, to introduce a cleavage or Nothingness into Being, to take a point of view on Being. We may say correctly that man is both Being and Nothingness, since it is he who brings Nothingness into the world. At the same time it would be wrong to claim that the Body is Being, and Consciousness the Nothingness. Consciousness is the process of introducing the Nothingness, of assuming the point of view. One cannot say that it is itself Nothing. It is the awareness of an object, along with an implicit awareness of not-being-the-object. These are, of course, not two separate states but a single intention with dual aspect. The best comparison perhaps is with *seeing*. Seeing is neither the object nor the light waves nor the rods and cones nor the brain cells. Seeing is always seeing *of* something, but it is not what it sees. The obvious difference is that whereas the dots of color, etc., which one may "see" with the eyes closed is of almost no significance, consciousness may find its objects in the body itself, in the rearrangement of its own earlier impressions, and in the invention of new ones via fresh brain synapses. The body may exist without consciousness for a short time after death, but it is noteworthy that we do not consider a corpse to be any longer a person or truly human. Thus the body both is and is not consciousness. It does not *have* a consciousness nor does consciousness *have* a body. Alive, the body is that through which consciousness effects its negations, thus standing apart from Being, and assumes a point of view. To have a body and to be a consciousness are one and the same for Sartre, who prefers to say that "consciousness *exists* the body." If consciousness appears to be characterized by certain regular structures, this is because the body is its means of relating itself to the object, without which consciousness could not exist. The fact that consciousness can take a point of view on its body indicates that in one sense it is *not* the body. For the point of view which consciousness takes on the body involves a degree of separation which consciousness can never attain in trying to reflect on itself. Yet pain or discomfort sometimes, and other sensations always—even vague visceral sensations and that slight sense of nausea which Sartre identifies with the taste of one's own mouth—these are inescapable accompaniments of all consciousness and indicate sufficiently that consciousness is a function of the body even if it is not to be identified with it any more than seeing is. Thus consciousness is a process which transcends its origin and its base of support as it transcends its objects—whether they are external and material things or physiological stimuli or the mental constructs of consciousness itself. Since consciousness is not an entity, it cannot be identified with body or viewed as a thing. Since it is a process which depends on a being—i.e., both body and the outside world—it is always localized as a point of view. Thus it is particularized and isolated. It is an *individual* consciousness because it is a process that must have a fixed and finite point from which it makes itself a point of view and a relating. Yet it is never determined by its past or present objects because—as a process—it is the constant setting up of a nothingness between itself and its objects.

After this long digression, we may return to the question of what happens in mystic or abnormal states of consciousness when the ordinary sense of self and outside world are strikingly transformed. Psychosis and milder mental illnesses pose no special theoretical problem. Diagnosis and treatment often may be radically different from conventional Freudian therapy with its use of the hypothesis of the Unconscious and its biological determinism. The basic assumption that the patient lives in a world dominated by fantasies because he feels incapable of confronting the real world remains true for all psychotherapy. Differences arise in appraising the degree to which the sufferer was responsible for choosing to escape and in judging the extent to which it is legitimate to distinguish the "real world" from the private world. Hypnosis might seem at first to be an insurmountable obstacle to the hypothesis of a free consciousness. Yet all that happens here is that a person wills—i.e., he *chooses* to regard the hypnotist's suggestions as absolute, even to the point of refusing to allow himself to be aware later of which suggestions have come from the hypnotist. Proof lies in the well-known fact that a person cannot be hypnotized against his will nor compelled to do something violently conflicting with his strong beliefs and moral code. I think the line of thought leading from consideration of hypnosis is a profitable one. Mystic states and such drug experiences as lay claim to noetic insight stress one or all of these things: that the sense of self is partly or wholly lost in a higher power or consciousness; that the physical world is all one and the subject coextensive with it; that material objects are overpoweringly real and incomprehensible; that pseudo-perceptions, which one intellectually knows "not to be there" are nevertheless present and uncontrollable; that time and space are altered or eliminated; that one understands "the truth about oneself" in a way no ordinary reflection could reveal.

Vedanta, William James, Freud, Sidney Cohen in his account of work with LSD—in fact, every writer I have encountered outside existentialism has assumed that these reactions must be accounted for by a hypothesis involving the bringing in of material usually contained within the Unconscious, if not from outside the person entirely. Some "opening of the sluices" is involved. James asserted, as the one bit of absolute knowledge we have of these baffling phenomena, our certainty that at least the near side of the experience is via the subliminal—or the unconscious. Sartre denies the Unconscious and insists that the very essence of consciousness involves at least an implicit self-consciousness. Obviously we confront a major difficulty and must—at the very least—prove that it is only that and not an insurmountable obstacle.

Since the problem of the loss of self, real or illusory, is the most knotty, we had best begin with this. It is easy to understand how the feeling that loss is imminent can be regarded as either threat or promise. All depends on the frame of mind of the one who experiences it, both how happy he is in his habitual personality and what his philosophical orientation holds to be the possible alternative to first-person-singular personal existence. Even within the framework of Vedanta, the seeker must overcome the tempting joys of individual existence just as the Christian must learn by painful struggle to recognize the worldly pleasures as the inferior shams which they are. In the passages from Huxley and Sartre, we saw that both Huxley and Sartre-Roquentin felt this fear of disintegration. To Huxley, the fear was balanced by the thought that greater reality and beauty accompanied the threat. For the atheist, disintegration of the separate consciousness denotes simple annihilation. But how in existentialist terms can we account for this sense of slipping away—let alone the feeling that one's consciousness has been expanded beyond the limits of the self to the point where the self as such does not exist?

It is important to be precisely clear as to what we mean by the word "self." Usually, at least in everyday terms and in psychological treatises, the term includes—if it is not limited to—the ego and the whole complex of personality structures which serve to differentiate one person from another in the judgment of others as well as in his own sense of being a separate creature. Even if psychotherapy induces in someone a new appraisal of this psychic material and a desire to modify it, the highly personalized self is what is meant in such expressions as self-understanding, self-analysis, or self-improvement. On this hypothesis, while the means by which it is accomplished remains obscure, we can easily conceive that a new self-awareness might exist in which all that had been recognized as an intrinsic part of the Self would be transcended and that a person might in his imagination regard the usual "Self" as totally alien or even forgotten. I maintain, in the face of all mystic assertions to the contrary, that even this exalted state is still a self-consciousness. If, as so many witnesses among mystics and drug experimenters have attested, I have the feeling of having left my usual Self behind, then clearly there is a new "I," contrasting itself with a former one in the same way that the adult views the child as a being which he was but is no longer. If ecstasy advances to the point of forgetfulness of the Past, when all that exists (or seems to) is awareness of being part of a greater awareness, there is still a self-awareness of Union. The final state of *Turiya*, according to Indian sages, transcends even the awareness of Union. One *is* Brahman so completely that one is no longer an Atman conscious of having been transformed into Brahman. I confess to never having reached this peak myself. Nothing I have read about it convinces me that self-consciousness, in Sartre's sense of *conscience* (*de*) *soi*, has been lost. Either of two things must be true. Either all awareness is lost, but this alternative is contrary to what has been written about the experience and would be equivalent to fainting or death if it did occur; or else we have a different sort of awareness. The experience is usually reported in terms suggesting sensation rather than thought. I do not mean sensation as a classifiable reaction to stimulus by any or all of the usual five senses. It seems to be rather a generalized feeling of intense euphoria, suggesting orgasm perhaps, but more accurately described as the positive equivalent of over-whelming pain, the kind that urgently blots out the possibil-ity of reflection so that for the moment one *is* the pain. Yet there is an implicit awareness of awareness. Even if we often find such expressions as "Time stopped" or "Only the imme-diate awareness existed," there are always telltale traces of the sense that "there is" an experience.

In Roquentin's abnormal fascination with the chestnut root, Sartre distinguishes carefully between the loose and easy formulation of what happens and the precise one. Ro-quentin says, "I *was* the root of the chestnut tree. Or rather, I was entirely a consciousness of its existence. Still detached from it, since I was conscious of it—and yet lost in it, nothing else but it." Of course Roquentin's ecstasy is lower down in the mystical hierarchy than the ultimate achievement of Nir-vana. But I think Sartre has put the essence of the matter in the words, "I was entirely a consciousness of . . ." and "I was *nothing else* but it."

We may tie together this somewhat discursive discussion by considering exactly what happens—in Vedanta terms and in existentialist—in the ecstasy (or ekstasis) which means, in experience as well as in its etymological origin, a standing out of (Self). For Eastern thought a buried separated fragment has emerged from the Self like a butterfly from a chrysalis. Since individual consciousness *was* the Self, any new, less restricted awareness is without a sense of self and is no longer even called consciousness. We are left with an ultimate mys-tery—how a fragment of an undivided eternal consciousness could ever become associated with the empirical individual consciousness. If we take the Sartrean view of consciousness, the situation is quite different. To start with, the individual consciousness is not to be identified with the personality structure. Thus one cannot say that consciousness *is* the self. Nor does consciousness *have* a self in the form of a finished entity which can be possessed. Sartre speaks of the self as that which is pursued but not finally attained so long as consciousness lives. From one point of view, it is hardly distinguishable from the Ego. The Ego (both the "I" and the

247

"me") is a psychic structure on the side of Being-in-itself. Considered in one aspect it is always in the Past, for it represents all those states of awareness which consciousness has been reflectively or nonreflectively, which are continually organized and reorganized by consciousness into some sort of unity, and which serve as a reservoir of data and a background to accompany each new act of consciousness. They are the psychic equivalent of the finite temporal and spatial environment on the basis of which a consciousness makes itself a point of view on Being, i.e., the outside world. Looked at another way, the Self exists only in the Future as an ideal totality of all those projects by means of which consciousness inscribes itself in being. The Self cannot exist as a fixed entity, for it changes with each new act of consciousness as consciousness decides how to remake the past and what sort of future it will choose for itself. For convenience we may designate the ideal unity of experiences and habits as "Self," but there is always the same psychic distance between this Self and consciousness as there is between consciousness and any other of its objects. The difference is that as consciousness contemplates its own products, its very reflection alters that which it contemplates. Thus we have that play of mirrors, that impure reflection or never quite effected scission of consciousness by self-reflection which Sartre has compared to a game of musical chairs.

In the mystic experience consciousness may find itself in either of several states. It may recognize the truth—that it is not identified with what is commonly called the Self. Such a realization is cataclysmic enough in view of our habitual ways of thinking. Of course there is still self-awareness in the Sartrean sense of *conscience* (*de*) *soi*. For consciousness is aware of not being the usual Self, and this implicit realization of not being that Self is consciousness' awareness of itself as the awareness. It is because of our ordinary thought patterns that this true self-consciousness is described as a loss of self. It is experienced as an expansion because it is an emancipation from the false idea of being identified with, hence limited by the accumulation of consciousness's earlier states and gradually formed ego-constructs. Since consciousness exists only as an awareness *of* something, even this liberation from the conventional Self must have an object. Thus if consciousness ceases to contemplate its own chrysalis, as it were, it will either focus on the objects around it, on the physical sensations accompanying its new awareness, or on some explanatory notion concerning this awareness. The last possibility may assume either a pure or an impure form. If the consciousness, reflecting on its sense of liberation, identifies itself with a separate higher power (i.e., God), it is introducing concepts borrowed from its earlier personalized experience. The state is impure in that consciousness is not actually concentrating on it alone but seeks to relate present and past awareness. The pure form may easily take on a vaguely pantheistic coloration without necessarily introducing intellectualistic concepts and learned philosophical commitments.

There may seem to be a contradiction here. Even if we grant that consciousness is not one with the personality, there is unquestionably a closer association here than exists between consciousness and any of its other objects. We cannot assume that liberation from the conventional Self would be replaced naturally by an exalted feeling of being one with everything else. Why should a true sense of separation (true always on the assumption that Sartre is right) be followed by the false illusion that one is a part of (or the whole of) everything else? I think the answer is that we cannot get accustomed to the idea that consciousness is nothing *but* the awareness, the process of relating, etc. Therefore, the realization that consciousness is not to be identified with what is "inside" tends to be interpreted experientially as the feeling that it is therefore "outside" and one with all that is "out there." Up to a point the feeling is a true one. Since consciousness is a form of "presence to" an object, I can say with Sartre that consciousness is in the street with the automobile I perceive—just as accurately (but no more so) as I can say that it is here inside my body. As a process of relating, it is both there and here; as nonmaterial, it is in neither place.

In the mystic experience, what I suspect really happens is

that consciousness realizes its existence as mere awareness, consequently its potentiality of being everywhere as presence to all things—or to everything, taken as a totality. We saw in Roquentin's account how his fascinated awareness of being *nothing but consciousness* of the chestnut root almost slipped over into a sense of *being* the chestnut root. Yet there was no point at which he felt that he might become *conscious as a chestnut root.* That is, there is never a suggestion that he might become a chestnut-root-consciousness. Had Roquentin's consciousness experienced itself, not as a relation to the particular objects which he perceived but to all the objects he *might* perceive, taken as a totality, then the feeling of *being* all of this totality might have hovered on the horizon, like that of *being* the chestnut root. It is the second step which the mystic takes, but I believe he reports it falsely when he says either that he is conscious of being the whole or that he is *the whole as consciousness.* What happens is that he realizes he is *nothing but* a (self-) consciousness *of* the whole. This is what I think Sartre had in mind when he wrote:

We find this same pure negation at the basis of those pantheistic intuitions which Rousseau has several times described as concrete psychic events in his history. He claims that on those occasions he *melted* into the universe, that the world alone was suddenly found present as an absolute presence and unconditioned totality. And certainly we can understand this total, isolated presence of the world, its pure "being-there"; certainly we admit freely that at this privileged moment there was nothing else but the world. But this does not mean, as Rousseau claims, that there was a fusion of consciousness with the world. Such a fusion would signify the solidification of the for-itself in in-itself, and by the same stroke, the disappearance of the world and of the in-itself as presence. It is true that in the pantheistic intention there is no longer anything but the world—save for that which causes the in-itself to be present as the world; that is, a pure negation which is a non-thetic self-consciousness as negation. Precisely because knowledge is not *absence* but *presence*, there is *nothing* which separates the knower from the known.[1]

[1] Ibid., pp. 177–8.

I have made no attempt in this discussion to answer the question as to why consciousness should suddenly abandon its usual way of confronting the world and either set up wholly different ways of perception or become preoccupied, as it were, with its own self-as-process. No one has so far come up with a conclusive explanation, either chemical, physiological, or psychological. (I disregard religious hypotheses as being affirmations of faith—at most descriptive evaluations, certainly not explanations.) Those who have discussed the matter acknowledge that two factors seem always to be steadfast. First there is a diminution in the quantity or variety of sensory intake. The religious devotee practices concentration or meditation to reduce "distractions" whether from outside or from within. One of the most interesting of the results obtained by Cohen in his LSD experiments is the evidence of similarity in the reactions of those who have been deprived of normal sensory stimuli as compared with both mystics and those who took LSD. Cohen makes a highly significant statement.

It appears that the human brain, unlike the computer, cannot be idle for long periods and still maintain its efficiency. Unless it receives a flow of varying sensory fodder, a dreamlike state emerges. We seem to need information for mental effectiveness as much as we need food for physical health.[2]

Cohen refers to the machine—the brain—rather than to the process—consciousness. All the same, what he says seems to me to furnish a valuable clue. If consciousness is *only* an awareness of objects, then naturally any reduction in the field of awareness is bound to alter the normal states of consciousness. If external stimuli are abnormally absent, consciousness will turn to the objects of its own psychic reservoir or concentrate in an unusual way upon the limited material available to it.

Add the second factor—that there seems to be some disturbance which impedes the usual nonreflective (if not wholly

<hr>

[2] Sidney Cohen: *The Beyond Within: The LSD Story* (New York: Atheneum; 1964), p. 55.

automatic) synapses in the brain cells. Once again science and religion recognize the same data while employing different terms. We observed, as examples, both Huxley and Sartre speaking of the failure of the usual concepts. It is the habitual, regulative, categorizing faculty which renders everyday experience smooth and void of novelty. Impeding the familiar response inevitably opens up the possibility or even the necessity for a new one and thereby undermines the entire pattern of ordinary perception and sensation. With these things in mind, I think we can see fairly readily what occurs in effecting the other mystic and hallucinatory phenomena characteristic of abnormal states—even if the over-all relation between the chemical-physiological and the psychological remains still a mystery, as indeed is true of thought and awareness in general. Within the Sartrean view of consciousness, we can see why objects on such occasions appear to be more real, unique, and incomprehensible to the point of being threatening. It is because we suddenly confront them as they are. Not as they are in or for themselves. Such a hope is naïvely anthropomorphic. A stone is not conscious of itself, and we can only by sentimental imagination partake of the quality of pure animal consciousness. But we may become acutely aware of the transphenomenal being of the object, of its existing forever as something outside us which we cannot absorb and into which we cannot enter. At the same time we realize that, as consciousness, we are nothing more than the awareness of such resisting objects. The hallucinations of peyote and mescaline are of a different order but related. Sometimes the experience is obviously a distorted interpretation of an objective external stimulus. I may give an example. When I tried an experiment with peyote, I was aware of a strong fragrance of cooking, slightly burning chocolate fudge. The impression was so overwhelming as to be more convincing than friends' denial that there was any chocolate nearby. It was quite conclusively demonstrated that the source of the aroma was a verbena candle. When it was extinguished, the smell of chocolate vanished. Nevertheless, if I tried deliberately to smell the candle, I could not sense it as the origin of the fragrance. Since I "knew" verbena candles did not smell like chocolate, the attempt at conceptual classification of the new impression altered the state of consciousness and caused the fragrance to disappear. The hallucinations which Sartre experienced—or the pleasurable pseudo-visions more commonly recorded—are slightly or not at all related to any physical stimulus. They more closely resemble the hypnagogic image. Many of us can recall that in-between stage, not quite either waking or sleeping, when we are nonreflectively aware of our immediate environment, yet are half-trapped in the illogical play of our own fantasies. Something of the same sort seems to happen in the drug experience except that there is a greater degree of reflective awareness. The psychic objects are in one sense the direct product of consciousness since they may result solely from consciousness, creating them either by reflective memory or imagination—as it assumes a new point of view on its own residue of experience, forming inward projects which may or may not be intended as actions in the outside world. In another way, since there is always the slight nothingness between consciousness and any of its objects, even these inward forms assume a certain opaqueness. Consciousness is aware of being nothing except its awareness of them, which gives to them an illusory weight and substance.

Alterations in the sense of time and space fit easily into the Sartrean theory of consciousness. In all human experience time and space have a subjective aspect inasmuch as they are lived as relationships, with the individual consciousness as a center of reference. It is this truth which consciousness experiences nonconceptually in the ecstasy. Since consciousness *is* neither in the conventional self nor in the body nor in the outside object, it can quite truthfully interpret this realization as the sense of being suspended in emptiness or of being simultaneously attached to the body and yet beside the object or in some far distant location on which its intention is focused. The slowing down of time, which is a characteristic of the hallucinogenic drugs, needs no special explanation. The doctrine of relativity has shown us the interaction of physical

253

motion, organic activity, and mental time. Long before Einstein, men and women were aware of the vast difference in hours lived as compared with hours indicated by the clock. The feeling that time has stopped is not essentially different. Time does "stop," but that way of putting it is misleading. Nothing outside has stopped, for nothing had ever started—if by such terms we refer to some external absolute entity or separate process. What really stops is consciousness' habitual attitude or way of intending its objects. Ordinarily, not only are we accustomed to view external action, including our own activity, as bearing an absolute relation to clock time, but we regard our inward processes as taking place in the same way. It is true that separate thoughts, like separate actions, have a "before," "same as," and "after" relation. Pure duration, however, cannot be measured unless the impression which endures is related to something else. In certain abnormal states, consciousness does not change its intention from one object to another. Its awareness consists wholly in its being aware of being a particular awareness. It has canceled out all past and future objects so that for the moment it has the illusion of being nontemporal. Perhaps, contrary to Sartre, we should say that in this state consciousness *is* nontemporal. The experience—if it could be compared to clock time—is possibly almost too short to be measured, though trances with suspended animation indicate that this is not necessarily true. At any rate, the feeling of the complete break in succession is likely to be interpreted in the following moment of consciousness as something of infinite duration. Reflective recollection may interpret it as years or as eons.

I have already suggested that the therapeutic value of LSD in psychoanalysis lies in the revelation of the truth of the perceiver to himself. I am referring to the self-understanding which is the goal of all therapy; that is, a comprehension, without self-deception, of the motives and results of what one has done and the ability to judge them in a manner consistent with one's genuine life-and-value-orientation. (I mean, of course, authentic self-understanding, not just an obedient response to suggestions from the therapist.) It seems indisputable that positive gain in self-understanding and constructive changes of personality often occur as consequences of the LSD experience just as they may in religious conversion—though in each case, it is the subsequent carrying through that is decisive. The answer seems to lie partly in the two factors already mentioned; that is, that the blocking of habitual, automatic synapses and the absence of the reassuring background of familiar sensory stimuli make it easier, if not imperative, to adopt a different point of view on whatever happens to occupy one's attention and particularly on present anxieties. Cohen suggests that the usual blocks set up to check repressed memories fail to function. Once the blocked material has broken through, consciousness is able and even compelled to re-examine these fragments of earlier experiences and may make them into a more constructively meaningful part of its present and future orientation. Put in Sartrean terms, consciousness not only reflects on what it had previously relegated to nonreflective levels; it also realizes more acutely the liberating nothingness between itself and all of the accumulated experience which it has structured into personality, ego, self-image—call it what you will. Thus the ecstatic trance is the most intense form of that health-saving moment of insight essential to all therapy—the realization that one can confront one's objectified psyche and make a new choice of being. LSD, when it does introduce the successful critical moment in psychotherapy—and shock treatment, too, I suspect—is able to effect this liberating self-realization by consciousness. Cohen suggests that part of the efficiency of the LSD treatment is due to the fact that under the drug's influence, consciousness finds it difficult to express even simple ideas verbally. We may differ as to whether this represents regression or an advance. The important point is that language gives form to experience; form, while it adds precision and order, necessarily limits and distorts the original experiential flux.

Language functions as surely as any of Kant's categories to make thought and emotion, too, into a product and to universalize them. The nonverbal, imagistic remembering or reflecting on one's present situation, earlier experience, and possibilities for the future is stimulated by LSD, probably *because* one can verbalize less easily. Failure to perform one activity with normal efficiency results in releasing the energies of processes usually inhibited.

I have tried to show that the phenomena of ecstatic experiences make sense if they are described in the context of Sartre's concept of consciousness and its relation to the outside world. If even this can be demonstrated, there is already much accomplished. For it means that neither the mystic nor the drug experience has opened "the sluices" or flung back the "doors of perception" in such a way as to force upon us some other religious certainty or definite philosophy. It does not, of course, oblige us to accept or to reject all other metaphysical hypotheses and cling to humanistic existentialism. Before leaving the subject of enlightenment, however, I should like to consider a special form of Oriental philosophy, which shares a view of consciousness that is much closer to Sartre's than we have found Vedanta to be.

Satori and Suchness

We might expect to find some kinship—at least an affinity of mood—between Zen Buddhism and existentialism inasmuch as both are movements of revolt against the transcendentalism of their respective traditions. Zen, early in its history under the influence of Mahayana Buddhism, rejected both the concept of self-entity and that of a transcendent Absolute. There is neither Atman nor Brahman. We can see this development in two poems supposed to have been written in China in the seventh century A.D. Shen-hsyi, assuming that a monk must struggle to keep the soul pure, wrote:

> This body is the Bodhi-tree,
> The soul is like a mirror bright;
> Take heed to keep it always clean,
> And let not dust collect on it.

Hui-Neng responded:

> The Bodhi is not like the tree.
> The mirror bright is nowhere shining.
> As there is nothing from the first,
> Where can the dust itself collect? [1]

Or, as Zen Buddhists are fond of saying, "From the first, not a thing is!"

Zen concepts of self and consciousness and their relation to the outside world will seem closer to or farther from Sartrean existentialism according to which authority on Zen Buddhism one is reading. Theoretically, followers of Zen resist the idea that its insights constitute a philosophy—much as Kierkegaard did. They deny that the essence of man's life and the solutions to his problems, or even the problems themselves, can be adequately treated by direct conceptual thought or ever fully communicated. Where Kierkegaard employed indirect devices—pseudonyms, semifictional characters, and even suggestions of novelistic plots, Zen devotees have written poems, painted pictures, and sought to demonstrate that what they were trying to convey could be best expressed where there were no words at all—in archery; flower arrangements; the tea service; in puzzles; seemingly banal, pointless remarks; and sometimes by deliberate vulgarity or physical violence. Even so, there have been many Zen scholars and writers about Zen (especially here in the United States) who have attempted to discuss the metaphysical and psychological outlook of Zen in terms meant to be both explanatory and justifying. It makes a great deal of difference which of these writers we read. Although it would be incorrect to classify such writing as belonging to one or the other of two distinct schools of interpretation, we may recognize that there are certainly two different tendencies. Alan Watts and Van Metar Ames, for notable examples, make of Zen a wholly naturalistic point of view although a nonconceptual enlightenment remains at its heart. In the work of D. T. Suzuki, on the other

---

[1] Quoted and tr. Daisetz Teitaro Suzuki: *Zen Buddhism* (New York: Doubleday; 1956), pp. 67–8.

hand, religious overtones and something close to pantheistic mysticism are certainly present. It is the naturalistic interpretation which, to my mind, offers the only reason for our making a special case of Zen for the present discussion.

As Watts describes the nature of individual consciousness and the self, it is easy to feel, much of the time, that here is a close parallel to Sartre, that a little verbal modification might bring the two together. Watts, who is clearly reformulating Zen precepts in Western terms, claims that the self is not an entity but a process of the nervous system and that it is at no time completely cut off from the external stimuli to which it responds. There is no valid distinction between act and actor, no doer behind what is done. Verbs, or at least gerunds, would be a more accurate way of expressing reality than the static substantive noun. Using the example of patterns in a shallow bed of sand, Watts says that there is no sand separate from the patterns and vice versa. The sand is at any moment one with whatever pattern it assumes. Continuity is an illusion. One pattern does not *become* another but replaces it. The sense of something's being there all the time stems from the fact that a particular twist or curve in a new form may recall an old one, and this is what we call memory. Our feeling that there is a definite permanent Self comes from our habit of restricting experience to conform with the image of ourselves, an ego-image which we have set up by abstracting the common elements of earlier patterns. Theoretically there are no limits to the Self, for there is no end to experience. Our insistence on being a distinct Self is like the act of narrowing a wide open floodlight to a small directed flashlight. So far we find much in common with the Sartrean position, that consciousness is a continuous process of attention, a constant refocusing. There are differences, too, but first we should consider the world outside and consciousness' relation to it.

The great insight of Zen (in part it is a restatement of an earlier school of Buddhism) is that the transcendent Nothing-yet-everything which the Hindus call Brahman, is present here and now in whatever object is before one—as well as in oneself. "There is no one to get back and nothing to get back to." There is no need to seek some Absolute behind the phenomena; one would find nothing which is not already fully manifested in the most ordinary of objects. *Sunyata* is *Tathata*. Nothingness is Suchness. Sunyata, which may be translated Emptiness or Nothingness, is not anything, and yet it is that without which no thing could be. Sunyata is what everything is when you stop saying of a thing that it is anything. But Sunyata is also Tathata—Suchness—the here-and-nowness, the being-thereness, the being-just-what-it-isness of any immediate experience. Hence this poem by Chao-Pien:

> A sudden clash of thunder, the mind-doors burst open,
> And lo, there sitteth the old man in all his homeliness.[2]

Or the frequently quoted, "When I began to study Zen, mountains were mountains; when I thought I understood Zen, mountains were not mountains; but when I came to full knowledge of Zen, mountains were again mountains." [3]

This acceptance of empirical reality is not simple naturalism or naïve realism as these philosophical positions are known in the West. The emphasis on Sunyata as Nothingness or Void is too important. In what sense, then, can we say with any consistency that things are simply what they appear (mountains are mountains) and yet that the real is Sunyata? The answer, as Watts has explained, is that Sunyata is not Nothingness in the sense of the unreal or of a nonmaterial, spiritual reality. It is an absence, an absence of form. What is unreal is the apparent fixedness of shapes, of things, of separations. At this point—if there were no need to go further—I think we might very well conclude that Zen thought offers precisely the same mid-point between idealism and realism which we have found in Sartre's *Being and Nothingness*. The central kernel, as it were, is indeed the same. At any given moment, in any act of consciousness, the world of nature is nothing other than it appears. Yet this specific, concrete appearance depends in large part upon the activity of the per-

[2] Quoted and tr. Alan W. Watts: *The Spirit of Zen* (London: John Murray; 1936), p. 81.
[3] Suzuki: *Zen Buddhism*, p. 240.

ceiver, who imposes *this* sort of structure rather than any one of many possible others.

Two things distinguish the Zen view from the existentialist. First, the Zen doctrine does not differentiate between the idea of the Self as complex entity and the immediate self-awareness of the individual consciousness. Second, it does not allow for a psychic separation between consciousness and the object. Sartre, who has described the For-itself as "a hole in being at the heart of being," grants that "for ontology it makes no difference whether we consider the For-itself articulated in the in-itself as a well marked duality or as a disintegrated being." [4] Zen is careful to preserve an ultimate monism. Watts, speaking of Eastern "ways of liberation," claims that regardless of doctrinal differences, they "all seem to culminate in the same state or mode of consciousness in which the duality of the ego and the world is overcome. Call it 'cosmic consciousness' or 'mystical experience,' or what you will, it seems to me to be the felt realization of the physical world as a field." [5] Watts himself speaks of such realization as a kind of insight rather than as a religious transformation. Yet he is willing to recognize that the seeming difference between Zen and Vedanta is partly only verbal and partly a matter of emphasis.

Buddhism emphasizes the unreality of the ego, whereas Vedanta emphasizes the unity of the field. Thus in describing liberation the former seems to be saying simply that the egocentric viewpoint evaporates, and the latter, that we discover our true self to be the Self of the Universe. [6]

D. T. Suzuki seems to me to go so far in the direction of blurring this difference of emphasis that his form of Zen is almost as antithetical to Sartrean existentialism as Vedanta is. Suzuki states that the Zen goal of "No Mind" involves not only giving up the control exerted by the conscious ego, but a

[4] Sartre: *Being and Nothingness*, p. 624.
[5] Alan W. Watts: *Psychotherapy East and West* (New York: New American Library; 1963), p. 52.
[6] Ibid.

falling back into an Unconscious rooted in a cosmic Unconscious. Moreover, Suzuki, deliberately challenging Sartre, asserts the identity of Being-in-itself and Being-for-itself. Once we realize that Sunyata is Tathata, he says, then "pure subjectivity is pure objectivity, the *en-soi* is the *pour-soi*, there is perfect identity of Man and Nature, of God and Nature, of the one and the many." [7] To be sure, Suzuki goes on to point out that this identity does not imply that either *en-soi* or *pour-soi* is annihilated. "Man as a subject facing the many remains conscious of himself." Nevertheless, one feels that for Suzuki, the manifold remains a superimposition upon some deeper oneness of being. "The mountains are mountains and yet not mountains. I am I and you are you, and yet I am you and you are I." *Tat tvam asi*—That art Thou.

The more naturalistic interpretation of Zen avoids this sort of mystical language. Watts, for example, tries as much as possible to use scientific analogies. He claims, "The final Buddhist vision of the world as the *dharmadhatu*—loosely translatable as the field of related functions—is not so different from the world view of Western science, except that the vision is experiential rather than theoretical." [8] "The field of related functions" is a well-phrased and accurate description of the Universe as Watts interprets Zen's picture of both human and nonhuman reality. At times his description of consciousness seems to identify it with the nervous system and sounds like the discussions of Behaviorists and old-fashioned materialists. "All our sensory experiences are states of the nervous system. The field of vision, which we take to be outside the organism, is in fact inside it because it is a translation of the external world into the form of the eye and the optical nerves. What we see is therefore a state of the organism, a state of ourselves." [9] Watts quickly qualifies his statement in two ways. There is the state of the organism which we call seeing but not a separate see-er. Furthermore, the outside world is not separated from the rest. "There is not the

---

[7] Suzuki: *Zen Buddhism*, p. 241.
[8] Watts: *Psychotherapy East and West*, p. 59.
[9] Ibid., pp. 69–70.

external world, and then the state of the nervous system, and then something which sees that state. The seeing is precisely that particular state of the nervous system, a state which for that moment *is* an integral part of the organism." Reality *is* related functions," a multitude of changing relations and interlocking patterns. Watts sums up his interpretation in a sentence which he apparently means to be taken both as literally true and as an image of the whole of things. "My outline, which is not just the outline of my skin but of every organ and cell in my body, is also the inline of the world. The movements of this outline are my movements, but they are also movements of the world—of its inline." [1] All human reaction is interaction. We are all aware that a color exists only when a certain physical component in the object, light waves, and nerve cells interact. Watts insists that a comparable situation exists in any awareness. If I touch a rock, "the rock is translated into nerve patterns." As consciousness deals with its environment conceptually, the world is "transformed into thought" as food is transformed into the body.

Sartre says that consciousness is always in-the-world. This is because it is consciousness *of* the world. But because it is present to the world by virtue of the nothingness which it brings into being, consciousness is at least nonreflectively aware of not being the world. In Zen thought, consciousness is in the world in the sense of being a part of it. Yet since we think of the world itself as being related functions, "to be a part" is misleading too. Watts is fond of asking, "What becomes of my fist when I open my hand?" It is our way of trying to pin down what can't be stopped which makes us insist on such inaccuracies as parts and wholes.

We can see now why Zen (as Watts presents it) and Sartrean existentialism seem to intersect at one point and then, like circle and tangent, sharply go their separate ways. Both insist that the ego is a secondary structure. For Sartre, the ego is a psychic structure which emerges as consciousness reflects upon its own—always past—states. For most people it

---

[1] Ibid., p. 60.

seems to be identical with consciousness itself, simply because most human beings are afraid to realize their possibility
of liberating themselves from accustomed patterns and choosing a new way of being. Watts claims that the ego is wholly a
social structure. As a matter of expediency, society assumes
that every man is to be identified with an ego or mind or self
which exists beyond the cortex and which controls the cortex.
"The ego is the unconscious pretense that the organism contains a higher system than the cortex." [2] Watts maintains
that the information about its own states comes into the
cortex only through other people and that this "complex of
social information relayed back into the cortex" is falsely
taken as a self-entity. "The ego feeling is pure hypnosis."
Watts denies the implicit self-awareness which Sartre postulates as one aspect of every conscious intention. Both Sartrean
and Zen psychology reject the primacy of the ego. Their
reasons for the rejection are as decidedly different as the
underlying vision of what consciousness is.

How great the consequences of what might at first seem to
be but a small doctrinal disagreement will become apparent if
we look briefly at two things which are of central importance
in Zen teaching: enlightenment and time.

Enlightenment in Zen Buddhism is called Satori and is as
important for Zen as Moksa or Nirvana is for Vedanta. Paradoxically, Zen insists that the insight gained in Satori is the
realization that there is nothing to seek, that what is found
was here all the time. Nevertheless the moment of illumination changes entirely the feeling with which one grasps the
fact that "the mountains are again mountains."

Zen writers vary in their descriptions and analyses. Frequently Satori is described in terms appropriate to traditional
mysticism, not as a trance perhaps, but nevertheless as a
complete *ekstasis* or standing out of oneself so as to realize
the oneness of all things as well as their manifold suchness.
Suzuki refers to Satori as the greatest mental cataclysm one
can meet in life, a "fiery baptism" and he discusses it at

[2] Ibid., p. 70.

length in concepts borrowed from James's discussion of mysticism in *The Varieties of Religious Experience*. Again, Zenkei Shibayama, abbot of a Zen temple in Kyoto, says that in essence Zen is "a sort of mystic personal experience which cannot be attained by thinking on the basis of ordinary dualistic knowledge, but is affirmed intuitively by the unitary spiritual power which exists in the innermost of the human nature." [3] Other writers, among them Watts, describe the experience in purely naturalistic terms.

With or without mystic overtones, Satori is essentially a "letting go." What one lets go of is the feeling that one is, or ought to be, or ought to want to be, in control of his own situation. This may seem to be in contradiction with the famous excellence of Zen-trained archers or the strict discipline of Zen temple schools, but it is not. The whole point is that "one" does not "do" anything. The "one" exists only as an immediate center of awareness, but this awareness is only a point, so to speak, in a complex of responses to an ever-changing environment, an environment which is, in turn, part of the totality of "related functions." Perhaps the closest parallel is dancing, which for full enjoyment must be performed and observed without any analytic awareness of separate parts or of a "dancer" separate from the "dancing." It is the central precept of Zen that if one gets over the illusion that there is an actor standing back of all actions, then every action functions harmonically and naturally as in any well-performing organism. It is the interposition of a false sense of self which impedes the function—like any foreign object thrust into the midst of a closely meshed mechanism. The blissful liberation in Satori stems from the sudden insight that "one" does not exist except as a closely integrated part of a whole. Over and over Watts refers to the "field." No event or thing exists outside a context. It is failure to include the context which gives the illusion of a separately existing consciousness or of any fixed forms. As in the interlocking patterns of a paisley tapestry, an observer can artificially isolate

[3] Zenkei Shibayama: "An Outline of Zen" in *Anthology of Zen*, ed. William Briggs (New York: Grove Press; 1961), p. 196.

a section, but the true pattern is "all of a piece." The tapestry is a less precise image than a kaleidoscope. One is nothing but awareness of experience; since all patterns overlap, there is quite literally no end to experience. Satori is the realization that what is simply is, that our own being is bound up with it, and that there is no necessity for us to do anything about it.

Satori may be viewed also in connection with the question of temporality. Suzuki has described Satori poetically as the intersection of time and eternity. More precisely in keeping with Zen teaching we may point out that in Satori one perceives that nothing exists or is real except the present moment —not just for the duration of Satori but absolutely. This doctrine is in some ways more difficult to comprehend than the Vedanta view that time is a superficial structure imposed upon a reality beyond time. It is far more radical than Sartre's doctrine which does, to be sure, put time on the side of Being-for-itself but which assigns an essential importance to the triple temporal dimension. In my opinion, this claim of Zen not only is false but strangely out of line with the rest of its teaching.

What can we mean if we say that only the present exists? One way is to be trapped in our own grammatical contrivances. Since we designate that something is or occurs in the present when and only when we can speak of it with the present tense, then it is obvious that "only the present exists"; for to say that "the past *is*" involves a grammatical contradiction. Or we can mean that only the present is real, inasmuch as past or future are never experienced *as such*, but only imagined by processes to which we give the names memory or anticipation. Zen takes us a step further. If only the present exists, that is because there is no separate entity or witness who endures through the constant shifting of patterns. There is not first a log which then becomes ashes. The ashes are not in the log nor vice versa. There is a log; there are the ashes; there are the various stages of fire and the diminishing chunk of log. Each one exists separately; there is no connection or internal relation among them. The same is true of the states of the nervous system. Moreover, since this system itself is inseparable from whatever state it is in, we cannot, strictly speaking, say that from one moment to another it is the same nervous system. We may recall the Heraclitean statement, "You can't step in the same river twice." And a later philosopher's comment, "You can't step in the same river once!"

All this reminds me of Sartre's attempt to show that such things as "destruction" and "the question" are impossible in Being-in-itself and emerge only with the upsurge of consciousness. But the Zen Universe, whatever we take to be its real moment, does not resemble Sartre's formless In-itself. It is at this point that we encounter what seems to me an inconsistency in Zen. All Zen thinkers stress the interconnectedness of things in the present real experience; the contexts, the farther reaches of events and existents must never be overlooked. It seems to me that if this is so horizontally and spatially, it is equally true vertically and temporally. Motion is meaningless, and so are related functions unless one brings in the idea of time as well as space. How long is the present moment?

A Zen poet exclaims:

> Miraculous power and marvelous activity—
> Drawing water and hewing wood! [4]

It is true that pleasure in humble tasks may be possible only if one refrains from asking what they are leading toward. Many of us have experienced in pure activity for its own sake a joy—a "small satori"—which would be quickly destroyed if one ceased to be absorbed in the action and had to relate it to the full purposeful context of a complex future. Yet we cannot reduce such activity to the instant either. For every single motion involved in drawing water or cutting wood or swimming is directed toward the future and is meaningful and satisfying only as a part of a continuing process. The temporal context is as essential as any other contextual relation.

I think that Sartre is right in insisting on the temporality

---

[4] P'ang-yun, quoted by Alan W. Watts in *The Way of Zen* (New York: New American Library; 1959), p. 132.

of consciousness. However humble and absorbing the activity, our performance of it and our nonreflective awareness of what we are doing involve a continued projection. Every motion is a preparation for that which is to follow; none of it would be even possible—let alone satisfying—without some sort of unifying theme and even, to some small degree, purpose. A nonreflective doodling nevertheless includes a sense of direction in the line being drawn. The performing tightrope walker cannot afford to reflect on the spectators' reactions or the feelings he will have when he reaches the other side; without a temporal context, he cannot perform at all. Zen does not deny, of course, that patterns of activity may bear the impressions of those which preceded, but the same is true with respect to the future. Here surely connections exist. Zen is right in declaring that the ashes are not in the log. It cannot easily deny that the potentiality of the log-become-ashes is in consciousness. It is there even in the poet's mind while he enjoys cutting the wood.

It is because consciousness is temporal that existentialism can defend its seeming paradox—that man is free and yet associated with a distinct personality. "Self" has meaning both as referring to a recognizable quality associated with the past acts of awareness of a particular consciousness in a particular body and as pointing to the kind of future which consciousness projects. Watt's cortex and neural patterns, because he refuses to grant them temporal connections, can have no enduring inner relations. Since they are not cut off from the surrounding environment, they have no individual identity.

Watts suggests that the split between consciousness and its environment may very possibly prove to be one of the blind alleys of evolution. Does it really result in a self-imprisonment? Or is it the attempt to deny the split, which becomes still another form of self-delusion, if not bad faith? Should we continue to resist the temptation of Eastern philosophy? Or are we blind to the persuasive evidence of an experience which our philosophical commitments prevent us from recognizing?

267

Why Not the Lotus?

To speak of the temptation of Eastern philosophy is to imply that it offers something alluring but dangerous and false. If anyone wants to point out that there is a certain presumption in referring in this way to the centuries of philosophical thought in several countries and languages, I can only agree. My defense is to state once again my purpose in comparing—superficially, I admit—a few of the basic doctrines attached to two "ways of liberation." My intent is twofold: it is to see whether humanistic existentialism, as some writers have suggested, may or may not work comfortably within the broad framework of Vedanta or Zen, enriching its own outlook by insights gained from a different but parallel approach; and to determine whether existentialism must modify its own position when challenged by philosophies which lay claim to an individual intuitive knowing as their starting point—as existentialism does too, but in a different way. If existentialism resists this temptation, and I think that finally it must, this does not mean that it rejects all of Eastern philosophy as false or condemns *in toto* the ways of life and the value systems which have been their consequents. Existentialism is neither contemptuous nor supercilious nor without profound admiration for the great minds of the past in the Eastern traditions and for the contemporary flowering of this *Weltanschauung* in the heroism of such men as Gandhi and his followers. In precisely the same way it may feel a sympathetic affection for Saint Francis of Assisi, an overwhelming awe at the intellect of Saint Thomas Aquinas. Yet, as an existentialist, I must at some point stand back and declare, "Their dharma is not my dharma!"

Ultimately humanistic existentialism says No to Vedanta and Zen, just as it rejects the nearer tradition of Judaeo-Christianity. When examined closely, Sartrean consciousness is fundamentally different from that of any Eastern view. Its way of knowing is different. Its values and sense of how man

268

may best live his life are still further removed from the prevalent attitudes of Eastern thought.

One way or another, all arguments and critical evaluation seem to refer back to two fundamental points of departure: reliance on special enlightenment as a nonrational revelation of truth; and the belief that the individual consciousness is but artificially and superficially separated from a cosmic consciousness. Actually these are but two aspects of one principle, for enlightenment *is* a realization of nonseparation. As a way of summing up our existentialist appraisal of Oriental philosophy, let us take one more look at this much talked of moment of illumination or ekstasis. In the discussion up till now, I have tried to show two things—that one can account for the abnormal occurrence of such experiences without departing from the premises of humanistic existentialism; and that the "truth" revealed is the truth of the individual subject and not that of a suprapersonal world. In connection with the latter I have stressed especially the variation in the types of noetic experiences, the part played by the predisposition of the subject, the difficulty of distinguishing between "mystic elements" and those hallucinogenic aspects which are clearly the result of a disordered nervous system, and (if we include drug experiments) the discrepancy between the subjective sense of heightened precision in awareness and the measurable lack of fine discrimination, and the intensification of suggestibility in the subject. I do not wish to discuss further these rational—if not conclusively scientific—explanations as to why I personally feel that enlightenment as such does not offer a proof that one should reject even the scientific, let alone the existentialist interpretation of man. Now I suggest another approach. Suppose, for the sake of the argument, we grant that some sort of cosmic consciousness does occur. What does it prove? How much is it worth? What consequence should it have in our lives?

It seems to me that the most we can reserve for any least common denominator of all experience of ekstasis is this: that by dint of great effort, or under highly unusual circumstances, one can *feel* a blissful sense of release from the restrictions of body and personality and that somehow this experience involves the active realization of one's connection with the basic energy (or spirit, or whatever word one prefers for this ultimate X) of which the universe is composed. Such realization is undoubtedly psychically and physically satisfying for those who have it, but it seems to me that it leaves the basic problems of life exactly what they were before.

The analogy with the sexual orgasm is almost inevitable. To claim that the mystic and the sexual union are intrinsically the same is not fair to either. Yet if the sexual experience were as infrequent and as difficult to attain as the mystic, we may well imagine that with its intensity, its sense of fulfillment, of becoming more than oneself, it would impel those who achieved it to claim that this in itself is a sufficient aim in life. Indeed, even as things are, some persons have tried to do so. Yet generally speaking, in this world where sexual fulfillment is taken for granted as a part of everyday living, it has presented its unique rewards, incentives, and problems. It has not served to justify all of existence nor to dissolve all other conflicts.

The mystic experience as such supplies no irrefutable evidence to support any particular view of the origin or destination of man or of the universe. If we allow—and I, personally, feel that it is more than we are compelled to do—that the "cosmic consciousness" is more than a sense of release from the habitual restrictions of body and personality, I cannot see that it offers either knowledge or any kind of awareness which points beyond itself. One grasps that all things are connected and that in a significant way one is part of them. In terms that a physicist might employ, we acknowledge the connections. Apparently we and material objects are all structured energy, made up of similar particles, which are certainly something quite different from matter as the inert tangible stuff postulated by the old materialism. Do we somehow *participate in* this dynamism in cosmic consciousness? Possibly, though I am doubtful. More important, what does it mean to be conscious of being part of the all or even of *being the all?* The sensation is doubtless overwhelming. Does it answer any questions? No matter how much the mystic feels he is one with sea and mountains, he never is aware of what it is to be sea or mountain. Nor is he—which would seem to be easier—ever aware of what it is to be conscious of being another person. The intuition that all men are one simply cancels out differences. It offers no keener comprehension of these differences. Even as I realize that my own consciousness is other and more than I have been accustomed to think of as my Self, I find that the host of other "Selves" remains as impenetrable as ever. Let us assume that Vedanta and Zen are right in insisting that the basic relatedness of all is in some way primary, more fundamental than the differences. Is this a place to stop or a starting point, an advance or a regression? So far as teleology is concerned, Eastern philosophy and science are agreed that the universe isn't going anywhere if by "going somewhere" we refer to some guiding purposeful plan. For science and—with different overtones—existentialism, the universe is at least open-ended. For Vedanta there is a succession of endless kalpas in which Brahma alternately manifests itself (i.e., makes itself manifold) and reabsorbs itself into itself in an ultimately meaningless cosmic play. Strict Vedanta seems to attach all value to the state of self-absorption. Even in India the disciples of Tantra, without doubting the metaphysics, questioned the evaluation. "If Nirvana means absorption, why seek Nirvana?" If separate existence is equally Brahman, why not declare it good and live it to the fullest? One can learn to love Lila, the cosmic dance, for the wonder of its shifting moments. It is not when he is at rest that the dancer holds our fascinated attention. In the world outlook of Hinduism and of those movements which sprang from within it without ever wholly separating from it—e.g., Jainism and Buddhism—there is no room for an open future where man himself may produce something wholly new, by his own acts creating significance in the universe and helping to alter its destiny as well as making his own.

Zen Buddhism theoretically holds that Sunyata is Tathata, that the specific suchness of the concrete experience is as real as the all-embracing formless void. Logically, one would think, the reality of Suchness ought to result in a positive this-worldliness in Zen Buddhists. Except in a narrowly limited sense, this has not been the case. We have observed how, as expressed in P'ang-Yun's poem, the Zen monk derived a sense of joy from such mundane activities as drawing water and cutting wood. In art and literature there are recorded a multitude of precious, fleeting experiences which Watts refers to as examples of the "small satori." They are those moments when a person simply lives to the fullest the absolute value of the immediate present—in the sight of something exquisitely beautiful or in the complete absorption in an activity performed for its own sake and with no further aim. Most often they involve a sudden intuition of the loveliness of something in one's natural surroundings—of the mountain peaks when the storm clouds lift, or the tremulous newborn colts in the field, or the call of a single bird over the water of a deserted lake at twilight. Such quiet ecstasies, I think, are lacking in the writing of Sartre, but we find them in Simone de Beauvoir's autobiography and in the work of Albert Camus —at the end of *The Stranger*, for example, or in some of Camus's "lyrical essays." In such passages, we feel on the part of these writers an intense love for the beauty of this world, not because it satisfies man's demand for order and meaning, but for its very indifference, for what it is in itself. I think it might be well for existentialism to learn to concentrate more fully on the joys of those happy moments which will come if we let them and on the small everyday pleasures. A bit of Zen laughter would be a real help in confronting the absurdity of existence. The existentialist might find that there is sometimes value in acceptance as well as in revolt. He may be right in declaring that an ecstatic, "Oh, the morning glory!" is an inadequate method of dealing with the evil and suffering of the world. But perhaps there is bad faith and evasion in spending too much time in the contemplation of our anguish.

All the same, I think that existentialism must conclude that neither the accumulation of small satoris nor the great Satori will satisfy it. On three counts it finds itself in disagreement. First, although it agrees with Zen that there is nothing back of suchness to give us reason to feel that there is any absolute external purpose in things, it finds that Zen deprives life of the meaning and purpose which we ourselves may put into it. The doctrine of separate moments, each of which alone is real, will not do. Van Meter Ames has pointed out that there are painful moments as well as moments of intense joy and quiet content. Vedanta can try to cancel them out by declaring them unreal for one who has advanced beyond the illusion of separate consciousness. Zen cannot deny that if the immediate state of the organism is painful, then the pain is as real as any other present. The Zen reply would be to tell us that even pain can be mitigated by a relaxed acceptance and by the simultaneous realization of transciency and of the connectedness of things. I find this but slight consolation.

"Going nowhere in a timeless moment" is the goal of Zen. Existentialism, of course, denies that any moment is truly timeless for a temporal consciousness. More than this, the Zen goal seems to have little to recommend it. Is retreat into the happiness of cosmic consciousness really so much higher than bovine contentment with a high standard of living? Echoing both Zen and Tao, Watts urges that we must learn to relax so completely as to relearn a dependence on the natural man. For Zen this involves two acts of faith which existentialism cannot accept: first, that nature is so marvelous an organic unity that related functions will act together by themselves—if left to themselves; second, that as soon as one gives up the illusion of ego as entity, then the person—i.e., a nervous system—reacts spontaneously with the "right" response to every situation. More accurately, he acts without reflection, for he is simply an integral part of the situation. In conduct where automatic responses are possible and appropriate, such advice is fine. In archery, in hunting, even in hand-to-hand combat, the cultivation of a supersensitive awareness of subtle variations in the environment and the ability to trust to automatic reflexes are essential. It is equivalent to recapturing the hypersensitivity and coordination of primitive man, and I am willing to grant that this is a value worth recovering. What I cannot see is its effectiveness in any situation where one is unwilling to live on the primitive man's level.

In choosing between the two values of genuine spontaneity and the creation of a coherent life plan and value system, Zen has chosen the former exclusively. Watts says that the ethics of Zen is nondirective rather than prescriptive. I would have no objection if he merely meant that when it comes to specific ethical choices, each one must work out the solution for himself in accordance with his own view of what he wants to make himself be. What disturbs me about Zen is that it seems to me to preclude the creation of a value system, both because of its denial of temporality and because it allows for no real sense of responsibility. In this respect, though for somewhat different reasons, it suffers from the same weakness that impairs Vedanta.

Much of what I object to in Eastern philosophy stems from two basic positions: its view of "desire" and its attitude toward human relations. Vedanta strives to uproot desire as being but an ignorant attachment to the world of Maya. The result is an extreme asceticism and quietism. The Indian saint feels compassion for the suffering of others inasmuch as they are all one with him. He may exert himself to help them realize the unreality of their pain and to teach them the necessity and means of attaining liberation. Except for refraining from any act of violence toward them, he will not feel any philosophical necessity to relieve their immediate situation in this life. In Sartrean existentialism man *is* desire as he is choice, as he is freedom. Through desire he relates himself to the world, carves out his place in Being. The aim is to live more intensely, more broadly, to enrich the pursuit of self via an ever-increasing network of desires, extending the horizon of experience until finally the needs of others too are included as significant to one's own consciousness. Complete liberation from desire would be the annihilation of consciousness. Zen rejects asceticism as one more aspect of self-centeredness, but it looks on all strong desires with suspicion, viewing them as examples of frustrated grasping due to the demands of the false ego-image. All that one should do is to respond to the need of the particular moment. Ikkyu wrote:

> We eat, excrete, sleep, and get up;
> This is our world.
> All we have to do after that—
> Is to die.[5]

A Zen Master, asked how to live after enlightenment, replies, "When I'm hungry, I eat; when I'm thirsty, I drink." One seeks no further; one merely does what needs to be done. Where nothingness and suchness are one, there is no choice, no imperative.

In Japan students of Zen Buddhism have in the past left the monastery schools to live as Samurai warriors, to take part in politics or whatever careers appealed to them. This is not necessarily inconsistent with Zen principles, provided that these activities are carried on with nonattachment—as complete an opposition to the existentialist ideal of commitment as one can find. The great Zen plea is for us to learn that none of it makes any difference. Like Brahman, we "play" at being ourselves, at living, at dying. Despite its emphasis on suchness, Zen assumes so completely the point of view of the whole that a corroding relativity takes away any real significance from all separate events. Even "life" and "death" are but two terms indicating our different ways of looking at events. Watts likens them to "up" and "down" or "left" and "right." If we worry about what "death is," we are asking false questions. As we might ask naïvely, "What becomes of my fist when I open my hand?" This attitude is reasonable only if we deny all validity to the individual consciousness. I myself believe that it is equivalent to rejecting man as himself. To learn not to care may relieve one of anxiety, but it is to take away all value both from the personal and the collective human adventure.

In our relations with others, both Vedanta and Zen lay great stress on Karuna or compassion. Karuna is rooted in the belief that all persons really *are* one. *Tat tvam asi* is both

[5] Ikkyu, quoted by Watts: *The Way of Zen*, p. 159.

present reality and ethical goal—"That art thou" or, as Chandhuri puts it, "I-and-thou-in That." I have sometimes wondered whether compassion based on the realization that others are really Me is truly altruism or magnified egoism. Nevertheless, this ideal has proved capable of admirable ethical development, probably reaching its peak in the mythical Bodhisattva of Mahayana Buddhism, where the Bodhisattva postpones his final entrance into Nirvana until all living beings (to whom he makes his help available) may enter with him.

Eastern writers admit that ethics as such is primarily the concern of "dualistic philosophers." Watts, even though he claims that the proper interpretation of the relations of this world may be described as love, confesses that no real ethics of brotherhood can be derived from the claim that all are one. The Orient offers no particular progressive social program derived from philosophical theory. Vedanta has been all too willing to cling to the caste system. Zen in Japan has fitted comfortably into the tradition of the Samurai warrior. Nehru, who has done as much for India as Gandhi, felt that India's religious tradition impeded her growth. Over the centuries most religious leaders in the East have held that the great thing one can do for an individual is to help him dissolve his problems via enlightenment rather than try to solve them. It has been argued by Aldous Huxley, among others, that if everyone pursued this ideal, there would no longer exist any ethical problems, either individual or social. Possibly this is true, but there remains the double question of the practicality of the method and the value of the ideal.

In the field of ethics, we encounter a paradox. The East, which begins by asserting the oneness of mankind, tends to be satisfied with the individual attainment of Nirvana or Satori. Humanistic existentialism, starting with the isolated consciousness, stresses social commitment and the need to reorganize society. One might say that Vedanta (and even Zen) moves from the theoretical collective "I" to the individual realization of this "I-ness," whereas existentialism proceeds from a pluralism of concrete "I's" to an ideal "We."

Eastern philosophy promises a higher irrationality which transcends the admitted limitations of human reason and opens the door to an infinite expansion of consciousness. It is my belief that this promise is an invitation to avoid working to achieve such progress as reason can make, despite its restrictions, and a temptation to escape the burden of responsibility which inevitably accompanies individual consciousness. It is neither self-expansion nor self-realization but a refusal to engage any longer in pursuing or making a self.

When Odysseus journeyed homeward to Ithaca, some of his men ate of the strange lotus which friendly strangers offered them, and they straightway refused to leave their new-found delight for a dangerous and difficult voyage. It has been customary to interpret this episode as an allegorical portrayal of how some men will settle for paltry pleasures of the flesh rather than struggle for nobler and more spiritual rewards. Yet who knows what sensations the lotus offered? Perhaps the Greeks entered into an enjoyment of cosmic consciousness which made the challenge to become epic heroes a paltry thing, a struggle for nothing. Why journey over the sea to Ithaca if one was already at home? Considering what happened to Odysseus' men later, possibly they would have been better off to stay with the lotus. We can hardly say the same of Odysseus unless we are willing to say it of all men everywhere who find a goal worth striving for.

PART THREE

RESPONSIBILITIES

IX

Existentialism and
Education

Spread across the front page of a tabloid in letters nearly three inches high were the words "Whole Town Doomed." Page 3 gave the story. It seems that the inhabitants of the remote town of Yolox in Mexico have been plagued for the last hundred years with blindness resulting from the disease onchocerciasis induced by a fly that breeds in the surrounding swamps. Since it is only a matter of time before everyone is bitten, the blind parents train their children for the inevitable darkness that is to come. Boys and girls practice walking and working blindfolded so that they may be prepared for their grim adulthood. The article explained that the Mexican Health Department has set to work getting rid of the flies but predicts a period of twenty to fifty years before the disease is entirely wiped out. Meanwhile a visiting doctor has been attempting to cure some of the children, for the infection is curable in its early stages before the blindness sets in. "To his amazement, he learned that the superstitious people didn't want to be cured. They didn't know what a doctor was, and believed that no man should tamper with their fate." [1]

[1] Report by Michael James, *National Enquirer*, October 11, 1964. Gould's *Medical Dictionary* indicates that a worm, not a fly, is responsible for this disease.

281

The moral of this tale is too obvious to need pointing out. Shocking as the story is, I found it no more so than a shorter news item tucked in as a filler at the bottom of page 24. This one had no editorial comment, but its headline seemed to me to suggest interested acceptance if not actual approval. I quote it exactly as it appears except that I have not given all of the proper names.

"Factory" Produces High School Grads

There were a few changes at C —— High School when it opened on September 14. It's now operating like a factory. When the school's doors reopened, pupils had to punch time clocks going in and out. They call their teachers "foremen." They do industrial work. They have regular coffee breaks. The only difference is they don't get paid. "The object," says principal M —— J ——, "is to train young factory workers of the future. The boys and girls are getting acquainted with factory routine and also with teamwork. They're learning about unions, shop stewards, safety and productivity. Our shops are turning out all sorts of products—cabinets, clothing, glassware, and so on. But our most important product will be kids who know all about factories before they ever set foot in a real one."

It seems to me that the two articles describe an identical process. I do not know how complete an industrialization the C —— High School authorities had in mind. I do not mean that factory life more than any other occupation resembles the blindness of the town in Mexico. But the Procrustean idea that education is meant to fit the pupil into the existing limitations of the social order seems to me to be essentially the same whether one uses literal or figurative blindfolds, whether the adult clothing is to be a work uniform or a gray flannel suit. No wonder that children wish to escape via torn levis or the black leather jacket or that they seem unable to get along without some kind of clothing symbol.

Whether or not it is explicitly formulated as such, the goal of education has generally been twofold: to instill in the child and student the values, the *Weltanschauung* of his society; and to provide him with sufficient mastery of inherited knowl-

282

edge to enable him to fit comfortably into the society, contributing his fair share to maintaining the status quo. I do not mean, of course, that a society may not think of itself as progressing. But the change envisioned is quantitative rather than qualitative. This was true even of the Enlightenment, which proposed inevitable progress toward a rational Utopia but always within the limits of a strictly defined view of a stable human nature.

In abstract formulation, the existentialist view of the proper relation between the individual and his society might not be perceptibly different from the basic assumptions of simple democracy. The ideal would be a state providing for the maximum opportunity for the free development of the individual's creative possibilities and happiness which is consistent with protecting the same opportunity for all others. Existentialism would, of course, emphasize the active, responsible side of government; that is, it advocates our responsibility to correct inequities and to foster freedom, not merely to refrain from interfering with the projects of free individuals. Its ideal is closer to the Welfare State than to laissez-faire capitalism. Despite Sartre's claim to have introduced the individual project into Marxism, I am unwilling to accept either the Communist or the Marxist society as the inevitable and appropriate setting for those persons willing to accept an existentialist ethics. To reaffirm the original principles of democracy as the New Radicals have done seems to me a more promising approach than Sartre's attempt to burrow back to the pure Marxism hidden beneath the layers of doctrinal encrustation. Both practically and theoretically, I see more hope of developing Sartre's ultimate philosophy of freedom in a democracy which consciously modified itself along socialist lines than in any existing or theoretical Marxist state into which one might try to introduce the values of democratic individualism. This does not mean, however, that I regard our present democratic state as being in good faith by existentialist standards. Quite the contrary. Aside from obvious injustices resulting from the discrepancy between theory and practice, existentialism mistrusts the manner in which the central aim of our democratic way of life has been gradually interpreted.

Inasmuch as it is individuals who compose and constitute the group and yet the group which sustains and supports the individual, I suppose any political theory must search for some sort of mean in reconciling the conflicting claims of freedom and responsibility—just as any individual ethics must do. But there are many variations in how the mean as such may be regarded. Even Aristotle recognized that the mean was not a fixed point. American democracy, in theory, recognizes that the mean itself must be balanced by a scrupulous concern for the extremes. Thus we seek in our Constitution a balance which will allow the maximum of liberty for the individual which does not jeopardize the good of the whole. The framers of the Constitution recognized that this aim proposes a problem as much as it offers itself as a solution, and they proposed a safeguard. Such a mean is progressively established by the will of the majority, but this will is prevented from infringing—even in the name of the greatest good for the greatest number—upon certain absolute rights of the extreme individual or minority groups. In jealously guarded areas of private concern, the privilege of being wrong is guaranteed against even the sincere effort of the law to enforce what the majority believes to be right.

In practice we have moved more and more in the direction of trying to define a proper mode of life for everybody. Our legal recognition of such obvious rights as freedom of religious belief, freedom of speech, equality of race and sex have progressed beyond the first intent of the Constitution. The more subtle pressures for conformity have increased and are perhaps more deadly because they are more insidious and offer less opportunity for clear-cut motives for revolt. It takes courage to fight for civil rights in Alabama, but at least it is clear that there is injustice to be opposed, that there is a principle worth defending. The half-secret attack on spontaneity and personal preference for one's own style of life is experienced without ever being fully grasped. It is like those thermal blankets in which the threads are so loosely woven that they seem to hold more empty spaces than substance, yet the result is an artfully contrived insulation against the outer environment more complete than any tight-woven textiles can provide. Against such suffocating pressure, one must fight one thread at a time, and each in itself seems too insignificant to justify a violent revolt.

If we are to have a reasonable hope that many people will succeed in living satisfying lives in good faith, society and its institutions must be in good faith. This is not to deny the responsibility of the individual. An honorable man may live a just life under bad emperors, and the knowledge that he has managed to do so furnishes its own peculiar reward. Christianity flourished under persecution. But while its otherworldliness transmuted even death into glory, the choice of an unpopular way of living on earth is not encouraged by a society which cuts off all possible channels for its development. A significant life in good faith is open to a one-armed man, but he and the society which cut off his arm have both lost any chance of his developing his talents as a great pianist. If he decides that he will commit suicide, we can hold him responsible for failing to achieve something more. Society's is the greater sin.

The Utopian social ideal is often represented in terms that suggest a "We," which is composed of a collection of "I's," each fulfilling itself individually, yet working in perfect harmony—like the players in a symphony. This is indeed comparable to Sartre's image of the football team, and Sartre has stressed the fact that the individual cannot fulfill his own personalizing talents as a player of football without the cooperation of the others. Thus the "We" makes possible the fulfillment of each "I" as well as the reverse. I think it was Sartre's intention to give equal weight to each side of this interaction. Yet both the typical Utopianist and Sartre suggest a hidden danger in these comparisons. This is the risk that we may interpret fulfillment of the "I" solely in terms of the common musical or athletic project. To pick up the simile of the symphony—there must be provision for solo endeavors somewhere in the program and for plenty of holidays during which the several musicians may go off on their own to become fishermen or to act in the community's Little Theater.

If we sincerely want a society which encourages each of its members to "make himself" as the existentialist expresses it, I think we must rethink the educational needs of the individual, whether child or university student. In earlier periods of the world's history there was an apparent reason for deliberate indoctrination, stern discipline, and even insistence on conformity; and it was something which even the child could grasp. So long as the idea of man is as clearly defined as that of fruit or flower, it seems logical and natural that standards and pruning should be applied. Today's society might, at first thought, be called properly consistent in relaxing the strict discipline of our schools and eschewing overt ethical training inasmuch as our vision of the adult ideal is blurred. But of course this is not a true picture of what happens. Paul Goodman attributes a large part of our trouble to the fact that we have adopted an attitude of permissiveness toward our youth without providing them any breadth of opportunity. It is like giving a prisoner full freedom to do as he pleases within the compass of an almost empty cell. In part I agree with Goodman, but I would put the matter a little differently. The idea of what man is and ought to be exists without being openly stated. What is worse, it is in direct contradiction with the permissiveness which appears on the surface. The permissiveness seems to imply (in "progressive" schools it does so on principle) that the individual is encouraged to discover his unique desires and to satisfy them. On two counts it is dishonest. First, it is out of harmony with an adult world which attaches the highest value to conformity. Second, even at the earliest stages, the apparent openness is accompanied by a hidden and subtle pressure pushing each child to desire the same things as everybody else. Even concern for others takes the negative form of not doing anything to hurt him rather than a positive respect for his right to be what he chooses.

On the university level, the situation is somewhat different. Permissiveness has already begun to give way to strict demands that certain objective requirements be met if one wants to stand well in the sequence of grades, recommendations, fellowships, and jobs. The professors whom the student encounters fall into three groups.

First there are those who as teachers (regardless of what they may do in the voting booth) are the eternal spectators. They are guardians of the past even though their field may be listed in the catalogue as contemporary drama or political science. Their ideal is objective, scholarly, analytical detachment. Yet they are not uncommitted. They are dedicated to their subject matter. Recorded ideas and emotions and ways of life are the material of their contemplative projects. They will not knowingly use their analyses as a point of departure for changing the world. For them students exist as recipients of trusts, as confidants for the story of the scholar's intellectual love affair. If the professor can persuade a gifted few to join him in the groves of Academe, he feels that he has performed the greatest of services, both to the young and to the inherited tradition of accumulated, ever-to-be-transmitted knowledge. There are many people in the world more harmful and less happy than these professors. If all people were like them, we would have fewer problems. In the world as it is, they are not the most helpful in solving the difficulties which beset us.

Those in the second group like to think of themselves as pragmatic realists. Secretly content with things as they are, they are at once cynical, optimistic, and effective. One might call them the modern Sophists. They are fully aware of the discrepancy between what is and what ought to be, and they have no hope that things will ever be any better. Yet they see nothing to prevent the individual from winning in the game. By learning the rules thoroughly, he may manipulate them to his own advantage. He may even become one of the leaders of men, and the thought of power is exciting. He may guide society farther; but if he is wise, he will continue in the established direction. Adjusting one's sails to the prevailing winds, sailing in the well-charted seas, a person may have a very pleasant voyage and even win in the boat races if he picks his contests carefully. The students who follow the advice of these professors almost never end up in the police court. Or if they do, it is with other high-ranking executives where the shared prestige protects their career. They seldom become psychotic or even neurotic. Ulcers, alas, are fairly common; at least doctor bills are no problem.

The third type is becoming more frequent, and they are the ones largely responsible for the growing distrust of academic communities on the part of those whose taxes support them. These are the professors who teach and genuinely believe that their task is to train the student to put everything into question, to evaluate critically, to accept as true only those things which seem to stand up as he himself judges them. Such teachers are oriented toward the future, and they hope that their students will participate actively in getting rid of existing evils. Whatever the subject matter may be, the professor treats it as in some way contemporary. Since he is usually committed to his own view of the present and his personal hopes for the future, he must recognize the danger of allowing his teaching to turn into indoctrination. Some fail, but I believe the majority will honor the right of the student to arrive at his own opinion more than they insist on his seeing the light from the professor's point of view. Frequently students take to heart the professor's exhortation that they commit themselves and act to change the world. Then there are student demonstrations and riots. At this point the community is usually reassured, for most professors—if they acknowledge any connection between their lectures and the students' actions—will proclaim loudly in Prufrock's words, "That is not what I meant at all." Sometimes faculty members decide that what is involved is genuine social action, and they actively support it. If they are lucky—and many of them are—the university will support them.

The young man or woman who has run the whole gamut from kindergarten through graduate school may rightly conclude that there is absolutely no common agreement among educators as to what we are educating people for or how we want to go about it. Such uniformity as we do have results largely from our concern that similar degrees should represent roughly equivalent amounts of study (measured in class hours and tested by examinations) and that graduates should be prepared to compete well for the jobs for which they have been trained. It does not derive from any well-thought-out concept of what the human being and his potentialities are or how education may deliberately direct itself toward one kind of future for mankind rather than another. In some respects diversity of aims and methods is to be strongly commended. The last thing in the world which an existentialist would want is a regimented program in which persons are bent on producing precisely the same type of human being. Too often, however, the somewhat haphazard character of a given student's educational career is due not to the different philosophical orientations of those whom he has met along the way but to the fact that few if any have ever formulated for themselves a coherent philosophy of education. An existentialist, whether parent, teacher, or simply taxpayer, ought certainly to raise the question of how and for what we are educating children and young adults and to offer certain criticisms and suggestions with regard to present practice. There is need of a comprehensive existentialist philosophy of education, one which would propose educational aims consistent with the existential view of man, which would develop an educational psychology along the lines of the new insights of existential psychology, and which would offer a concrete program to implement its proposals. This task is obviously far beyond anything which I can hope to accomplish in this short chapter. I will limit myself to a few basic observations.[2]

The very idea of education presents in acute form the paradox inherent in the concept of responsible freedom. The existentialist realizes as keenly as Rousseau the contradiction involved in the decision that we must force people to be free. No matter how firmly the teacher—or parent—resolves to respect the freedom of the child, he cannot help influencing it. Freedom is not exercised in a vacuum. It is meaningless

[2] Some of the material which follows is adapted from my article, "The New Humanism in Education," pp. 193–209.

except where there is an obstacle to overcome—i.e., a choice which must be made. Freedom is always "in situation." Thus whatever the teacher may say or do, he is helping to create the situation in terms of which the student will make his free choice. That the choice is free is attested by the anguish with which the parent watches the child determine by himself whether the adult's word is to be taken as something to guide him or a thing to react against. Nevertheless the child chooses within the situation which we have to some degree structured for him, just as any person's present choice has a particular past as its background. There is no escape from this Original Sin. As Sartre has pointed out, even if we want to give the student's freedom an unlimited range, we restrict it by our very reluctance to impose limitations. If we provide him with a world of absolute tolerance, we thereby prevent him from developing qualities which he might discover in a world less permissive. It is recognition of this fact that has caused many persons to criticize the more relaxed forms of elementary education. Its critics feel that the child is being denied the opportunity of developing intellectual self-discipline and the ability to resist and endure in frustrating situations which he is bound to meet later.

There are two illegitimate ways to cut this Gordian knot. One is to assume that since, in any case, influence is inevitable, one may as well set out to influence the child deliberately and absolutely in the direction which one assumes to be right. In extreme form this results in unabashed indoctrination, which I believe should under no circumstances be defended, not even in wartime and for the armed forces. The alternative is to aim at making our influence as small as possible. Or to put it more attractively, we will seek to use our influence for one aim only—to persuade the student to think for himself. On the higher levels of education, at least, this goal, in the form of the ideal of detached neutrality, is in truth the guiding principle of many honest teachers. I do not believe that it is a solution which existentialism can accept as adequate. In the first place, the teacher who tries to be a wholly impartial arbiter will not perfectly succeed. In spite of himself, he will weight the scales on the side which he believes to be correct—either in a summarizing reformulation of what has been said or by his examples or by his choice of subjects for discussion —not to mention such things as facial expressions and gestures, which for some reason students often take more pleasure in interpreting than the spoken word. If the teacher has committed himself as a person and as a scholar outside the classroom, his students may know already where his convictions lie. It is more honest and more effective to state plainly where one's own bias lies and then to the best of one's ability present the other sides as well. (It goes without saying that I have in mind only the conscientious teacher who really wants students to express their own ideas, who will listen to them, and sometimes himself be influenced by them.) Furthermore, our ideal is neither the indecisive adult nor the indifferent adult, but the person who is concerned about his world and the world of others, who will be ready to act by what he believes to be best and true without closing his mind to the possibility of a future change of mind. Finally the teacher should *teach*, not merely serve as referee. He *should* be able to impart some wisdom to the student beyond what members of the class can find for themselves. Otherwise all that is needed is a master of ceremonies.

On the upper academic levels and within the classroom, the mean between noncommitment and indoctrination is delicate but not formidably difficult to attain. Particularly when we realize the variety of professional personalities to which any one student is exposed, it appears that the infringements on his freedom are relatively small so long as teachers are honest and administrators scrupulous in respecting academic freedom. The more difficult problem arises where the subject matter to be discussed is not intellectual ideas but emotional and ethical attitudes. These are not wholly separate from academic pursuits at any point. They are present implicitly, if not overtly, in any discussions of human conflict and achievement. The professor confronts them directly when the student comes to his office for advice. Most urgently and in purest form, they appear long before that in the kindergarten and early grades, even earlier when the child is under the exclusive care of parents and baby-sitters. This is the time when direct training in conduct cannot be avoided. The parent confronts the ethical choice full face. The dilemma of the elementary teacher differs from that of parents only in that the teacher must justify his or her teaching to employers and the community whereas the parents have for the most part only their own consciences as judge.

There is a great paradox in American education, and I do not think either that it is a healthy one or that it is inevitable. From a strict point of view, it would be fair to say that most American children receive absolutely nothing of what can in any significant sense be called education in ethics. The average parent assumes that this is the task of either the school or the church. The public and nondenominational private schools will usually not tackle the problem directly because educators tacitly hold to the traditional belief that moral precepts are the outgrowth of religious doctrines, and of course such schools cannot teach religion. This already eliminates a great many children. What happens to those who go to church-linked schools or to Sunday schools? Perhaps in a few cases they receive positive teaching in self-understanding and in ways of meeting real problems which they are likely to confront. The majority are either trained in church doctrine only, or are given largely negative prescriptions, or are pleasantly entertained with cheerful stories in which the moral is obvious enough but detached from all realistic setting. Worst of all, any elements of sound moral instruction are so closely connected with church doctrine that if the child later rejects the religious teaching, he too often jettisons the ethical content along with the rest of the cargo. If we thus connive in the production of a generation of moral illiterates, we should not be surprised when they fail to read the obvious signs of warning. The secular school, theoretically concerned solely with the development of the mind, must nevertheless cope with the coexistence of large numbers of unruly bodies and troubled psyches. In the absence of open instruction in ethics, it imposes some sort of formal discipline.

Here we see the other side of the paradox. In indirect fashion the child is molded, even indoctrinated from the moment of his first appearance in the classroom (leaving out, for the present, all question of pressure or influence exerted by his family and by other children). The never more than half-formulated principles seem to me to be something like this:

1. Everyone is supposed to be happy.
2. It is easy to be happy in America because this is the land of opportunity where there is enough for everybody.
3. All school work—or any work—ought to be fun.
4. Although people seem to be different on the surface, they are all alike underneath. This is true even of people in foreign lands. A few wicked leaders make trouble for America because they are greedy, but the people themselves are just like us. We would all like one another if we could meet together freely.
5. Since we are all alike, we must never hurt other people's feelings.
6. In this blessed and just society, one must not be a troublemaker.
7. All violence and aggression are bad. Besides, such conduct is stupid because it makes the aggressor unhappy as well as the one he hurts.
8. Things which are dangerous are bad.
9. Forbidden things are dangerous. One must resist them for one's own good.
10. If anyone acts or looks different from others—unless he is from a foreign land and hasn't had a chance to learn—he is doing this just to call attention to himself. This shows that he is selfish and conceited, which means that he needs help. Anyone who feels like this or anyone who is unhappy should talk things over with the friendly school counselor.

This decalogue is not an all-inclusive formulation; I would not claim that it is a fair presentation of the values of all schools or of all teachers. I believe that it does represent the crystallization of a prevalent attitude. "Trust Uncle Sam. Don't rock the boat. You ought to be happy." This seems to be the gist of it all, and tremendous effort is exerted to hide any inherent contradiction.

As an existentialist, I object both to the content of this collection of half-truths and falsehoods and to the fact that it is never brought out into the open for direct examination and discussion. An existentialist approach would formulate very differently its view of what man and society are and ought to be; it would commit itself to a definite program of implementing its ideals and values.

I freely admit that the existentialist view of man may be presented abstractly in such a way that it seems to preclude any idea of education, at least of education in good faith. Yet while it may lay more stress on the difficulties involved and the need for constant flexibility, existentialism can commit itself as forcefully here as in any other sphere of human activity.

To start with, existentialism does not believe that at bottom everybody is, or ought to be, like everyone else. Existentialism does not even hold that everyone should on all occasions be like, or *be*, himself. Ludwig Lefebre, following Heidegger, has well phrased the existentialist goal in saying that the psychotherapist's aim should not be to help someone to "be himself" but to "come to himself." [3] Sartre, too, has pointed out that "to be oneself is to come to oneself." [4] The emphasis throughout is on the "coming to," not on a self finally attained. The idea that a person is a free, continuous process of self-making introduces several corollaries. Obviously we will be doing violence to the individual if we try to persuade him that in order to be his real or best self he must fit into some ready-make mold. Furthermore, one of the most important consequences of freedom is that a person can change and radically; that he may at some point or points in his life effect so total a reorientation in his relations with the world that he makes what Sartre calls "a new choice of

[3] Ludwig Lefebre: "Inclusion of the Negative," *The Christian Scholar*, Vol. XLVI (Fall, 1963), pp. 219–34, cf. especially p. 233.
[4] Sartre: *Being and Nothingness*, p. 538.

being." If we believe what we say when we state that man is free, we must face the fact that even in childhood a boy or girl may be at one time a quite different kind of person from what he or she has been at an earlier date.

Finally, we should take a new look at those famous latent possibilities. Not everyone insists on the "acorn theory of man": that in each of us there is one given set of traits and potentialities which determine us or which we ought to develop as the one and only real self. Yet almost everybody will agree that what we ought to do is to find out as early as we can what sort of person we want to be and then develop consistently. When a man has not done this, we are accustomed to say, "He took a long time to find himself." Or "He made several false starts before he discovered what he wanted to be." As though he had never wanted to be what he was earlier! And what *was* the self which he was before he found himself?

Obviously no single consciousness can ever develop all of its possibilities. Even in a theory of reincarnation, the opportunity to live a particular situation in more than one way is excluded. For finite mortals, freedom is choice; what one does not choose is rejected forever. If I decide not to go to New York today, my going next week is a different experience, not the one I am presently refusing. To acknowledge this quality of the finite is not the same as to demand that one should make a virtue out of choosing as narrowly and repetitively as one can. Consistency may easily assume the form of a strait jacket. To sum up, the view that man is a free self-creation requires that we convince the child to see himself as a never-ending open process. We will encourage and provide the opportunity for him to define for himself what sort of person he wants to be. We will realize that this self-creation may result in his modifying or profoundly altering his self-definition as he grows older and that the definition itself may involve a decision to explore many ways of being rather than settling upon any one to the exclusion of the rest.

Someone may object that we are failing at this point to do

either of two things which are not only expedient for a stable society but necessary for the consistent adherence to the premises of existentialism. These are the development of concern for others and the responsibility which is inseparable from freedom. This I admit, but let us postpone the problem for the moment as we look at things from the point of view of the self-concerned individual. It is with him that we must start. Unless we convince him to choose freely what is offered and to internalize it as his own way of being, we will be ineffectual. Unless we make it possible for him to be there at the end, finding in good faith that the goal was worthy of his efforts, we will have failed him and we will not have justified ourselves.

I maintain that three needs of the child are being ignored if not deliberately frustrated. They are: the right to live the extreme choice, the right to change, and the right to spontaneous self-realization.

It has been interesting to me to observe the renewed popularity, especially among university students, of Hermann Hesse's *Steppenwolf*, a book which less directly makes these same three assertions. Hesse's solutions are unacceptable, at least to me as an existentialist. He solves his hero's problem artistically by bringing in imaginative experiences induced by drugs. Philosophically the resolution is arrived at by an appeal to Eastern doctrines of metempsychosis and "*tat tvam asi*." Yet in presenting the Steppenwolf's problem, Hesse does not confine himself narrowly within the area of his own philosophical predilections, and he has some important things to say. He claims that the bourgeois—that is, the average man or that collectivity which we call society—"is nothing other than the search for a balance." He fears extremes in others and in himself. Hesse maintains that many persons—if not all—sense the appeal of the unconditioned life.

If we take any one of these coupled opposites, such as piety and profligacy, the analogy is immediately comprehensible. It is open to a man to give himself up wholly to spiritual views, to seeking after God, to the ideal of saintliness. On the other hand, he can equally give himself up entirely to the life of instinct, to the lusts of the flesh, and so direct all his efforts to the attainment of momentary pleasures.[5]

It is Hesse's idea that for the average man, "the absolute is his abhorrence." He will do anything in order to avoid the extreme. He chooses the temperate zone "at the cost of that intensity of life and feeling which an extreme life affords." Hesse says that the motive for clinging to the colorless mean is fear of losing one's identity. "A man cannot live intensely except at the cost of the self." I cannot accept Hesse's words in quite the sense which he intended. I do not believe that passionate commitment to intense living is a giving up of oneself to something else. It is rather the choice of being the kind of person who lives this sort of life rather than another. I can agree with Hesse's statement, however, if we assume that the "self" which is lost in intensity is the idea of self which is imposed by society and which, in bad faith, a man accepts as his essence. Living a passionate commitment inevitably takes one beyond the horizons of conventional social ethics, and one is obliged to chart one's own way. In this sense authenticity and the extreme choice have a certain affinity. The right to choose the intense one-sided rather than the balanced life is perfectly consistent with existentialist ethics. One's choice will in itself demonstrate whether one views the mean as the Greeks saw it—μηδὲν ἄγαν (nothing too much) or as the Romans phrased it, *aurea mediocritas*, the Golden Mean, reading into the term the English connotations of mediocrity.

At this point I must forestall one obvious objection. The existentialist emphasis on passion and commitment has often been interpreted as if Kierkegaard and others after him had meant that passionate activity of any kind is to be valued and judged right in preference to any attempt at neutrality, non-commitment, or passivity. Walter Kaufmann in particular has attacked existentialism from this point of view.[6] He objects that if passionate commitment is of prime importance

[5] Hermann Hesse: *Steppenwolf* (New York: Modern Library; 1963), pp. 56–7.
[6] Walter Kaufmann: *The Faith of a Heretic* (Garden City: Doubleday; 1961), Ch. iv.

without consideration of that to which one is committed, then the dedicated Nazi directors of concentration camps would be pronounced models for our admiration, whereas the all-tolerant man, wanting simply to live and let live, would be a monster. Even granting that neither represents the ideal commitment, Kaufmann is certainly correct in objecting that under no circumstances can we support an ethics which would bestow laurels on the officials at Buchenwald.

Two things should be said by way of explanation. First, commitment is indeed an existentialist virtue, but it is not the only one. We can better understand the idea of commitment if we consider the closely related concept of action. Existentialism emphasizes action for two reasons: First, as Inez says in *No Exit*, "You *are* your acts." A man will have been what he will have done, not what he kept as a daydream or potentiality. It is by his actions that man defines himself. Man acts, man chooses, man makes himself. These assertions come close to being synonymous. To refrain from action is in itself an act just as not to choose is already to have chosen. Therefore we must agree that action is primary for existentialism, but this is not to say that all action is good. By his act a man may define himself as being in good faith or in bad faith. It is entirely consistent to pass two judgments simultaneously upon either action or commitment as we do when we say that someone performed an act which was kind but mistaken. At times the degree of commitment may very well be the factor on which our judgment is based. The humanistic existentialist would usually, I believe, give his approval to the fully committed religious believer who acts consistently with his faith rather than to the social or polite churchgoer who only half-believes, who timidly refrains from all questions, who is content with a secondhand experience, who is quite willing to profess one code and live by another. The believer may be mistaken in the eyes of the humanist, but he is in good faith. He has chosen to justify his life by acting in harmony with what seems to him the true view of man and his destiny. The lukewarm Christian has refused all challenge to justify his life. He implicitly accepts the values of the Serious World, avoiding the task of creating a value system of his own.

This same example can be further developed so as to show how a judgment may waive the factor of commitment as irrelevant or even attach to it a negative value. If in the interests of furthering my own religious goals I begin to treat others as objects, denying and abusing their freedom, perhaps killing them in the name of the true Faith, then clearly I have trespassed against values more sacred to the existentialist than passion. He might still declare objectively that I was willing to risk all for my belief. Like de Beauvoir with regard to some of the very young idealistic Nazis, he might commend my courage and my self-transcendence. Yet he would ultimately condemn both me and my actions as guided by a false view of man and devoted to false absolutes.

A second point to be made is that genuine commitment is not the same as blind devotion to a system set up by somebody else. The wish to avoid the necessity for thinking through each choice and recognizing one's responsibility for each act is what engenders loyalty to extremist groups whether they be fascist, communist, racist, or fanatically patriotic. Surrender of self and self-transcendence are opposites, not synonyms. Self-transcendence alone involves true commitment. In speaking of the right of the individual, whether child or adult, to make the extreme choice, I am referring only to a commitment which is justifiable in existentialist terms. With these qualifications, I would defend the right to the extreme choice in good faith, whether the majority of men call it sensible or not. Narrow it may be, but intensity, as well as breadth, can be a value.

Another possible objection we must take more seriously. The extreme choice, if it represents a way of life and is for a lifetime, is of necessity a choice which satisfies only—or almost solely—our need for reflective self-realization. This is true even if, as in Hesse's example, it is a choice which places the highest value on the sensual. So long as we maintain it, we must close off all spontaneous reactions to other possibilities. At most, we will deliberately renew the choice, sustaining it *as a choice* but giving it our unswerving allegiance. Only if the choice is renewed, without being accompanied by the refusal to put everything into question, does it remain existentially pure.

For all that he defended the right to the unconditioned life, the Steppenwolf does not find the once-and-for-all commitment to be the most desirable. Despite its intensity, there is danger that its self-restriction will leave it somewhat impoverished. The situation is altered somewhat if our defense of the right to make the extreme choice is accompanied by insistence on the second assertion, the right to change—that is, to choose again. I realize that the idea of making a succession of unconditioned choices can easily be made to appear ludicrous. We think of Don Juan falling in love forever—with every woman he meets. Still I maintain that the life which reveals a series of radically different reorientations is not necessarily a sign of insincerity, emotional instability, or even of a growth process unduly protracted. Speaking still abstractly, I would argue that the possibility of so choosing is the most obvious way of satisfying one's need for spontaneous self-realization without giving up all possibility of temporal self-realization. For we must not forget that our third assertion, too, is vital—that man needs the opportunity to act spontaneously in a new way, "out of character," in response to the strong appeal of an immediate situation.

Sartre seems to be thinking along somewhat these same lines in an introspective passage toward the end of *The Words*. Although he explains his attitude as derived from his sense as a child that he was living for the sake of future fame, and although he speaks of himself as perpetually fleeing forward because of dislike of what he is and has been, nevertheless Sartre admits to a certain pride in claiming that he never feels at any moment that he is identified with the man he was formerly. Neither criticism nor praise of his past achievements touches him deeply, for he feels that the one praised or blamed is no longer there before the critic. Sartre himself judges the past self with a certain detachment. One small section of this discussion seems to me worth quoting, particularly because it contains a suggestion of a way to reconcile the demands of the two types of self-realization.

I became a traitor, and I am still one today. I try in vain to put myself wholly into any undertaking, to give myself up unreservedly to my work, to anger, to friendship; a moment later I will deny myself. I know this, it is what I want. At the height of passion, I already betray myself by the joyous presentiment of my future betrayal. On the whole, I stand by my commitments, like anyone else. *Steadfast in my affections and in my conduct, I am unfaithful to my emotions.* Monuments, paintings, landscapes— there was a time when the one I had seen last was always the most beautiful. I have annoyed my friends by recalling cynically, or simply in fun, a common memory which could have remained precious to them—and all in order to convince myself that I was detached from it.[7]

Sartre goes on to say, albeit a trifle condescendingly, "Yet I like and respect the humble and faithful tenacity with which certain people—especially women—cling to their desires, their former projects, festivals long past. I admire their will to remain the same in the midst of change." Obviously he himself prefers to be loyal to commitments, steadfast in affections, unfaithful to his emotions. I do not claim that Sartre's personal ideal should be that of all of us. It does seem to me that he suggests here one resolution of the dilemma.

For obviously there is a dilemma. It stems from the same fact about man's being which we discussed in connection with bad faith. I both am and am not my past. To disclaim all connection with it is as false as it would be to deny that at the moment of secretly taking a stranger's money, it is I who am stealing it. Even if my consciousness is process and not entity, even if it separates its objects from itself by a nothingness, still this consciousness I call mine is aware of having been a consciousness which initiated certain acts; it sustains now in memory a particular closed relation to these acts, one which is inaccessible to any other person. The earlier activity of consciousness is a part of that background which goes to

[7] Sartre: *Les Mots,* p. 198. My italics.

make up the situation within which it initiates any project or intends any object. Simultaneously, however, we must recognize that the present relation which a consciousness sustains with its earlier activity is not necessarily the same as it was earlier. We observed how bad faith sought to blur these distinctions as a way of avoiding responsibility. The task of good faith is to keep them distinct and at the same time to reconcile the demands of freedom and responsibility, of spontaneous and reflective self-realization, the truth of the immediate response and the reality of temporal continuity. Sartre suggests that he has effected the reconciliation in his own case by demanding of himself fidelity to commitments or engagements while holding himself open to the spontaneous emotions evoked by new experiences.

We may return now to the student and our problem of educating him, considering these three needs or rights of his in terms of what we owe to him and to ourselves as members of the society which his acts will affect. If we work within an existentialist orientation, I think we cannot do better than to adapt to our own purposes Sartre's early description of the New Revolutionary. Sartre presented this in an article called "Materialism and the Revolution," published in 1946, when Sartre was still trying to distinguish between the positions of existentialism and contemporary Marxism rather than viewing existentialism as a parasitic ideology, seeking to modify Marxism from within. The view of man and society which he then presupposed as underlying any specific program could be summed up as follows:

Man is "unjustifiable," and his existence is "contingent." There is no Providence or inner law of history which determines the course of human events, nor is there any fixed human nature to enable us to predict how man will behave or to serve as a yardstick by which we can say how he ought to behave. Man alone is responsible for his destiny; better yet, each individual man decides what mankind will be by his own choices as he makes his life. Therefore any given society exists without any guarantee of its ultimate "rightness" and may be transcended toward another kind of society. The values of any existing society are always those which both reflect the social structure and tend to preserve it. Therefore men may always seek to go beyond an existing set of values since the new values are anticipated, even invented by men's very effort to pass beyond the present social order.[8] On the basis of these premises, Sartre feels that an existentialist philosophy of evolution must allow for continued self-transcendence in the direction of greater freedom and an open future.

It seems to me that the same sort of open future may be posited as a legitimate goal for the individual. In each case the possibility of progress toward a more satisfying level of existence is kept open. It is not the easy inevitable progress of the Enlightenment. Genuine self-transcendence means a *new* goal and *new* values, not merely a closer approximation to a Utopia clearly envisioned in all of its details. I suppose one could represent such a life diagrammatically as a series of plateaus, resembling the upward curve of the learning process. There is no final level of attainment, unless it is that which is formed artificially by death or by the destruction of the human race. Naturally one hopes that each plateau will be higher than the earlier one, more inclusive in its view. We must expect, however, that even when this is true, the greater spaciousness of the later landscape will be accompanied by loss of certain closer delights which the earlier afforded. It is entirely probable, too, that the vista of the later plateau will be no more spacious but simply different. In the history of the arts, we can easily perceive the achievement of such plateaus. There are the eras (e.g., the Elizabethan or the Renaissance) when artists, with no sense of restriction, work out their individual visions, develop their own unique capabilities in forms which they gradually crystallize. Then comes the period of imitations, of second-raters, who do not realize that they are seeing only secondhand, that they are seeking to express the synthesis of a particular moment of human expe-

[8] Jean-Paul Sartre: "Matérialisme et révolution," *Les Temps modernes*, Vol. I (June–July, 1946). The ideas which I have sketched here are discussed in the July issue, pp. 1–39.

rience which is already a step behind the movement of experience itself. There is a staleness, an overripeness which has something false about it; we must await a fresh voice or eye willing again to look at life itself and not at the concepts that others have formed of it. Similarly the society which perhaps best satisfied the needs and ideals of justice for a given group goes on functioning in the usual way for a long time before anyone realizes that those values and ideas that inspired it are no longer the same. In the individual life, whether or not the person who lives it believes in the possibility of his freedom to change, there occurs this same development with respect to the plateau which one has reached. There is first the awareness that all things work together in spontaneous response to a new, totalizing view of reality. Both the freshness and the genuineness of unified, consistent action are exhilarating. It is at this point that we can come closest to accepting Alan Watt's direction to us to let go and trust the natural man. The view of reality which we have chosen for ourselves, which we have chosen to *be*, sets up a requiredness in our decisions and acts which seems to us to exist both in things themselves and in us. Sometimes we meet open discrepancies which force upon us the incorrectness or inadequacy of our orientations, and we recognize intellectually the need for advancing to a more inclusive or quite different view of things. Most often we remain fixed without recognizing that our reactions have become mechanical, automatic responses to stimuli, that we look at things in terms of an old classification without investigating to see whether it still fits or whether we are still classifying the same objects. Neither freshness nor genuine spontaneity remains. At this point, it depends on us whether or not we find the energy and courage to move on. It is now that we must battle it out between those two needs of our organism—growth and safety,[9] being and becoming. As existentialists, we must recognize that the plateaus of being must be left behind if they are not to be transformed into pockets of bad faith.

[9] Abraham H. Maslow: *Toward a Psychology of Being* (Princeton: D. Van Nostrand Company; 1962), especially Ch. iv.

Successful adjustment, whether personal or social, is a series of plateaus and not a mountain peak. The only absolute knowledge is a dynamic knowledge which is ever in process. If we, as teachers or parents, believe this, then we must seek somehow to present uncertainty with the positive highlights of the challenge, not merely as the negative threat of insecurity.

I am convinced that there has been no period of history more congenial to the idea of educating for an open future than our own. We are obviously in a state of transition. I say this with full awareness that there is no decade or even a single year which is not transitional in one way or another; if nothing else, it at least marks off a period of time until a change is perceptibly underway. That our own era is transitional to a marked degree seems obvious, whether for evidence we point to the breakdown in the Judaeo-Christian morality in the West, or to the breathtaking revolutions in science and technology, or to the emergence on the scene of world history of new nations in Africa and a new form of ideological conflict. It would be ridiculous to suggest that we have come to a resting place in any of these areas.

A transition which is in the past always appears as an interesting blend of old and new elements, all stamped with a well-defined orientation toward some new goal. When we *live* a transition, it shows itself in three heterogeneous aspects: by vague thrusts toward an undefined future; by sudden violent returns to the past, suddenly reinstated as an unsurpassable Absolute, and by strips of no man's land where people wander convinced that there is *no* pathway leading out. Of this despairing or indifferent aimlessness we can see examples on all sides, both in life and in much of contemporary literature. It is the attitude that because the older values have been uprooted, the earth must remain the Wasteland which Eliot so well described a generation ago. The return to the past is typified, of course, by such movements as that led by Billy Graham or—less innocently—the extreme right wing political parties, which have in some cases allied themselves with Protestant fundamentalism. It is the thrusts toward the future

305

which chiefly concern us. Granted that no one can say which of these actually carries the imprint of that future which will be; it is equally true to say either that there is not as yet *any* future or that the outline of many futures is clearly before us in each human project. A philosophy of education in a transitional period should be aware of these qualities of the transition. It must be prepared to resist regressive tendencies but not fail to take them into consideration; it must search for new ways of appealing to the disillusioned; and it must remember always that as it chooses to view certain movements as significant, the very choice will cause these movements to be *actually* indicative of the future synthesis.

Finally an existentialist philosophy of education ought to commit itself in the form of concrete proposals for specific changes in the existing educational system—its institutions, its methods and requirements, as well as its ideals and goals and the concepts of human psychology on which they are founded. Two types of problems are involved. We need persons with the courage to plan for a future still remote from us when our educational institutions would be as strikingly different from our own in organization and function as that longed-for society which will have solved its problems of production. We should not be afraid of the Utopian in our thinking, for it is only belief in the possibility of what has not yet been attained which makes progress even conceivable. A willingness to rethink all of our aims and to throw the whole system into question will prevent our painting the walls when we ought to be getting rid of the termites and strengthening the foundations. At the same time education cannot wait for Utopia any more than politics can. We are going to be living within our present structure for a long time yet. Internal improvements simply must be made; in fact, it is only by working with them now that we will learn how to build a better building later.

In these areas everything still remains to be done. It would be a long and tedious task to list all of even the more obvious needs. Moreover everything hinges on everything else until one may easily get the impression that the little red schoolhouse has proved to be a Pandora's box from which only Hope has escaped. In concluding this chapter I will limit myself to indicating a few of the problems which seem to me particularly pressing for one with an existentialist orientation.

There is first the question of how to foster the unique individual in a graded system designed to classify people according to the length of time spent in it and to reward them with tangible symbols of their performance as compared with that of others at the same level. Free development ought not to be hampered by the need for some means of measurement, but it frequently is. Educators have rightly pointed out that for the child prodigy to be pushed rapidly through the established curriculum and find himself sitting amidst classmates seven years his seniors is not a good solution. The opposite alternative is no better—to provide him with only such mental nourishment as the majority in his age group can and will digest so that he comes more and more to resemble them.

At present we make some provision—never enough—for the students who are willing and able to master academic subjects more swiftly and easily. Occasionally we provide special classes for the "gifted students." The designation is revealing and dreadfully accurate. These boys and girls are indeed gifted; they possess the particular abilities and have developed the personality traits which society has chosen to recognize as desirable and to encourage. I am all in favor of special classes and opportunities for these special students. Indeed I should like to see their opportunities expand and the students become far more special and less like one another.

It is important not to let children with a high I.Q. (i.e., abilities which society not only values but has learned to measure) wither from boredom instead of coming to full bloom. It is just as vital and more difficult to do something about two other groups, which are usually neglected. There are those whose interests and talents find no place to develop within the standard curriculum. The student who can perform comfortably in traditional ways is encouraged to engage in extra independent projects of his own. The one who most

307

needs and could best profit by a different approach is forbidden to try it because he has not first mastered the conventional assignments. There is simply no time to let the apparently poor or indifferent student experiment. He is judged incapable of doing something other than the standard because he has not shown himself capable or willing to meet the standard. In fact, even the so-called superior student is rather unlikely to make radical use of his special privilege. By the time he has proved himself worthy of it, commonplace habits of thought are so ingrained in him that his "original" work will almost surely be at best a progress along lines already clearly mapped out. Besides failing to develop the unique possibilities of those who will with more or less success at least complete high school and college and merge into the indistinguishable mass of other Americans who make do without being really happy, we are guilty of downright injustice toward the much too large minority of underprivileged Americans who enter the primary classroom as if coming into a foreign land. With "no vocabulary" for understanding the teaching which is offered them, they are carried along, a sullen burden, from grade to grade until they reach the age when they may legally attain the status of high school dropout—unless sheer desperation pushes them into overt delinquency long before that.[1]

I do not know how we can solve the problem of offering equal educational opportunity for all without impressing upon our youth a boxlike mold which would prevent anyone from pushing out at the top and sides and would crush all those who can't fit in at the bottom. Somehow it has to be done if our goal for both the individual and society is an open future.

What is required is not merely revision of the curriculum

[1] "No Vocabulary" is the title of a lecture presented by Professor Higman of the University of Colorado. Professor Higman was reporting on the program of research and social welfare which the Department of Sociology carries out under his direction in Denver. His concept of "action research," in which the process of investigation results in changing (and improving) the conditions investigated, is one which existentialism enthusiastically endorses.

or even more latitude in choosing the particular subjects which one will study. We need to work out a totally new concept of the proper relation between the formal course of study and the individual's personal needs and interests. I recognize that we immediately find ourselves in a dilemma. If we allow students to follow byways of their own, how are we ever going to find some common set of criteria to determine when their education is to be pronounced complete? How will we be able to decide who is prepared for college or graduate school and who is not? And how can the teacher at the more advanced institution possibly teach individuals so differently and so unevenly prepared? I do not pretend to have the full answer to this difficulty. Partly, of course, the problem would be made easier by the fact that our increased flexibility and practice of allowing students to meet requirements in a variety of ways would apply all the way from the primary grades through graduate school. We would not merely make a game of learning in the early years and then expect the student to follow instructions so as to learn in earnest when he reaches maturity. The original and truly creative approach is harder as well as more rewarding. Moreover, I do not urge that we eliminate subject matter in the interests of emotional self-expression but that we seek ways by which each person may gain knowledge in the manner most effective for him and conducive to his making active use of it rather than receiving it passively and storing it away like a buried treasure. If there is any one place where a fresh creative approach is most desperately needed and should be easiest to arrange, it is the graduate school, particularly in the areas of the humanities. At the moment its smug complacency renders it almost impregnable. Graduate students may rightly regard their stay there as an initiation or ordeal with the Ph.D. as a medal of valor and ticket of admission to freedom. Unfortunately, most of them will insist that other candidates go through the same endurance tests that they themselves have passed.

There still remains, however, the question of how to distinguish those students who are capable of going further in the strictly academic life from those whose choices in high school have led them in other directions. Possibly we could institute the policy of giving two kinds of diplomas. One would certify that the graduate was in fact ready to enter college, and I mean by this that he had achieved a level of knowledge beyond that presently attained by the majority of entering freshmen, most of whom have never worked to full capacity because of the low average of expectation in the schools from which they come. The second diploma would indicate that the graduate had completed the minimum of general education which society requires of its members. This should not be the equivalent of a dishonorable discharge or token of failure. If primary and secondary education consistently consider the varied needs and abilities of the pupils, the group of those who will not go to college will no longer be composed solely of those who studied the same subjects in the same way but didn't make it. The more flexible program and the recognized policy of finding avenues suitable for every boy and girl will result in sending to college some who could never conceivably arrive there in our present system. On the other hand, there will and should be some persons who will receive the second diploma although at present they and their parents would take college for granted. I do not say this because I want to tighten the entrance requirements or because, with the pressure of increased population in an affluent society, I should like to make higher education a privilege for the intellectual elite.

I hold quite the opposite view. Even those who receive a supposedly terminal diploma ought to be offered every opportunity to prove by some tangible evidence that they are eligible for the chance of working toward a higher degree. In addition I should like to see universities and colleges do far more in opening their classes to persons who want special training in certain areas without working toward a degree and in providing courses for people of all ages who would like to devote their leisure hours to the sheer pleasure of learning. I should like nothing better than to see education become a major area of recreation. On the other hand, I do not believe that either the full- or part-time academic life is or ought to be for everybody. One of our gravest errors has been to equate "intelligent" with "intellectual." If we could somehow get rid of the idea that one's worth as a person is measured by his years of formal academic training, there might be many a now unhappy undergraduate leading a much more rewarding life far away from the institution where he feels himself a voluntary prisoner or less articulately knows he is unhappy and vaguely blames the system. Here, of course, we are dealing with social attitudes, a problem even bigger than that of education. Yet certainly education molds as well as reflects social opinions and indeed furnishes one of the clearest accesses to a vantage point from which to change them.

Perhaps one of the best ways to induce an individual to strive for the kind of life most truly satisfying to him is to show that there is a great variety of types of lives which he can respect and among which he can choose that most congenial to him. Most Utopian planners have included the idea of dividing people into groups according to their talents and have assumed that all will be happiest doing what they can do best and will recognize the justice of rewards being given proportionate to the value of the service rendered. These systems are vitiated by their insistence on classifying people, assigning them to one class, expecting them to stay contentedly in it, and making of the structured society an unabashed hierarchy with a pyramid at the top held by the best, the most valuable members (valuable from the point of view of their ability to keep the society going along the lines established). What I propose is not another class system, not even a benevolently intentioned one. I am utterly opposed to any attempt to assign a child to a group where he seems to fit and then direct him in a planned program. We are educating men and women, not breeding strains of animals. If I speak of types of lives, it is only with the purpose that they may be used as exemplars of a world of choices and widely diverse possibilities. If from the start we imbue the child with the idea that he should not only pursue happiness but decide for himself what happiness really is and the path which he wants to follow in searching for it, then I do not think we have to worry overmuch lest he live imitatively and lose himself in the social role. We should in any case constantly emphasize that in the later career and adult life, each individual should live his situation freely in his own particular way—just as he will have grown accustomed to doing in his school projects. We must remember, too, to allow for new choices. We should provide not only a head start but a fresh start. Even in our present over-rigid system of grading and evaluating, we inflict unnecessarily severe penalties on the student who changes his mind—whether he merely picks a new major in his junior year at college or drops out of school for a while or fails his courses for two semesters while he concentrates on some personal problem. A friend of mine suggests that we ought to allow any student who feels the need of it simply to drop from his record any one year which he feels represents an aberration or a false start. This might be an idea worth adopting.

I am fully aware that everything I have mentioned here raises new difficulties as great as those which I insist we ought to overcome. There is a whole army of Scylla-Charybdis monsters to beset us once we stray from our present well-trodden middle path. There is the old problem of how to combine the liberating education of the mind with the specific requirements of the vocation for which the student is being trained. Certain related questions are still harder: If we allow the student to follow where his own inclination leads him, how can we prevent him from choosing what is merely easy and pleasant rather than what is potentially most rewarding? How can we keep him from choosing so narrowly that he fails to see even the possibility of other approaches and makes of his freely selected path the road to a prison? If we demand less by way of imposed requirements, can we reasonably expect a student to emerge better educated? What incentives for higher performance remain once we have removed the uniformity of expectation which allows us to measure and reward? Where will the student learn the self-discipline and responsibility for commitments if we encourage him to follow

312

his own bent and to begin over again every time he makes a mistake? These and many other tensions of conflicting demands will have to be squarely confronted. The solutions will not be easy to find. For myself I will say only this: It is my firm conviction that we should demand more, not less of our students from kindergarten through graduate school. Is this determination consistent with the resolve to foster individual freedom? I am convinced that it is, for I believe that the person who lives in a situation which is conducive to his realizing himself both in becoming and in being will find that growth is more appealing than stagnation.

Another large problem area is the field of counseling. Here I refer not only to the staff of school counselors and psychiatrists but also to teachers and professors, all of whom—unless they deliberately avoid it—are from time to time in the position of advising troubled students concerning problems which may or may not be philosophical but which are certainly personal and not academic. I am sure there will still be unhappy individuals who need help even in institutions nearer to Utopian than our own. I cannot anticipate the particular problems likely to be encountered in an educational system which has been brought into harmony with the ideals of existentialism. I know that there are several aspects of our present procedure which undermine our best efforts and which need correcting.

In the first place, while there are numerous exceptions, too many of the counselors and of the teachers who send students to them still cling to the idea that successful adjustment to the established social order is the desired goal. If the student's inability to cope with his world stems directly from family or interpersonal relations, or from certain types of sexual maladjustments, then—given an intelligent counselor —any one of the traditional therapeutic approaches may prove helpful. If, as so often happens these days, the student's problem is less personally psychological and stems from bewilderment at what seems to be our human condition and from hostility toward contemporary society, he will rightly resent being told that adjustment to what he has rejected is the only solution.[2] In the eyes of those who are rebellious as well as unhappy, the counselor is often the epitome of the flat mediocrity against which they are revolting. The counselor or psychiatrist who has never seriously questioned either the authenticity or the philosophical foundations of his own life is ill equipped to meet this new kind of challenge. He is tempted to see it as merely a surface symptom of the "deeper," more familiar conflicts which he is used to treating, e.g., resistance against parental authority or sibling rivalry or an Oedipus complex. The students resent this procedure. In mingled disgust and amusement they sometimes play the game of inventing the expected confessions and then watching for the predictable reactions. At least the stronger ones do, for all that they may regret this effort to flatten out their philosophical crisis and wipe it away without resolving it. The weaker may accept with gratitude the new Absolute which comes their way to shelter their dependency. God is dead, but don't worry. The psychiatrist is in charge and will see you at eleven.

There are certain efforts which I think we ought to make—both to keep the student from having to present himself for some sort of therapy and to help him more effectively when he does ask for help. First, we must rid people of the notion that abnormality is in itself a sign that the psyche is like a machine in disrepair which needs to be taken to a mechanic. In part we can help by simply easing up on the pressure to conform. Many a well-intentioned adviser has endeavored to persuade a teen-ager that it is a foolish waste of energy to get into trouble over such meaningless symbols of defiance as particular hair styles. The same adult will fail to realize that in his very plea, he is asking for compliance with a trivial regulation as a token of willingness to conform! Certainly in general we should grant to the student the maximum of social freedom that we can persuade the public to accept. We must

[2] I have discussed some of these ideas in an article, "The Ivory Tower Rebel and His Philosophy," *Journal of the National Association of Women Deans and Counselors*, Vol. XXVIII (Winter 1965), pp. 66–73.

imbue in him the idea that to be different is not in itself a sign either of natural superiority or an indication that something is wrong with him. We must go much farther than this. We should seek some way to persuade people to be willing to bear a degree of psychological pain. The habit of self-analysis (I do not mean morbid introspection) can be learned as well as the ability to understand others. But it is not enough merely to be aware of what goes on inside one's self. Lefebre proposes as the goal of existential therapy, the patient's "ability to stand ultimate situations." [3] A legitimate aim of teaching—and perhaps one way to ease the crowding in the counselor's office—might be this: to instill in the individual the realization that the process of making oneself is never-ending, that the interest and rewards it offers are directly commensurate with the psychic labor and anguish which one is willing to put into the task. The sickly, fond contemplation of one's neurotic image is indeed a destructive narcissism. Learning to comprehend the full meaning of one's own growth and to find the process interesting even when painful is one of the prime sources of human satisfaction and quite legitimately so. To experience one's self as both creator and created, to welcome the playing of one's own part, even if the play prove to be a tragedy—this is to me the profound meaning of Nietzsche's Yea-saying.

Not everyone who would like to say Yes to life can manage by himself to clear the frustrations which seem to block every attempt at authentic self-making. When we are appealed to for counsel, what kind of response is consistent with our existentialist premises? To begin with, we must recognize that the student's social dilemmas are posed against the background of a society whose codes of conduct are rapidly changing and which offers a wide discrepancy between our half-open practice and our theory. In giving specific advice to one who moves uncertainly and is troubled, we must be sure first in our own minds of what we believe to be a defensible position and we should be honest in presenting it, no matter how contrary to established opinion it may be. If it is opposed

[3] Ludwig B. Lefebre, "Inclusion of the Negative," p. 233.

to the policy openly embraced by local authorities, we owe it to the student not only to show all the reasons why the alternative views have seemed desirable to the majority of persons but to remind him both of the probable consequences when he is judged by those who still at least pay lip service to the law or regulation, and of the grave responsibility which anyone incurs when he acts contrary to a law he regards as unjust. So far mere honesty would demand. It seems to me important to let the student know that he is not alone in refusing to measure his actions by a given social yardstick. Instead of leaving him with the feeling that he is a hostile aggressor against the community, we should urge upon him his responsibility to change the social structure for the good of the community.

There is no perfect solution to the tension between the demands to respect the other's freedom and the acknowledged obligation to share the wisdom of one's own experience and convictions when one feels that it will help. An existentialist must recognize the absoluteness of each requirement and choose, without guarantee, which he will put uppermost at a particular moment without totally waiving the other. I believe that we should openly and deliberately teach certain ethical attitudes. Naturally I do not mean that even one sympathetic with humanistic existentialism should indoctrinate by preaching the unassailability of such specific social commitments as I have been presenting in this book. There exist, however, some principles and views of man which do not represent the commitments of an engaged freedom but are the conditions of any life which is to realize the full possibilities of its freedom. We ought to teach people that we are responsible and free, that authenticity and the ethical life are values worth striving for. We should show them the difference between being-with others and being-one-with others. We should help them to understand their relation to their own emotions, to realize that they are not enslaved to their past and that they will themselves determine the quality of their own future. We should unashamedly proclaim the doctrine of the irreducibility of each independent subjectivity and affirm that nobody should ever be relegated to object status because of some accident of his birth or social circumstances. To enlarge this list of presuppositions and aims and to implement them is the task of an existentialist philosophy of education which has yet to emerge.[4]

[4] Although I have not encountered what I am willing to call a fully developed existentialist philosophy of education, I gladly acknowledge that some writers have been working with the possibilities of introducing existentialist concepts into educational theory. In particular I should like to point out two works: Van Cleve Morris: *Existentialism in Education: What It Means* (New York: Harper and Row; 1966); and George F. Kneller: *Existentialism and Education* (New York: Philosophical Library; 1958).

X

Personal Pronouns

Note on "It" and "They"

Existentially "It" and "They" are impersonal pronouns and have no place in a discussion of human relations in good faith. "It" belongs properly to the realm of Being-in-itself. Illegitimately "It" creeps into the human world when one person regards another as an object. "They," as the equivalent of the German *das man*, is Heidegger's famous term for the unauthentic anonymous crowd. We have encountered both of these pseudo-personal pronouns in our discussion of the Serious World and will leave them there.

"You" and "I" and "We"

It would be almost—not quite—correct to say that in the two kinds of self-realization we have two kinds of values—an I-value and a Me-value. True, it is the "I" which realizes the value in either case, but there is a difference.

In spontaneous self-realization, it is the sense of my subjective "I-ness" which emerges. In reflective self-realization, what is important is that I recognize with approval the responsible relation which my present "I" sustains with both the past "I's" and the anticipated future "I's," now viewed temporally as objective "Me." Thus even within my own consciousness there is need for more than one pronoun to designate this person which I am. In a world where there are others, any person—*potentially* at all times and *actually* most of the time—exists as not only an I but as He or She, We, You, and They in both the subjective and objective cases. "Human relations" is simply the term we use to describe the fact that every "I" is a multiple of pronoun forms.[1]

Religious existentialism—including both the openly theistic position and the being-philosophies of those writing under the strong influence of Heidegger—has linked authentic existence with love. In these writers one finds love presented as the Unconditional, as the highest value, as the natural reality and only true fulfillment of the human creature. By contrast, when one thinks of humanistic existentialism, what immediately springs to mind is the climactic moment of Sartre's *No Exit:* Garcin's declaration, "Hell is Others." Even further thought on the subject is likely to stick with Sartre's brilliant analysis of the "battle to the death of consciousnesses" in *Being and Nothingness.* Religious existentialism seems to offer a personalized world in which the individual centers of consciousness, through the radiant power of transcendent Being, unite in their essence with one another. Sartrean human relations appear more reminiscent of the Lucretian universe, composed of isolated atoms, endlessly clashing, entering into transient combinations where there is contiguity but neither merging nor interpenetration. For the moment I prefer to waive the question as to whether the description of love in religious existentialism is realistic and concrete or senti-

---

[1] In Sartrean psychology, of course, a consciousness is originally nonpersonal. The "I" is used here partly for greater ease in communication and partly because the sense of an "I" is present in everyday experience even though the ego is not an a priori structure of consciousness.

mental and abstract. Let us instead confront head-on the negative limitations of Sartrean existentialism. Do they allow any reasonable reaction other than cynicism or despair?

For the record, we may note that Sartre has stated explicitly that his analysis of human relations in *Being and Nothingness* applies only to relations in bad faith. In a footnote following his description of the collapse of all attempts to resolve the subject-object conflict, he says, "These considerations do not exclude the possibility of an ethics of deliverance and salvation. But this can be achieved only after a radical conversion which we cannot discuss here." [2] Sartre's theoretical discussion of relations in good faith has been confined to the social or political context, rather than the personal. In his plays and novels, he has written movingly of commitments in friendship and has at least sketched the possibilities for love in good faith between men and women. The literature of Camus and de Beauvoir is still richer in illustrative material. [3]

Still we must admit that the absence of any philosophical justification by Sartre of love as a positive existential structure of human reality is a serious lack. The picture of human relations presented in *No Exit* has an intended universality which is not wholly offset by the individual portraits of significant loves or friendships in the rest of Sartre's work. Hostile critics maintain that the reason Sartre has not offered a philosophy of love and of human relations in good faith is that he *cannot* do so consistently with the view of human consciousness presented in *Being and Nothingness*. I do not accept this judgment. At the same time I certainly recognize that Sartre has raised serious difficulties. Without repeating his analysis of the abortive circular movement from love to hate via masochism and sadism, I wish to begin by pointing out briefly certain fundamental principles of his which I feel we must accept—both because they seem to me to be true and because if we do not accept them, I cannot see any justification for continuing to speak of my position as being existen-

[2] Sartre: *Being and Nothingness*, p. 412.
[3] I have discussed existentialist literature from this point of view in a chapter entitled "Engaged Freedom" in *Humanistic Existentialism*.

tialist in the Sartrean tradition. The problem then is whether, on these terms, any acceptable positive view of human relations is still possible.

I would like to start with the most concrete and personal— with the possibilities for an intimate relationship between two people. In the discussion of guilt and sin, we have seen that I cannot, in good faith, deny or seek to destroy the Other as a free subject. This we recognized to be a factual restriction of my own freedom. So far the Other appears to exist primarily as an obstacle or at best as recalcitrant material which is a negative but necessary ingredient for my projects—as the hardness of the stone is for the sculptor. Clearly we must go beyond this point. Perhaps it will be best to begin by marking out what I cannot expect from this relationship and indicating some of the complexities which make for difficulty.

There are two fundamental concepts in Sartre's picture of human relations which have understandably created the impression that the only existential structures presented by his philosophy are conflict and frustration. The first of these is *Le Regard*. We may translate it neutrally as The Look. The contexts in which Sartre introduces it suggest either The Stare or The Judgment. I am suddenly aware of being looked at as I perform some awkward movement suitable only for privacy. Or I am caught as I am myself looking through a keyhole. As the object of such looks, I am naturally overcome with shame or embarrassment; the hostile subject confronting me threatens my subjectivity. We must not forget, however, that these are but two examples of many different types of looks. Even if we exempt those which please me by designating me as an approved object, there are others where the whole existential status of the Look as that which bestows object-ness is called into question. There is also the Look which is an exchange. And there may be two people looking together at the world. Sartre has not adequately explored either of these dimensions.

The second source of difficulty arises from the fact that Sartre says—or is taken as saying—that I never communicate with another as subject-with-subject, that although I seek to reach him in his subjectivity, I can never grasp more than his object-self, his self-for-me. This is the more complex problem and the more basic. We will consider it first.

For existentialism, as we have seen, each life-world is a private world, ordered by the unique subject who lives in it. Within my life-world everything points to my consciousness as a center of reference. If the Other appears on the horizon and is aware of me, if he assumes a point of view upon me, then—as Sartre puts it—he effects a hemorrhage of my world; it "bleeds in the direction of the Other." I am suddenly aware that the world and I myself possess—for someone else—a dimension which does not exist for me, one which I can neither grasp nor control. I realize that I possess an object-side. This awareness includes more than the knowledge that since I possess a body, I share to some degree the fragile materiality and "being-thereness" of all existing things. Mere forces of nature could bring that illumination. The stare of the Other is different. His awareness is directed at an object which is not a thing. Even the man who stares idly at a woman's legs is not looking at things-in-the-world; through the legs his gaze is directed at a living consciousness. Conscious of the Other's look, I sense the emergence of a new structure of my existence—my self-for-the-other. To the Other, this self is always an object, whether the Me whom he meets is the result of conscious, careful, molding on my part or an encounter in which, without restraint, I simply let myself be seen. In either case this self exists *only* for the Other. I may have my own ideas as to how I have appeared to him, but I can never see or know that self with his eyes or with his consciousness.

Freud has claimed that in every sexual union four persons are present: In each of the pair there is the set of dominant and developed masculine (or feminine) characteristics which constitute the individual as man (or woman), and there is in each the subordinate, mostly repressed feminine (or masculine) traits which nevertheless color both the physiological and psychological responses of the man (or woman). Freud's view suggests a mysterious chemical reaction in which the precise quantity of active elements is on principle unknown. In the Sartrean encounter, too, there are four selves involved. There are the subjective "I" of each one of us, his self-for-me, my self-for-him. This is a minimum. Given a few minutes of tension and embarrassed "self-consciousness," the quartet may become a veritable crowd—the self-which-I-think-I-am-for-him, the self-which-I-remember-being-for-someone-else, the self-for-me which he was yesterday, the new-self-for-him which I am determined that he will find in me, and so on indefinitely.

I do not see how anyone could deny that these structures are present in at least most contacts between two people. The question is whether there ever occurs a moment in which the two selves-for-others are simultaneously transcended so that the subjects meet directly. Poets and song writers, some philosophers, a few psychologists claim that they do. If this meeting is to be defined as a merging or union of souls or consciousnesses, Sartre denies that it is possible. I believe that Sartre is right. *Ego te amo. Tu me amas.* Reciprocity is via the objective case.

Is there any way in which we may legitimately speak of consciousnesses as being united? Although people speak loosely of union, of oneness, of sharing, as if these terms were clearly understood, those who feel that some breakthrough in the private worlds occurs do not necessarily have the same idea as to just what happens. Some of these unions and meetings of souls are indisputably outside the sphere of humanistic existentialism. To start with possibilities which we must exclude, we should reject any recourse to the hypothesis of a pan-psyche or any theory of the Eastern sort which claims that all separation is illusion or Maya. Consciousness for us involves a nihilating withdrawal, a psychic separation from Being-in-itself. Obviously we cannot consistently state that the Nothingness which Consciousness introduces into the World has never been really there save as an unreal limitation due to ignorance. I may add that such hypotheses seem to me, in any case, to dismiss the problem of communication and love between two persons without resolving it. If we all are

really one, then karuna or compassion for all living creatures
is a natural consequence. It does not provide any basis for an
intense emotional bond between two particular people. On the
contrary, it cuts the very foundation away from any love or
friendship which rests on an appreciation of what is unique in
the Other. Eastern monks who renounce all erotic love are
entirely consistent.

In the Western tradition, that oneness which is said to be
the ideal of lovers does not generally depend upon the literal
breaking down of the boundaries of the personality. I suspect
that most persons who speak of "two become one" would, if
pressed, admit that the expression, even if applied to minds
and not bodies, is largely metaphorical. I strongly suspect
that more than half of a fair cross-section of the population
would insist that there still remains some form of union hard
to define but believed to be somehow not mere metaphor.
Many who denied it would do so chiefly in the interest of
precision of language but with the uneasy sense that the
feeling of oneness was left unaccounted for.

Both on the basis of existentialist psychology and by appeal to empirical observation, I reject the idea that there is
any merging or full identity of two consciousnesses. Except
in certain examples of science fiction, people simply do not, in
life or in literature, have a total comprehension of each
other's minds or emotions. Even in the shared moment of
orgasm, there are two sensations of pleasure. If consciousnesses seem to unite more fully then than at any other time,
this is only because at that moment the intensity of the
experience allows the consciousness to focus on nothing but
the immediate sensation. I do not mean, of course, that the
physical pleasure is the focus of a reflective consciousness or
that a person is not significantly aware of the Other. The
experience would appear to be, on principle, nonreflective. As
in any conscious state, there is a Gestalt unity of figure and
ground. The quality of the physical sensation as it is experienced is thoroughly imbued with the surrounding emotional
aura. The lover is nonreflectively and simultaneously aware

324

of several things: of the pleasure itself, of the fact that this pleasure comes from contact with the body of the beloved, that the beloved is gladly giving and receiving in this experience in which both are fully absorbed. Insofar as each consciousness is at this moment aware only of the pleasure given and received and made possible in physical contact, the two are defined only by their immediate shared-present. Yet there is no identity. What makes for the illusion of identity is the exclusion of almost all content from the two consciousnesses except for the immediate present. At this point the two selves-for-others are not present as the objects of a reflective consciousness, and this may give rise to the illusion that they are not there at all, that they have been completely transcended. This does not mean that there has been a union of I-subjects. Part of the value of the shared orgasm may arise from my nonreflective realization that the other as subject is as gladly engaged as I am in a gladness of physical and emotional pleasure which we effect together. But I am aware *of* this awareness of his. I do not feel it directly.

When all is said and done, Sartre is probably right in stating that the orgasm, however successful it may be in momentarily satisfying the desire for physical possession of the Other, is less effective than the caress in conveying some sense of possessing the Other in his uniqueness. In either case the degree of satisfaction depends on the willingness of each partner to allow his consciousness to be incarnated, to be wholly present to and in the body. This is altogether different from the contact of transcendent subject-consciousnesses. At most it is a consent on the part of each one that for a little while, he will not be—in any active sense—that which separates him from the Other. It is not truly an opening of the private worlds. Someone will say that the willingness to be wholly present to and in the body for the sake of another is dependent upon an agreement of consciousnesses and that what marks the difference between the physical union of lovers and the simple satisfaction of two lustful bodies is precisely the degree to which personalities have already intermingled. This is true, but it does not solve anything. It merely refers us back once more to the question of how and to what degree such blending of consciousnesses is possible.

I think we need not belabor the point that there is never any actual merging of consciousnesses where one person fully comprehends the whole of what goes on in the mind of the Other. If we are to think of two consciousnesses as being like two circles, which might be precisely fitted together to form one, this is obvious nonsense. Even if we went so far as to grant that two people could live a present experience in identical terms, the recollection of the past as a background against which the present must be focused would color everything and constitute two distinct experiences.

At this point someone may grant that naturally two people never become identical or share all of each other's experiences as if they had but one central nervous system. But he will point out that two circles can overlap so as to share a common area even though the boundaries are different. Is the same true for two consciousnesses? Or can we not think of the subjects of our two circles as producing by their joint efforts a third figure which would encompass them both? It is this idea which has often been presented in literature—that when two persons love, a new self is created which is not either one of them but both together.

To my mind there are both a legitimate and an illegitimate way of holding to this last hypothesis. Since I am at the moment speaking of views to be rejected, I will say that if by such overlapping of selves or common self we mean any sort of two-in-one consciousnesses in which the subjective "I" is the same for both or where two "I-subjects" are merged, once again we reject the claim both as inconsistent with the Sartrean view of consciousness and for total lack of evidence. Granted that all of us have experienced occasions when two people at almost the same moment have had the same not too obvious thought. There have been other times when the sense of certainly sharing an emotion was so strong as to make confirmation by word, touch, or glance, superfluous. Even so the awareness of mutuality comes only via an interpretation of the Other's behavior or by an intuitive comprehension based on previous knowledge. It is exactly what occurs as we try to decipher the meaning of any human conduct. If we need proof, I may point to the fact that in a pathetically large number of instances, the sharing turns out to be illusory, the flash of comprehension a misunderstanding. What seemed to be the pregnant silence of the Other's understanding of me and appreciation of the beauty of the present moment may have been due to his preoccupation with a new love or plans for a business trip.

Most of these claims of oneness involve a touch of mysticism, a reliance on something that is more than the emotional and which belongs strictly to the realm of the irrational, and the mysterious. There is a modified point of view which would speak less of merging than of meeting. Erich Fromm, for example, says: "In love the paradox occurs that two beings become one and yet remain two." [4] Fromm emphatically does not believe that the boundaries of the personality are destroyed or that such a state of affairs would be desirable if it were possible. To the degree that any man does lose himself in another or two people in each other, Fromm calls the result a "symbiotic union" in which there is a mutual parasitism stultifying to both partners. "In contrast to symbiotic union, mature *love* is *union under the conditions of preserving one's integrity*, one's individuality." [5] Yet Fromm, at the same time that he insists on recognizing the Other's separate uniqueness, uses language which suggests a meeting of subjects. He speaks of my knowing the Other "in his essence," of overcoming my sense of isolation by being known "in my essence" by him. With apparent approval, Fromm proceeds to say that in love, we make promises based on a twofold faith: my belief that the Other will not essentially change and my confidence that I too will remain the same "in my essence." [6]

[4] Erich Fromm: *The Art of Loving* (New York: Harper and Brothers; 1956), p. 21.

[5] Ibid., p. 20 (Fromm's italics).

[6] Ibid., pp. 31 and 123.

I cannot accept Fromm's statements. In the first place he does not explain just how one person knows another in his essence. Fromm implies, without actually stating, that this is by some sort of intuitive total comprehension which lets me suddenly see the Other and his world from within. Nothing in the rest of Fromm's work shows how this internalization is possible. In fairness we must admit that Fromm does not explicitly claim that it is, nor does his theory of human relations entirely depend on such inwardness. The alternative is that he means that I grasp the Other's essence as an object, as his self-for-others, and that by my choosing it as a value I include him and his happiness as a part of my own projects. The only difficulty here stems from the question of what is meant by "essence." If we refer to an abstraction of those personality traits displayed in my present encounter with the Other, and to the history of his past acts insofar as I know them, then I see nothing wrong with the idea that by a process both intellectual and emotional, I should be able to arrive at a fairly accurate idea of the basic quality and "life style" of the man, his fundamental "choice of being" or attitude toward the world, his value system—in general, a knowledge of "what makes him tick." What I thus achieve is a comprehension of the core of his personality and its diverse modifications. For Fromm, if my appraisal is deep and broad and correct, I have in truth grasped the Other's essence; there is only a minimum of danger in making a commitment for the future. This is because Fromm's view of man is still linked with the Aristotelian. Fromm does not deny that a person is free to change. Yet the fundamental choice which this freedom enjoys is that of choosing whether it will pursue its own self-realization or allow others to stunt and distort its growth. In other words, we are back with the acorn theory. To know a person's essence is possible for Fromm, at least in theory, because a person is an entity, even if part of what he is remains potential. I do not see, however, that accurate knowing makes the knowledge other than objective.

Existentialism allows for this same objective knowing of what a person has been. A man's essence *has been* exactly this abstract unity of which I have just spoken. If we seek in the present to know what a man's essence *is*, then we can only say that it is a freedom; that is, a consciousness, a process, an ever-future project, or—as Sartre puts it—"an always future hollow." One can never fully grasp such a freedom-essence even objectively. In committing oneself for the future to a person who knows that he is free, one risks everything. One may perhaps trust the Other's good faith to keep specific promises. That he will never significantly change is more than one has the right to demand. Nor will we regard any essential core of ourselves as beyond the possibility of changing—except for the recognition of the requirements of good faith in a being-who-is-a-freedom.

Viktor Frankl, whose "Logotherapy" is rightly considered to be either a branch of existentialism or at least closely affiliated with it, has spoken of love in terms much like those of Fromm.

In the spiritual act of love we apprehend a person not only as what he "is" in his uniqueness and singularity, his *haecceitas* in scholastic terminology, but also as what he can and will be: his *entelechy*. Let us call to mind the definition of human reality as a possibility—the possibility of realizing values, of self-realization. . . . It is part of the metaphysical mystery of the spiritual act we call love that out of the beloved's essential image it succeeds in reading the potential image.[7]

In some respects this passage is less clear than Fromm's statement. Lucidity is not helped by references to "metaphysical mystery" and to "spiritual" acts, as though these represented certain states of conscious activity distinguishable from all others. Like Fromm, Frankl insists on speaking of essences. The result is that his magnificently open definition of "human reality as possibility" is subtly modified to suggest that in the individual human, possibility is restricted and made to refer to specific, innate potentialities. But Frankl is more satisfactory than Fromm in stressing the uncertainty

[7] Viktor E. Frankl: *The Doctor and the Soul*, tr. Richard and Clara Winston (New York: Alfred A. Knopf; 1965), p. 150.

and risk involved in committing oneself to another, and he noticeably refrains from asking for any commitment not to change.

Both Fromm and Frankl emphasize the importance of valuing the Other as a separate being in his "uniqueness and singularity." Neither quite satisfies our wish to know just how we are to apprehend this unique quality which the inward life of the other possesses. Frankl, more than Fromm, seems to me to suggest that it is by our own sympathetically imaginative insight. His use of the term "image" implies that it is our idea or feeling of what the Other is in himself which causes us to value and love him, not some mysterious ability to experience his inwardness directly. I do not believe that Frankl, or Fromm either, means to say that in our apprehension of the Other's essence we have succeeded in penetrating his private world and attaining his total view of reality. Such an achievement would offer even more obstacles than the problem of merging consciousnesses as we encountered it earlier. To live the experience of another in its uniqueness and singularity would be to become the other. It would be also to cease being myself. For even if, by any of the irrational methods hinted at by some writers, I could comprehend directly the contents of another's consciousness, even if by extrasensory perception I could have all of his thoughts and sensations put into my own consciousness, I would still not be living his experience as he lives it. I would still possess my own consciousness as a background for his experience. No matter how sympathetic and tender my feelings toward him, I as subject would be assuming a point of view upon his life-world; that is, I would still encounter him as an object. But of course even this Jonah-in-the-whale type of incorporation of another is impossible. The truth is that since to be an I-subject means to be a center of reference for a consciousness, I-subjects can never merge nor even overlap, if by overlapping we mean that they actually have an identity of experience. Let us recognize once and for all that claims of united essences and merged I-subjects and stepping into the center of another's life-world must be taken for metaphorical exaggerations or for sentimental wish-fulfillments. Human beings meet as existents, not as essences.

There remains one other view which we should consider briefly before returning to possibilities which are consistent with the Sartrean theory of consciousness. This begins by acknowledging our ultimate separateness as individuals living our particular lives in the world. Superficial attraction or interest may stem from what is unique in the Other. Then we are told that love is possible because of that common humanity which is the same in each of us. If this argument holds any truth, which is debatable, it applies to the sphere of our relations with all others, to my respect or affection for mankind. I do not see how it is valid for the intense, very particularized emotion which leads two people to bestow on each other a place apart from the rest of the world. Yet some would insist that in true love the object of my love is the particular manifestation in the Other of Universal Being, that essential nonchanging reality which inevitably is sooner or later linked in such discussions with the Ground of Being or God. Yet atheists can and do love one another, and I do not think it fair to insist that they do so in ignorance. The wonder of love is not that, by a metaphysical chemistry, like elements seek out each other. It is that separate beings, on their own impulse, resolve in some way to bridge the gap between them and to move on in a direction which both choose together. It is the creation, not the discovery of mutuality which needs to be explained. Even if God exists and we are a part of Him, the bond between two lovers is between them, not between them and the Universe. Love between humans is a human triumph, whether God exists or not.

It is time now to search for a view of love which we can accept. We may begin by reminding ourselves that metaphors are used when one wants to express a truth which ordinary language seems to express inadequately. It would be folly to deny that something happens in human relations which is of a different order from my encounter with any other object in the world. Obviously this difference stems from the fact that the Other in himself is *not* an object. If we

331

refuse to admit that the I-subjects are united, we must explain just what does happen which so universally has given rise to the feeling of some kind of psychic union.

Let us return to that Look by which I first became aware of the existence of the Other. Sartre has emphasized that it is the Other's Look which makes me realize my own existence as an object. This realization is, of course, inseparable from my awareness *that he is a subject*, for I cannot be an object except to a subject. Knowing that he is a subject is obviously not the same as knowing him from within as subject, and we have shown that the second is impossible. Nevertheless, as a step toward a positive view of human relations in good faith, we must recognize that even hostility and hatred, in Sartre's theory, stem from the fact that the Other *is* irreducibly a subject, no matter how hard I try to prove that he is only an object for my manipulation. The wearisome struggle to reduce him from subject to object and the attempt to lose my own being-as-subject in his subjectivity are each one an abortive attempt to flee from the fact that free subject is what each of us irretrievably is. It is surely illogical to insist, as some critics have tried to do, that the only human relations possible for humanistic existentialism are those in bad faith which pretend that we are what we are not.

Obviously any human relation in good faith will retain at its heart the awareness on the part of each one that the Other is a free subject and not an object. As one of de Beauvoir's characters says, "Between us there is reciprocity. . . . At the moment when you recognize a consciousness in me, you know that I recognize one in you too." [8] If we stopped here, we should have accomplished at least something. We could establish that upon the basis of my approving appraisal of the objective aspect of the acts of another as they appear to me, I recognize and value his being as a consciousness. I resolve to protect and further the well-being of this subject whom I cannot grasp in order that I may continue to enjoy my contact

[8] Simone de Beauvoir: *L'Invitée* (Paris: Gallimard; 1943), p. 312. The French says, "Dans le moment où tu me reconnais une conscience, tu sais que je t'en reconnais une aussi."

with his self-for-me. Of course there is much more than this. If consciousness were in fact an entity, then the impossibility of my *being* the Other would indeed result in closed-off selves. Then it would be hard to think of communication as anything more than radio messages in code. Consciousness is not an entity, and it is nothing *without* an object. Remembering the peculiar nature of the relationship between consciousness and any of its objects, we can begin to see why the relation of one subject to another is not that of simple contiguity any more than it is a merging.

I mentioned earlier that the Look need not be limited to the Stare. It can be an exchange or a looking-together-at-the-world. What happens in the exchange? The content may vary. I think the underlying meaning remains the same. There is a simultaneous recognition by each one that the Other is a free subject and recognizes him as a free subject. If this were all, the exchange would come close to that intuitive grasp of our common humanity which we rejected earlier as inadequate to explain particular human loves. Perhaps some exchanges do not go beyond that. There are others which do; those are more than the Look itself although they presuppose it. In close contact with another, I take something from him. It would be better if we could put the expression in French— *de lui.* For I take both *from* and *of* him, and he necessarily (since we are speaking of an exchange) takes from and of me. There is nothing mystic or mysterious here. The Other, through words, gestures, actions, reveals to me new possibilities, new dimensions of the world. These are not exclusively conceptual. I read in him the emotional aspects of a world that is fearful, beautiful, disgusting, . . . I learn from him new ways in which a consciousness may relate itself to its own products. All of this I take in from my own point of view, to be sure. But the point of view is modified by that of which it *is* a point of view. Once I have recognized his possibilities as real possibilities of the world, my own world must include them. Although our worlds have not merged, each one will henceforth include structures which the Other has led me to embrace. Something of this kind happens in any human contact, even a hostile one. The difference is both quantitative and qualitative. In indifference or hostility, I try to ignore or to challenge the validity of the Other's organization of the world. At most I seek to make of it an object-as-obstacle, which I will incorporate into my field of consciousness as if it were a piece of resistant matter overcome. In love, I open myself to the inward life of the Other. What I desire most of all is that he and I may both comprehend and live the new relations to the world which each reveals to the other. Although I encounter his self-revelations as objects coming from the outside, I strive to internalize them in such a way that I relate myself to the world and to his experiences *in the same way that he has done*. It is no wonder that in the first stages of reciprocated love, each member of the happy pair experiences simultaneously an enlargement of himself, a fulfillment, and a sense of insulated isolation from the rest of the world.

As novelists and authors of columns of advice to the love-lorn never tire of pointing out, a love which endures must return to the world. This brings us to that other sort of Look, the looking-together-at-the-world. Most often, I suspect, this follows after the exchange, but there is naturally no fixed order. In most instances there is probably some degree of each. By "looking together at the world," I refer to the making of a life together which is the ideal of romantic love and marriage. In two ways, consciousness as Sartre has described it is eminently suited to live this experience significantly as more than a sentimental illusion. So long as consciousness is taken to be some sort of determined or fixed entity, it is difficult to comprehend how living a life together involves a relation of more than juxtaposition. When, on the other hand, a consciousness is seen as nothing other than a free process of relating itself to its objects, then we can understand how, particularly on the nonreflective level, the simultaneous intention of the same object and the same goal would produce not a merging of consciousnesses, to be sure, but certainly a harmonious close similarity. We can go further. Consciousness *is* its own project. If the two consciousnesses are absorbed in projects which can be identically defined and involve the same modifications of identical objects in the world, then—while Sartre is right in denying that a common "I" has appeared—we must recognize, as he has done, that there has come into being something more than two already existing I-subjects. This is the "We," which gives rise to what Sartre has called "the common self."

It is unfortunate that Sartre has chosen to discuss this "We" only in terms of the group, not as it arises between two people in erotic love or close friendship. (The single seeming exception which he gives is the union between two who feel themselves to be the object of the hostile stare of a Third; this is an Us-object, not a We-subject. *No Exit* is a brilliant demonstration of its quick disintegration.) What Sartre has written of the We-subject in the group may be helpful to us in our understanding of relations *à deux*. But to effect the necessary modifications is to recognize how completely Sartre has neglected the inquiry into love that is not in bad faith.

In *Being and Nothingness* Sartre allowed for only transitory and relatively unimportant manifestations of the We-subject; for example, the rowing team, men cutting down a tree, a group of people following direction signs in a train station or witnessing together a funny incident along the road. No actual analysis of these fleeting states was provided. In *Critique of Dialectical Reason*, Sartre attached far more value to the "We," which he develops under the concept of the "Group-in-fusion." This is any group involved in immediate action in a common project to accomplish the same objective goal. Besides giving the example of the football team, which I mentioned earlier, Sartre describes the group-in-fusion as composed of hitherto noncommunicating individuals suddenly united in political activity. His example is the taking of the Bastille.

Sartre points out several characteristics of the group-in-fusion. First, my self—in so far as I *am* my project—is not lost in the group. What happens is that my goal, which I could not accomplish alone, is now in process of being attained—e.g., resistance to the police. Second, Sartre points

335

out that the We which arises is of course not a hyperorganism. There is no substantial community of men, there is unity of action out there *in the world*. Possibly this is to overstate the case. The Bastille by itself certainly does not provoke the action of the individuals who attack it. It is only insofar as each one sees it as a threat to his free projects that it has any meaning at all. Yet Sartre is right in maintaining that the We has arisen as a response to something external, out there, and that the experience of unity and the action develop simultaneously. It is the fact that I see my neighbors doing what I myself want to do and can do only along with them that produces the impression of union. The union does not precede the action. Formerly this was only a collection of separately experienced feelings of frustration.

In the heart of action, Sartre recognizes that I am no longer an object to the group, nor is the group an object to me. Instead there is a relation of reciprocity. The unity is the practical unity of action, not a substantial unity of consciousnesses. Nevertheless it is not a unity which I as subject perceive as a unity which is bestowed on me as object. It is a unity which is not in me *and* in the group but *in us*. When Sartre speaks of a group in flight fleeing with its one hundred pairs of legs, he, too, seems to be passing into metaphor. His analysis of how reciprocity functions in the group almost seems at first to break down the We. He describes the group-in-fusion as an assembly of third persons (*les tiers*) in which each member turns himself into a means for achieving a common end which each one has freely chosen and internalized as his own project. In some individual enterprise, I may regard my body and skill (i.e., myself) as instruments for accomplishing a task. In group action it does not matter who accomplishes which detail of the action at hand. In so far as I am my project, each third is equally a "myself." The word of command is mine whether it is my lips which utter it or my hands which execute it.[9]

This is a bold use of language—to declare that in the

[9] Jean-Paul Sartre: *Critique de la raison dialectique* (Paris: Gallimard; 1960), pp. 391–411.

group-in-fusion everyone is in the third person and yet "myself." If we are to let Sartre get away with it, it will be because he is describing activity which is nonreflective, in which consciousness is almost wholly absorbed in its object with only the barest minimum of self-awareness. The obvious parallel on the individual level is the task which I perform with total concentration and a total blending of conscious intention and automatic reflexes. Although nobody thus absorbed is ever wholly lost in the action, one's marginal consciousness is certainly insignificant in relation to the whole.

If we move from Sartre's group-in-fusion to the dual looking-together-at-the-world of two lovers, we find a closer parallel than the "assembly of thirds" might seem at first to permit. Here as in the group, there is a unity of action, a oneness of attitude which is effected outside and then internalized. Absorbing themselves in the achievement of common projects, each one of the pair temporarily puts in parentheses those parts of himself which would intrude in the present enterprise. Each consciousness becomes close to being *nothing but* the awareness of the progress of the project which they have launched together. In its most intense form, this sense of two equivalent selves as instruments of the common end is as short-lived as that of the group-in-fusion. The constant renewal of such action and the awareness that the possibility of it is always there in abeyance produces the continued sense of sharing and participating.

What Sartre leaves out is the "You." Or if one insists on the archaic, he omits the "Thou." Because he does so, we are left with the uneasy feeling that even the group-in-fusion, although each one puts his "I-ness" in parentheses, hardly becomes a true "We." Why Sartre has altogether omitted all discussion of the second-person pronoun, I do not know. To speak of all encounters with the Other as if only first and third persons were involved is to do violence to experience as well as to language. De Beauvoir, too, somehow conveys a feeling of first and third persons even in the passage where she has her character introduce the idea of reciprocity. "At the moment when you recognize a consciousness in me, you

337

know that I recognize one in you too." Surely in the intensity of love, what matters is not that I recognize *a* consciousness but that I am acutely aware of *your* consciousness or—still better—of *You* as a consciousness.

In many communications, the "You" is little more than a grammatical convention. If I ask a stranger for directions, my contact with him is not necessarily any different in essence from my relation with a city guidebook which would furnish the same information. To greater or less degree my personal relations with others involve the "You" directly. It is vital to the look-as-exchange, which could not otherwise exist. The existential "You," as contrasted with the merely grammatical, can derive from either a reflective or nonreflective consciousness. There are occasions when my interest in the Other is such that in so far as is possible, I suppress all concern with my own future project. The "I" is present only as an active agent engaged in helping the other further his own chosen projects. Extreme examples are those cases in which one person saves the life of another with no thought of his own safety. More frequent are the occasions when a teacher or counselor or simply friend is absorbed in attempting to solve the other's problem in a way acceptable to him. This You is closer to Sartre's union of third persons inasmuch as the object intended by both consciousnesses is the objectification of "Your" self as project.

On the reflective level, the "You" is not posited along with the partial suppression of the "I." Rather there is an intensification of both and a special bond posited between them. In purest form, the only content of this "You" is precisely this positing of the relation. It is as though this "You," whether spoken or expressed in some other way, conveyed these two things: first, that an I-subject is at the moment making itself nothing except an awareness of the Other and an awareness of that awareness; second, that the I-subject seeks to transcend the Other as object and asserts both the existence and absolute value of the other as "I-subject." Of course this is not an assertion *about;* it is a recognition *of.* It is given and received without intermediary. Clearly this "You" aims at transcending the Other as object. It is directed toward the subjectivity which the self-for-others never includes. Sartre has chosen to emphasize the abortive aspect of the attempt, and it is true that I cannot possess as an object the other's being-as-subject. I do not think that such possession is the intention of the "You."

The parallel between the reflective "You" and the reflective "I" is amazingly exact. As I look into myself and confront my existence as a freedom, I simultaneously grasp an objectified "Me" and realize that there is something which has escaped all attempt at reflection. I realize that there is no self to be grasped because this so-called self is already a projection toward what is to come. Yet it would be nonsense to say that because consciousness cannot fully and simultaneously both be itself and comprehend itself, there is no comprehension at all of one's own subjectivity. The realization that one is not fully included in the object which one is to oneself constitutes the fullest revelation that one *is* a subject. In the existential "You," I affirm with equal certainty the "I" of the Other. If the "You" is reciprocal, there has been a joint affirmation of two I-subjects even though—as we have seen—there is neither possession nor merging.

In the Look as exchange, the "You," jointly asserted, is uppermost. In the looking-together-at-the-world, there is a stronger sense of "We." The difference between this "We," as I see it, and Sartre's assembly of third persons in the group-in-fusion is that the unity of action in common projects has as its background the remembrance of the "You." On the margin of consciousness is the realization that I and this other "myself" have established that a part of the value in the goal which we are pursuing lies in our pleasure that the other has freely chosen it. This is in truth a meeting of existents. We cannot legitimately call it a union of essences.

I do not believe that there is ever more than a grammatical "You" involved in hatred or in indifference. Either attitude sets out to deny the validity of the Other's organization of the world into his private world. I cannot ignore or seek to destroy the Other's I-subject at the same moment that I strive to affirm it and modify my own world so as to form in it structures equivalent to his. Sartre is right in claiming that hate and indifference strive to reduce the Other's subjectivity to his objective Self-for-others, which is to deny him as a freedom, to transform him from person into thing.

This raises the interesting question as to whether or not one can hate another in good faith. The strictly honest answer is No. Hate involves either the will to destroy or a total condemnation or both. Either wish can be sustained only so long as I judge the other person solely in relation to my own value system and by ignoring all those aspects of his life and personality which are not in opposition to my own values. Good faith compels me to realize that his acts have another aspect and color when seen within the framework of his own private world and that "the one who" performed these acts does not stand in the same relation to them as the man whom I condemn. His being is not exhausted in the acts which have aroused my hatred. We all recall the annoyance which we feel when someone tries to show us that the person we hate is not truly depicted in the portrait our anger has painted of him. This is because we sense the fact that once we allow ourselves to recognize his subjectivity, either we must give up our hate or acknowledge our guilt in denying to another free consciousness his right to organize the world as it appears to him. In hate we feel a pleasure akin to that we have recognized in a certain experience of spontaneous self-realization; the recognition that we do not *have* to be ethical. To admit and not repress our flashes of hatred is both psychologically wise and philosophically honest. Such an admission should be accompanied by the confession that insofar as one has indulged in these emotional outbursts, one has failed to live up to the ideal of good faith.

No Exit is concerned only with the negative aspect of human relations. All three of the characters are in bad faith. No one of them posits a genuine "You" or even seeks a "We." They try to use one another as a means of bolstering false images of themselves, to convince themselves that they are in truth the Self-for-Others which they try to persuade the

Other to accept. More than anything else, the play is concerned with the way in which there is always a third subject to break down the fragile pretense which the other two try to construct as a mutual protection. Even as we recognize that this particular study of Sartre's is deliberately restricted and one-sided, we are forced to admit that Garcin's agonized "Hell is Others" goes beyond the immediate situation. It would be nice if we could say that "Hell is Others" applied to human relations in bad faith and that there is a counterpart "Heaven is Others" for relations in good faith. The fact is that we do not have two precisely equivalent poles of value and disvalue, of perfection and corruption. One can avoid the sort of Hell which comes into being when people struggle to destroy each other's subjectivity and to assert themselves as sole subject with their own object-side wholly transcended. To acknowledge that others are subjects and to be reciprocally recognized is certainly possible. Yet here as in all phases of self-fulfillment, to choose one possibility is to forego another, to engage one's freedom is both to make it meaningful and to restrict it. The structures which make it possible for human relations to be Hell are transformed but not wiped out. The most we can say is that when human relations are at their best, one feels no need of Heaven. Possibly this is enough.

"He" and "She"

If there is anywhere that man's bond with Nature appears to be particularly obvious and secure, it is in the pattern of the sexes. That long procession led by Noah and his wife into the Ark seems to image basic duality, the union of opposites which lies at the heart of the Universe and keeps it going. Paradoxically, this appeal to nature has evoked two antithetically radical positions. At one extreme there is the *Playboy* philosophy, which argues with evangelistic fervor that man should exploit the pleasures of his natural animality. Sex in the pages of *Playboy* is hardly distinguishable from the elegant pleasures of the moneyed gourmet. The only suggestion that this sphere of sensory delight is more complicated than that of the culinary epicure appears in impassioned articles against those remnants of Puritan morality still present in our culture. Midway in the spectrum are writers such as D. H. Lawrence, who glorify man's bodily existence but make of sexuality a mystique of spiritual fulfillment. At the extreme on the far right are those who use God's manifest Plan in Nature as a reason for looking on sex with suspicion. The very fact that man does share sexuality with the animals is made into an argument for transcending his "lower nature." Hence the grudging acceptance by the early and the Medieval Church of matrimony as a second-best way of fulfilling the divine purpose. The true end of love finds its culmination in the dedicated celibacy of nuns and priests and in the erotic mysticism of a St. Theresa.

Humanistic existentialism is free of theological and churchly claims. It regards all traditional mores as at least open to question and re-examination. It is equally insistent that within the limits of his finitude, man sets up his own relations with nature. Therefore our existentialism rejects any argument that either asceticism or natural animality is the "right" solution. Nor will we be satisfied to say simply that the position of humanistic existentialism lies between these extremes—as if that would solve anything.

Any statement of an existentialist attitude toward sexuality ought to be developed with two different problems in mind. There is first the question of morality; that is, what we believe to be the correct relation between the individual's sexual life and the demands of the society in which he lives. Second, there is the question of how sexuality fits into the over-all value system of the life in good faith.

The first question is easy to answer theoretically. Except for safeguarding the welfare of children and protecting persons against sexual violence (either rape or taking advantage of the ignorance of the very young), it is not the province of the law or of anybody to dictate to individuals in any way whatsoever. Naturally I respect the right and duty of parents and educators to offer guidance here as in any other area of human conduct. Indoctrination is unacceptable.

That busy visitor from another planet who is forever commenting on human institutions would hardly find any better example of social bad faith than the contemporary American sex code. We may ignore as unimportant the rarely if ever enforced blue laws which threaten fines and imprisonment, not only for adultery and fornication, but against the so-called "abnormal" ways of sexual gratification between married couples. Furthermore, I do not claim that we are the first society to live in bad faith. Within the Christian era prostitutes have always been both condemned and kept in business. The American call girl is but a quieter, less flamboyant version of the courtesan celebrated in European literature, art, and opera. If I insist that there is a more serious falsification today, this is partly because I believe that the number of persons whose sex lives are at variance with the professed code is far greater than formerly. This statement cannot be proved. We have for earlier centuries no Kinsey reports and no sociological treatises on "The Changing Mores of College Students." Literature is admittedly untrustworthy since it always searches out the dramatic and focuses on the conflicts of persons living and rebelling against the conventions. Even so, the difference in the prevailing attitude of almost all contemporary fiction and that of the nineteenth-century novel in England and America seems to me a significant indication. More serious is the fact that there is little or no connection between the reasons which supposedly underlie our laws and community judgments and the actual values in relation to which persons privately work out their own sexual behavior.

Except in cases involving personal violence, I can think of only two things which could conceivably justify the intervention of society in the individual's sexual life. The first would be the belief that divine powers were in some way interested in or connected with human sexuality. In primitive tribes this has been very real indeed, and it is not surprising that various sexual taboos were enforced. The life of the tribe, as well as the safety of the individual, depended upon the proper observ-

343

ance of the numen, which frequently was hardly differentiated from the sexual power in the human being. A fundamentalist interpretation of Christianity gives a different but related sort of justification, this time based on the idea that God, as the antithesis of the bodily, begrudges our earthly concerns and pleasures, favors our denying them, but provides in literal commands the regulations for their enjoyment. I honestly cannot see how any but a fundamentalist Christianity can retain any connection between God and the specific nature of man's sexuality. It would seem that here as in the matter of eating and drinking, it is up to humanity to regulate strictly human activities.

The second excuse for society's interfering in sexual matters is obviously concern for the children who will be born—either that they should be as numerous as possible or restricted, depending on the birth rate, or that they should be born only to parents who might be held responsible for taking care of them. Obviously this involves the problem of the father's being able to recognize the child as his own and the mother's being assured of the father's help in rearing it. Such is indeed the appropriate province of the law, and I cannot imagine a society in which it would not be necessary to have some formal, enforced regulation concerning the responsibilities and obligations of fathers and mothers and the legal recognition of a union between two people who wish to have a child. At the same time I cannot believe that society will long continue the practice which it has observed in the West for about two thousand years. This has been the attempt to solve problems of paternity and parental obligations by means of regulating the entire sexual life of every individual. The medieval chastity belt is only one of the more obvious symbols of this drastic solution. Even before any but the crudest methods of birth control were known, there was a certain highhanded quality about the decree that all sexual activity should be restricted to legalized monogamy. Certainly now we have reached the point where it seems that existing laws should be modified. In the near future society ought to take the position that it is concerned only with matters of parentage and economic obligations, not with sex as such.

I hope to show later that I do not hold the inevitable result of this tolerance to be a promiscuity even less restrained than that advocated by *Playboy*. Not everybody reads worthless pornography simply because it is published, and there is no reason to think that those who do will read *War and Peace* because they can't find *Candy*. Yet in the same way that I feel that the absolute removal of censorship is necessary for a free literature, so I would hope that society would someday allow the individual to work out his own sexual problems without the burden of guilt which comes from living contrary to what society upholds—or pretends to uphold. Speaking, for the moment, wholly from the point of view of the individual's freedom from social punishment or pressure, I urge that the only proper existentialist attitude is that each man and woman should be allowed to work out his or her own destiny without hostile interference. If a woman is forced into prostitution by economic pressures, we may feel that it is right to change the structures of a society which offers her no other recourse. For many reasons, we may feel that the life of the prostitute does not recognize a full development of human potentialities in good faith, and we may work for programs which would make more easily available the possibilities of more significantly satisfying ways of living. The question of whether any man or woman wants to engage in sexual activity for financial reward—inside marriage or out of it—should remain the private problem of that individual. Love affairs of all sorts, adultery, homosexuality, incest, and the varied catalogue of nonviolent sexual deviations—all these, if they are to be opposed, should be discouraged by informative discussion and for reasons other than that they are outside some normative pattern established by God, nature, or society. The problems of sex belong to the realm of personal psychology. In so far as sexuality becomes one of the legitimate concerns of ethics, it is not the biological question which is important but the problem of commitments between human beings.

345

Removing sex from the province of law and sociology (with the exceptions already mentioned) and allowing the individual to work out his own solutions as he does in other matters involving personal human relations would be a tremendous step forward. So far I sympathize with the earnest endeavors of the *Playboy* staff. It is only the first step. Like any liberation from outside constraint, it frees the individual to choose for himself what he will do with his possibilities. It does not relieve him of responsibility for his choice and its consequences. If civilized man could separate from the rest of his life those qualities he shares with other animals, then sexual freedom would indeed be a solution instead of the posing of a problem to be solved. But as we have all been told too many times, man does not eat and drink and have intercourse in the simple, monotonous fashion of animals. Even Lawrence is aware that his neo-primitivism is a *return* to the Garden of Earthly Delights and not to be confused with the ignorant innocence of its first inhabitants. And Freud, despite his claim that man's psychic suffering stems from the social restrictions which frustrate his instinctual drives, is well aware that man is more than his Id. "Where there was Id, there shall be Ego" is the analyst's goal, not the opposite. In human beings, sex and *human* consciousness are inextricably bound together.

Sartre argues that sexuality is so inseparable a part of the human condition that it exists prior to and independent of the specific sex organs. In a startling paradox, he claims that the human person has sex organs because to be human is to be "sexed," and not the reverse.[1] This attempt to confuse logical and biological priority does not seem to me to result in one of Sartre's most lucid statements. If he means what I think he ought to have meant, he is making two very important claims: First, that the human condition includes the potentiality for desiring the possession of or sharing in a communication with another person and that the body plays a part in this. Sexual desire, for Sartre, uses the sex organs as instrument, so to speak, but is not reducible to their tumescence

[1] Sartre: *Being and Nothingness*, pp. 382–4.

and satisfaction. Second, Sartre claims that we choose our own way of living or condition as men or as women. Our *human* being is not determined by our being male or female.

The first of these claims, although it perhaps appears the more untenable at first reading, really is not startlingly new. It is a commonplace observation that sexual attraction and impulses can be felt even when there is no perceptible stimulation of the sex organs. Sartre's reference to children, the very old, and eunuchs is scarcely necessary. It is equally trite to point out that much as we may talk about the difference between love and sexual infatuation, the precise dividing line is impossible to locate. Just as a handclasp may mean much or nothing but is never the mere meeting of flesh without reference to the persons who extend their hands, so the sexual act cannot be a thing in itself but is a meeting and, however slight, the contact of two consciousnesses.

This we have always known. Are there any specifically existentialist observations which are pertinent here? I will not claim that existentialism has a view of erotic love which can be arrived at only from existentialist premises by an existentialist dialectic. I do say that an existentialist will have definite attitudes about what does or does not constitute what he —in good faith—will call love in good faith.

In the first place, an existentialist will never countenance conduct which aims at reducing the Other (or himself) to being nothing but a sexual object as an instrument of pleasure. Such conduct is as much in bad faith as sadism, masochism, or an indifference which pretends that people are only objects or, at most, their selves-for-others. This principle at once eliminates the conduct of a Don Juan, of any exploiter of others' love for the sake of one's own vanity or pleasure. It condemns the attitude of any man (or woman) who feels that he can buy or rent or own the body of another as a piece of property.

Does this position rule out all enjoyment of sex to which we would not give the name of love and where there is no question of a long-term commitment? No. But this is a No which we must speak with great care and surround with all

347

kinds of qualifications. There are many human activities where we take it for granted that a "We" of limited duration or the Look as exchange may evolve without the total involvement or full commitment which we have come to associate with love. We are accustomed to grant the desirability of the exhilarating meeting of two minds when strangers come together for the first time in discussion. Is the shared pleasure of bodies necessarily to be kept on an altogether different plane? Fully aware of the danger of acting by analogy, we may grant that there may be some occasions when sexuality without love or commitments for the future may take place. Existentialism does not seek to ally itself with Puritanism. If there exists no question of betrayal of one's commitment to another, if the sexual pleasure is shared, freely bestowed and appreciatively received, if there is mutual respect, and if neither partner has any secret sense of merely using the other or of being used, then there seems to be no theoretical reason why such a relationship is in bad faith. With painful honesty, we may even admit that in exceptional cases we may admit within the purview of good faith certain sexual exchanges where money is part of the agreement. They will be rare, for it is hard to envision a situation in which one could offer oneself for sale without feeling that the Other was accepting the right to treat one as an object. *Love* cannot be for sale under any circumstances. Still at the risk of defending a situation so infrequent as to be of no interest save as an irritation to statisticians, I will argue that there may occasionally be shared commercial sex where nobody is degraded into an object, not any more than the expensively procured lecturer who speaks to an appreciative audience on a subject of his own choosing and their interest. We must observe, however, that in these casual unions, good faith demands a certain commitment even if it is one which does not significantly involve the future. The affirmation of the Other as subject requires putting one's own subjectivity in abeyance to the extent of letting oneself become involved in the mutual evoking of pleasure, not passing detached judgments. There is, in short, a rudimentary approximation of

348

that exchange and looking-together-at-the-world which forms
the essence of the "We" in love.

Having granted this much to the champions of uncon-
cerned sex, I will add further qualifications. First of all, these
associations, while they may involve a minimum of ethical
concern, are but little removed from spontaneous, nonreflective self-realization. We have already seen that this holds a
legitimate place in existentialist ethics but that it is only a
part. If it is theoretically possible for a person to find contentment in a life that does not seek more than transitory erotic
experiences, we still have the right to say that he has settled
for less than his potentialities allow. In the vast majority of
cases this choice does not result in either good faith or happiness. Even so unlikely a person as Norman Mailer recognizes
that there may be an advantage in "saving up sex" until one
finds a person with whom one can experience it significantly.
It is a truism that actions, like words, lose their value if too
often repeated and cannot be easily restored to their original
significance. It is only abstractly that we can for very long
keep sexuality free from the complicated interweaving of
personalities. Viktor Frankl remarks that one of the dangers
of early sexuality lies precisely in the fact that the adolescent
is trapped in a maze of psychological intricacies before he has
the knowledge or experience to deal adequately with human
relations.[2] In sexual desire, as Sartre says, a consciousness
incarnates itself, but even an incarnated consciousness has
not lost its subjectivity.

Love demands some sort of temporal commitment whether
in marriage or nonlegal liaison. Western convention, of
course, recognizes only matrimony and has decreed that the
couple should demand and give absolute fidelity, "forsaking
all others." Divorce, which dissolves the agreement entirely,
is allowed if not really approved. There is no public acceptance of any other alternative. Existentialism would say that
the good faith or bad faith of lovers' being-together bears
very little relation to the formal observance of conventions.
To start with, we may point out the obvious truth that the

[2] Frankl: *The Doctor and the Soul*, pp. 170–5.

supposedly happy marriages are not necessarily in good faith. Consider first the ways in which couples try to resolve the subject-object conflict.

If we contemplate the marriages of those around us, we will probably find that in most of them the battle has been fought and settled long ago. One subject is definitely in power, and the other has accepted object status, often gratefully. There are several variations on this theme. The boldest and clearest pattern, and one which society has only recently begun to question, is the open assertion of the authoritarian male. In extreme form this rests upon the fiction that the human species is defined in terms of the male; woman's role is to contribute to the welfare of the species of which she is only an instrumental, subordinate member. This is, of course, the idea which de Beauvoir has attacked in *The Second Sex*. Although the overtly patriarchal family is less common today, we all know too many cases where the woman has ceased to develop since her marriage except as a talking mirror for her husband. She has made of herself nothing but a project to support his projects. Her ideas and values are unauthentic reflections of his. The husband values his wife as a support to his ego. If he is frequently unfaithful to her, our condemnation of his ingratitude ought to be tempered with sympathy. Only Narcissus could find her exciting. Many times the woman is the subject. Where her ascendancy is obvious, the husband appears both pathetic and ridiculous. In his case there is no social approval to console him for his acceptance of the inferior place; consequently he is likely to arouse more indignant sympathy than the object-wife. In existentialist terms, the violence done to a human freedom is equally indefensible. The situation which I personally find most distasteful because it seems to me most deeply permeated with bad faith is the familiar situation in which one partner (it is more often the man) is deliberately flattered with a carefully prepared picture of himself as subject, whereas he is actually manipulated in such a way that he has become scarcely distinguishable from the object the woman wishes to possess.

Glorified as a power behind the throne, such a woman seems to me to betray her husband and herself.

Another type of marriage fits almost literally the "battle to the death of consciousnesses." Since the goal of each one to reduce the other to an object is never won, only the death of one of them—or of the marriage—can end the struggle. Occasionally such a marriage manages to survive the violent outbursts of the pair and to avoid the divorce court. We are tempted to say that the participants value drama and emotional catharsis more than love. In some cases possibly the marriage is held together by bonds of good faith which are there all the time, covered up by the excitement in the foreground. Here the jousting is not in earnest but a sport. Each one knows that he cannot permanently reduce the other to object-status and values him for that very reason. Yet in that mingled spirit of respect and slightly hostile rivalry which one feels for a worthy opponent on the playing field, each one tries to win as many specific skirmishes as possible. Instead of seeking to modify their private worlds harmoniously, each one tries to force the other to make all the changes. Since the victory shifts back and forth, there are reciprocal remodelings, after all, until finally even the memory of the battles lost gives pleasure as the two look back together over the common battleground. If nothing else, the two have been so preoccupied with their conflict that their worlds have come close to touching, simply because neither has let the outside world intrude.

A third attempted resolution of the subject-object relation is the situation in which each one tries to become only an object to the other. Logically, any relation between two objects—without any subject as mediation—would seem to be impossible. Strictly speaking, this is true, and of course no subjectivity is ever wholly destroyed. It is the false claim that man is or may become only a object which constitutes all of these relations as being in bad faith. Yet in the same way that there is an attempt to deny the subject-being of one of the pair, so there may be unions in which neither member fully lives his subject-status. I refer here to marriages or long-lasting liaisons which appear to be perfectly happy and which we might mistakenly be inclined to call associations based on love in good faith. We all recall those gentle couples who are wholly absorbed in one another, living in complete unanimity, hardly distinguishable from one another. It is usually about them that we hear the amused comment, "They have come to look alike." Unless contentment is to be made our sole ethical criterion, we will not envy them. We must, as existentialists, say that they, too, are in bad faith. There is something pathetic about their relationship and a smell of failure—though they would not recognize it as such. This is because the two people have found still another way to avoid confronting the perils of freedom whether in oneself or in the Other. Each one seeks in the Other's Look a guarantee for every choice. In order to support this constant reciprocal confirmation, they have had to cancel out of their lives anything which could not be fully shared and all possibility of anything new which might shatter the precarious unanimity. They have not significantly grown—together or separately. They have reduced themselves to a least common denominator, and their love for one another is hardly distinguishable from narcissism.

The fourth relation is, of course, that between two people who accept each other and themselves as subjects; it is the only personal relationship which is in good faith. Such a marriage is the embodiment of the "We" which I have already discussed. Whether within marriage or without, the We-union of subjects in love involves a paradoxical value structure. Looking from one point of view, we seem to find self-expansion, self-assurance, self-aggrandizement. Through my interest in the other, I enlarge my projects, expand the scope of my freedom. Yet since this is possible only because I have engaged myself in affirming the value of the other as subject and of his private world, there is—in the conventional everyday sense—a loss of self. Heidegger has pointed out that a consciousness is always outside, "in the street." He means, of course, not that consciousness is outside itself in ceasing to be its own center of reference but that even as a self-consciousness it always has an object other than itself. In love I am acutely aware of my consciousness as reaching out, as coming to rest "over there"; but in a strange way it is both "outside" and "at home." My entire life is a process of objectifying my subjective consciousness in my temporal relations with the world—what Sartre calls "inscribing myself in Being." In relating myself to objects in the world and in my less personal involvement with other people, there is danger of my no longer recognizing my own freedom in the acts which I perform. If we may adapt the Marxist terminology, "Man becomes the product of his product instead of his own product." The love which the other gives to me guarantees this objectified aspect of myself in two different ways: First, he bestows upon me and my acts an objective value by making my well-being a part of his own projects. Second, he constantly refers my acts, my objective being-in-the-world back to my being-as-a-subject, at no time trying to imprison me in my self-for-him. Thus in a curious way he makes me aware of my being-in-the-world without causing me to lose my sense of being-for-myself. And of course I do the same for him.

Even for two people who genuinely respect their own and each other's being-as-subject, the continued life of love in good faith is a difficult undertaking, and there are innumerable unsuspected pitfalls. To start with, we may note that many people destroy this fragile structure by demanding too much of it, by wanting those things which, if they could be attained, would destroy love. The ideal of perfect understanding is a pertinent example. Adolescents almost always long for someone who will perfectly understand everything that is in them; most of us as adults are grateful that nobody does.

The approximation to perfect communication and total comprehension of one person by another is one of the treasures of love. It is the rarity of such moments that makes them so precious and the fact that we never get beyond the approximate which makes possible their being repeated. If there is anything at all which we can completely understand, it must be something which is nonconscious and inanimate. If I *could* know the Other so thoroughly that nothing new or unexpected could emerge from him, then I could hope for no future enrichment. Moreover, he could no longer offer to me anything more than I could find in myself. It is only love in bad faith which mistakenly seeks this goal. Love in good faith, perilous though it be, demands the constantly renewed pledge that each will seek both his own and the Other's continued growth. There is no evading the possibility that one will move in a direction which no longer allows the two worlds to remain close together. Even so the risk must be taken, for the love which recognizes and values human freedom can make no other sort of commitment. There is one consoling thought. Two people who continue to face honestly the responsibilities of their freedom are more likely to look together at the world as a We-subject than a couple one of whom insists on keeping his eyes fixed on the same objects.

It is often claimed that love is enough in itself to give meaning to life. There is a modicum of truth in this view. For many persons, the establishing of one genuine love relationship enduring throughout the years is enough to weld together in a significant pattern both the frustrations and the successes of other projects. Yet generally speaking, I do not believe that the person who does not find existence itself an incentive for making his life worthwhile will discover that reciprocated love magically bestows an absolute meaning on the whole of things—at least not one which will last. Granted that the sheer interest of enlarging one's experience by learning to know the complexities of another personality and of the world as it appears to him has the fascination of a story and can carry us along with its continued suspense, its promises, fulfillments, surprises, reconstructions of past events, and hopes of still more tales to come. Unless we have already looked on life and our own lives with some of this same kind of fascination, we are not likely to be satisfied with the meaning we find in another's existence.

It is legitimate and desirable to find pleasure and interest in the semi-detached observation of the way in which one's relations with another unfold. Yet we must recognize the temptation of substituting absorption in the involvement for any genuine concern for the other. Living literature is not an adequate substitution for either love or responsibility toward another. What often happens is that one gradually supplements one's fascination with the expectation that one's relation with the Other should be like that which one experiences with characters in the book one reads. The peculiar *mitsein* which I enjoy with fictional heroes and heroines is the only form of being-with-another in which the Other and I do in truth maintain a common center of reference. This is true, of course, only because my relation with the fictional being is wholly in the imaginative mode. The author has laid down the paths which I am to follow, but it is I as reader who gives life to the printed words and re-created persons and events of the imaginary world. The result is that I am magically with the hero without intervening distance. His reactions may surprise me, but nothing lies hidden. It is true that in later rereadings I may constitute things differently and observe things which I had not noticed before. But within each single encounter, I enter into the private world of the hero. My comprehension of him is perfect. Yet I do not see him as an object only since I react and feel what he is feeling. My meeting with him may very well result in my ultimately modifying the structures of my own private world. Having once forced my way into his, I must give to him a place in mine. Yet, as does not happen with a living person, I can separate myself from him at will. There is no chance that, once I have assigned to him the role he is to play, he will suddenly offer resistance because of his own choice to become a new kind of person. There are persons who can love only in this way. They love in recollection and in letters—or perhaps in phone calls. The actual encounter with the beloved is disturbing and can be appreciated only in rearranged remembering. Love here is love of love and not of the beloved. I have forgotten the Other as subject and made him into an object that is not even real.

The greatest threat to love in good faith is but a more

subtle form of the danger which freedom encounters in any of its projects. Freedom is not meaningful unless it is in some way engaged. If it engages itself too closely, forgetting the psychic nothingness which consciousness sets between itself and its objects, then it denies itself as freedom. In our discussion of love, we confront now the most serious problem and one which allows for no single theoretical answer to fit all cases. This is the question of the degree to which we should be bound by commitments made to the Other. Here as much as anywhere else in human experience we are painfully aware of the clash between personal fulfillment and responsibilities toward others. The situation is complicated and at the same time rendered more open to a possible solution by the fact that there is a conflict between qualitatively different demands upon the individual—even if he thinks solely in egoistic terms.

I should like to begin with an example: A student of mine, whom I had reason to believe on the verge of suicide, discussed with me the problem of finding some way of finding life worth living. He himself had decided independently that the one and the only thing which could make life significant for him would be an ideal love, one supported by mutual full commitments and permanent union. He had been involved in a number of liaisons which inevitably failed him, either because he made such extreme demands on the girl that she rejected him, or because he decided she could never hold any value for him except as a means to immediate sexual pleasure. Gradually the boy straightened out his problems, rejected suicide, learned to form a more realistically human ideal of what love should be, and married a remarkably attractive and intelligent girl. Within a few months of the marriage, he came to tell me two things: First, he wanted me to know that this time love was in truth the wonderful thing he had been searching for and that he and his wife were in close harmony working out a life that they found meaningful. Second, he somewhat sheepishly confessed to a new difficulty. He had come to believe that one of the highest values in living and in self-realization derived from the achievement of close understanding and communion in friendships with other people. In exploring such possibilities with women, he felt that so long as sexual relations were forbidden, this constituted a barrier. Fidelity to his wife seemed to be purchased at the cost of sacrificing rich possibilities for his own self-realization, for "full living." What was my advice?

I confess that I had to fight against the temptation to answer with impatient indignation. It would have been easy to call this presentation of the problem nothing but an attempt to rationalize and excuse the boy's irresponsible wish to acquire a bit of added sexual variety cheaply and to flatter his vanity with further conquests. I could not help remarking that his interest in exploring the personalities of other people seemed to be restricted to females. In fairness I must say now that I think he was not so much rationalizing as trying to find out whether I considered the conventional response to be the only one in good faith. Well then, is it or not? And why?

We must try to avoid falling into either of two types of answers which would not be in good faith. On the one hand, we want to avoid simply repeating the distilled "wisdom of the ages," representing what society has found to be best with respect to the code of behavior which society has itself set up. At the same time, we must resist the fallacious idea that promiscuity is the natural and right solution and that only Puritan prudery would see in it a betrayal of love. To make either kind of reply is to beg the question.

In the example I have chosen, it is possible to arrive at certain conclusions quite in harmony with the "wisdom of the ages" without invoking religious commands or any abstract morality. Any form of deception was certainly out of the question. The Look-as-exchange and Looking-together-at-the-world are both impeded by any willed areas of opacity. To deceive is to use the other as an object, for it is to make him an instrument to an end he has not chosen. Even by a purely selfish calculation, the young man would be foolish to enter into light liaisons if it meant attempting to deceive his wife. The same applies to the decision that he tell her the truth and knowingly cause her to suffer. For in love one not only

357

acknowledges the Other as a subject; one affirms that one values this subjectivity and its well-being. Furthermore, if a person finds life meaningful and happy because he has been able to make a reciprocal commitment with one person, he would be stupid to jeopardize the relation for the sake of trivial affairs which he had found insufficiently rewarding when he had nothing beyond them. Even the argument that to enter into any close knowledge of a member of the opposite sex must involve sexual relations is dubious when used as an argument for promiscuity. Where one is unwilling to devote the time and care necessary for love, recourse to sex may serve to narrow the possibilities of knowing another rather than broadening or deepening them. The physical may be a short-cut to attaining an illusory sense of breaking down separation while it by-passes completely the exploring of those intricate traits of personality which constitute the Other and his private world as unique.

Even without the social taboos against adultery and the almost universal condemnation of the infidelity of lovers, it appears that those who are actively engaged in discovering and creating the possibilities of erotic love are right in committing themselves to exclusive fidelity and in expecting a reciprocal commitment. The body which each one caresses as the incarnation and means of communication for the Other's consciousness is so wholly infused with the love lavished upon it that it is no longer for either one a thing in itself detached from the emotions it has aroused. To some degree this remains true forever for those who choose to renew their love by ever new exchanges and looking together at the world. For some the maintaining of this sacred status is a trust gladly undertaken, and the temptation to infidelity carries more taint of defilement than promise of pleasure. Most people take it for granted that one feels possessive regarding the beloved's body but will acknowledge that with time and familiar habit, the possibility of realizing oneself in close union with another takes on a positive value, at least as a temptation. Conventionally, society has solved this problem by mutual renunciation. Each party agrees to forego this type of enrichment of his private world for the sake of the other. If either one openly breaks the agreement, the liaison is broken, the marriage is dissolved or remains a union of expediency without love. What happens most often, of course, is that there is secret deception with the careful preservation of appearances in a relation that is no longer in good faith.

From the existentialist point of view, the only absolute demand is honesty and mutual agreement on the part of both persons as to what their commitments to each other really are and what each wants them to be. In society as it is presently set up, a mutual commitment to the love which forsakes all others is probably the most rewarding for most people. I am not sure that it is necessarily the right solution for all or even the best solution—if by "best" we mean that which most fully satisfies both the demands of a freedom to realize its own potentialities and the concern to allow and help the other to do the same. There has been much criticism of the Sartre–de Beauvoir relationship, and one might, I suppose, take a different view of it if one were involved on the periphery. Certainly from the standpoint of those two, the relation has been an enduring one in good faith for the greater part of their lives. "There has been one absolute success in my life—my relationship with Sartre," [3] says Simone de Beauvoir. And Sartre replies, "My complete confidence in her has always given me complete security." [4] If two people are able to maintain a We which allows them to enter into other We relations as well, this is an achievement which I can see no reason to condemn, particularly when, as in the case of de Beauvoir and Sartre, they themselves have only grateful appreciation for each other.

Until now we have discussed love and sexuality with little concern for the distinctive roles played by man and woman. From one point of view existentialism, more than any other

[3] De Beauvoir: *La Force des choses*, p. 672.
[4] "Sartre Talks of Beauvoir," an interview with Madeleine Gobeil, tr. Bernard Frechtman, *Vogue*, Vol. 146 (July, 1965), pp. 72–3.

philosophy, does not consider the ethical requirements for men and women as being in any way different. It is a philosophy which refuses to define any person by his or her social role or biological function—either descriptively or normatively. On the other hand, existentialism is particularly concerned with the problems of living beings in their concrete situations. From this approach, one might expect that masculinity and femininity would be themes of major importance in existentialist psychological and sociological studies. Indeed they are, but we must be very careful. It is legitimate to speak of the psychology of women, as we might speak of the psychology of men, provided that both are treated as special investigations within the broader framework of a human psychology. The reactions of women to pregnancy and childhood and to all the psychosomatic complexities of their rhythmic sexuality certainly merit more serious and far-reaching analysis than can be found in marriage manuals and the *Kama Sutra*. The equivalent is true for the sexual life of men. Similarly the problems which women and men confront as they seek to relate themselves to the world will vary significantly according to the expectations and demands which society has set up. There may be a psychology of woman and of man as there is a psychology of city-dweller and farmer, of civilized cultures and of primitive. Yet just as it is important to recognize the truth of what one's past has been and at the same time freely choose what its meaning is to be for present and future, so one's acceptance of one's sex— its limitations and its possibilities—must be viewed as the material out of which one makes oneself, not as the determinant of a life.

There is another sense in which we as existentialists will stubbornly resist the idea of a special psychology of women (or of men). We will do so in the same way that we would reject any psychology of Negroes or of Indians which tried to see them as in some way different from the standard human. When Sartre said that human sexuality is ontologically prior to the possession of specific sex organs, he meant— or I hope he did—that one's being as a person precedes and determines the way in which one lives one's being as man or woman. This is the antithesis of the Freudian view. It is opposed to the position of most psychologists of all schools. Abraham Maslow, for example, who is generally very sympathetic with the existentialist position, states explicitly that "Of course, femalehood is prepotent over personhood." And again, "One must first be a healthy, femaleness-fulfilled woman or maleness-fulfilled man before general-human self-actualization becomes possible." [5] Erich Fromm, too, insists, "There is masculinity and femininity in *character* as well as in *sexual function*." [6] We have seen that even the writers whom I have called negative rebels seem to feel that fulfillment as a woman precludes the necessity for any other kind. Paul Goodman adopts without question the Freudian portrayal of woman, whose life is first blighted by penis envy, then fulfilled by the child as penis-substitute. With mingled envy and contempt, he states flatly that only men have to worry about finding meaning in something beyond their biological role. Without Puritan sexual restrictions, there would be no delinquent girls. Evidently the mutiny of the young is as masculine in character as the hand-to-hand combats on the plains of Troy.

Simone de Beauvoir in *The Second Sex* has magnificently demonstrated that men and women both are responsible for perpetuating the fiction that women are objects for men-subjects; she has shown the impossibility of continuing the legend if members of either sex are to fulfill themselves and live in good faith with one another. Betty Friedan's *Feminine Mystique* provides ample documentation to show that neither men nor women nor children have benefited from the postwar flight of the educated American woman back to home and family, away from the difficulties and the responsible opportunities of the public world. I do not intend to repeat their arguments in summary here nor to quote from others of the many available works to support the obvious truth presupposed by both de Beauvoir and Friedan: In the present state

[5] Maslow: *Toward a Psychology of Being*, pp. 121 and 196.
[6] Fromm: *The Art of Loving*, p. 36.

of technological achievement and in a world where overpopulation, not tribal diminishment, is the threat, society has no justification in demanding that women devote their full time to bearing and rearing children and looking after home and family. In short, one might argue that at an earlier stage of civilization the individual's very existence depended on putting the welfare of the species first. This is no longer true for either man or woman in any but the most general sense.

Put abstractly, the rule for good faith between the sexes, whether on the personal or the social level, is the same categorical imperative which we have encountered everywhere: everyone is a subject and must be valued as such. Or we might use that other formula: everyone is totally responsible and wholly without excuse. A little more concretely, we find certain obvious corollaries for both men and women. If we consider first the situation of the contemporary male, we find that his dilemma historically is not altogether unlike that of the Western white Gentile with respect to a minority group. The centuries-old assumption of superiority is hard to shake off. Even when one regulates one's overt conduct by the principle of recognizing equality, there is often an implicit enjoyment of one's gracious waiving of privilege. For the privilege is certainly there, thanks to the social structure. Constant vigilance is required if one does not—at least on the emotional level—equate it with natural superiority. Giving up the feeling that he belongs to the more gifted, dominant half of the species threatens more than man's vanity. The sense of having been born with a higher intrinsic value contributes significantly to one's feeling that one has a meaningful role to play in life. True, it is not a very distinctive honor since one shares it with half the race, but then there are the ever present members of the other half against whom to feel the positive merit. In the same way that many a woman has felt justified by responding with loving care to the dependent child she has brought into the world, so the need to provide and take care of the endearingly helpless woman has given to men a feeling of purpose, the security of being needed. If the woman has trained and made use of her intellectual qualities,

362

she is no longer dependent, and the man not automatically necessary in the same ways that he used to be. He must justify himself in her eyes and in his own by achievements specifically his own, not by the mere fact of his having been born a man. To many men it seems that wife and home are no longer a secure refuge from the public arena but rather one more area of competition. Some critics have commented on the degree to which modern literature is permeated with overt dislike of women. One reason for it and perhaps also for the increase of male homosexuality (I do not pretend that it is the only or the most important one) is resentment of the object turned subject. It is distressing enough to realize that one has an object side which any stranger's look may suddenly call into being. To find it there where one has been led to believe it will be kept carefully in abeyance can be devastating.

The most common masculine lament expresses a sense of loss in the possible disappearance of those prized qualities which seemed to derive precisely from women's acceptance of their earlier role. This "femininity" is made to include anything which the man who is speaking has found valuable— grace and charm, softness, nonaggressiveness, tenderness, sensitivity, sympathy, unselfishness, receptive understanding, shyness, motherliness, gentleness, passivity, carefully tended beauty, and the faculty of never openly being quite as intelligent as the male. It should be obvious that none of these supposedly feminine traits is restricted to women who remain at the fireside unless it is those spurious qualities assumed for the sole purpose of flattering the male ego. As a consolation, I may point out that even ego-building need not be lost. Men and women both can and do learn the art and use it for those who demand it. If the new pattern must be fitted to the individual as himself and not merely a member of the species, it could be more satisfying than ever. Sartre, in an interview with a representative of *Playboy*, spoke more realistically and significantly about the probable loss of peculiarly feminine qualities if women ceased to be an oppressed group. He remarked that he had a special preference for women as friends in the same way that he especially liked many Jews, who had responded to anti-Semitism by developing a particular "gentleness and subtlety."

There are qualities in women that derive from the feminine predicament, from the fact that she is both a slave and an accomplice. That's why her sensibility ranges so much wider than a man's. . . . Like Simone de Beauvoir, I'm in favor of total feminine emancipation. But when the day comes, of course, the special qualities of sensibility for which I prefer the company of women will be due purely to chance; sometimes a woman will have them, sometimes a man. They'll cease being a feminine prerogative.[7]

The danger of making equality into sameness confronts us everywhere, and we must constantly be on our guard against it. We can hardly deliberately promote tragedy because of the purified knowledge which is said to be one of its consequences. We cannot justify the oppression of Negroes because we admire the art which they have produced as an expression of their sorrow and their rebellion. Moreover, the consequences of injustice and tragedy are more often negative than positive. If sensitivity and compassion are two of the compensations for women's subjection, so are the deception, shallowness, and petty vanities which gave Schopenhauer the excuse to say, "Women are directly fitted for acting as the nurses and teachers of our early childhood by the fact that they are themselves childish, frivolous and short-sighted; in a word, they are big children all their life long—a kind of intermediate stage between the child and the full-grown man, who is man in the strict sense of the word."[8]

One may sympathize with man in his ejection from the Paradise of privilege, but there is no way for him to go back. He may retreat into bad faith of course, and he may easily find a woman still willing to help him sustain his fictions. But she will be using him as much as he is using her and this

[7] Quoted in "Playboy Interview: Jean-Paul Sartre—Candid Conversation," *Playboy*, Vol. XII (May, 1965), pp. 69–76.

[8] Arthur Schopenhauer: *The Pessimist's Handbook: A Collection of Popular Essays*, tr. T. Bailey Saunders, introduction by Hazel E. Barnes (Lincoln: University of Nebraska Press; 1964), p. 199.

symbiotic union—to use Fromm's term—is not good faith. I am reluctant to call it love. Like all relations in good faith, the free coexistence of male and female subjects is filled with perils; the stakes are higher than ever before.

Whether in business encounters or in personal relations, the man in good faith will grant the same degree and range of choice to a woman as to a man. This is fairly easy in matters where simple justice and equality of opportunity are concerned. It is more difficult in passing judgments. Among those men who are willing to grant women equal opportunity, most are not so crude as to attribute the errors and shortcomings of a specific individual to the fact that she is a woman. The same men will find it more difficult not to demand that a woman who enters a hitherto masculine world should come in without introducing any changes. Neither a corporation executive nor a professor is supposed to cease being a man when he enters his office or classroom. Women are asked to make their sex as unobtrusive as possible—unless, indeed, the position is one in which their sexual assets are specifically meant to be involved, as in the case of entertainers and some men's secretaries. I agree that sex and business are better left unmixed—unless indeed sex is the business. The case is different with regard to the so-called masculine and feminine ways of looking at things. Either there exists no difference, hence no problem, or else men and women, because of their different physiologies and social experience, do have certain peculiar ways of approaching reality which exist along with—not opposed to—objective knowledge and rational ability. In that case neither approach can be identified with the "human"; both are partial. Their pertinence or nonpertinence depends on the project at hand. For full understanding, it seems logical that both are better than either one alone. Most important of all, no individual man and no woman is wholly or even primarily defined by those things which he shares with the rest of his sex. Even in the so-called masculine and feminine traits as defined by the most regressive of psychologists, the members of the human species are found strung out in a continuum, not in two separate compartments.

If the position of the sexes in recent centuries has been determined primarily by the dominant males, we may fairly say that its present and probable future depend primarily on the good or bad faith of the females. The resentment toward women, which we recognized as an important theme in contemporary literature, is not solely the result of the disgruntled hostility of the dispossessed man. Women are guilty of both noisy and quiet forms of bad faith. They, too, try to make both others and themselves into objects. Some seek to deny their being-as-women, others to exploit it illegitimately. The most obnoxious kind of woman is the one who feels that she must prove the superiority of women in general by demonstrating her personal superiority to whatever man she meets. Such a woman does not honestly want a relation of free equality between the sexes. It is her own subjectivity which she must assert at all cost; usually she is just as incapable of relations in good faith with other women. Perhaps less objectionable but just as wrong is the woman who feels that the only way for her to hold her place in the world of men is to develop those qualities which traditionally are associated with men. Thus she will ape men in language, dress, and mannerisms. It is quite true that this kind of woman secretly hates her femininity. I do not believe that the Freudian explanation is the right one. The motivation is more probably the fact that she has accepted the prevailing view of her environment that women are inferior and wants to do everything in her power to deny that inferiority, to show that she personally is not like the rest of this subspecies. She resembles those Negroes who hate their race as much as any prejudiced white and who try to make themselves as much like the typical white as possible. This parallel should, however, serve as a warning. There is inauthenticity in all Negroes, Jews, and women who want to be what they are not, merely because they have accepted the value which the dominant group has attached to itself. It is just as important to remember that outside of biological distinctions there is no single quality or value to which any group has sole claim. Men jealous of their privileges are quick to view any nontraditional conduct of women as an aggressive imitation of the masculine, as if it were trespassing on a field already owned by another. In many cases it is the genuine expression of a free consciousness choosing authentically its own self-project.

Some women, in resentment at the attempt to force inferior status upon them, seem to have elected hostility and suspicious vigilance as their way of life. As in all conflicts, defense against injustice is likely to do some violence against others and results in some loss to oneself. Other women have chosen the opposite strategy. Instead of denying their femininity, they retreat into it, making of it an excuse to avoid the responsibilities of a free human being. Women already engaged in careers may use prejudice as a rationalization for failure when the prejudice either does not exist or might have been overcome. Out of lack of self-confidence or from fear or laziness, a woman may use her sex, her "woman's destiny" as an excuse for not taking up a career or for settling for a position not equal to her potentialities. Or she may try to use sexual attraction to substitute for talents she does not have or is too lazy to develop. Most common of all is the woman who, having chosen marriage, has decided that the way of self-fulfillment is to make herself an object to husband and children, to live for them and through them. For all its superficial resemblance to noble self-sacrifice, such conduct remains an evasion for the woman and a poisonous gift to husband and children. "A woman to a man is just a woman, but a man to a woman is her life." The old words represent neither the ideal nor a cynical view of what inevitably must be. They contain in essence a statement of those traps which society has made easy for each sex to fall into. *He* is encouraged to want and to find only "a woman"; *she* tries to be no more than that.

When it comes to the socially recognized institutions within which we are supposed to work out our love relations, I would extend what I have already said with regard to sexual regulations. Actual legal provisions do not at the moment constitute a major difficulty. Prevalent social attitudes do, and very few people have the authenticity or the courage to oppose them. Laws do not compel men and women to marry,

367

and they permit the marriage to be dissolved. Yet there is reason to believe that many marry at a time when they are not ready for parental responsibilities and to people they would never have married if the social pressure to gain security by "going steady" and "getting settled" were not so great. Reverence for the values of the Serious World, carried to the point where one decides some of the most important decisions of one's life by giving in to the need to be like everyone else— all this is so far from authenticity that it is no wonder so many of these marriages in bad faith soon end in divorce and frequently in lifetime neurosis. People ought to regard marriage and the time of marriage, celibacy with or without sex, and the type of partner one chooses, as belonging entirely within the sphere of authentic personal choice. If a girl of eighteen marries because she is afraid she may have no better chance and will be branded a social failure in her early twenties, both she and her society are deplorably in bad faith. If a man of thirty marries in order to get a responsible job and because his employer will otherwise reject him as possibly homosexual or irresponsible and not to be counted on, then we may ask how much our purely legal rights are worth.

The same is true with regard to the particular arrangements which people may wish to make with regard to careers and marriage and the economic problems attending on both. I do not believe Betty Friedan is right when she states that the only way for a woman to be happy and live significantly is to combine a career with being a wife and mother. Friedan's great contribution lies in her forceful demonstration that a creative career and domesticity together are possible and that when a woman is forced to choose one without the other (or believes that she is), the results are disastrous for her, often for her family as well, and certainly a loss to society at large. I do not accept Friedan's further claim that the married woman ought to feel guilty and will of necessity be less happy if she does not find a career outside the home. There are many other possibilities. The community activities Friedan sneers at are not all mere busy work. Some women, too, make their lives meaningful by constantly broadening their horizons in reading and systematic study, in an intelligent and genuinely appreciative pursuit of the arts, in learning to live more broadly and deeply the wide range of experience which the human and nonhuman world have to offer and which the more active of us long in vain for time to explore. If the woman who stays at home is happy because she is growing in ways she has herself chosen, we are not always right in describing her state as that of bovine contentment. She may have chosen the path that is in reality the best both for her own self-fulfillment and for her responsibilities toward husband, children, and community. Genuine happiness tends to overflow and to become in a peculiar way a value for those who surround the happy person. Similarly I proclaim against Friedan the right of women not to marry, and I assert that for many this is the more rewarding choice. Of course one loses something by not having children. One also gives up something in order to have them. One has here, as everywhere, the right to choose one's own values.

There are certain positive steps which society ought to take in order to bring its recognized social patterns in line with actual practice. That we should get rid of outdated laws providing penalties for infringement of Puritan morality goes without saying. Learning to associate responsibility with sex, the problems of commitments in love—these things cannot be enforced by law. Everyone has to learn for himself what is best; parents and teachers can help if they have successfully solved their own problems and are honest about what they have learned. There remains one area where community action seems necessary. This is the problem of the increase in very young marriages. Youthful marriage has the merit of solving the old problem of enforcing chasity on young couples until they were finished with their educational training, a point which for many persons today would come in the mid-twenties or even later. Obviously this solution is better than either prolonged repression or guilty indulgence in forbidden sex. Yet one wonders if it has not created as many problems as it has solved—even if for the moment we ignore the tremendously frightening threat of overpopulation. First, there is the fact that commitments in marriage are theoretically for life and that few high school students or college undergraduates are in a position where they can intelligently make such a commitment or where it is to their best interests to do so. A divorce, no matter how easily secured, almost always leaves the adults with some psychic scars. Children of these broken marriages, although they are spared the social stigma, share many of the disadvantages of the illegitimate. It is no great help to say that they are better off than they would be in the tension of a hostile marriage, although this is frequently true.

A second danger in the young marriage is that the pair undertakes responsibilities too soon. I am not sure that they "grow old before their time." On the whole, Americans seem more open to the charge of immaturity than to that of premature old age. But this is perhaps the point which should concern us. If they have a sense of responsibility for their children, the young parents are forced to settle as quickly as possible into a way of life which is intended to continue, particularly for the man, with promotions and perhaps transfer from one place to another, but with no radical change for the rest of his life. Margaret Mead has pointed to the genuine loss which such a pattern entails. The young man has no time to feel his way, to investigate several possibilities before committing himself to the project which promises to be richest in his chosen values. More than this, he has no chance to explore what are perhaps only byways but excursions rich in immediate value and in contributing to the background structures of the world within which he will carve his future projects. He cannot take the time to see whether or not he has it in him to write a novel, win recognition as an artist, or satisfy his thirst for wandering and living from day to day on what his own hands and ingenuity can provide.[9] In short, early marriage and paternity compel him to work out a coherent life plan for responsible reflective self-realization. So far

[9] Margaret Mead expressed this point of view in a public lecture at the University of Colorado. She discusses the problem in an article "The Young Adult" in *Values and Ideals of American Youth*, ed. Eli Ginzberg (New York: Columbia University Press; 1961).

so good. What is lacking in too many cases is both the experience necessary for intelligent choosing and any opportunity for immediate and spontaneous self-realization, without which a life may be somewhat impoverished in value even if it has been freely chosen so that we have no right to call it unauthentic.

For the woman the consequences are often still more serious. In one respect she is more fortunate than the man. The problem she confronts is so obvious that neither she nor society can avoid seeing that it exists, whereas her husband is unlikely to recognize what it is that makes him discontented with what he has chosen and wanted from the beginning. The young mother is aware that she is sacrificing her further education or failing to use the training she has had. She does so willingly, sometimes because she feels that she gives up the lesser for the greater reward. Or she may think that she is merely postponing the fulfillment of her other potentialities until the children no longer need her constant care. When in a few years she finds herself with time on her hands, she seeks employment. For many women the problem is solved at this point. They obtain employment to bring them out into the world again, to give them tangible reward as productive members of society, and they find it sufficient. For others this is the moment of disillusion. The woman who wants not just a paying job but a professional career finds that her educational training is inadequate or out of date. Some employers, including some public school boards, will not hire older women. Graduate schools may admit women over thirty-five; not many will encourage them to hope for a position on the college or university level once the degree is attained. In every area it is usually the jobs of lesser importance, the part-time and temporary positions which represent the older woman's only possibilities.

There are two quite different solutions which we can envision. Both have been proposed, and I believe that society ought to try to work out the possibilities of both, not choose between them. Here as elsewhere we should not try to replace an old pattern by imposing a new one. What we want to do

371

is to provide a wider set of possible patterns among which people can freely work out what they believe to be best for them.

One obvious thing to do is increase the opportunities for continuing education for women. As Mary Keyserling, director of the U. S. Labor Department's Women Bureau, has phrased it, "We need rust removers and rust preventers. . . . We need to give them back this sense that ability is a precious thing and that they still have it." Educational institutions must be made to be more alert to the needs of women, both young undergraduates and older women returning to the classroom. Mrs. Keyserling recognizes the necessity for more realistic counseling. "Better professional and life planning, counseling at the high school and college level will help. Girls need to plan, not just for the next step: College, a job, or marriage—they should plan for an entire lifetime." [1] More is needed—fellowships for women who want to return after some years of not studying or working, course schedules adapted to housewives' hours, perhaps provision for refresher courses and special programs for those who want advanced training but do not wish or need the degree with its specific requirements. Some of this is already being done, but not enough. Its real success depends on another factor, our ability to persuade employers to hire the women. The difficulty here is that in addition to the prejudice against women, we confront the almost universal reluctance to hire anyone who has begun late in his field, whatever the reason may be. Legislation can hardly help here. Persuasion on the part of an interested public and by educational leaders will accomplish more —even if slowly.

What I have said in this connection should be extended to those men who decide to change their careers to work in a sphere they find more challenging and creative. One of the criticisms raised against Friedan's book was that men as well as women are bored and frustrated with uncreative lives and that merely liberating women from household drudgery is not enough. The argument, while it hardly seems to me justified

[1] Mary Keyserling, quoted in The Denver *Post*, July 8, 1965.

against a book which posited and tried to solve only one problem, is valid if we take it as a comment on the social situation as a whole. We may even go so far as to say that if her husband and community are sympathetic, the woman has an advantage. Presupposing that she has her husband's salary to insure their economic existence, she can choose her career without giving the most important consideration to the financial aspect, to guaranteed means of subsistence and the certainty of continued future employment. For the few men who are willing to start over again and lose, at least in part, the advantage of years of experience in one field, we should be ready to create such opportunities as I have suggested for women.

The first solution has been based on the assumption that people prefer to marry and have children when they are biologically ready or at least in the years soon after puberty. This sort of proposal is closer to nature, if you like, and does not seriously upset traditional mores. It does not, of course, solve all of the difficulties I have mentioned. The second suggestion has met with such forceful opposition that society as a whole has never given it serious consideration. Yet it has been proposed and by a highly respected member of the legal profession. I refer to Judge Lindsey and his suggestion in 1927, so shocking to most people, that society recognize as legal the temporary unions of young men and women, trial marriages without the full legal commitments of traditional matrimony and with the agreement that there be no children. Now forty years later, I am not sure how many people would entertain such a possibility long enough to reach a really thoughtful acceptance or rejection of any form of "companionate marriage." Probably very few. Yet we may ask seriously whether something of the sort would not be more satisfactory and more moral (in the sense of introducing responsible commitments) than the present situation. The improvement of contraceptives has made childless sex more easily possible. If unplanned conception should occur, any couple could be forced by law to do exactly what they usually do now—that is, marry or arrange for legal adoption.

373

Rather than being immoral, irresponsible, degrading, giving in to man's basic animal instincts, and all the other vituperative things which have been said against it, some sympathetic recognition of unions between people not yet ready for parenthood and lifetime monogomy would seem to me a great improvement over what exists today. As it is, the majority— or at least great numbers—of teen-agers and early twenty-year-olds are not the sexual innocents their not-so-innocent parents would like to believe they are. Secrecy may, to be sure, sometimes add to the romantic spice and intense feeling of togetherness. Often the initial attraction and affection becomes tainted with guilt-feeling, or the pair is so preoccupied with the fact of rebelling against authority that possibilities for love and tenderness are suffocated. Promiscuity replaces the meaningful attachment which might have been.

In love, consciousnesses do not merge, but private worlds are affected and reflect each other. In love I may indeed arrive at the point at which I place so high a value on the life and happiness of the Other that at critical moments I will choose to protect his well-being at the expense of my own. Strictly speaking, this preference for the Other is neither egoism nor self-sacrifice. It is self-transcendence of the highest order. Man *is* a self-transcendence, which means that he lives by going beyond what he has been toward some further relation between his consciousness and the world around him, one more step in "inscribing himself in Being." In loving another, a person recognizes that the self which he is is not simply the pure awareness of immediate consciousness. It is all that which consciousness has internalized as a part of its private world. The Other whom I love is an object in my world. I can never perfectly know him as he is in and to himself. Yet this object and the subjectivity which I recognize as existing there beyond my grasp may come to represent the highest value which I have found in my self-projections. If I choose to perpetuate this value even when my consciousness is no longer there to enjoy it, I am not denying my freedom.

374

Neither am I making myself an object. Rather I engage my freedom in a final act of self-realization. If a man dies for another as the result of a contemplative decision, he blends in one unique tragic and heroic act the two forms of self-realization. He affirms the ultimate validity of that objective value hierarchy which he has set up as his coherent life plan, and he asserts the freedom of his consciousness to posit a value higher than its awareness of those values which it has chosen. Man is an always future project, Sartre has said. In love I can project myself in a project which is no longer my own future.

PART FOUR

BEING

HERE AND THERE

XI

Being and "Thou": The New Theologians

Man makes his being-in-the-world, but he is not the maker of Being. Whether or not we are religious in temperament, we have to recognize that with this statement of the obvious we introduce the necessity of choosing our attitude toward transcendence, mystery, and faith. Material being existed before man and will continue to do so even if man carries out his threat to destroy himself. Man can enfold in his nihilating questions more than tangible mass and energy. "Why is there something rather than nothing?" asks Heidegger. Why "Is"? Man puts into question not only his own being and the being of the Universe—not only beings but Being itself. Is this universal immaterial Being of all beings an ultimate reality? Or has man simply evolved it as the abstract essence of his own questioning? Is Being really there? Or are there only beings?

In the most significant sense the problem of Being is religious. Or, to put it more accurately, the first question to be answered about Being is whether our attitude toward Being

379

allows for such categories as sacred, holy, God, and the like, or not. In short, our initial decision as to whether the problem of Being is properly philosophical or theological or religious is in itself a solution which determines the nature of all subsequent investigations of the problem of Being.

In the twentieth century many theologians seem almost to welcome Nietzsche's proclamation that "God is dead," provided they may put Being in His place. Thus Bishop Robinson writes, "Indeed, though we shall not of course be able to do it, I can at least understand what those mean who urge that we should do well to give up using the word 'God' for a generation, so impregnated has it become with a way of thinking we may have to discard if the Gospel is to signify anything." [1] In place of God the Father, sitting on His throne in Heaven, Robinson would accept Tillich's "God beyond God," preferably called by Tillich "Being-itself." That Christian theologians, having rejected the personal deity of fundamentalism and the social gospel of earlier "liberals," would identify the heart of the religious experience with Being as the ultimate reality is not surprising. What else was left for them? More interesting is the avowed connection with Heidegger's existentialism. This is sometimes merely the sympathetic awareness of parallel paths, proceeding from close but distinct starting points to view a common reality. On the other hand, Tillich's thought is frequently all but inextricably bound up with ideas derived from Heidegger. Rudolf Bultmann goes so far as to write, "Heidegger's existentialist analysis of the ontological structure of being would seem to be no more than a secularized, philosophical version of the New Testament view of human life." [2] Heidegger himself has never allied himself with Christianity or with any specifically religious position. Nevertheless there is no question as to the primacy of Being over beings in his philosophy.

In the midst of all this talk about Being, the contemporary

[1] Robinson: *Honest to God*, pp. 7–8.
[2] Rudolf Bultmann (and five critics): *Kerygma and Myth: A Theological Debate*, ed. Hans Werner Bartsch (New York: Harper and Row; 1961), p. 24.

atheist has a hard time of it. On the one hand, he is still liable to lose a job or a vote if he does not pay lip service to some vaguely defined deity. Admittedly the true believer has to take care as well. If his belief is too precise, he may be taken for a bigot. But the atheist has other worries. Not only must he defend himself against those who hold—quite contrary to the experience of their own lives—that all moral integrity, idealism, and love of mankind is inextricably linked with belief in the existence of a God. The atheist must confront as well the charge that he himself does not exist. First he is told that he is illogical and self-contradictory. God is defined in such a way that it is impossible for one not to believe in Him. For He is identified with whatever *is*. Thus, for example, Bishop Robinson: "God is, by definition, ultimate reality. And one cannot argue whether ultimate reality *exists*. One can only ask what ultimate reality is like." [3] Then the atheist is accused of pettiness of spirit, of misrepresenting the God others believe in so that he can cherish his own sense of removal from "the religious." After all this, it is small consolation to be told by the New Theologians that they feel closer to the atheist who rejects God for the right reasons than to the faithful who believe for the wrong reasons in an outdated concept of God. Theologians, I suppose, must be allowed to forgive the atheist if they insist, but the atheist will not be grateful for this charity if it comes at the price of his not being permitted to point out a difference between his position and the theologians'.

We must raise two fundamental questions: First, is there after all a reconciliation between the claims of humanistic existentialism and of religious existentialism (for the moment I should like to use this term loosely enough to include both the Being-philosophy of Heidegger and Christian existentialism)? Is Sartre's existentialism atheistic only in contrast with a supernaturalism now rejected by the new religious leaders? Can humanistic existentialism still be called religious in any meaningful sense? Or does the old distinction still apply? Second, regardless of the answer we establish to the first

[3] Robinson: *Honest to God*, p. 29.

381

question, we must face the problem of how we look at those aspects of existence still not explained. In short, we must determine our own attitude with regard to transcendence, faith, and the still unfathomed "mystery" of existence.

I will begin by flatly stating my conclusion to the first of these questions and then attempt to justify it. I do not believe that religious existentialism is compatible with a position based on Sartrean premises. I do not find in Tillich's Being-itself a concept which is logically tenable or a reality existentially meaningful. I cannot see that Heidegger's Being is a valid or more valuable alternative to Sartre's Being-in-itself. For the sake of clarity, I will divide into two parts this discussion of why I prefer another commitment. I will speak first of the New Theology and then of the philosophy of Heidegger.

My first objection to the theological claims of Tillich, Robinson, Bonhoeffer, and Bultmann—to use them as examples and speaking of what they share in common without implying that they are in full agreement—is that they claim to be Christian while denying what has been essential in Christianity whereas they subtly retain Christian assumptions when they profess to establish philosophical truths independent of sectarian commitments.

In their plea for a revolution in Christian thought, these theologians seem at times to argue for a position scarcely discernible from naturalism. The idea of a God "out there" somewhere in or beyond space, or the concept of any Being which is separate from us and the world is as offensive to Bishop Robinson as the medieval God who dwelt "up there" in Dante's three-level universe. Tillich argues against all use of "supernatural" concepts of God. Bultmann urges that we must "demythologize." Bonhoeffer suggests that Christianity should advance to the point where it no longer needs the "religious premise," that the Christian must "plunge himself into the life of a godless world, without attempting to gloss over its ungodliness with a veneer of religion or trying to

382

transfigure it."[4] There is no question that the scholarship and earnest persuasion of these men and of others working with the New Theology have resulted in a tremendous achievement. They have restored the possibility of being Christian to thousands of thoughtful persons who were finding that science, especially biology and psychology, and the study of comparative religion had sounded the death knell to any fairly literal belief in the Bible. The theologians have secured Christianity against all possible criticism at its hitherto most vulnerable points: its unscientific cosmology and anti-evolutionary science; its childish concept of a much too human God; its reliance on dubious, unprovable historic events, its tendency to equate the Christian life with worship; its primitive eschatology of reward and punishment. What is left?

From the point of view of the traditional Christian, not very much. I confess that I sympathize with the fundamentalist ministers who argue that whatever else it may be, this new religion is not Christianity and should be given some other name. The distance between Jesus' disciples and the Old Testament prophets seems to me no greater than that which separates St. Paul from Paul Tillich. It is the fashion today to interpret the New Testament writers as if they had been fully aware that they were using myth and allegory to convey philosophical truth and to argue that we are wholly free to reject whatever seems primitive or inadequate without in any way impairing the essential message. By what reason? These men were not sophisticated philosophers, nor were many of those who read and listened to them. An unforced reading, even of the books by Paul and John, reveals little more than an attempt to make use of the most obvious insights of Mystery and Logos doctrines. The principal doctrinal problems are those of the date of the end of the world and the relation of Christianity to the old Jewish law. A century or two later, intellectuals who wanted to be Christians set about transforming Jesus' simple message into a total philosophy. Even here it seems infinitely more likely

[4] Quoted by Robinson in *Honest to God*, p. 82.

that Tertullian's *Credo quia absurdum* was an anguished attempt to believe the doctrine despite its improbabilities than that it was an attempt to brush them aside as extraneous to the religious "proclamation." To suggest that the early Christian writers did not believe that Jesus was more than human is to maintain that everyone in those centuries conspired to write with deliberate obscurity if not downright hypocrisy. By "more than human" they certainly did not mean simply that we can read God's purpose in a human event. Contemporary theology does not always, of course, insist that the early Christians, even including Paul and Jesus himself, were speaking directly to us albeit in the language of their contemporaries. Bultmann in particular argues that it is our task to unveil a truth which earlier people were incapable of seeing. To demythologize is precisely to abstract kerygma, or proclaimed teaching, from its husk of myth and superstition. However commendable and necessary this step may be, it is a complete transformation of what Christianity has been. It amounts to saying that the New Testament, instead of being a Revelation from God, is an event in History within which we are free to search for Truth—a Truth hitherto concealed and forever subject to diverse interpretations.

The God whose existence nobody can deny is not, in strict truth, the God of the theologians—even though they do claim to make God identical with Being-Itself. Robinson makes this clear in the very passage in which he seems to assert the contrary.

God is, by definition, ultimate reality. And one cannot argue whether ultimate reality *exists*. One can only ask what ultimate reality is like—whether, for instance, in the last analysis what lies at the heart of things and governs their working is to be described in personal or impersonal categories.[5]

The God of the Christian theologians is *never* an ultimate reality defined in impersonal or scientific categories. God, for them, is not identified with reality as such but with reality seen in a particular way. This is particularly clear in a fa-

[5] Ibid., p. 29.

mous passage from Tillich. After insisting on the folly of believing in God as *a* being, rather than Being, Tillich says:

The name of this infinite and inexhaustible depth and ground of all being is *God*. That depth is what the word *God* means. And if that word has not much meaning for you, translate it, and speak of the depths of your life, of the source of your being, of your ultimate concern, of what you take seriously without any reservation. . . . If you know that God means depth, you know much about Him. You cannot then call yourself an atheist or unbeliever. For you cannot think or say: Life has no depth! Life itself is shallow. Being itself is surface only.[6]

Two pages later Tillich continues:

The name of this infinite and inexhaustible ground of history is *God*. That is what the word means, and it is that to which the words *Kingdom of God* and *Divine Providence* point. And if these words do not have much meaning for you, translate them, and speak of the depth of history, of the ground and aim of our social life, and of what you take seriously without reservation in your moral and political activities. Perhaps you should call this depth *hope*, simply hope.

Robinson quotes both of these passages approvingly as though they were elaborative statements of what he has said in identifying God with ultimate reality. They are not. The New Theologians regularly follow a pattern which is something like this: It is as though we were to say, "Nobody can deny the existence of Terra, for Terra is whatever we live on. Terra is a flat object made of fire." Then we proceed as if the Terra nobody can deny and Terra as further defined were indisputably one and the same.

At this point I wish to raise two questions. First, what justification is there for saying that the New Theologians' God or Being-Itself is a specifically Christian view? Second, is there any adequate reason for holding that reality is actually what they claim that Being is? Before anything else, of course, we must attempt, however reluctantly, to determine

[6] Paul Tillich: *The Shaking of the Foundations* (New York: Charles Scribner's Sons; 1953), p. 57.

with some degree of clarity what is meant by this Being-itself which God is. Obviously it is not simply the everyday world as the scientist sees it. Nor is it a pantheism, either of the Indian or of the neo-Stoic variety. Supposedly it is both transcendent and imminent, the Universal manifesting itself in the individual. It is the Transcendence beyond all transcendence, the Unconditioned which makes possible the commitments of our conditioned relationships, it is the Unworldly in the midst of the world. It is the Suprapersonal which is revealed in the personal. Above all, it is Love, seen by faith, in defiance of all outward appearance, as the essential structure of the Universe and History. Finally, *It* is *I-Thou*.

I find a curious and somewhat frustrating blend of objectivity and subjectivity in all of this. Tillich attempts to place the blame on our own faulty thinking. The subject-object problem enters in only when God is conceived of as *a* Being upon whom we may take a point of view. God as Being-Itself allows no such distinction. *Being-itself* is the ground of *our* being; we already participate in Being even as we try—in vain—to separate ourselves from it. Yet we may at least lay claim to the right to discuss the objective or subjective quality in the theologians' descriptions of Being. Here I personally am unable to find much consistency.

Consider, as a start, the two passages quoted from Tillich. If we looked at them detached from the rest of Tillich's writing, we might be tempted to equate God with any object of an attitude of serious and ultimate concern or even with the attitude itself (hope). I do not believe that Tillich means to be read in this way. Nevertheless, it is hard to see how his words could not be applied to communism, for example, which is certainly a cause which many persons have chosen as the regulating principle of their lives and as something worth dying for. Some people, of course, would gladly settle for this interpretation. A popular, though to my mind indefensible, use of the term "religion" applies it readily to whatever is the dominant interest of an individual, be it God, patriotism, beauty, or money. It would be stupidly insulting to accuse Tillich of holding a view no more profound than this. Obviously he must mean that whether they are aware of it or not, men and women are ultimately concerned (or ought to be) about a relationship with Being, more profound than is found in the surface aspects of human existence. Has Tillich not argued that we *cannot* say, "Life has no depth! . . . Being itself is surface only"?

At the end of one of his books, Tillich writes, "The courage to be is rooted in the God who appears when God has disappeared in the anxiety of doubt." [7] Evidently Tillich here refers to Robinson's underlying ultimate reality, which is objectively there even if subjectively experienced. It would be easy to jump to the conclusion that Being-Itself is either a Jungian type of Pan-psyche or something resembling the Indian Brahman and that our participation in it is that of the superficially separated part which may mystically realize its identity with the whole. But Tillich states explicitly that "Eastern mysticism is not the solution of the problems of Western Existentialism." [8] He and other New Theologians seem to share two major objections. First, mysticism is too closely dependent on the psychological make-up of the individual and comes dangerously near to resembling a specialized technique of "knowing." It cannot be the principal path of revelation to that Truth of Being which underlies our daily experience of ultimate concern. Furthermore, it destroys the importance of everything that is personal and individual. Instead of conferring meaning, it provides an "abyss of every definite meaning." Tillich says, "The God above the God of theism is not the devaluation of the meanings which doubt has thrown into the abyss of meaninglessness; he is their potential restitution." [9] Yet Tillich, even though he tells us that mysticism too must be transcended if we are to reach the God beyond God, finds a truth in mysticism that is broader than the mystic's own claim. "Mysticism is more than a special form of the relation to the ground of being. It is an

[7] Paul Tillich: *The Courage to Be* (New Haven: Yale University Press; 1952).
[8] Ibid., p. 186.
[9] Ibid., pp. 158–9 and 186.

element of every form of this relation. Since everything that is participates in the power of being, the element of identity on which mysticism is based cannot be absent in any religious experience." [1] So there remains something more than our individual selves and the good earth around us, and it is important that we find it. Being-Itself is not the three-personed Trinity (except mythically). It is not simply the object or goal of an attitude, like Santayana's ideal good. It is not an All-Soul or Brahman deceitfully cloaked in Maya. What then are we to make of it?

At times Being-Itself seems to be only the quality of the real and the existent, in contrast with the unreal and the nonexistent—in short, only the totality of what is as opposed to what is not. Here it is the abstraction of this common category which chiefly interests Tillich rather than the tangible world of matter. It is as though we were to make a reality out of the *fact that* all that is possesses being. Sartre has warned us against being trapped by this kind of expression. To say that everything which is has being sounds as if we were uttering an innocent pleonasm. It easily becomes a dangerous reification. Subtly implied is the idea that existents somehow *possess* being as if it were something added on. As Sartre says, it would be better to think of being as the condition of all revelation of reality. The being of the phenomenon is not reducible to the phenomenon of being. [2] Either the two statements "All existents *are*" (which is already pleonastic) and "All existents have being" are identical, or else the one who asserts them is surreptitiously introducing the idea that all existents share a form of reality which is not what it seems to be on the surface and which has consequences.

The New Theologians obviously mean still more than this. What they finally claim is that all existents have being and that human existents have something more too—the possibility of sharing in and communicating with a *power* that includes but certainly is not the same as the simple being-there

[1] Ibid., p. 160.
[2] Sartre: *Being and Nothingness*, pp. l–lii.

of living creatures and objects. Tillich would doubtless inter-
ject that the word "power" is symbolic, and I accept the
correction. I do not know what other word to use, particularly
since I do not accept Tillich's Being-Itself as a legitimate
synonym for all reality.

"Paradox" is a favorite word with the New Theologians.
Walter Kaufmann, an unkind but persuasive critic, argues
that "ambiguity" would be a better term and that it represents a deliberate defense of concepts they would like to hold
but cannot rationally support.[3] I myself feel that they are
offering us a new form of the medieval "doctrine of the
twofold truth." In faith, both the Universe and History take
on a new dimension. Without in any sense challenging the
conclusions of either the historian or the scientist, the theologians insist that an entirely different view of the world and of
events is also true. They are ready to declare that the future
of Christianity depends upon the world's being willing to
accept this paradoxical interpretation of the events in the
New Testament. Bultmann's summation of this position is
concise, typical, and as clear as any such statement can be.

Thus the ἐφάπαξ is understood as never before in its true sense of
the "once" of the eschatological event. For it does not mean the
datable uniqueness and finality of an event of past history, but
teaches us in a high degree of paradox to believe that just such
an event of the past is the once-and-for-all eschatological event,
which is continually re-enacted in the word of proclamation. This
proclamation is a word which addresses me personally, and tells
me that the provenient grace of God has already acted on my
behalf, though not in such a way that I can look back upon this
act of God as a datable event of the past, but in the sense that
God's having acted is present as an eschatological Now.[4]

I cannot and I do not wish to attempt any full discussion of
the problem of how supposed events in history can be revelations of God and at the same time perfectly mundane happen-
ings which took place—if indeed they did take place—in a

[3] Walter Kaufmann: *Critique of Religion and Philosophy* (New
York: Harper and Brothers; 1958), pp. 124–31.
[4] Bultmann: *Kerygma and Myth*, p. 209.

fashion quite different from the way in which the mythologized account has come down to us. The position is nonrational, and of course faith has always maintained that there is an irrationality above reason as well as the subrational. This new irrationality strikes me as potentially more dangerous than the older forms. The fundamentalist faith in a seven-day creation, the virgin birth, miracles, and occasional visions was supported chiefly by the belief that God as the Creator of the Universe could suspend His own laws for His own purposes and reveal Himself and His will to man. In itself there is nothing illogical about the idea that the deity who made the world should continue to be interested in it and should be above the regulations he has set to govern it. There is something disconcerting about the possibility of a sudden divine irruption into natural law, but the occasions have always been reassuringly rare. The old irrationality had one great merit. It was confined primarily to events which happened long before history or after death; it referred to things for which no other explanation and no proof were available. Thus in a strange way it was not, in principle, in conflict with science and rationality. Even the doctrine of twofold truth was applied chiefly to such problems as the first creation of matter *e nihilo*, the resurrection of the body, etc. Miracles, which might seem an obvious exception, are actually a case in point. The believer clung to them as miracles because they appeared to be a defiance of natural law. If scientific proof were offered to the contrary, one either acknowledged he had been mistaken or declined to accept the proof as adequate. Self-deception, wishful thinking, prejudice frequently decided the response. The believer might compromise by saying that in this instance God had chosen to manifest His will through natural law. But one was never called upon to hold simultaneously two contradictory ideas—that things were exactly what they seemed and at the same time were something more. One was not asked, for instance, to separate Jesus from Christ, to assume that what never happened was nevertheless a specific revelation of God in history. If the New Theologians were willing to say that they find in the New Testament a semifictional portrait of an ideal human being and a way of life which they believe we would do well to follow, we might agree or disagree with their evaluation; we could certainly not call their procedure illegitimate. But this is the position of the old liberal Christianity and social gospel which they so scornfully reject.

An alternative would be to state that out of the events recorded in the New Testament, one can, by a subjective creative process, derive an allegory to fit a particular view of reality and set of values which one already holds. This is what I believe Bultmann and the others have done, but they will never admit it. Naturally, for if they did, there would no longer be any good reason to call their theology Christian. The world's literature is full of stories of those who suffered for truth or for man—Socrates, Prometheus, Bruno. Dying gods who were resurrected are innumerable. The Bodhisatt-vas do not give up life for three days; they postpone salvation and bliss for eons—until the millennium when all may share it with them. Kaufmann has argued convincingly that the Christian eschatological myth, with its doctrine of original sin and damnation for all but the saved remnant, is intrinsically far less adaptable to an allegorical interpretation of God as love than are numerous other examples of the world's hagiology.[5] Tillich's reference to Grace by which the unacceptable are found to be acceptable does not seem harmonious with the parable of the tares and wheat. Yet even if we were to grant—as I do not, except for the sake of the argument—that the New Testament represented a purer allegory of a universe of love and salvation than any other religious document, I cannot see that, as allegory, it can serve as more than illustrative myth for the philosophical and ethical position. Once the story and preaching are stripped of the supernatural elements and of all those things which do not fit in with the new kerygma (imminent world-damnation, Jesus' comments on divorce, Paul's on marriage and on women, etc.), it holds no compelling force. The philosophy of Tillich, Bultmann, and others has determined the meaning which these theolo-

[5] Kaufmann: *Critique of Religion and Philosophy*, pp. 141–7.

gians find in the New Testament; neither myth nor Jesus'
clear teaching has contributed to their philosophy much that
is still recognizable.

The kerygma which the theologians find as the kernel of
the myth seems to proclaim that Being is Love and that our
relation to Being is personal even though Being is not a
person. Robinson makes a great deal of the distinction between "God is Love" and "Love is God." The second is a
statement the naturalist might make; the first is not. Robinson argues that God is revealed only in personal encounters;
yet He is not to be equated with these encounters any more
than He is the same as man or nature. Thus Being, while it
never exists separate from us and from the world, is something other than we and the world are.

To assert that "*God is love*" is to believe that in love one comes
into touch with the most fundamental reality in the Universe, that
Being itself ultimately has this character. It is to say, with Buber,
that "Every particular *Thou* is a glimpse through to the eternal
Thou," that it is "between man and man" that we meet God, not,
with Feuerbach, that "man with man—the unity of *I* and *Thou*—
is God." Nevertheless, as Bonhoeffer insists, "God is the 'beyond'
in the midst"; "The transcendent is not infinitely remote but close
at hand." For the eternal *Thou* is met only *in, with and under* the
finite *Thou*, whether in the encounter with other persons or in the
response to the natural order.[6]

We may note that Robinson claims that Being can be described in terms of love. Elsewhere he writes, "God, the
unconditional, is to be found only in, with *and under* the
conditional relationships of this life: for he *is* their depth and
ultimate significance." [7]

I confess that I find a difficulty here. Robinson seems to say
that we meet God only indirectly as that which makes possible our loving encounter and unconditional commitments to
others. This idea is strengthened by his parallel remarks on
prayer. In a radical break with tradition, he insists that the
most meaningful prayer to God is usually an active wrestling

[6] Robinson: *Honest to God*, p. 53.
[7] Ibid., p. 60.

with the problems of existence where one is not directly worshiping or even thinking about God as such. Naturally one is approaching these problems in a spirit of responsible love and concern for one's fellow creatures. Nevertheless I cannot myself see that God is necessary in these human struggles any more than he was needed in the mechanistic universe of Laplace. Robinson apparently holds, as Tillich does, that true love for others comes about when we recognize that the Ground of our being is the same for all of us. It is doubtless true that we could hardly have a relation of love and sympathy with others if there were no common ground between us. I do not see that more is called for than the obvious realization that as human beings we all partake of the same finite human condition and that the same Being-in-itself is the stuff of our projects. We need not postulate any other source or medium. The difference between our specific situations is significant as well as the general similarity of our condition. French existentialists have recognized, as one cause of the feeling of human solidarity, precisely the awareness of our mutual loneliness.

Bultmann gives more emphasis to the direct encounter with God, apart from personal relations with others, but his words are disappointingly obscure. He, too, insists that the world is more than "a closed weft of cause and effect." Faith asserts that God acts in history, but "the encounter with God is not objective like a worldly event." If a man speaks of an act of God, he says something about his own personal existence. It is an existential affirmation without the usual sort of objective reference. At the same time, we are not to think of the encounter with God as simply a subjective experience to be explained by psychology.

When we say that faith alone, the faith which is aware of the divine encounter, can speak of God, and that therefore when the believer speaks of an act of God he is *ipso facto* speaking of himself as well, it by no means follows that God has no real existence apart from the believer or the act of believing.[8]

[8] Bultmann: *Kerygma and Myth*, p. 199.

Bultmann uses as illustration for this paradoxical position both the experience of "self" and our relation with others. First, he points out that I have already transcended the world, objectively viewed, when I speak of myself. "For I myself, my real self, am no more visible or ascertainable than an act of God." That transcendence is involved here I do not deny. The experience of oneself as consciousness *is* a process of transcendence. We have observed, however, that the realization by consciousness that it is *not* its object does not bring in as a corollary the existence of the self as an entity. Quite the contrary. The true comprehension of one's own existence as freedom reveals precisely the fact that there are no hidden depths or opacity in consciousness. Bultmann's other appeal is to the personal encounter with another:

The love of another is an encounter whose essential character depends upon its being an event. For it cannot be apprehended as love by objective observation, but only by myself who am encountered by it.

Everything seems to me wrong in this parallel. It is true that the ultimate evidence of love lies in the subjective experience of the lover, although even here one might argue that the objective conduct of the lover toward the beloved sometimes gives the lie to what the lover has persuaded himself is love. The fact that the beloved is sometimes even unaware of the lover's love seems to me to argue against Bultmann's claim that all love is a genuine existential encounter between two persons. In any case, the existence of the beloved is never called into question. The analogy with the God who can be seen only through the eyes of faith is a false one. Bultmann must finally conclude, as countless others have done, that "We cannot say what God is like in himself, but only what he does to us." [9] This is equivalent to saying that we do not know what ultimate reality is like but only our own relation with it. Unfortunately there is not sufficient unanimity in the relations which individuals enjoy with the rest of reality for

[9] Ibid., p. 202.

us to form any firm conclusions as to just what it is that God or Being does for us or whether either *does* anything.

One way or another, all of the New Theologians end up by ascribing an active role to Being, one which is suspiciously reminiscent of the personal God whom they claim to reject. Bultmann speaks of what God does to us. Bonhoeffer, while his appeal to us to learn to live "without religion" might seem to put him farthest of all from tradition, writes in terms almost anthropomorphic.

God allows himself to be edged out of the world and on to the cross. God is weak and powerless in the world, and that is exactly the way, the only way, in which he can be with us and help us. . . . Only a suffering God can help.[1]

Tillich brings in unmistakable reference to something which comes to us, which happens to us from outside—even while he constantly insists that Being-Itself is not something apart. We have observed that Tillich spoke of God as being that depth which we cannot fail to recognize in ourselves. Even in the single passage quoted, there was a puzzling vacillation between the purely ontological concept of Being-Itself, as the Ground of all reality, and the psychological (ultimate concern). I find a similar uneasy movement in all that I have read of Tillich. He speaks constantly of the Ground of my being as that which I cannot escape (for it is what I *am*) and that from which I may be estranged. Estrangement from God and our reconciliation to Him are, of course, the central motif of almost any religion. What is different in Tillich is that he tries to remove all that is supernatural or distinct from man and nature while at the same time retaining all of the old values bound up with divine salvation. But to reject the term "supernatural" on the basis that the natural is everywhere imbued with the divine is to quibble with terms if it is not deliberately to mislead or to construct a convenient ambiguity.

In one passage Tillich argues that the decision for "a *secular* world" has "excluded those deep things for which

[1] Quoted by Robinson in *Honest to God*, p. 75.

religion stands: the feeling for the inexhaustible mystery of life, the grip of an ultimate meaning of existence, and the invincible power of an unconditional devotion. These things *cannot* be excluded. If we try to expel them in their divine images, they re-emerge in daemonic images." [2] If instead of "secular," Tillich had used "scientific" in the narrow sense of the word, I should agree with him wholeheartedly. There is more in man than can be explained by scientific formulae, and the "how's" of science do not pretend to answer the ultimate "why" or "what for." These are human questions, not questions which the universe sets for itself—or for us. Certainly neither the universe nor Being provides a clear answer to them, particularly not in the same terms as those of the questions. Yet Tillich claims that a kind of answer is there ready at hand. In order to do so, he must take two steps. The first, although it has assumed a much different form on the surface, is a descendant of the old arguments about the First Cause, the noncontingent source of contingency, etc. Because all human actions, all relations with others and with nature involve transcendence, Tillich assumes that "the finite world points beyond itself." Hence it is "self-transcendent." I do not see that human transcendence necessarily entails a self-transcendence on the part of the world. Transcendence implies some sort of consciousness. Furthermore, the transcendence which is indeed an essential aspect of every conscious intention does not require another, more inclusive transcendence as its origin or goal. To postulate such an ultimate transcendence would necessitate a radical alteration in our concept of what a transcending consciousness is. In the process of going beyond its objects—whether they be external and physical, or internal and psychic—a consciousness always retains itself as an implicit center of reference. A consciousness *is* a transcendence. There is no need to posit Being-Itself as the ground for individual transcendence and self-transcendence.

Similarly Tillich goes beyond both empirical evidence and

[2] Tillich: *The Shaking of the Foundations*, p. 181.

logical necessity in providing Being-Itself as the sustaining foundation of human love. Neither the passionate devotion of lovers nor the feeling of concern and compassion for all humanity demands more than an awareness that other subjects like ourselves exist. The world of matter in which we all simultaneously inscribe ourselves by means of our projects is admittedly the medium by which consciousnesses can know one another and communicate. There is no necessity to endow it with love and hate. Nor is there any reason to assume the existence of some nonmaterial medium to enable consciousnesses to communicate. I confess that I do not understand what the theologians mean when they argue that beneath all conditioned relations we must postulate the Unconditional. Either this is a mere playing with words and a reification of abstractions, or it is the equivalent of the old argument that God as perfect being must exist in order to explain our concept of perfection in an imperfect world. If there *were* some central consciousness to which we belonged in some special way and from association with which we might derive more significant existence, then it might be right to argue that this allegiance ought to be put first. This does not seem to be exactly what Tillich and the others mean. In fact they explicitly deny that God is a Spirit or that reality is pantheistic. We seem to be left simply with the idea that Being is the Unconditional because it is always there.

Once more we are brought back to the question of what Being is, which brings us to the second step which Tillich has taken without ever quite admitting it. Being-Itself, while Tillich has stripped it of the more obviously anthropomorphic qualities associated with God the Father, and although it is now to be found within us and no longer located either "up there" or "out there," is endowed with much the same spiritual activity and power which religion has always bestowed on deity. Despite himself Tillich speaks of Being or God as a personal force. In *The Courage to Be* he writes:

Faith is not an opinion but a state. It is the state of being grasped by the power of being which transcends everything that is and in which everything that is participates. He who is grasped by this power is able to affirm himself because he knows that he is affirmed by the power of being-itself. In this point mystical experience and personal encounter are identical.[3]

Even more mystical and emotional overtones occur in Tillich's discussion of Grace in *The Shaking of the Foundations*.

Grace strikes us when we are in great pain and restlessness. . . . It strikes us when we feel that our separation is deeper than usual, because we have violated another life, a life which we loved, or from which we were estranged. It strikes us when our disgust for our own being, our indifference, our weakness, our hostility, and our lack of direction and composure have become intolerable to us. . . . Sometimes at that moment a wave of light breaks into our darkness, and it is as though a voice were saying: "You are accepted. *You are accepted*, accepted by that which is greater than You, and the name of which you do not know. Do not ask for the name now; perhaps you will find it later. . . . *Simply accept the fact that you are accepted!* . . ." In the light of this grace we perceive the power of grace in our relation to others and to ourselves. . . . We experience the grace of being able to accept the life of another, even if it be hostile and harmful to us, for, through grace, we know that it belongs to the same Ground to which we belong, and by which we have been accepted.[4]

Finally we may note that for Tillich, Jesus is the revelation of God exactly insofar as he represents the possibility of surrendering his finite self to the ground of his Being. Robinson sums up the doctrine with his usual precise lucidity.

It is in Jesus, and Jesus alone, that there is nothing of self to be seen, but solely the ultimate, unconditional love of God. . . . It is in making himself nothing, in his utter self-surrender to others in love, that he discloses and lays bare the Ground of man's being as Love.[5]

---

[3] Tillich: *The Courage to Be*, p. 173.
[4] Tillich: *The Shaking of the Foundations*, pp. 161–2.
[5] Robinson: *Honest to God*, pp. 74–5.

398

Who or what accepts us? Is the love of God man's love for Him or His for us? Presumably it is both if the "I-Thou" is reciprocal. Since we are told that reality in its very structure is personal, that personality is the ultimate value, it is hard not to call the "Thou" Someone rather than Something. Still God is not a person, and Tillich tells us it is blasphemy to make Him so—or to make It so. Yet it seems that if I-Thou is a dialogue, either there is personality at each end, or I am talking to myself. Not necessarily. Others have written of a nonpersonal Being which nevertheless speaks to me. Let us turn now to Heidegger and see if he can help.

Letting Being Be: Heidegger

Martin Heidegger, writing without any commitment to Christianity, finds it easier to avoid making the Universe personal; he is scrupulously careful to avoid anthropomorphic overtones. Being, in his work, does not appear as a Thou, nor as Love. Heidegger has stated explicitly that Being is not to be equated either with "God" or "Nature." All the same, the problem of whether or not to call his existentialism "religious" is a difficult one. We have seen that Bultmann finds in Heidegger's approach the secularized philosophical equivalent of the New Testament. Sartre, in a lecture in the midforties, declared himself and Heidegger to be atheistic existentialists in contrast to the Christian Jaspers and Marcel. It was only about a year later (1947) that Heidegger in his "Letter on Humanism" stated that his thought, at least up until then, could not properly be called either theistic or atheistic. He explained that he had been concerned exclusively with "the existential determination of the essence of man." Consequently "nothing has yet been decided about the 'existence' or 'non-existence' of God, nor about the possibility or impossibility of God." [1] Inasmuch as Heidegger has still not explored the theological problem directly, it is perhaps best to accept his statement at face value and not insist on assigning him to one side or the other of the religious issue. Yet it is fair to observe that those who have adopted Heidegger's description of *Dasein* and Being as a springboard or support for their own thought have either—like Bultmann and Tillich—found it congenial to the openly theological point of view or have freely combined it with reference to God and the religious needs of man, as so many of the existential psychotherapists have done. This is not surprising. Heidegger speaks of Being as something which has been lost and must be recovered. Man must learn to find his way home in Being. Heidegger speaks of man as the "shepherd of Being," as the "guardian of Being," as one who "ex-sists" in "the clearing of Being." These expressions could, as metaphors, be applied to the Sartrean For-itself without straining them to the breaking-point. Yet there is something in all of them which does not quite fit. There is an air of the numinous about Heidegger's Being which we do not find in Sartre's ontology, neither in Being-for-itself nor in Being-in-itself.

The fact remains that Sartre's statement that he and Heidegger both belonged on the side of atheism seemed perfectly reasonable to most people at the time; yet Sartre would certainly not have made it in the years since then. The "Letter on Humanism" represents a definite change in Heidegger's thinking, at least in his published thought as it was generally interpreted. I do not presume to distinguish between the extent to which Heidegger himself changed and the degree to which *Sein und Zeit* had represented his thought inadequately or partially or had been misinterpreted. What is clear is that Sartre, for his part, recognized his indebtedness to Heidegger and did not consider even his original developments in *Being and Nothingness* to represent a radical depar-

---

[1] Martin Heidegger: "Letter on Humanism," tr. Edgar Lohner. The essay is included in the anthology *Philosophy in the Twentieth Century*, Vol. II, ed. William Barrett and Henry D. Aiken (New York: Random House; 1962). The quotations are from p. 293.

ture from Heidegger's over-all philosophical *Weltanschauung*. It is significant that in the same work in which
Heidegger rejects both theism and atheism as inadequate
descriptions of his approach to Being, he claims that he and
Sartre do not mean the same thing when they speak of existence. It was at this same period that Heidegger expressed the
wish that his own philosophy no longer be called existentialism. Supposedly this was because he wished it to be absolutely distinguished from Sartre's. I would argue that it
might very well have been also because Heidegger's later
work definitely gives priority to essence over existence and
attaches an absoluteness to Being which is no longer appropriate to "existentialism."

It is always risky to conclude that an original philosopher
could not have developed his philosophical system if he had
never read the work of the man who admittedly influenced
him. Still it is hard to imagine what *Being and Nothingness*
would have been if Sartre had not encountered Heidegger.
The emphasis on authenticity and unauthenticity (further
developed by Sartre in the concepts of engagement and bad
faith), the view of man as a free self-project and of the world
of matter as an instrumental hierarchy, the ecstatic projection
of *Dasein* in temporality, the idea that the human person is a
"being of distances," the importance given to existential
states of anguish, despair, forlornness, abandonment—these
are only some of the fundamentals of Heidegger's view of
human reality which Sartre adapted to his own philosophy
with varying degrees of modification. Yet if in 1943 (the
publication date of *Being and Nothingness*) Sartre's Being-
for-itself was but a first-cousin to Heidegger's *Dasein*, the
gap between Sartre's ontology and Heidegger's more recent
discussion of Being can no longer be bridged.

In his lecture, "Existentialism Is a Humanism," Sartre
said that all types of existentialists hold one premise in common: "Existence precedes essence." In the "Letter on
Humanism" Heidegger claims that this "key phrase of 'existentialism' has not the least thing in common with the same

phrase in *Sein und Zeit*." [2] Sartre, according to Heidegger, uses the words "existence" and "essence" in their traditional metaphysical sense whereas when Heidegger speaks of Being, his approach is prior to such distinctions of potentiality and actuality. For Heidegger, man's essence does indeed rest in his *ex-sistence*, but the sentence means something quite different. "The sentence says rather: man is essentially such that he is 'Here' (*Da*), i.e., within the clearing of Being. This 'Being' of the Here, and only this, has the basic trait of ex-sistence: i.e., it stands outside itself within the truth of Being." [3] Heidegger is not quite right in accusing Sartre of putting nothing more into the concept of existence than actuality. Man's being, Sartre holds, is characterized by its standing apart from the rest of Being by its power of effecting a nothingness between itself and its object in each intentional act of consciousness. It would not be inaccurate to say that for Sartre too, human existence is "ex-sistence." Despite this objection, I am willing to agree that the two philosophers in their understanding of the nature of this ex-sistence and its relation to Being hold almost nothing in common.

Both Sartre and Heidegger try to maintain a middle path between old-fashioned idealism and realism by insisting that man is the revealer but not the creator of Being and that Being appears to man without any sort of Kantian distinction between the noumenal thing-in-itself and the phenomenal thing which I perceive. There the similarity ends. We have observed that Sartre postulates a "transphenomenality of being," but he means by the expression only the fact that existing objects are not exhausted by their appearances. In short something is really there outside us which we have not created by our perception although we must not say that it exists as substance independent of its appearances. Sartre at no time abstracts this Being as if it were something apart from existing things, nor does he make it an object of knowledge or of reverence. One does not *know Being;* one knows

[2] Ibid., p. 280.
[3] Ibid., p. 278.

existing things and is *aware that* they exist outside of the
consciousness which is aware of them. Their significance,
wholly, and their differentiation, partly, depend on the intending consciousness. In terms of meaning, Being-in-itself is
more, not less, when it becomes the object of a consciousness.
Furthermore, while Being-in-itself may be approached in
practical activity as well as by thought, perception, and imagination, it is always revealed through specific beings to a
consciousness which exists in a situation and which takes a
definite point of view on the world. A consciousness may, if it
likes, think of Being as a totality and of the fact that there is
Being or more abstractly, that *Being is*. We cannot, even by
an act of abstraction, attain to any direct contact with a Being
which is behind all beings. No such Being is there.

All is quite different with Heidegger and Being. He sums
up the difference in French in a passage quoting Sartre directly. Sartre, Heidegger reminds us, had said *"Précisément
nous sommes sur un plan où il y a seulement des hommes."* [4]
Heidegger writes, "Instead of this, if we think as in *Sein und
Zeit*, we should say: *précisément nous sommes sur un plan
où il y a principalement l'Être*. But whence does *le plan* come
and what is it? *L'Être et le plan* are the same." [5] The distinction could not be put more clearly. When Sartre says, "We
are on a plane where there are only men," he uses *le plan*
merely as a linguistic device to contrast his own position with
that of theism. It means no more than if he had written: Our
opponents believe there is a God or some existing overarching
value structure from which man may derive his ethical commands. We, on the other hand, hold that man exists without
deity or fixed human nature to guide him or to serve as any
ultimate guarantee that his choice is "right." Therefore man
cannot look beyond himself. It is he who must make himself
what he will have become—individually and collectively.
Heidegger rejects this sort of humanism. "We are on a plane
where there is, above all, (*principalement*) Being." "The

[4] Sartre: *L'Existentialisme est un humanisme*, p. 36.
[5] Heidegger: "Letter on Humanism," p. 283.

plane" and "Being" are the same. *Le plan* is something real. It is not a region of discourse or a vague "situation" or "circumstance." It has existential significance. It is that in which we dwell—almost, but not quite, that which we are. Heidegger's restatement and interpretation establish two things. There *is* an all-embracing reality encompassing us. And this Being is the all-important. "Being is the essential as the dimension of the ecstatic of ex-sistence."

Heidegger regards the whole of Western philosophy "from Anaximander to Nietzsche" as a departure from Being. Thus man is homeless, estranged, and Heidegger would call him back. Heidegger's first step for recovering Being is an attempt to purify language which, as it is used today, chiefly conceals the truth of Being. Heidegger refers both to the meaningless platitudes of the "anonymous they" (Sartre would call them the inhabitants of the Serious World) and to the metaphysical terminology employed by centuries of mistaken philosophers. The second constitutes a formidable obstacle, and I am not convinced that Heidegger has taken the right path to get around it. He states as his point of departure:

In thought Being is taken up in language. Language is the house of Being. In its home man dwells. Whoever thinks or creates in words is a guardian of this dwelling. As guardian, he brings to fulfillment the unhiddenness of Being insofar as he, by his speaking, takes up this unhiddenness in language and preserves it in language.[6]

A few pages later Heidegger writes:

Man, however, is not only a living being, who besides other faculties possesses language. Language is rather the house of Being, wherein living, man ex-sists, while he, guarding it, belongs to the truth of Being.

For Heidegger, the unhiddenness and the truth of Being are one and the same as he tries to show by interpreting the Greek word for true (ἀληθής) in terms of its etymological

---

[6] Ibid., p. 271.

roots—"uncovered" or "unconcealed." Thus truth is something which belongs to Being in its relation to *Dasein;* it is not a characteristic of propositions or statements *about* Being. With some qualification and insofar as I can understand Heidegger's mingling of metaphor and philosophy, I am willing to go along with the idea that Being is revealed in language. Usually, if not always, discoveries are not lucid and fully comprehended until we put them into words—even if the words are never spoken aloud. Once in verbal form, this transfixed thought influences our future actions and revelations of Being. So far so good. I think all would agree that language sets man apart from other creatures far more decisively than the opposable thumb. It is easy to see how he might make of language either a fortress, a factory, or a prison.

Heidegger advocates two methods of insuring that language may reveal Being and not conceal it. The first is his well-known attempt to return to the pre-Socratic philosophers and to discover the language which housed Being before both were distorted and lost in "metaphysics." Unfortunately Heidegger has translated and interpreted pre-Socratic fragments with a willful disregard of what the Greek actually meant. What he does is to work with the etymology of certain terms instead of searching for their meaning in actual usage. Even on those occasions when his etymology is correct, Heidegger has no evidence that the writer had the historically literal denotation in mind. One might as well argue that the English word "good-bye" indicates today the intention to invoke the deity since the word "good-bye" derives from the expression "God be with you." A single example from Heidegger will suffice. I choose it because he himself uses it as an example of fruitful linguistic discovery.

Among the philosophical fragments of Heraclitus is one which reads: ἦθος ἀνθρώπῳ δαίμων. A natural and justifiable translation is, "A man's character is his Fate." Slightly more literal would be, "A man's characters is his deity" or even "A man's characters is his guiding star." "Daimon" commonly referred to a minor god or demigod. It was often used in philosophy for a divine force in man—for example, the inner voice so important to Socrates. The term is as rich in varied connotations as "democracy" is for us. Heidegger, however, is not primarily concerned with "daimon." His attention is focused on ἦθος.

"A man's character is his daimon." This translation is modern but not Greek thinking. ἦθος means abode, place of dwelling. The word designates the open sphere in which man dwells. The openness of his abode allows that to appear which approaches toward the essence of man and so arriving abides near them. The abode of man contains and maintains the advent of that to which man in essence belongs. This, according to Heraclitus' saying, is δαίμων, God. The fragment says: Man, in so far as he is man, dwells in the nearness of God.[7]

This is surely "preaching and not teaching," the equivalent of that advantageous misreading of biblical texts which so aroused Kaufmann's ire against Tillich and Bultmann. As indicated in Liddell and Scott's Greek dictionary, the most fundamental meaning of ἦθος seems to be "an accustomed place." That the emphasis here is on "custom" and not place is borne out by the fact that the form with the short e, ἔθος has retained the meaning "custom" or "habit" but no suggestion of locality. The plural of ἦθος may indeed mean "haunts" or "abode"; an equally common meaning of the plural is "manners" or "customs." The singular can mean only "custom" or "usage." Heraclitus uses the word in the singular. Heidegger may, of course, challenge the dictionary, but the evidence from passages where the meaning is beyond doubt is against him. Heraclitus did not say nor intend to say what Heidegger attributes to him. Defenders of Heidegger argue that it does not matter whether ἦθος meant "abode" or what Heraclitus actually meant. They say that Heidegger's achievement is neither philological nor historical. He does not treat the philosopher as dead and his words as uttered once and for all, his work finished. Instead Heidegger enters into a living dialogue with him so that new truth may emerge. I agree that it is permissible and necessary to build upon earlier thought and to de-

[7] Ibid., p. 296.

velop it beyond the point at which its author might still call it his. This is the classical pattern for the advance of knowledge. But then I do not see why Heidegger should be allowed to claim that certain of the pre-Socratics knew and spoke of Being in a way which we must now recover. Nor do I believe that Being is revealed by mistranslating a foreign language and attributing to a philosopher ideas he never had and would not have accepted. If Heidegger has a new comprehension of Being, let him bravely take us forward to meet it, not pretend that it has lain buried for centuries in the past. Deliberate distortion of fact and the meaning of another's words results in our having unkind suspicions of the fashion in which Heidegger himself uses language. The shepherd of the truth of Being seems not to recognize the wolf which comes to threaten it.

Heidegger's second prescription for finding the Thought which guards Being is an attack upon conceptual thinking. He maintains that if we confine ourselves to the kind of thought which has characterized Western philosophy during most of its history, then we must agree with Nietzsche that Being and comparable metaphysical concepts are "the last cloudy streak of evaporating reality." [8] But "there is a mode of thinking more rigorous than the conceptual." [9] At this point we may be reminded of the claims of Eastern philosophy. We will not find anything suggestive of mystic absorption in Brahman. The mood is rather that of Zen Buddhism. Indeed Heidegger has remarked that insofar as he understands Zen, he and the Zen masters have been saying the same thing. [1] I do not believe that we may thereby assume that *Sein und Zeit* might as well have been called *Sein und Zen*. Yet it is indisputable that Heidegger's comments on Being and man's proper relation to it have certain things in common with Zen.

[8] Martin Heidegger: *An Introduction to Metaphysics*, tr. Ralph Manheim (Garden City: Doubleday; 1961), p. 29. The German edition, *Einführung in die Metaphysik*, was published in 1953.

[9] Heidegger: "Letter on Humanism," p. 297.

[1] William Barrett quotes a remark by Heidegger to this effect in his Introduction to Suzuki's *Zen Buddhism*, p. xi.

Like the Zen thinkers, Heidegger insists that man's most genuine existence is on a level which precedes the subject-object split. Heidegger claims that the world is not a being nor the realm of beings. It is "the openness of Being." Man is not a subject relating himself to the world. He is "ex-sistent in the openness of Being." As Zen argues that Sunyata is always there and yet cannot be grasped by one who deliberately searches for it, so Heidegger argues that Being is both nearest to us and yet most remote. "The strange thing in this thought of Being is its simplicity. This is precisely what keeps us from it."

Being is further from all that is being and yet closer to man than every being, be it a rock, an animal, a work of art, a machine, be it an angel or God. Being is the closest. Yet its closeness remains farthest from man. Man first clings always and only to beings. But when thought represents beings as beings it no doubt refers to Being. Yet, in fact, it always thinks only of beings as such and never of Being as such. The "question of Being" always remains the question of beings.[2]

This passage possibly appears to give more emphasis than Zen would give to an abstract reality back of actually existing things. I do not believe, however, that Heidegger intends us to think of Being as separated from beings but rather as revealing itself by means of them. I think we would not misinterpret his intention if we related what he says here to the Zen argument that individual things, while they are exactly what they appear to be, must not be taken as ultimate in their separateness but must be viewed as a part of the encompassing ground of reality. Heidegger is still closer to Zen when he tries to define the nature of that thought which encounters Being directly. The distinction between "thinking the truth of Being" and thinking conceptually about beings is, so far as I can see, precisely the same as the Zen pronouncement that knowledge about is not the same as that knowledge which is participation in Being. For Heidegger,

[2] Heidegger: "Letter on Humanism," p. 282.

the thought which speaks the truth of Being is characterized by *lassen* or "letting be." It is neither theoretical nor practical, for it is prior to such differentiation. It is superior to science because it does not cloak reality with human organizations. "It lets Being be." We may be reminded here of Suzuki's "The flower speaks to me."

Heidegger, too, puts activity on the side of Being, not merely in the attentive subject. Or more precisely, he denies the separation. Thought is "l'engagement *de l'Être*." Heidegger prefers the French *de*, which allows "of Being" to be both a subjective and an objective genitive. "Thought is of Being, in so far as thought, eventuated by Being, belongs to Being. Thought is at the same time thought of Being insofar as thought listens to, heeds, Being. Listening to and belonging to Being, thought constitutes what it is in its essential origin." [3] Heidegger dislikes the expression "there is" or "*il y a*" in connection with Being. He prefers "*Es gibt Sein*" or "It gives Being," where the "It" which gives is Being Itself. "Being is the *transcendens* as such." It is Being which projects *Dasein* into the world, and Being itself is the relation between *Dasein* and Being. In short, Being is both transcendent and immanent as we found it to be in the philosophy of Tillich. In *Being and Time*, Heidegger told us that consciousness is always outside in its objects: *Dasein* was homeless, always in the streets. Now we find that man is the prodigal with a welcoming home he may return to at will. Man exists outside himself, to be sure, but he "ex-sists" outside himself "within the truth of Being." Thus Heidegger's "existentialism" ultimately makes essence and being prior to existence. "The humanity of man . . . rests in his essence." Man *is* before he acts (*if* he acts). We cannot say of *Dasein* as Sartre says of the For-itself, that a man *is* his acts.

Furthermore, the objective ultimately has precedence over the subjective, however much Heidegger may try to deny the distinction. This point is made very clear in his attack on all

[3] Ibid., p. 272.

thought which is value-centered and which judges things in terms of their meaning or value for man.

What a thing is in its Being is not exhausted by its being an object, much less when the objectivity has the character of value. All valuing, even when it values positively, subjectivizes the thing. It does not let beings be, but makes them valuable as the object of its action. The extravagant effort to demonstrate the objectivity of values does not know what it is doing. When one proclaims "God" as altogether "the highest value," this is a degradation of the essence of God. Thinking in values here and in general is the greatest blasphemy that can be thought of in the face of Being.[4]

It is easy to see why so many of Heidegger's readers feel that his philosophy is religious. Being remains It and not Thou. But it speaks, it heals, it is the home in which man "belongs." Supposedly Heidegger's philosophy enables the individual person to live authentically by finding his unique Self in the Truth of Being. To me there is a contradiction here. Authenticity comes about when the individual freely establishes his own relations with the world, acknowledging that their origin lies within himself. The instant we give priority to absolute Being, we undercut not only the anguish of freedom but freedom itself.

Followers of Heidegger are right in recognizing that ultimately Sartre's philosophy and the later Heidegger works are irreconcilable. What I object to is the bland assumption that Sartre leaves us with only despair, cynicism, and arbitrary whim whereas Heidegger provides hope, community, and a sustaining ideal. Despite Heidegger's objection to looking at things in terms of their human value, I think that a few evaluative comments relative to the two philosophers are in order. Which concept of humanism gives more dignity to man? And I dare to ask, What is Being worth to the man who guards it? Still more concretely, what practical connections have these men allowed between their ontologies and the specific concerns of their contemporaries?

[4] Ibid., pp. 292–3.

The contrast between the two seems to me most strikingly illuminated in an area, which—for our purpose—can be approached by examining one of Heidegger's key phrases. We have spoken of Heidegger's insistence that we must "let Being be." The statement seems to me to comprise metaphysical, epistemological, and ethical consequences which are opposed both to Sartre's explicitly formulated position and to the particular possibilities of an ethics based on Sartrean premises which I have attempted to develop in this book. Heidegger's pronouncement refers, first of all, to the attitude which we as humans have toward the natural world. He finds totally repugnant the old idea that man is the master of beings and that we should learn to know nature in order that it should serve us. Although he himself delineated man's relation to the things around him as that of the user of instruments in an instrumental hierarchy, still for Heidegger this by itself is an unauthentic relation. Sartre does not designate man as the Lord of the Universe with all the old-fashioned connotations of that expression. Yet man encounters Being-in-itself as the matter in which he carves his projects, in which he inscribes himself, by means of which he makes himself known to himself and to others. Sartre certainly does not deny that there is an influence coming to me from the external world. The *pratico-inerte*, even without any other human intervention, may "steal my action from me," may cause it to "deviate," may produce a "counterfinality" quite opposed to the end at which my act had aimed. Sartre is as acutely aware as Heidegger that in seeing myself objectified in the self-image which I have projected into the world, I may, if I am not careful, become the prisoner of this object form of myself, of the "me" which is *out there*, as a degraded replica of the free consciousness which I really am. In all of this interaction with nature, there does remain for Sartre a sense of mastering, of using Being-in-itself, and this is what Heidegger dislikes.

I do not argue that the right is all on Sartre's side. If Heidegger will allow us to speak of value, I will point out that there is indeed value to be derived by one who "opens himself" to Nature. The appreciation of the potential beauty of a landscape, the sympathetic awareness of forms of organic life radically different from the human, an interest in both the unique variations and repetitive similarities which one can find (or reveal) in natural objects, and awed admiration for the sheer abundance and extent of all that brute being-there which surrounds us—all these may enhance the significance and worthwhileness of a life for the one who lives it. Sartre has paid too little attention to the fact that there is a genuine, nonexploitative *Mitsein* for man and the nonhuman as well as between people—though its structure is radically different. I do not believe, however, that this sort of aesthetic and sympathetically imaginative relation to the natural world is all that Heidegger has in mind. The idea that Nature "reveals itself" to a consciousness is true for both Sartre and Heidegger, but it means something different to each one. For Sartre, things do not point beyond themselves except insofar as a consciousness transcends them. For Heidegger all things, by being what they are, point to Being. In Sartre's ontology, beauty is introduced by consciousness as much as fear, wonder, hate, or any other attitude. Heidegger would agree that Being reveals itself only to *Dasein*, but there is a curious passivity introduced into the consciousness which "lets Being be." Man becomes in some way the *recipient* of a revelation in which more is revealed than appearances. If we think of beauty and meaning as concepts, Heidegger would grant that they are products of *Dasein*. Yet he seems to feel that in some preconceptual way such experiences as we would normally define by terms like these are conveyed to man *by* Being. For Heidegger Truth is openness to Being, not correctness in our statements or beliefs. While we are not justified in reifying it, Truth nevertheless *is*, independent of all concepts. Either it is something experienced or it is the experience itself. In either case Truth is something other than the Rational. Thus Heidegger's plea to "let Being be" turns out to be something quite different from merely letting beings be what they are. When it comes right down to it, Heidegger seems to be interested in cutting down the claims of man to make himself the center of his own world, more than he is concerned to restore dignity to nonhuman beings. Hence the strange remark that man is closer to the divine than to animals [5]— though in the absence of any elucidation of the meaning of "divine," I confess that I do not wholly understand this statement. To sum up—"Letting Being be" calls upon us to give reverence to something there behind appearances. Heidegger enfolds this something in mystery, gives it preeminence over the human although he seems to feel that it is in this very acknowledgment that man best fulfills himself as human. Sartre argues that Being simply *is* and that it is up to man to decide what to make of it and how to make himself by means of it.

If here I choose Sartre over Heidegger, it is for two reasons: First, I do not believe that Heidegger's Being *is*. He has presented us with an abstract concept, which he defends by telling us that it cannot be grasped conceptually. Things are, forces are, consciousness is (though not as an entity). Being is, as the whole of existence, contrasted with nonexistence. "Being" is a term which we use when we mean that something, potentially or actually, directly or indirectly, is capable of being made the object of a consciousness—though even here we distinguish between "being" as the condition of things existing outside a consciousness and the condition of those existing only within the imagining consciousness. Being as something separate from all the beings that are or Being as a spiritual accretion entwined about whatever exists or Being as the Ground of the existing—this Being *is not*. I cannot find in any of the pages of either Heidegger or Tillich any evidence, empirical or conceptual, that it is. If Heidegger were willing to bestow on Being any discernible quality or effect whatsoever, I should be willing to be persuaded. Whatever Being may say to Heidegger, when he listens to it, Heidegger has kept it a deep secret. I am well aware that since the language of Being is nonconceptual and preverbal, there would be some difficulty in conveying the specific content.

[5] Ibid., pp. 278–9.

But surely there should be some effect. Traditional mystics have always grappled with the problem of how to convey to another the quality of an experience which was personal and ineffable. Nevertheless, there has never been any question as to the connection between the experience and the spiritual orientation and values of the mystic. As Heidegger presents things, I really cannot see what ultimate difference it makes to living persons whether Being is or not. This Being is not ultimate reality. It is not real. To postulate it as an absolute seems to me the equivalent of arguing that there is a hidden backside of a TV image.

Of course the idea of Being has made a difference to the later philosophy of Heidegger; its chief result, to my way of thinking, has been the total lack of any specific concern with the problems of living men and women. Side by side with the comparison implied in contrasting "Letting Being be" and "inscribing oneself in Being"—we may place the concepts of Care (Heidegger's *Sorge*) and Engagement (Sartre's term). As the Guardian of Being, Heidegger's *Dasein* cares for Being or has concern for it. In addition *Dasein* cares for itself that it may find its own self-center in its relation to Being. And *Dasein* may have care for others since it is with-them in the world. *Being and Time* contained the possible genesis of an ethics of responsible freedom. These first beginnings Sartre has fostered and developed in working out specific problems both in his fiction and in his essays—though not as yet in any formally complete ethical system. As first principles Heidegger laid down the necessity of authenticity in one's relation to oneself and the obligation to respect and foster authenticity in others. In each case Heidegger used the word "conscience" in discussing these imperatives. Conscience in the authentic man is the call which comes from the inner being of *Dasein*, demanding that he fulfill his unique possibilities of Being, that he remove himself from his "fallenness," his subservience to his immediate, external present, and that he live creatively for the future the possibilities which he brings with him out of the facticity of his Past. Conscience, in short, is the recognition of the necessity to choose freely what one will be, not denying the Past but re-creating its meaning in an authentic future. In a splendid phrase Heidegger extends this "call of conscience" (*Der Gewissensruf*) to the *Mitsein*, appealing to *Dasein* to "become the Conscience of the Other" and thus free the Other to realize his own possibilities. To become the conscience of the Other does not imply that one sets the standards for the Other. Just the opposite. One tries to awaken him to his own possibilities for being and to inspire him to choose himself authentically.[6]

If anyone wants to point out that in these premises Heidegger has stated in essence the demand for good faith toward oneself and others which I have laid down as the foundation stone of a humanistic ethics, I will gladly agree. My objection is that Heidegger has vitiated these possibilities by failing to provide a context that would make them meaningful and by returning to an idealist concept of Being which undermines the earlier humanistic promises. Already in *Being and Time* and in reiterated declarations since then, Heidegger has emphasized that the call of conscience and *Dasein*'s authentic choice of himself are transmoral, that they have nothing to do with either ethics or religion and are prior to both. That they are existentially prior, I agree. Yet to say that one should choose one's unique possibilities is one thing if the statement is made within a philosophical framework based on the supposition that there is nothing above or beyond the human from which man may derive knowledge, direction, meaning, or purpose. It is quite another if we are to introduce a God. During the forty years since the publication of *Being and Time*, Heidegger has steadfastly refrained from committing himself one way or the other with regard to the existence of God. He argues that man can live authentically only if, in all aspects of his living, he embraces the necessity of his death, but Heidegger refuses to propose either annihilation or some sort of immortality as his own chosen hypothesis as to what happens after death. All possibilities are left open. Yet the quality of this being-unto-death is hardly even definable with-

[6] Martin Heidegger: *Sein und Zeit*, 7th edn. (Tübingen: Max Niemeyer Verlag; 1953), cf. especially pp. 295–301.

out reference to some such hypothesis. Finally, the concern for another *Dasein* remains too abstract to be meaningful unless there is some recognition of the concrete situations within which we confront other people.

I have expressed my dissatisfaction with Sartre for his unwillingness to formulate an ethics until society has solved its immediate social and political problems, but at least two things may be said in his favor. First, he has proved by his acts—and much of his writing should be considered political and social action as well as literature—that he believes it is important to do what one can to alleviate the suffering and injustice in the world. Second, he has made it abundantly clear that his own commitment lies in the direction of what he feels to be a liberating, revitalized Marxism. One may not always approve of his individual judgments or of the means which he finds efficacious. I do not think one can doubt that his sincere aim is a classless society where every individual may enjoy practical freedom from material pressures so that he may work out in his projects the possibilities of that inward freedom which he is. Sartre has on occasion worked with the Communists; he has sharply criticized them at other times, both theoretically and apropos of specific events. He has never allowed the Party Line to become his own conscience. He enjoys the peculiar distinction of having at one time or another disappointed almost all of his close followers; yet he continues to win respect for his integrity even in the minds of hostile critics. This situation is the result of Sartre's constant public commitments on all sorts of issues, usually on the unpopular side. He has moved from almost total disengagement in his youth to an intense involvement so complete that it might easily have put an end to Sartre the philosopher except for one saving factor—that the philosopher and man of action are united in a single choice of a way of being. Sartre as political activist acts through his philosophical writing and speaking; Sartre as philosopher has always held the position that man makes himself by his actions, that he *is* his acts.

Heidegger's career in this respect has been the antithesis of Sartre's. Both the man and his work have become increasingly removed from the concrete problems of the contemporary world. This has happened in spite of the fact that *Being and Time*, with its ontological description of *Dasein*, and its investigation of essential characteristics of humanity and the most general problems was supposedly paving the way for the study of more specific questions whose answers depended upon this ontology. During these four decades, Heidegger's philosophy has shown a steady movement away from living men and women toward a Being which certainly cannot be called human and has tenuous connections with humanity, if any.

The one exception to Heidegger's consistent noninvolvement in contemporary affairs was his unfortunate speech supporting Hitler and the Nazi party on the eve of the national elections, on Armistice Day in November 1933. I do not feel that it is right to judge Heidegger, either as man or philosopher, solely on the basis of this speech. Not long afterward he resigned from his professorial chair. There is no evidence that he did further writing or speaking on behalf of the Nazis. While we can hardly excuse him on the plea that the true nature of Hitler's plans was not yet clear in 1933, we must acknowledge the possibility of change in a man and at least be charitable with regard to an action in circumstances whose inner context we do not know. At the same time I am unwilling to follow the lead of those devotees of Heidegger who, since they cannot pretend that the speech was never given, ignore or soft-pedal it, at most acknowledging it as an evidence of human frailty but admitting no connection whatsoever between what Heidegger said on this occasion and what he has written in his philosophical works. The speech is not a mild, innocuous oath of allegiance but a strong exhortation to the Germans to vote for the Nazi party in the first "single party election." Its intent is clear, much more so than in Heidegger's frequently obscure philosophical writing. It is not fair to argue that because a philosopher supports a nihilistic movement, his philosophy in its total outlook may be properly characterized as a nihilism. Nevertheless the speech exhibits a disturbing use of Heidegger's own philosophical terminology in instances where common usage would not demand them. For example, the first paragraph:

The German People [*Volk*] has been called by the Führer to vote. The Führer, however, does not beg anything of the People; rather he is giving to the People the most direct opportunity for the highest kind of free decision as to whether the whole People does or does not want its own existence [*Dasein*].[7]

Dasein replaces the more normal word *Existenz*. In *Being and Time*, *Dasein* was used both for individual human existence and for human existence as such—just as we may speak of each man as being *a* for-itself or of *the* for-itself in contrast to Being-in-itself. To use it for the existence of the German people is to suggest exactly the concept of the People as an organic unity, which fascism demanded, which existentialism has always opposed, and which I believe Heidegger's later use of Being tends to support. Heidegger, in this address, consistently uses *Dasein* when speaking of the German people, including the highly significant expression "the necessity of the self-responsible existence of the People" (*die Notwendigkeit des selbstverantwortlichen völkische Dasein*). These words, minus the "*völkische*" are used in *Being and Time* to describe authenticity. One can hardly avoid hearing echoes of the authentic individual resolve in another sentence (the German text sets it in capitals): "This revolution brings the complete upheaval (*Umwälzung*) of our German *Dasein*." In other places Heidegger employs the term Being (which, it is fair to note, would in any case be capitalized as a noun in German.) In each instance it is preceded by the word "human" and suggests an overarching, natural potentiality. For example:

[7] *Bekenntnis der Professoren an den deutschen Universitäten und Hochschulen zu Adolf Hitler und dem nationalsozialistischen Staat*, Überreicht vom Nationalsozialistischen Lehrerbund, Deutschland/Sachsen (no publisher or date or place of publication given), pp. 13–14. The translation is by Ulrich Goldsmith. I am indebted to Professor Dietrich Goldschmidt for locating this speech and drawing it to my attention.

It was not ambition, not thirst for glory, not blind willfulness, nor was it lust for power, but solely the clear will to absolute self-responsibility in the shouldering and mastering of our People's fate that prompted the Führer to leave the "League of Nations." This is not a turning away from the Community of Peoples; on the contrary, our People by this step places itself under the natural law of human Being [*Sein*] which every nation must obey first and foremost if it wants to remain a nation.

A bit later Heidegger goes on to say:

When the will to self-responsibility becomes the law of the Community of Nations, then every nation can and must be mentor for every other nation, teaching it the richness and the strength of all the great deeds and works of human Being [*Sein*].

It is disconcerting to see the self-responsibility of the authentic individual transferred to the Nazi party's choice to constitute itself and the German State (as the Nazis defined it) as the teacher of the potential and actual achievements of human Being. Still more distressing is Heidegger's use of "Truth" when he indicates the role to be played by Science and Scholarship in the new State (the German word "*Wissenschaft*" includes both).

What then is the nature of this event? The People is regaining the TRUTH of its will to existence [*Dasein*], for truth is the manifestness [*Offenbarkeit*] of that which makes a people sure, bright, and strong in action and knowledge. Out of such truth springs the genuine will to know. . . . Science [*Wissenschaft*] is tied in with the necessity of the self-responsible existence [*Dasein*] of the People. Scientific endeavor, thus, is the pedagogic passion for wanting to know in order to convey knowledge. To *have* knowledge, however, means to master things with clarity and to be resolved to act.

This presentation of Truth (*die Wahrheit*) contains two other terms which are frequent in Heidegger. *Entschlossen* (resolved) is the adjectival form of the famous *Entschlossenheit* (resolution) which *Dasein* assumed as the means of delivering himself from unauthenticity. It is significant that at this stage the resolution is not for a quiet "listening to Being" or "letting Being be" but for heroism. Heidegger goes on to urge that scholars must have the courage to embrace "the unwonted and the impredictable," to know and to endure the "depths of *Dasein*." The other term is "*Offenbarkeit*," which in this context, and to satisfy the demands of English sentence structure, is translated as "manifestness." Literally it is "openness" or "unhiddenness," the word which Heidegger uses over and over in speaking of Being. In the later works, Truth *is* the *Offenbarkeit* of Being. In the speech Truth is given a pragmatic interpretation, but it is a pragmatism geared to the needs of the *Dasein* of *das Volk*.[8]

If I have given more attention to this speech than good taste and respect for a distinguished philosopher seem to allow, it is not because I wish either to fix attention on one regrettable and long past moment of Professor Heidegger's creative career. Nor am I attempting to show that the philosophy of *Being and Time* led naturally and inevitably to fascism. I am trying to make quite another point which seems to me extremely important: that Heidegger's superficially objective analysis of human essence and existence is actually so barrenly abstract that its practical consequence is a radical and arbitrary subjectivism. In *Being and Time* the resolve of *Dasein* to live authentically involved only the decision to realize his own possibilities. Specific content and moral considerations were put outside the realm of discussion. In the Freiburg speech, the *Dasein* of the *deutsches Volk* is represented as making this same kind of resolve. Evidently Heidegger himself did not for very long approve of the kind of commitment which the German people chose to make in the 1933 elections. Nothing in his later writing shows why the choice was wrong or what sort of political and social choice

[8] A recent article in *Der Spiegel* discusses a new book by Alexander Schwan: *Politische Philosophie im Denken Heideggers* (Cologne: Westdeutscher Verlag; n.d.). Schwan, according to the writer of this column, argues that Heidegger was never a "political opportunist" but that his political attitude stems directly from his essential philosophy. Schwan claims that Heidegger, while not a Nazi, was and still is sympathetically inclined toward some sort of totalitarianism. *Der Spiegel*, February 7, 1966, pp. 110–13.

is appropriate for one who lives in the "clearing of Being." In the speech Heidegger makes vague references to human Being. In his work since then, Being is no longer restricted by the designation "human," and man's ultimate purpose and destiny seem to be to "stand in the Truth of Being." In the "Letter on Humanism," Heidegger explicitly relates Being and ethics.

If now, in accord with the basic meaning of the word ἦθος ethics dwells in the abode of man, then that thought which thinks the truth of Being as the original element of man as exsisting is already in itself at the source of ethics. But then this kind of thinking is not ethics, either, because it is ontology. For ontology always thinks only the being (ὄν) in its Being.[9]

The Freiburg speech and Heidegger's writing since then reveal the great drawback and positive danger of Being-philosophy. The idea that truth is a direct communication with absolute reality not only serves as an excuse for not investigating political and social problems and for not committing oneself to action which one can justify. It positively impedes the development of any consistent human value structure. "Love God and do as you will," said Augustine. Bishop Robinson, arguing that this is the very opposite of an invitation to ethical irresponsibility, is content to accept Augustine's advice as the ultimate solution to the ethical problem. So long as God had discernible qualities and stood for something definite, it was possible to agree that if one committed himself to God and what He asked, then he had chosen his way of life and all fell into line. God as unconditional Love seems to me to open up ethical dilemmas as much as to solve them. But Love and concern are at least something on which one can build; an ethics without them is hard to conceive. Heidegger's Being is said to come to us "in the clearing." I cannot help feeling that it simply stands in the way and blocks the light. To define truth as a direct contact with Being results in removing all criteria of truth other than the immediate experience. Furthermore, we have only the word

[9] Heidegger: "Letter on Humanism," p. 297.

of the subject to assure us that the Being he thought was actually what he thought and not an amalgamation of what was objectively there and what was introduced by his own subjective expectation. We find ourselves in the worst sort of irrationalism from which there is no exit. Whatever Being is, *if* it is, it offers no clear apodictic message as to what we should do about it. We must still make, each of us, our own being by means of our specific projects in the world. Heidegger's Being seems to call to us to come back to it beyond the things of the world. I am convinced that if man obeys the summons, he will do so at the expense of what ought to be his ultimate concern for himself and for mankind.

PART FIVE

EXISTENTIALIST
FAITH

XIII

Death
and the Cooling Sun

Albert Camus said: "The future is the only transcendent value for men without God." Camus was convinced that for the individual living consciousness there was no future after death. But he recognized that because of our feeling of human solidarity a person may find such meaning and value in the possibilities of others that he will give up his own life for their future. So much of my life, of Me is caught up in my projects that I view as *my* future even that part of time which extends beyond my consciousness. The individual who has broadened the horizon of his immediate self-interest so that he may find meaning and significance in the lives of his contemporaries may hope realistically, not just sentimentally, that his future extends beyond himself in the life of man. What of the future of man? Here we encounter the problem all over again.

Sartre has posed it in a chilling admission of dismay. Toward the end of *The Words*, after renouncing his early hope of salvation via literary immortality, he writes:

427

In order to assure myself that the human race would perpetuate me, I implanted firmly in my head the conviction that it would never come to an end. To be extinguished within it was to be born again and to become infinite. But if anyone put before me the hypothesis that someday a catastrophe could destroy the planet, even if it were fifty thousand years from now, I was terrified. Even yet today and disillusioned, I am unable to think without fear of the cooling of the sun. That my contemporaries may forget me the day after my burial matters little to me. So long as they live, I will haunt them, inapprehensible, unnamed, but present in each one of them—like the millions of deceased whom unknowingly I preserve from annihilation, but if humanity finally disappears, it will kill its dead for good.[1]

Yet it was this same Sartre who commented with admiration on Giacometti's almost joyous welcoming of an accident which might have ended his career and destroyed him.

I admire that will to welcome everything. If you like surprises, you must like them all the way, to the point of liking even those rare illuminations which reveal to its lovers that the world is not made for them.[2]

The problem of individual mortality and the question of the final destiny of humanity are closely linked; they are not the same. That there is no post-mortem continuation of our highly individualized psyche, no crystallized unembodied Self which lives on, carrying its unique memories along with it—this seems almost certain. In question here is the attitude to be assumed with regard to an all but established fact. What the future of humanity will be we cannot predict or more than dimly imagine unless we resort to the unjustifiable procedure of denying the possibility of any further development in human knowledge and of any event not now foreseen in the Universe around us. Although our hypothetical answer to the question of the individual's death on the one hand and to the demise of humanity on the other inevitably influences the attitude which we will hold in looking at either problem, there is no necessary correlation between the answers. The

[1] Sartre: *Les Mots*, p. 208.
[2] Ibid., pp. 193–4.

mortality of the individual neither demands nor precludes the continued existence of the species—and vice-versa.

Humanistic existentialism declines to build its philosophy upon the "almost" in the "almost certainty" of annihilation after death. This refusal is not from cowardice or reluctance to risk anything. Despite the accusations of irrationality which have been made against existentialism, the humanistic branch does not count it a virtue to act counter to reason whenever evidence and human desires are in conflict. To "believe *because* it is absurd" remains to this way of thought simply absurd. It is not only scientific evidence which stands in the way of accepting the hypothesis of personal immortality. While it is true that psychology has tended to reinforce the old Lucretian arguments for the interdependence of psyche and body, we must admit that most claims for the continued existence of the soul involve the theory that there is in man something more than is revealed in empirical tests or observations of human behavior. The laboratory technician cannot prove or disprove the hypothesis of immortality any more than he can identify the "substance" of bread and wine as being mere food and drink or the Body and Blood of Christ. It is the irresolvable contradiction in the very idea of human immortality which has led even the New Theologians to give it up, at least in its traditional form. Man is individualized by his finiteness, his factual limitations, his temporal memories and his concrete situation—in short by his mortality. To remove all these is to make him infinite; it is also to destroy the person he is.

Nobody has seen this dilemma more clearly than Unamuno, who nevertheless clings to the "almost" in spite of all that his own mind can do to undermine it. In *The Tragic Sense of Life* he attacks those who, like the New Theologians, claim to cling to a belief in immortality while stripping it of everything which makes it valuable to the man who wants to live on as himself. Continued existence of Ultimate Reality or of Being or of anything other than the personal self is not immortality for the would-be believer who longs for it. Unamuno will have all or nothing and he insists that what is not all is worth nothing. Unamuno patiently goes through all the rational arguments to show the impossible self-contradiction involved. Then in a Kierkegaardian leap, he resolves to hope and to believe in the very face of reason. In his story "The Madness of Dr. Montarco," Unamuno shows this movement of thought and its climax.

Reason, which we have acquired in the struggle for life and which is a conservative force, tolerates only what serves to conserve or affirm this life. We don't understand anything but what we must understand in order to live. But who can say that the inextinguishable longing to survive, the thirst for immortality, is not the proof, the revelation of another world, a world which envelops, and also makes possible, our world? And who can say that when reason and its chains have been broken, such dreams and delirium, such frenzied outbursts as Dr. Montarco's, are not desperate leaps by the spirit to reach this other world?[3]

It is a tribute to Unamuno as a philosopher that he never offers his personal faith as a proof to others. His fictional hero, Dr. Montarco, dies insane even though we are made to feel that his madness contained a truth and grandeur. Unamuno's ultimate conclusion is not quite a certainty that faith will be rewarded. It is closer to Pascal's wager but put in a more attractive, less calculating form. Live *as if* you were immortal, he says. Better yet, live so as to deserve immortality.

The ideal of living so as to deserve immortality is a legitimate goal for the ethical choice even if it cannot by itself serve as a clear directive for any particular brand of ethics. The value of the exhortation to live as if we were immortal is ambivalent. Unamuno did not intend to make of it a reason for denigrating the importance of life here and now, but the notion of other worldliness has often been so used by others. Provided it is not intended as an excuse to avoid responsibility for action in correcting social injustice, I can see that the decision to live as if one is immortal might be either an

[3] Miguel de Unamuno: *Abel Sanchez and Other Stories*, tr. Anthony Kerrigan (Chicago: Regnery; 1956), pp. 201–2.

authentic choice or an evasion. If a person honestly believes, despite all apparent evidence to the contrary, that the desperate desires and aspirations of human beings are in some way fulfilled by the Universe, then he certainly has every right to live with the hope that in some way now incomprehensible he will himself endure after death. Those of us who do not so believe may think that he is mistaken. We cannot legitimately say that he is in bad faith. He will remain in good faith so long as he does not attempt to make of this hopeful hypothesis an evidence which would justify his attempt to deny his own responsible freedom or to do unnecessary violence to the freedom of others. Most often the attitude of living as if we were immortal is not a conscious resolve to accept a belief about what happens after this life. It is a refusal to confront the inevitability of the death which brings this present life to a close. Tolstoi in *The Death of Ivan Ilyitch* and Heidegger, who refers to this story, have delineated in penetrating, sometimes painful detail the way in which the cowardly refusal to face the fact of one's own mortality may result in a life and a society almost totally unauthentic. The life thus protected is no longer worth preserving and is without savor for the one who lives it. Tolstoi and Heidegger have magnificently demonstrated the truth contained in the New Testament assertion, "He who would save his life must lose it." Ivan Ilyitch at the moment of death found his life again in a neo-Christian revelation purporting to show that death is but a new beginning. Heidegger stresses death as the prime constituent of individuality in each *Dasein*. Realizing that I and I alone will "live my death," I become intensely aware of my uniqueness. In *Sein zum Tode*, often translated as Being-unto-Death, *Dasein* lives "toward death." Grasping his existence as finite, he develops to the fullest possible extent the particular possibilities of this Self which will die. It is as though the recognition by *Dasein* that at one time he will not be impels him to resolve that he will have been what he alone can be.

At this point we have come full circle. Starting from the authentic choice of living as if we were immortal, we have encountered two examples where the refusal to confront the inevitability of death was an evasion. In one case the awakening in good faith led to an affirmation of eternal life, in the other a resolve to live one's mortality to the fullest. As a humanistic existentialist, I will henceforth confine myself to the second choice—to reject the "almost," to accept death as the end for every particular consciousness, as the moment when the Self is finally attained in the form of the unity of a life which has been and is no more. As Sartre puts it, death is the point at which I cease to be a for-itself and become part of Being-in-itself—for others.

It is a mistake, I think, to try to propose any one attitude as the correct or best way to regard death. I do not mean merely that one's personal situation may legitimately influence the way in which one welcomes or shrinks from his own death, though this is certainly true. More than this, however, I hold that inasmuch as each consciousness exists both as an immediate presence to its present object and as a temporal process, no single and simple point of view on death is adequate. We have established that there is often an irreconcilable conflict between the demands of spontaneous self-realization and temporal self-realization in the same consciousness. Death may appear differently to us, depending on which type of urge to self-realization is dominant on a given occasion. Reflections which genuinely satisfy the consciousness which is concerned with its temporal pursuit of self may initiate only rebellion in this same consciousness when it is engaged in its enjoyment of immediate presence. I will not go so far as to assert that only rebellion against death is appropriate for spontaneous self-realization and that death may be accepted as a fulfillment for the temporal self-realization. I do maintain that this is largely true albeit with some qualifications. Either/or may be a legitimate demand when it comes to ethical commitment. I do not believe that our response to death can be truthfully said to be more than "Yes, but—" Revolt and resignation will remain as ingredients even if we feel that the final product may be fairly labeled acceptance.

Simone de Beauvoir has been most vivid in expressing

revolt. In her autobiography she showed openly her resentment at the signs of imminent old age, her reluctance to cease living, and an envy of those who would continue to enjoy a world which she had loved. In the account of her mother's death from cancer ironically entitled *A Very Easy Death*, de Beauvoir referred to letters which she had received from readers of her autobiography. Some with "a malicious commiseration" had written that she would not be so afraid of death if she had not lost her Faith. Others said, "To pass away is nothing. Your work will remain." To both alike de Beauvoir replied that they were mistaken. She and her Catholic mother were alike in their passionate love of this earthly life. Neither celestial nor terrestrial immortality nor hope of posthumous fame was adequate consolation for death. When her mother died, de Beauvoir felt the emptiness of the conventional expressions of comfort, particularly the banal, thoroughly rational reflection that the death of the old is a natural thing and not to be lamented.

One doesn't die from having been born, nor of old age. One dies of *something*. To know that my mother was doomed by her age to an end that would soon come did not lessen the horrible surprise. She had a sarcoma. A cancer, an embolism, a pulmonary congestion: it is as brutal and unforeseen as the stopping of a motor in midair. My mother encouraged optimism since crippled and dying, she still affirmed the infinite worth of every moment. But also her futile persistence wrenched away the reassuring curtain from the banality of everyday. There is no natural death. Nothing which happens to man is ever natural since his presence puts the world in question. All men are mortal. But for each man his death is an accident. It is, even if he recognizes and consents to it, an unreasonable violence.[4]

There is a bitter truth in these words which we may attempt to sweeten a bit with other reflections but which we can never wholly wipe out. Why should we try? Whether or not this is the best of all possible worlds cannot be decided when there is no way of determining what else if anything

[4] Simone de Beauvoir: *Une Mort très douce* (Paris: Gallimard; 1964), concluding paragraph.

could have been. Certainly the human condition as it is and even the most modest ideal of what we would like it to be are separated by an unfathomable gulf. Of all saccharine palliatives ever uttered, the statement that nothing which is natural and necessary can be evil strikes me as the most fatuous. One might as well argue that old age is a good thing because the only way to avoid it is to die young.

Sartre, too, stressed the difficulty of making death in any way a meaningful part of life. In a wry image, he reworks the old picture of human beings in a condemned cell, knowing they must be executed but uninformed as to the precise day and hour. Sartre remarks that we indeed resemble these prisoners, but he adds to the story. Let us suppose that certain ones among these condemned prepare to meet their execution with courage and dignity—then die unexpectedly from flu. Death, Sartre says, cannot come as the aesthetically fulfilling resolving chord of a life inasmuch as we have no way of knowing when that musical moment will be. I would suggest in line with Sartre's thought that our situation resembles the absurd antics of players in a game of musical chairs. We know that the music will come to an abrupt end without warning. Meanwhile we keep moving and hope that each passage from chair to chair may be completed.

This wholly negative attitude toward death is admittedly but a first moment, so to speak, in the dialectical consideration of our mortality. Yet against Hegel, I insist that it is a moment never wholly resolved in any reconciling synthesis. If we love life, we are reluctant to leave it. Watching our own or another's power to live diminish with the encroachment of senility is a pain for which there is no reparation. The premature gratuitous death of a Camus is an offense against all justice. Strictly speaking, Sartre is right in claiming that the For-itself, which lives as an always future project, cannot find in its own death either meaning or possibility. Death is the end of all meaning—for the one who lives it, for "a meaning can come only from subjectivity." "Death is not my possibility of no longer realizing a presence in the world but rather an always possible nihilation of my possibles which is outside my possibilities." Death is not an ontological structure of Being-for-itself but, like birth, "an external and factual limit of my subjectivity." As several commentators have pointed out, Sartre's position resembles that of the Epicureans, who passed it off as a consolation: Death is solely the absence of awareness. So long as I live, I am aware. When I have died, there will be no awareness of my having ceased to be aware. Sartre goes beyond the Epicureans to a further point: Death is a form of alienation still more radical than the discovery of my object-side in my encounter with the other. "To be dead is to be a prey for the living." The moment of death witnesses my transformation from Being-for-itself to Being-in-itself. My physical body quickly comes to have no more meaning than the elements of which it is composed. At most a skeleton may end up as a forlorn exhibit in an anthropological museum as an example of a biological type. It is noteworthy that while the resting place of the famous dead may become a shrine, their remains are not usually exhibited. The relics of saints or heroes may hold value for devotees but only on the magical level and in exactly the same way that their clothes or personal possessions become fetishes by association. The carefully preserved body of Lenin is an object of the same sort—midway between fetish and authentic portrait. In any case, the lifeless remnant is but the object, meaningless in itself, of the associations which others build around it. The past life of the deceased continues to exist in a totally different way. When he was alive, this person was constantly deciding the meaning of his acts, remaking his past in the light of the future he was choosing. Dead, his past continues to be remade and given its significance in terms of men's choices of their future. But it is other people who decide the meaning of this past. The dead man's life is forever a "transcendence transcended." My death has meaning, not for me but for those who survive me. The Look of the other has won.[5]

It is at exactly this point that we find the seminal possibilities for a more positive view of death, but I am not quite

[5] Sartre discusses death in *Being and Nothingness*, pp. 531–48.

ready to discuss these. Let us for the moment postpone the consequences of seeing in my outlived life and in my death a meaning for others and look at it as the point of cessation of all awareness of meaning—for me. The Epicurean comfort is no great help to contemporary man. It is only the fundamentalist who fears pains and punishment after death, and for him the alternative of Paradise far outweighs the Epicurean promise of nothing at all. What makes death so unattractive to most of us is precisely the lack of consciousness which seemed to the Epicureans a deliverance. In answer to this deep-rooted reluctance to give it all up and not be, all arguments are, at best, of the Pollyanna type. It does not help to call death a rest and peace after the weary struggle of life. "Rest" and "peace" exist only in relation to awareness. Objects do not experience rest and peace, nor do dead bodies and vanished consciousnesses. Annihilation is not rest and has no value except for one who does not wish to live. At this level, Heidegger is no help either. *Dasein* confronting the inevitability of his death resolves to live authentically, developing those possibilities which are uniquely his. There is nothing in *Being and Time* to console the *Dasein* who would like to prolong his authentic existence beyond the particular span allowed him. Revolt at the human condition may quite legitimately take the form of the declaration that old age is obnoxious, death at an unknown date repugnant, and the final cessation of our individual consciousness an evil—even if a necessary one. Just as we may love a person and still disapprove of a particular trait, wishing that in this respect he were different, so I believe that our final acceptance of mortality usually does and probably ought to include and give recognition to this one moment of negative revolt—"the great indigestible."

Admittedly, Pollyanna arguments have some value if they are based on the perception of comforting truths in a generally unpleasant situation. The best of these which I know is Viktor Frankl's. Frankl advocates that we change the quality of our feelings about the approach of death by reversing our attitude toward what we have already experienced. "Having been is also a kind of being—perhaps the surest kind. . . . Time that has passed is certainly irrecoverable; but what has happened within that time is unassailable and inviolable. Passing time is therefore not only a thief, but a trustee." Frankl goes on to say that the older man may think of himself as having exchanged possibilities in the future for realities in the past.

The pessimist resembles a man who observes with fear and sadness that his wall calendar, from which he daily tears a sheet, grows thinner with each passing day. On the other hand, the person who takes life in the sense suggested above is like a man who removes each successive leaf from his calendar and files it neatly and carefully away with its predecessors—after first having jotted down a few diary notes on the back. He can reflect with pride and joy on all the richness set down in these notes, on all the life he has already lived to the full.[6]

In thus contemplating the past *as it was*, a person attains a kind of absoluteness which he can never wrench from the future. Frankl's words are comparable to de Beauvoir's analysis of the festival as a deliberate attempt to stop the continuum of means and ends. The festival, whether it is a celebration of a particular achievement, such as the liberation of Paris, or a recognition of time traversed (a birthday) or the reaffirmation of the meaning in a past event (religious and some national holidays), may in some cases be the occasion for resolves touching the future. Its primary function is to assert the absolute value of what has been achieved. It is a triumphant proclamation that no matter what may happen henceforth, this particular structure of being has come about and cannot be made not to have been. It is interesting to observe that while the lack of any further future is what appals us in death, we seem to hold, while we live, a desire to cut off the constant movement toward the future by this assumption in the present of a view which looks backward. The thought

[6] Viktor Frankl: *The Doctor and the Soul*, pp. 33–4.

437

that there will be no more presents may come to cloud the pleasure of this present. The idea of each present giving way to an endless succession of future presents tends by sheer weight to remove all significance from any present.

At this point we meet a second consolatory argument which, while still a bit on the Pollyanna order, carries a certain finality. This is the realization that for finite creatures such as we are, death is not only necessary but preferable to any alternative which we are capable of imagining. (I speak here of earthly immortality rather than of the Christian or the Indian variety.) Without going so far as to agree with Euripides' character that "not to have been born at all is best," I think we ought to grant that a life without the possibility of either temporary unconsciousness and death would be intolerable to contemplate. To be compelled to live on forever with all of our finite limitations except mortality would be in very truth the Hell which terrifies the fundamentalist. Of course we could hypothesize an endless life in which these limitations were somehow nonexistent, but that is to propose immortality for some other species, not for us. We meet the same sort of logical block which we encounter in imagining any sort of personal life after death. We, the persons who long for it, could not endure it. The person who could would no longer be one of us. A corollary of this argument has been discussed by a number of existentialists. In particular de Beauvoir, Frankl, and Peter Koestenbaum have stressed the idea that it is our mortality, as well as other aspects of our finitude, which gives value to our projects. If choices were nonexclusive and if time were reversible, no choice would hold any importance. If one lived on forever, there would be no sense of urgency, no intensity, no possibility of giving significant pattern and form to life. De Beauvoir's heroine in The Blood of Others discovers that life finally has meaning when she has found something she is willing to die for. The hero of All Men are Mortal is allowed to drink an elixir of immortality, and he bitterly regrets it. He learns that when one can pay no price, one can buy nothing of any value.

Koestenbaum carries this idea to the limit—if not a little

beyond.[7] "Paradoxically, the most vitalizing fact of life is the utter inevitability of death!" It is death which allows ethical responsibility.

Only through the constant awareness of death will an individual achieve integrity and consistency with his principles. Since there is, basically, no threat other than real or symbolic death, and since he has accepted that threat, he is well beyond fraudulent bribes and threats alike. In the last analysis, all man owns is the integrity of his character. . . . What criminal would think of holding up a convict on the way to the death chamber?

Here Koestenbaum goes too far. Awareness that death will come ultimately may or may not make it easier to risk a particular death now. Furthermore, there are many things, other than moral principles, which give courage in the face of death, not the least powerful of which is the failure to love life.

Koestenbaum again makes everything too easy in another passage where he is more obviously echoing and developing Heidegger's teaching concerning the relation between death and authenticity.

The person who is aware of his death and the consequent limit to his time on earth will thereby concentrate on essentials. He will not waste time in useless details, since detail is often but an excuse to avoid the real issues in life. Recognizing his death, man is prompted to get immediately to the point of his life—and to stay there. He will always look ahead; he will see every action of his in the light of a total plan. The realization of death leads automatically to what in the business world is called "thinking big."

Koestenbaum represents a curious reversal. Instead of overcoming our abhorrence of death by counseling that we gloat over what we have absolutely achieved, as Frankl did, Koestenbaum puts all his emphasis on the future. There is only one flaw in this rather facile presentation: it is exactly what Sartre pointed out in his criticism of Heidegger's attempt to

[7] Peter Koestenbaum: "The Vitality of Death," *Journal of Existentialism*, Vol. V (Fall, 1964), pp. 139–66.

make death a meaningful part of life. This is that the death which I thus postulate as that which gives form to my life is not really my death but death as the universal conclusion of all lives. If the date and style of my fatal hour were precisely known, then I could in fact confront my death and live toward death. It is not. Consequently, the man who wants to give form to his life is—to use Frankl's comparison—like a sculptor with an unknown deadline. This image is more realistically subdued than Koestenbaum's portrait of the man "thinking big." Frankl does not see it as wholly negative, and I think that he is right.[8] If all that mattered to the sculptor were the finished product and this a single statue, then I can see no alternative to the blackest pessimism. But the obvious point is that the sculptor enjoys the artistic process and that his aim, if I may add a detail, is a group of related figures, each one of which is intrinsically satisfying even though its value is increased when related to a group which will never be finished. One may recall here those medieval cathedrals which were never quite completed. Perhaps this is the best of such symbols. One wishes that the spires of Chartres had been finished and that the later parts equaled the artistic achievement of the earlier portions; these imperfections are but slight in our estimation of the whole.

Enough of such symbols and of Pollyanna. So long as our lives satisfy us sufficiently so that we would like to live on forever or indefinitely or just a little bit longer, there is a bitter pill to swallow in the realization that we will not do so. The greatest consolation is probably the realization that we cannot—except by accepting mortality—enjoy the values which make us want to live. It is the price we must pay. What we get in exchange depends primarily on us ourselves —if we believe that man is free. Lucretius pointed out that some people out of fear of death so poison their lives that they long to die. Schopenhauer and Camus, from widely separated approaches, both demonstrated that suicide is a surrender to the absurdity and meaninglessness against which man's mind

[8] Frankl: *The Doctor and the Soul*, pp. 65–6.

440

revolts. Our mortality, like all other factual obstacles to our freedom, becomes ultimately part of the material out of which we make the meaning of our life. I myself prefer a position midway between Heidegger and Sartre. I do not live my death. Sartre is right in saying that it is others who live it and decide its meaning. But my awareness that I will thus one day become the "prey of the living" is an essential part of my human condition. The way I deal with it will determine in large part the quality of my life. Thus, my death, as the future toward which I project myself, does have meaning in my life. But its reality is that of the future itself, which *as future* is never realized, although it is always there at the heart of my projects. "My death" has a place in the meaning of my life even though my consciousness cannot grasp it except abstractly. When I actually encounter death, others will "live" it and will constitute its meaning.

If we are to equate the being of the person with his living consciousness, which, as Sartre has shown, always includes an implicit self-awareness, then death and the Other win out. The longest possible postponement of the final defeat is the most anyone can hope for. On the level of spontaneous self-realization, such an identification is necessary, for this is a recognition of my own freedom, of my existing as simply that part of Being which brings Nothingness into the world and which chooses without constraint its immediate presence to objects in the world and its own construction of Being-in-itself into a world. Death, although we think of it as annihilation, is actually the suppression of Nothingness, not of Being. With the absorption of Nothingness into Being, consciousness disappears. We have observed that the moment of spontaneous self-realization occurs as a sort of rupture in time. One could almost say that it is the realization by a consciousness that it can nontemporally assume a point of view upon its own temporality. To put it another way, consciousness can—if it will—sever all concern for the content of its own past and future projects. At this point it realizes that it is not to be identified with the world of which it is conscious. At the same time consciousness *is* temporal. Even the refusal to maintain a consistent point of view upon the past is an acknowledgment of the reality of the past for consciousness. The same is true with regard to the future consequences of one's present acts although the reality here is imaginatively projected and not reconstructed in memory. We have no difficulty in feeling that a person's concern for his projects is a part of him, is "he," as much as his body is. We can accept the idea that a person *is* his acts. Is the identification of the person with the projects and the future consequences of his acts a kind of sleight of hand? Or is it a legitimate extension of what "he" is? We must be very careful here. No matter how fascinated by an object, a consciousness is not the object. A mother does not *become* the child for whom she voluntarily gives up her life. Yet the well-being of a living Other may constitute a real value for the one who cares for him. The choice and enjoyment of this value are in truth a part of him integrated in the structure of his conscious life. There is no existential difference if this chosen Other is not yet born or will live after our death. Someone may object that our consciousness will not then be aware of the Other's well-being. It is only by sympathetic imagination that we experience it now. The presumption *that* he is or will be benefited by us is independent of time. All futures for the For-itself are only probable whether one minute hence or a million years from now. Reflective self-realization links outlived and anticipated states of consciousness in a significant pattern. It includes both one's immediate subjectivity and one's objectified self-for-others. It involves the recognition that my world and the Other's touch and affect one another even though they are never one. This self-realization has no end. Insofar as it is based on concern, it extends infinitely—or as far as I allow myself to be concerned.

Sartre has pointed out that even those whose names have been forgotten are still part of reality for the living who look back upon human history and seek to learn from it.

To be forgotten is, in fact, to be resolutely apprehended forever as one element dissolved into a mass (the "great feudal lords of the thirteenth century," the "bourgeois Whigs" of the eighteenth, the "Soviet officials," etc.); it is in no way to be *annihilated*, but it is to lose one's personal existence in order to be constituted with others in a collective existence.[9]

It is these nameless dead who make it possible for historians to draw up those generalizing descriptions of the *Zeitgeist* of a period. For example, in the Middle Ages—European man was on the whole content to accept the place in the Universe which the Church allotted him and the social status into which he was born. Or—In the first fifty years of the United States, men were restlessly pushing on to new frontiers, scornful of newly acquired stability and anxious to wrest a still greater empire from the wilderness. Or—The twentieth-century American was so happy in the material comforts which he was understandably proud of achieving that he was suspicious and resentful of those who sought to arouse him to the realization that all was not well. Or—

We have found that there are two ways in which we may defy mortality. Or, if you prefer, there are two ways in which each person may reconcile himself to accepting his own death. The first lies in simply asserting the absolute value of that which is and has been, without reference to the future which one does not claim for it. The second involves self-transcendence toward the future, asserting that one's chosen project is the future of the whole human race. We arrive now at the second problem of mortality—the future of man. Again there are two possible attitudes, one of which is the equivalent of the first of the two just discussed. That is, we may assume that the end of the earth and of mankind together is as assured as that of the individual, that only the precise date and specific cause are uncertain, that the significance of humanity will vanish when man does. In this case, we cannot but conclude with Sartre that when this time comes "humanity will have killed its dead for good." The only recourse for those who share Sartre's fear is to assert the absolute value of what will have been and which as "having-been" can never be

[9] Sartre: *Being and Nothingness*, p. 542.

wiped out. The spirit of positive revolt may give to this attitude a bittersweet dignity. There is in addition something moving, something which may inspire in us a melancholy pride in the human courage which dares to pronounce itself an epiphenomenon of no ultimate significance. Yet somehow such predictions of the fate of man and his world usually fall short of tragedy. Revolt becomes resignation and pathos. A classic example is Bertrand Russell's.

That Man is the product of causes which had no prevision of the end they were achieving; that his origin, his growth, his hopes and fears, his loves and his beliefs, are but the outcome of accidental collocations of atoms; that no fire, no heroism, no intensity of thought and feeling, can preserve an individual life beyond the grave; that all the labor of the ages, all the devotion, all the inspiration, all the noonday brightness of human genius, are destined to extinction in the vast death of the solar system, and that the whole temple of Man's achievement must inevitably be buried beneath the debris of a universe in ruins—all these things, if not quite beyond dispute, are yet so nearly certain, that no philosophy which rejects them can hope to stand. Only within the scaffolding of these truths, only on the firm foundation of unyielding despair can the soul's habitation henceforth be safely built.[1]

We observe that this attitude implicitly adopts an unproved hypothesis about man—that the human condition will not essentially change. If we wanted to quibble, we might point out that even on this assumption, we do not necessarily link man's demise and the death of our planet or even of the solar system. The scientific view of man includes faith in the continued growth of his technology. The possibility of his moving to other planets and systems exists, and there is a reasonable hope that he will be allowed the time he needs in order to work out the difficulties of getting there. Of course the persistent pessimist may quote the second law of thermodynamics at us and point out that if all energy ultimately dissipates in the form of heat, any solar system we may find

[1] Bertrand Russell: "A Free Man's Worship" in *Mysticism and Logic* (New York: W. W. Norton and Company; 1929), pp. 47–8.

444

will finally disintegrate. We postpone the end by some billions of years, but that is all. At this point I confess to a feeling of impatience at the idea that a creature with so brief a history behind him would so cavalierly brush aside a future calculated in billions. Still we may grant the point. Even if the entropy theory is wrong, even if the new "heartbeat" hypothesis is the correct one, it seems unlikely that the fragile human being we know could survive such cosmic travail.

Here I frankly admit that I personally have chosen the second of the alternatives which I suggested in the chapter on finding a meaning in life. To me there is something illogical in assuming that humanity may live on through even the paltry millions of years until the cooling of the sun without undergoing or itself inducing radical modifications in what we now think of as our fixed human condition. Particularly as existentialists, we are all but compelled to follow up our fundamental premises with a commitment to further change. That man is free and self-transcending, and that there is no determining human nature are empty mouthings of dogma unless we believe that man has the possibility of becoming something quite different from what he has been—and this existentially, not just socially and technologically. To say that he *will* do so is to make a statement of faith, not merely to hazard a guess as to whether man will or will not live up to his potentialities. Humanistic existentialism too recognizes that faith is a necessary ingredient, perhaps even an ontological structure of the human being. It is time for us to consider what sort of faith it finds appropriate in a world without God or semi-deified Being.

The faith of humanistic existentialism is not merely a reaffirmation of the eighteenth-century belief in progress. It differs in two ways. First, our faith in the possibility of human improvement is not a conviction of inevitable progress. To hold that humanity moves by some inner or outer necessity toward some distant perfection is to deny that man is the arbiter of his own destiny as surely as the doctrine of inevitable decline denies it. The existentialist is acutely aware that man might blow himself up. He is frightened by the possibility that man will allow himself to be suffocated in the population explosion, or tranquilize himself to torpor in conforming comfort, or put himself into such a straitjacket of repressive political structures that the nineteenth century may forever stand as the high peak of human happiness—as some twentieth-century writers have already begun to designate it. If as existentialists we believe that this will not be the future of man, this faith has nothing metaphysical about it. We believe in man in the same way that we believe in individuals, knowing that our hopes may be disappointed but committing ourselves confidently to the belief that they will be fulfilled. Like both James and Dewey, existentialists acknowledge the validity of an ideal which will become a reality only if we believe in its potential existence sufficiently to work toward it. The second difference between the existentialist faith in progress and that of the Enlightenment lies in the greater openness of the ideal future. The progress of Rational Man was quantitative. The goal envisioned was the perfect happiness to be achieved by all and already grasped by a few. Reason was to solve existing problems but had no expectation of being itself modified in the process of solution. Human Nature was fixed like the precious kernel of gold in the nugget. Reason had seen it shining and was already sharpening tools to remove the encrusted layers of ignorance. Existentialist faith does not clearly foresee its goal. Its confidence lies in the conviction that if it moves forward, it will discover points worth climbing to.

Since humanistic existentialism finally ventures into such wide-open fields of faith as these, a question arises: Why does it reject the faith of religious existentialists, or at least of those among them who do not insist on specific ties with Christianity? This question has been partially answered in earlier chapters, but more is needed. I think our reply should be extended to show, not only why we are not content with Being-Itself as the ultimate answer to our concern but why I am unwilling to say that our existentialist faith is also in its own way a religious commitment.

446

Let us grant at the start that we recognize the ultimate mystery. Why should there be something rather than nothing? What happened first and what is the meaning of "first"? What *is* energy—or whatever material or nonmaterial stuff one wants to pose as ultimate? Existentialism does not pretend to hold answers to such queries. It suspects that these seemingly profound interrogations are incorrectly formulated —on the order of "Why are circles green?" or "Where are the four corners of the earth?" But it confesses that it is unable either to rephrase them or to be convinced that they are unimportant. Man is a self-transcending being whose life is an ever-renewed self-projection toward a future. Thus he continually lives "beyond the evidence." It is natural and entirely proper that he should form hypotheses concerning a future that is beyond his future and hazard answers about ultimate reality even before he knows how to phrase the correct questions. Appropriately too, his conduct will be influenced by these half-intellectual, half-emotional extrapolations. Here as elsewhere, not to choose is already to have chosen. In acknowledging the existence of the mystery, we do not necessarily postulate something sacred and holy but merely the existence of that which is not understood—or not yet understood.

There are two ways in which we may regard a mystery. One is to view it as something to be solved. The other is to declare that it is on principle unknowable. Religion, of course, has always taken the second position, but it has never been content with simple agnosticism. Surrounding the unknown with an aura of the sacred, it then proceeds to take two more steps. First, the claim is made that in various ways one may experience the power and effects of the mysterious center and to some degree manipulate them to one's own advantage. Second, despite the assertion that the divine transcends our understanding, its nature is described or circumscribed in conformity with the needs, values, and imaginations of man at his present stage of evolution. God created man in His own image, we are told, and this may or may not be true. What is certain is that man has returned the compliment over

447

and over throughout his entire history. That this is true for fundamentalist Christianity, for primitive religions, and for any concept of a personal deity is obvious. The New Theologians vehemently deny any anthropomorphism, but how can we believe them? Not only do they maintain that ultimate Reality has been most adequately revealed to us in the mythically shrouded content of the New Testament. Being-Itself is personal, is love, is the content and form of our ultimate concern. Heidegger avoids anthropomorphism better than the theologians, but he, too, assumes that reverence and quiet submission to the power of Being are the appropriate attitudes. To me they are indistinguishable from the more inward types of traditional worship.

Attempts to identify the mystery with the Holy end up by doing exactly what they seek to avoid. They begin by declaring that there is an aspect of reality which man must admit is beyond his comprehension. They end up by showing that this Unknown is the *answer* to man's questions, is directly or indirectly his origin, goal, his source of strength and power. In short, the unknown aspect of Being is made into a numinous Being-Itself. The mystery is kept like a tight ball at the heart of all experience, as though all unfolded from it and looked back toward it. Its secret is continually made manifest although in code. There is no movement forward. The attitude of contemporary Christian theologians and philosophers of Being toward science is thus simultaneously permissive and amusedly contemptuous. Science is credited with all sorts of achievements, both beneficial and otherwise, which mark out paths on the circumference of life and make our superficial movements much easier. It cannot touch, it has no relation to that central core of Being wherein each life-world has its deep roots.

In a series of lectures which Paul Tillich delivered on concepts of history, he developed the stages of Western man in three images. The Greeks and Romans, Tillich claimed, thought of history and human existence cyclically, not penetrating or rising to more than human possibilities but making the most of what the moment offered. The early Christians and medieval man lived vertically in ever present awareness of paradisial ecstasy and demonic despair, with little awareness of any need to cope with earthly problems of society and politics. The Enlightenment and the nineteenth century moved horizontally. Ignoring spiritual heights and depths, it sought perfect happiness in a straight forward movement on earth. Tillich concluded his lectures by suggesting that twentieth-century existentialism is seeking a synthesis of these three movements. Tillich did not describe a visual symbol for this new trinity—but I think he can hardly have failed to see that it would be ⊕, a circle with a cross in the middle.[2] My complaint is that the symbol and the thought expressed by it are equally closed off and self-contained.

Humanistic existentialism is unabashedly horizontal and forward in its outlook, but the terrain ahead is uneven and shows no well-marked pathway. The existentialist's resolve directs itself toward clearing a path and is nourished by the hope that the way already traversed has never failed to allow a forward movement for those who worked at it. Short cuts and newly invented tools he may expect to discover, but he has long since given up the hope of guiding voices from heaven.

Existentialism regards Being-in-itself, not as something Holy or infused with the Holy or even regulated by the Holy. It is simply that within which man makes his individual being-for-himself. This does not mean that we are uninterested in Being-in-itself or that we do not hope that our understanding of it will advance as we ourselves develop. Sartre goes so far as to acknowledge that there might be a dialectical movement in nature.

Ought we then to deny the existence of dialectical connections at the center of inanimate Nature? Not at all. To tell the truth, I do not see that we are, at the present stage of our knowledge, in a

[2] I am aware that this symbol is used by the United World Federalists, but my comments are not in any sense directed toward this group.

position either to affirm or to deny. Each one is free to *believe* that physico-chemical laws express a dialectical reason or *not to believe* it.[3]

It would be easy to jump to the conclusion that Sartre has belatedly acknowledged that there just might be a Purpose in things after all. We would be wrong. The possibility which Sartre suggests is that there might be patterned development of a kind that we are now unable to detect. He certainly does not intend to say that things in nature are moving in obedience to some higher Spirit's command or that they are purposefully developing themselves toward some higher goal, not even one indiscernible by us. Sartre's choice of words in this paradoxical suggestion of a dialectical reason in "inanimate Nature" strikes me as unfortunate. A class struggle amidst the minerals would come close to justifying the final atom bomb, and it is hard not to make some such associative connotation. More soberly, the term "dialectical reason" serves to explain what I think Sartre really meant.

When Sartre speaks of the dialectical development of history, he never wants to claim—as many Marxists would—that human events are determined by economic laws functioning as impersonally and independent of human desires as the force of gravity. It is always men who make history, working together but acting, each one, as individuals. The public human structures which go to make up the situation into which each person is born and within which his freedom chooses his particular way of existing are included by Sartre in the "*pratico-inerte*," that impersonal, not wholly malleable environment in which man carves his being and in which his projects deviate. We may say that the existence of gold mines in a country whose economy is based on gold provokes, demands, or forbids certain human activity. We do not thereby bestow any purposive force or determining meaning upon the gold itself. In precisely the same way, we may attribute causal force and pattern to human events as they

[3] Sartre: *Critique de la Raison Dialectique*, p. 129.

450

have influenced individuals without our introducing regulative inner laws distinct from the events themselves. "Dialectical reason" in history refers both to the connected unfolding
of human events and to the intellectual process by which we
trace those connections. Presumably a dialectical reason in
nature would be comparable. What I believe Sartre means is
that if we had the required knowledge we *might* be able to
reveal relationships in the centuries of inorganic changes
more coherent and unified than those displayed in the simple
listing of geological ages and the like. That at least is as far
as I feel safe in trying to interpret what he meant. I admit
that if we stop at this point we are left dissatisfied and with
the feeling that further questioning is demanded. What possible sort of patterned development in Nature could Sartre
possibly have in mind which would be neither the simple
enlargement of scientific knowledge about molecular structures and the like, nor the endowment of nature with qualities
hitherto reserved for human consciousness? I do not know.
What I should like to think, and what I indeed believe to be
possible, is that Sartre intended something like the following:
There *may* be an aspect to Nature which we have not yet
grasped, one which—if we could comprehend it—would reveal the possibility of a history of nature as complex, as
fascinating in its superficial unity and inner diversity as human history. It would not be human, and it would still remain
the stuff of human projects. The relations which human consciousness might establish with a Nature thus understood are
totally beyond our present comprehension.

Sartre complains that conventional Marxists have transformed the bare hypothetical possibility that there is a "concrete dialectic of Nature" into a clearly understood, unconditioned law of nature which totally conditions human societies.
This sort of dialectical materialism Sartre rejects with the
statement that it is to substitute science fiction for truth.
What the Marxists have done is not different in essence from
the procedure of the New Theologians. Both groups, acting
on the tenuous hypothesis that reality is capable of yielding

451

up more meaning than we have yet discerned there, rush to fill in this space still empty of knowledge; and they put there whatever is needed as regulative ideas for their otherwise partial philosophies.

In preference to either mechanistic dialectical materialism or religious reverence for Being-Itself, Sartre has chosen to disregard a hypothesis which cannot be proved one way or another and to concentrate on ways of improving those social and political areas of human existence which do not depend on our uncovering the deeper secrets of reality. His attitude is somewhat reminiscent of the comment on God, spoken by Camus's hero, Dr. Rieux: "Since the order of the world is ruled by death, may it not perhaps be better for God if we do not believe in Him and fight with all our strength against death without lifting our eyes toward the sky where He sits in silence?" [4] Sartre, of course, is concerned primarily with what is better for man, not with what is good for God or Nature, whether it is a Nature infused with dialectical reason or not. So, I believe, was Camus.

If we are unwilling to settle for Sartre's indifference, and if we are averse to either Marxist or theological fill-ins, what alternatives have we? There is pure agnosticism, the conviction that we can never have knowledge that is more than a peripheral extension of what we now possess. On the surface, this position appears not only safe but irrefutable. As human beings, we cannot assume anything but a human point of view. To hope that we might someday achieve a qualitatively new view of internal patterns of Nature seems to demand more than the sort of difference represented in the advance from the Greek atomists and nuclear physicists. So far I am in agreement, although even in this example one wonders if mere quantity of knowledge has not begun to induce a qualitative modification of what is properly called human understanding. Certainly the Greeks would have been content to identify "human" and "terrestrial" whereas we cannot now or will not do so much longer. Then there is faith in the

---

[4] Albert Camus: *La Peste* (Paris: Gallimard; 1947), p. 147.

possibility of those radical existential changes which I mentioned earlier. If man changes, his relations with the external world and his understanding of it will change. Being-in-itself will certainly reveal far different profiles to a for-itself which has learned new forms of transcendence.

 # XIV

Ethics and the Future

We sustain three types of relation with the future of the world. Two are strictly ethical: At least for so long as humanity continues to exist or to leave its imprint in a universe where there might conceivably be some other form of consciousness, we know that we are responsible for helping to make the future. And we know that we will be judged by the future. The third relation is metaphysical: As members of the human species, our view of our own existence is inevitably colored by our speculative "over beliefs" concerning the probable future story of mankind. Indeed at this stage of history metaphysical faith and social planning are sometimes surprisingly difficult to keep separate and tend to meet in areas which up until now were reserved for science fiction. We cannot solve these problems of future humans, even if we are able to see in dim outline the situations which they will confront. And indeed we have conflicts more pressing than the question of whether government or private enterprise will manage transportation routes to Mars. Yet our preliminary excursions into outer space have made it obvious that it is not

454

too soon to start thinking of how we are going to reconcile the conflicting claims of nations to the Moon's territory. Similarly there are other areas where we can, with very little strain on the imagination, see the results of our sins or our virtues inscribed in the situation within which later men and women will make their lives. As we envision these various possibilities, I think it is appropriate to indicate certain cautionary principles which existentialism might establish as natural corollaries of its view of the human. Instead of speaking generally and abstractly, I should like to work with an example—the problem of birth control—stressing its possible future dimensions rather than limiting myself to facts and statistics as they can be established at present.

Overpopulation is already at our doorstep. The ultimate solution may easily be more akin to what we read in science fiction than in any of the pages of history. Will they belong to the nightmare laboratories of the *Brave New World?* Will they be a streamlined version of Plato's "Great Lie"? Will we, for our part, do nothing at all, tacitly assuming that, if things get too bad, our descendants can fight it out in a war that by then would really solve this particular question—for a while? Existentialists, like most other thinking people, would reject all three of these procedures, the first two because they deliberately constitute the majority of human beings as objects to be manipulated and the third as an evasion of responsibility. We can assert confidently and comfortably that only one course of conduct is in good faith so far as the present and immediate future are concerned. Obviously the first step is to prevent the birth of unwanted children. Existentialism recognizes no divine or natural imperative to regard sex as solely for purposes of reproduction. Obviously it recognizes no obligation to bring into existence as many consciousnesses as possible, regardless of the sort of future they are born to. Its immediate responsibility would be toward those now living, that they might control their lives as fully as possible and bestow their intelligent devotion upon children who are desired and who may enjoy the opportunity of leading satisfying and significant lives. At the moment this course provides no insurmountable obstacles. It is primarily a matter of working to provide information and clinical facilities for those who need them. Conflicts arising from religious taboos and disagreement over questions such as whether unmarried women should be allowed to buy the pill can be gradually solved by the process of public education and the growing realization by church authorities that new crises need new solutions. At present we can still afford to let the individual parents choose. Nobody is forced to restrict the number of his progeny, nor do I believe that anyone ought to be so long as there is hope that enlightening propaganda will suffice to keep the birth rate from accelerating. To hope that persuasion alone will suffice is naïve, perhaps, but not necessarily stupid. We have deplored the extent to which regard for public opinion results in conformity which is stultifying or downright injurious to the individual. If one is aware that disapproval is justified, even those in good faith may be wary of incurring it.

We must face the fact that voluntary birth control may not be enough for very long. In this event, those who are sensitive to the just needs of human freedom will realize our immersion in Original Sin more keenly than ever before, more bitterly even than in our encounter with the criminal and the substandard. As always it is easier to say what our approach and attitude should not be than to offer realistic positive proposals. Clearly we should avoid the greatest temptation of all: We will not conclude that since we will inevitably do violence to some, we will simply accept the arithmetical calculation of the greatest good for the greatest number and let the chips fall where they may. Or if we do ultimately find that there is nothing better than this old utilitarian principle, we shall at least not be misled by its surface simplicity. The equation of the greatest good with the greatest number is the most difficult of all mathematical calculations, for it is to balance two incommensurates—quality and distribution.

Suppose that the world has to resort to legal decisions as to who may have how many children. Obviously child-bearing should never become the privilege of an upper economic or social class. I have heard as a serious proposal the suggestion

456

that in the United States parents having more than a specified number of children would be taxed for each additional child instead of being allowed the usual exemption. At first thought the idea sounds quite reasonable. In an overpopulated world why should one not pay for the privilege of having a family larger than the average? Can we not rightly demand that those who have children should be in a position to support them? This argument, while not entirely specious, cannot hide the unacceptable proposition that both birth and bringing to birth would depend on cold cash. A second procedure sounds more impartial but is equally objectionable when examined closely. I refer to the various proposals concerning a legally enforced, systematic eugenics program. Existentialism rejects such a plan for several reasons. First, we insist that an individual is more than his genes, that human beings make themselves and cannot be bred like horses. Second, we refuse to accept a plan whereby a small group or even a majority of the world's inhabitants would assign an absolute value to each person, appraising him like an object, then deciding whether or not he is to be judged worthy to reproduce himself and with what partner. The primary objection here is not the one sometimes offered, that there is no way to be sure what are the best traits to perpetuate (although this is certainly true) and that there is danger in breeding out the diversity in human beings. Existentialism believes too firmly in the unpredictability of human freedom to feel that such fears are very realistic. The more serious error in this kind of thinking is its willingness to sacrifice the present generation for the sake of a vague future and to suppress individuals for the abstract good of the whole. Even if it could be proved (and we must not discount the fact that it cannot) that the human race would progress faster toward its selected goal if some low-achieving persons did not have descendants, this is no justification for demanding so great a price of individuals. The absoluteness of private worlds still holds. The less intelligent are not objects and should not be treated as such. If a program of eugenics could be voluntary, existentialism would have no theoretical objection to those who wished to experiment. Marriage itself has always involved some degree of eugenic concern. Huxley's Utopian novel *Island* portrays a society in which some parents, after their first child, choose artificial insemination in the hope of producing particular physical types or musical talent or other potentialities which appear to be determined by genes. We may laugh at the idea that people would ever come to accept so radical a divorce between sexual love and reproduction. Whether or not we would be right to find the idea ridiculous, I cannot say. There is nothing immoral about artificial insemination. Nor does the existentialist view of freedom deny the importance of the physical body, including the brain cells, which consciousness uses as the material from which it makes itself. It is compulsion exerted against an already existing consciousness which we oppose and the idea that any group—large or small—has the right to decide by itself the future of all humanity.

Someone may object at this point: This is all very well except that you are still evading the real issue. It might for a time to be a solution to say that every couple who so choose should be permitted to have a fixed minimum of children—let us say, one child—and that nobody should be granted extra privileges. But suppose the population had reached the point where even this was too many for the world's resources? And what would you do in the case of those who broke the rule? Fines are no solution. Would you regress to infanticide, imprisonments, and public branding? With some trepidation, I will attempt at least a partial answer.

From our vantage point, we may first point out that it is our responsibility not to allow matters to arrive at so desperate a state. In this respect we are inescapably as responsible for the situation of future men and women as we are for that of our contemporaries. I admit that this remark by itself resembles the answer given to the stranger inquiring how to get to Cincinnati, "You can't start from here." Let us assume then that we or our descendants might actually find ourselves in this waking nightmare.

With apologies for a roundabout approach, I would like to refer to Edmond Cahn's remarks (in *The Moral Decision*) concerning what he calls the "morals of the last days." Cahn discusses a case in which survivors of a shipwreck were dangerously crowded together in a longboat. In an effort to save the rest, the members of the crew of the *William Brown* threw overboard fourteen male passengers. On the following morning the survivors attracted the attention of a passing ship and were rescued. At the trial of one of the seamen, the judge stated that if any passengers had to be sacrificed in order that some might be saved, the decision should have been made by casting lots. Cahn, whose concern is to demonstrate the intricate reciprocity between morals and laws, objects for two reasons. First, one must not sacrifice lives on the basis of mere probability, when there is any chance at all that a later solution may make the sacrifice unnecessary. One must risk the possible destruction of all rather than choose the certain death of some. Second, Cahn argues that at such extreme moments, the usual distinctions among people are nullified.

In a strait of this extremity, all men are reduced—or raised, as one may choose to denominate it—to members of the genus, mere congeners and nothing else. . . . I am driven to conclude that otherwise—that is, if none sacrifice themselves of free will to spare the others—they must all wait and die together. For where all have become congeners, pure and simple, no one can save himself by killing another. . . . Under the terms of the moral constitution, it will be *wholly* his self that he kills in his vain effort to save himself. The "morals of the last days" leave him a generic creature only. . . . Whoever saves one, saves the whole human race; whoever kills one, kills mankind. So, in all humility, I would put aside the talk of casting lots, not only because the crisis involves stakes too high for gambling and responsibilities too deep for destiny, but also because no one can win in such a lottery, no one can survive intact by means of the killing.[1]

[1] Edmond Cahn: *The Moral Decision: Right and Wrong in the Light of American Law* (Bloomington: Indiana University Press; 1955), p. 71. Simone de Beauvoir has proposed this kind of problem and arrived at much the same sort of solution in her play *Les Bouches inutiles*, which I have discussed in *Humanistic Existentialism*, pp. 269–70.

I am not certain that I understand precisely what Cahn intends by his statement that all humanity is saved or killed in the single life or death. Perhaps he has the same thing in mind as Sartre had in claiming that, in choosing for myself, I choose for mankind; that is, in my choice, I make manifest my own concept of what man is; furthermore, inasmuch as man is only what individuals make themselves to be, each act is a restatement, a total definition. There are two other aspects of Cahn's conclusions which I find more important. First, he recognizes the incommensurability of persons. Where simple survival is concerned, we cannot rightly allot the privilege to one rather than another. All criteria by which we would judge are sustained by the living. A particular individual, who has devoted himself to artistic or intellectual achievements or to the social benefit of mankind, may rise to the point of choosing the survival of others rather than himself because he feels their contributions to what he values will be greater than his own. We have no right to demand of others that they sacrifice themselves to the more socially useful. The privilege of maintaining one's own private world, its absolute existence, simply cannot be impartially weighed against the greater enrichment of the worlds of others. Cahn's second idea is that survival at the cost of betrayal of our responsibility to realize this ultimate incommensurable value of each human freedom does such violence to the ethical man living in good faith that he ought to choose probable death in preference. Some will argue that this position is naïvely noble but indefensible either logically or pragmatically. I believe Cahn is right. We are working on the premise that when we accept the bare idea of "ought," we imply that we ought to do that which we believe we can justify. We cannot justify the choice to live if to live means going contrary to all that we have laid down as the justification of a life. At the end of his discussion, Cahn asks, "Finally, would it be permissible to suggest that this planet we live on is not entirely unlike the longboat of the *William Brown?*"

We return now to our hypothetical future decision concerning the limitation of Earth's population. I would argue that all of the points made by Cahn apply. The right to reproduce (i.e., to have one child) ought to be given as absolute a status as the right to preserve one's own life. It ought never to be made a privilege to be won by calculations of social utility. Here we are all simple "congeners." Even at the risk that we may all drown, we must cling together in the hope of lasting till the now indiscernible rescue appears as it did for the shipwrecked survivors. Still more in our case, for we have more means at our disposal to search for a way to save ourselves—e.g., the possibility of sending colonies to other planets. A life on an overcrowded planet might be hardly worth living. It would be no worse than life in a laboratory where only a privileged few were the experimenters. The species we want to preserve is not the one which is defined solely by its biology but a collection of free self-transcending beings. Cahn, opposing both force and the drawing of lots, does not rule out voluntary self-sacrifice. Nor should we discount the will to cooperate in members of a society that offers men and women the maximum encouragement to choose freely what they wish to be.

What of the transgressors against our fair, equally shared regulations? It would be foolishly Utopian to expect that there would be no infringements of the laws passed. I confess that any perfectly satisfying solution seems hopeless. There would have to be some penalties, and the solution here is obviously not a lenient temporary imprisonment for rehabilitation. Certainly the vengeful penalties of the past are out of the question. Neither infanticide nor forced abortions is acceptable. Probably at this stage the best we can suggest is that penalties should take the form of the loss of certain privileges. Possibly the time will come when those unwilling to exist under earthly restrictions may lead elsewhere a life that is harsher in some ways but which allows more free scope in others—as in the early days of American history.

The issue of overpopulation and birth control can hardly be called a problem of the future. It is a present reality. A few scientists have already suggested that we are on the threshold of a problem at the other end of life—the question of the

461

artificial prolongation of life. Dr. Ervine Page, a director of research at the Cleveland Clinic, claims that within the last quarter of a century there has been a biological revolution that gives rise to a whole new set of ethical problems for which we are wholly unprepared. He points to two critical areas: First there is the possibility of prolonging a persons's life by the transplanting of human organs. Dr. Page asks:

When we are able to transplant human organs, who shall get them? Will a costly kidney be given to an old man who also has an ailing heart or liver, just to give him a few months more of life? Will parents agonize whether they should donate kidneys to help some child other than their own? [2]

To put the ethical questions in this way is to assume that survival itself is the highest value and asks "For whom?" Dr. Page recognizes that there is a still deeper question.

People go to church and say they believe in immortality. But ask them—or give them the opportunity as will come—if they want to survive beyond their natural span on earth, and whether that survival is worth any cost, then they do not know what to believe.

Besides the question of who should have the privilege of living longer, we find Dr. Page proposing seriously the possibilities which Huxley followed through so grimly in *Brave New World*.

Scientists have taken first steps in the long journey to understand the genetic code of life, perhaps ultimately making it possible to substitute good genes for faulty, to avoid inborn defects, to ordain the birth of highly intelligent, long-lived healthy humans—or droves of uncomplaining slaves.

Dr. Page feels a sense of urgency about these problems. If society does not anticipate its crises, then it is likely to become hysterical, to pass ill-thought-out laws and regulations that will not work. Furthermore, the social dilemma is indis-

[2] Dr. Page is quoted by Alton Blakeslee, Associated Press science writer, in "Should Life Be Prolonged?" *Boulder Daily Camera*, September 7, 1964.

tinguishable from the most fundamental philosophical problem, for it "will bring our whole philosophy of life into question. We shall have to ask more keenly, what is the meaning of life, of death, of survival? And we had better start thinking of it now." Dr. Page admits that doctors are not prepared to provide the right answers any more than anyone else. These are questions which science must face, but they cannot be answered scientifically. They are too urgent to be made exclusively the problems of philosophers although one wishes that philosophy departments were more inclined to help. They are, of course, questions for all of us.

I will not be so rash as to suggest that humanistic existentialism is in a position to provide specific answers to the many concrete questions which already are being suggested to us by both social developments and the spectacular achievements of recent science. It is, I believe, less likely to be caught off guard than most philosophies. It has always proposed an open future; it believes firmly in human self-transcendence. It searches for new solutions and new meanings, new ways of relating oneself to Being. Yet it safeguards this openness with those limits which stem from its resolve never to ignore the subjective reality of individual freedom. Just as it recognizes the demands of both temporal and spontaneous self-realization in the person, so it balances the needs of the "We" with the jealous preservation of each differentiated "I." Humanistic existentialism, unlike the religious branch of existentialism, is not antiscientific. It will not replace God with the computer, for it considers that man has made both in his own image and must decide their destiny, not let them determine his.

Index

Absolute, 42–7, 50, 81, 96, 217, 256
activism, 151, 153, 197
addiction, drug, 177–83
Advertisements for Myself (Mailer), 195
agnosticism, 452
altruism, 135, 136, 139, 144, 148, 276
Ames, Van Meter, 214, 257, 273
anguish, 18, 88, 126, 133, 272
apolitical left, 150–96
Aristotle, 56, 91, 95, 104, 126, 131, 132, 284
"as-if" fictions, 88, 91
assimilation of minorities, 170
atheism, 43, 64, 211, 217, 239, 245, 331, 380, 381, 401
Atlas Shrugged (Rand), 122, 127 n.
atom bomb, 157
Augustine, St., 112, 422
authenticity, and unauthenticity, 18, 19, 59–60, 402
Ayer, A. J., 235

bad faith, 81–9, 90 and n., 93, 110, 134, 298, 302, 320, 347, 350, 351, 352, 366
Baldwin, James, 154, 173; quoted, 174
Beatniks, 122, 152, 154, 159, 160, 162, 163, 166–71, 192, 196, 213
Beauvoir, Simone de, 29, 32 and n., 37, 38 and n., 41 and n., 45, 62 and n., 95, 116, 231, 272, 320, 332 and n., 337, 350, 359, and n., 361, 432–3, 437, 438; quoted, 433
Behaviorist psychology, 10, 57, 83, 85, 121, 126, 261
Being: and Nothingness, 11, 18, 37, 54, 56, 57, 62, 79, 242, 323, 441; in Heidegger's philosophy, 65, 380, 381, 382, 400–6, 408–16, 418–23; transphenomenality of, 132, 236, 237, 403; problem of, 379–80, 397; as Love, 392
Being and Nothingness (Sartre), 29, 42, 45, 46, 47, 50, 53, 56, 59, 67, 87 and n., 105 and n., 217, 220, 234, 238, 239, 240, 259, 319, 320, 335, 401, 402

Being-in-itself, and Being-for-itself, 11, 13, 51, 53, 55, 67, 114, 235, 237–42, 248, 260, 261, 265, 266, 401, 435
Being-Itself, 380, 382, 384–9, 395, 396, 397, 446, 448
birth control, 455–6, 461
Branden, Nathaniel, 131, 146; quoted, 127 and n.
Bultmann, Rudolf, 382, 384, 391, 393, 400, 401; quoted, 380, 389, 393, 394
Burroughs, William, 154, 169, 178, 181, 185; quoted, 178–9, 181, 183–4

Cahn, Edmond, 458, 459, 460, 461; quoted, 459
calculated culpability (Camus), 111, 208
Camus, Albert, 71, 74, 93, 94, 105, 111, 116, 159, 205, 208, 211, 272, 320, 427, 434, 440
capitalism, and Objectivism, 124
categorical imperative, Kant's, 95, 96, 97
choice, to be ethical, 3–28
Christianity, 8, 10, 46, 56, 80, 92, 102, 103, 113, 123, 133, 146, 147, 212, 218, 221, 224, 285, 344, 383–4, 390, 448; *see also* New Theologians
civil rights, 141, 142, 143, 152, 153, 158, 197, 200, 284
Cohen, Sidney, 245, 251, 255; quoted, 251
commitment: involved by self-transcendence, 299; loyalty to, 301
conscience, call of (Heidegger), 416
consciousness, 11–17, 22, 52, 88, 96, 126, 127 and n., 237–44, 249–56, 301, 319 and n., 323, 333, 334; personalized, 12; as freedom, 15; reflecting and reflected-on, 67–8, 324; function of, in assigning distinction and meaning (Sartre), 96; expansion of, 176, 177, 186, 226, 245, 248, 277; oneness of, in Vedanta, 218, 219; Sartre's definition of, 241–3; Zen concepts of, 257, 258, 260, 261, 262, 267; cosmic, 260, 269, 270, 273, 277; psychic

i

A Note about the Author

HAZEL E. BARNES was born in Wilkes-Barre, Pennsylvania, in 1915. She received a B.A. *magna cum laude* from Wilson College and a Ph.D. from Yale where she was the recipient of several prizes. She has done postdoctoral work in modern philosophy and Indian philosophy and holds an honorary Doctor of Letters from Wilson College. Dr. Barnes has taught (among other places) at the Woman's College of the University of North Carolina, Pierce College in Athens, Greece, Ohio State University, and—from 1953—the University of Colorado where she has been a full professor since 1962, teaching in both the classics and humanities departments. Dr. Barnes is the author of *The Literature of Possibility* (reprinted as *Humanistic Existentialism*), co-author with Donald Sutherland of *Hippolytus in Drama and Myth*, and the translator of Jean-Paul Sartre's *Being and Nothingness*, *Existential Psychoanalysis*, and *Search for a Method*, for all of which she wrote introductions. She has contributed articles and reviews to numerous journals of philosophy and classics, as well as to various literary reviews, and is a member of several philosophical societies.

A Note on the Type

THE TEXT of this book is set in MONTICELLO, a Linotype revival of the original Binny & Ronaldson Roman No. 1, cut by Archibald Binny and cast in 1796 by that Philadelphia type foundry. The face was named Monticello in honor of its use in the monumental fifty-volume *Papers of Thomas Jefferson*, published by Princeton University Press. Monticello is a transitional type design, embodying certain features of Bulmer and Baskerville, but it is a distinguished face in its own right. *Composed, printed, and bound by Kingsport Press, Inc., Kingsport, Tenn. Typography by Vincent Torre.*